Let Newton be!

PRÆCLARISSIMUS·ISAACUS·NEWTON·EQUES.
ECCE PHILOSOPHORUM PRINCEPS

Let Newton be!

Nature, and Nature's Laws lay hid in Night.
God said, *Let Newton be!* and All was *Light*.
Alexander Pope

EDITED BY
JOHN FAUVEL, RAYMOND FLOOD,
MICHAEL SHORTLAND, and ROBIN WILSON

OXFORD NEW YORK TOKYO
OXFORD UNIVERSITY PRESS
1988

Oxford University Press, Walton Street, Oxford OX2 6DP

Oxford New York Toronto
Delhi Bombay Calcutta Madras Karachi
Petaling Jaya Singapore Hong Kong Tokyo
Nairobi Dar es Salaam Cape Town
Melbourne Auckland
and associated companies in
Berlin Ibadan

Oxford is a trade mark of Oxford University Press

Published in the United States
by Oxford University Press, New York

British Library Cataloguing in Publication Data
Fauvel, John
Let Newton be!
1. Physics. Newton, Sir Isaac. 1642–
1727. Critical Studies
I. Title
530'.092'4
ISBN 0–19–853924–X

Library of Congress Cataloging in Publication Data
Let Newton be! / edited by John Fauvel . . . [et al.].
Bibliography Includes index.
1. Newton, Isaac, Sir, 1642–1727—Knowledge—Science. 2. Science—History.
3. Physicists—Great Britain—Biography. I. Fauvel, John.
QC16.N7L47 1988 509.2'4—dc19 88–9911
ISBN 0–19–853924–X

Printed in Great Britain by
Butler & Tanner Ltd, Frome and London

Contents

H. Gravelot delin.

H. S. E.
ISAACUS NEWTON Eques Auratus,
Qui, animi vi prope divina
Planetarum Motus, Figuras,
Cometarum semitas, Oceanique Æstus,
Sua Mathesi facem praeferente,
Primus demonstravit,
Radiorum Lucis dissimilitudines,
Colorumque inde nascentium proprietates,
Quas nemo antea vel suspicatus erat, pervestigavit.
Naturae, Antiquitatis, S. Scripturae,
Sedulus, sagax, fidus Interpres
Dei O. M. Majestatem Philosophia asseruit
Evangelij Simplicitatem Moribus expressit.
Sibi gratulentur Mortales,
Tale tantumque exstitisse
HUMANI GENERIS DECUS
NAT. XXV. DEC. A.D. MDCXLII OBIIT MAR. MDCCXXVI

Introduction

In April 1727, the French writer Voltaire viewed with astonishment the preparations for the funeral of Sir Isaac Newton. The late President of the Royal Society lay in state in Westminster Abbey for the week preceding the funeral on 4 April. At the ceremony, his pall was borne in a ceremonious pageant by two dukes, three earls, and the Lord Chancellor. '*He was buried*', Voltaire observed, '*like a king who had done well by his subjects*'. No scientist before had been so revered. Few since have been interred with such dignity and high honour. To see why this was so, and to learn more about the relevance of Newton today, are among the aims of this book.

The boy from rural Lincolnshire had come far. His academic career was not especially outstanding, either as a schoolboy or as a university student. Yet by the age of 26, he had become the professor of mathematics at Cambridge, and gradually his reputation spread as the foremost mathematician of the age.

Newton's interests were not confined to mathematics. He applied himself with unresting dedication to what may strike anyone today as a quite unmanageable range of concerns. In the privacy of his study, a host of investigations poured from his pen—in optics, dynamics, history, astronomy, alchemy, chemistry, music theory, theology, and other subjects.

Not content with the life of a reclusive Cambridge scholar, Newton in his fifties opted for a more public role as a civil servant in London—at first Warden, then Master of the Mint. Soon after, he became President of the Royal Society. By the time of his death, Newton had established a reputation as the greatest of scientists and the most powerful scientific administrator in the country. He had come to ordain the spirit and direction of British science as autocratically and effectively as he had once directed his own researches.

In this book we explore the richness of Newton's life, labours, and legacy. What kind of scientist was Newton? What connections are there between the different strands of research he undertook? Why were his contemporaries so in awe of him? How has Newton's work left its mark on our understanding of the world? These are some of the questions addressed in the chapters that follow.

Hercules of the fable?

Something of what Newton's contemporaries saw in him was expressed in Alexander Pope's well-known epitaph:

> Nature, and Nature's Laws lay hid in Night.
> God said, *Let Newton be!* and All was *Light*.

The tomb of Isaac Newton in Westminster Abbey, designed by William Kent, was erected in 1731. The rich symbolism alluded to the many fields of Newton's influence. The boys on the front of the sarcophagus are playing with a prism, the reflecting telescope, a furnace, and newly-minted coins, while one boy weighs the Sun and planets. Above Newton is a celestial globe showing the path of the 1681 comet and the solstice position by which Newton dated the ancient Greek expedition of the Argonauts.

Newton himself reclines on a pile of books, labelled *Divinity*, *Chronology*, *Optica*, and *Phil. Princ. Math.*, while the cherubs at his feet hold a scroll picturing the solar system and a mathematical series.

And the French mathematician Pierre-Simon Laplace, a century later, explained wistfully that since there was only one universe it could be given to only one person—the fortunate Isaac Newton—to discover its fundamental law.

After the many scientific upheavals of the twentieth century, we have lost confidence in the belief that there *is* only one fundamental law, or that Newton had the good luck to discover it. But Newton's work still governs the way in which we try to describe, analyse, and predict the motion of physical objects in all kinds of circumstances, as well as the way in which many of us think about science.

It was Newton's great achievement to reduce to mathematical laws the complex relations between heavenly bodies, and explain these by means of the concept of gravitational force. Indeed, the physical theory he set out provided a complete account of the structure and motion of the universe. Newton's masterpiece *Philosophiae naturalis principia mathematica* (1687) laid out the most coherent 'System of the World' since the days of Aristotle and Plato over 2000 years before. It is little wonder that his contemporaries viewed his achievement with awe and admiration. The antiquarian John Aubrey declared that the *Principia* was, quite simply, '*the greatest highth of Knowledge that humane nature has yet arrived to*'.

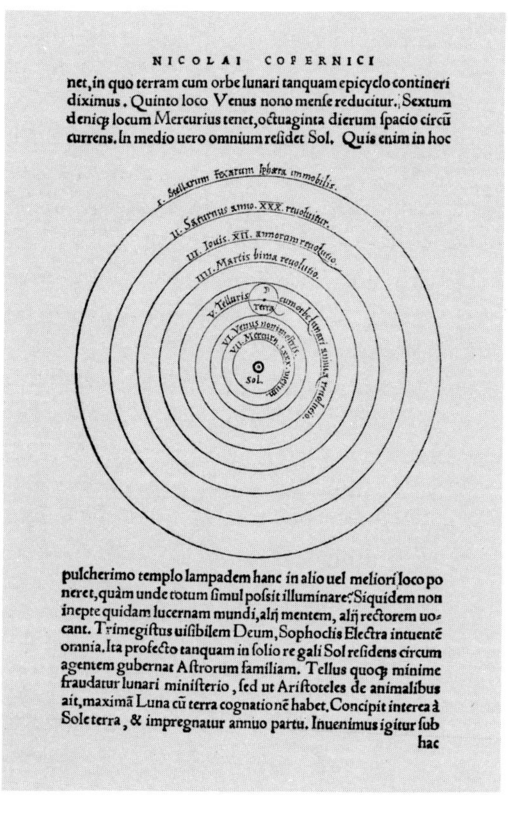
NICOLAI COPERNICI

net, in quo terram cum orbe lunari tanquam epicyclo contineri diximus. Quinto loco Venus nono mense reducitur. Sextum denique locum Mercurius tenet, octuaginta dierum spacio circũ currens. In medio uero omnium residet Sol. Quis enim in hoc

pulcherimo templo lampadem hanc in alio uel meliori loco poneret, quàm unde totum simul possit illuminare? Siquidem non inepte quidam lucernam mundi, alij mentem, alij rectorem uocant. Trimegistus uisibilem Deum, Sophoclis Electra intuentẽ omnia. Ita profecto tanquam in solio regali Sol residens circum agentem gubernat Astrorum familiam. Tellus quoque minime fraudatur lunari ministerio, sed ut Aristoteles de animalibus ait, maximã Luna cũ terra cognationẽ habet. Concipit interea à Sole terra, & impregnatur annuo partu. Inuenimus igitur sub

hac

No single person to this day has reached higher—Newton's achievements remain unsurpassed. Nor is his influence confined to cosmical dynamics: in optics and in mathematics, Newton's legacy remains a potent living force, throwing up problems for investigation and inspiring research.

Despite the passage of three centuries, Newton's reputation stands high for another reason, which relates to popular perceptions of the scientific enterprise. Voltaire acutely put his finger on part of Newton's appeal when he compared him with the earlier French mathematician and philosopher, René Descartes:

> Very few persons in London read Descartes, whose works have in fact become totally useless. Newton also has very few readers, because it requires great knowledge and sense to understand him. Everybody however talks about him.

Like Albert Einstein in our own century, then, Newton's fame spread far beyond the small number of people who could understand his work in depth. Maybe some part of his widespread fame was precisely *because* his books seemed obscure and difficult. That so few people could or would read Newton's *Principia* helped, perhaps, to turn it into a classic: a book many want to have read, but few want to read.

This makes the role of a book such as this a rather delicate one. In fact, Newton's work can be simplified only at the risk of banality and distortion. In Chapter 12, Sir Hermann Bondi, a distinguished scientist in his own right, suggests that Newtonian ideas are in fact *still* much harder to teach and understand than, by comparison, Einstein's. Of course, we must distinguish between the difficulty of understanding the fundamental technical Newtonian concepts, and the general belief, which we have absorbed in some measure due to Newton's work, that the course of events is predictable and that nature is controllable.

The end of the twentieth century is a good time to attempt popular expositions of the full range of Newton's labours and legacy. In recent years there has been much historical research on many aspects of Newton's life and work, which it is now timely to disseminate more widely. This growth of scholarly activity, which might not unfairly be called the *Newton industry*, has had at its centre the major editions of Newton's correspondence and his mathematical papers, details of which are given in the 'Further reading' section on p. 20. These, and other editions still in progress, have depended upon a renewed interest this century in Newton's manuscript papers. At an auction sale in 1936, the economist John Maynard Keynes bought the alchemy manuscripts in Newton's hand, which he gave to King's College, Cambridge. This has ensured that, together with the mathematical and other manuscripts given to Cambridge University by a nineteenth-century Earl of Portsmouth, much of Newton's enormous manuscript

In *On the revolutions of the heavenly spheres* (1543), Nicolas Copernicus argued that the Sun, not the Earth, is at the centre of our planetary system. This belief was quite widely shared by the time of Newton, whose work explained the motion of the planets within this framework. The diagram pictured is too simple—planets move in elliptical orbits, as Kepler discovered in the early 1600s. The word *Trimegistus* four lines below the diagram refers to a sacred-mystical tradition which influenced both Copernicus and Newton, and is discussed in Chapter 6.

René Descartes (1596–1650) was one of the key influences upon Newton, in several respects—notably in his approach to mathematics, cosmology, optics, and dynamics.

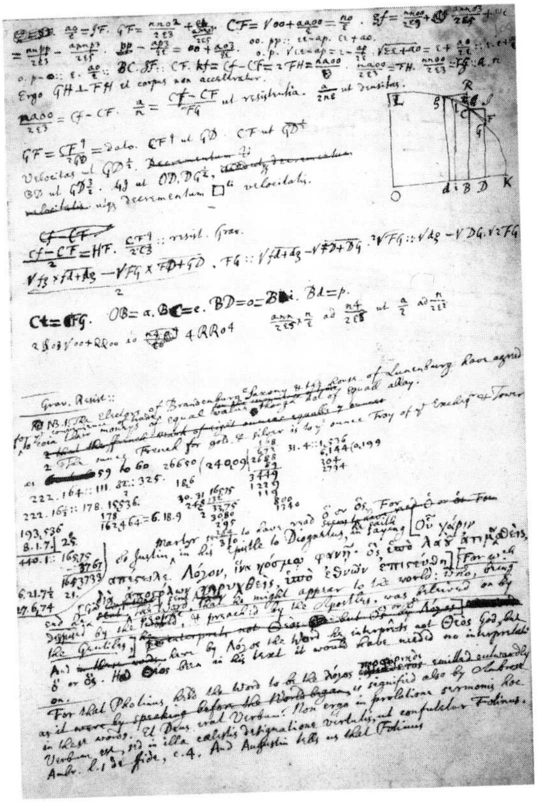

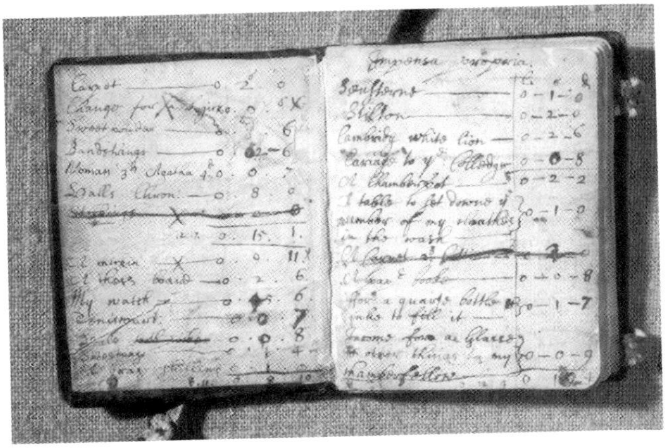

This Newton manuscript of about 1685 shows the range of Newton's concerns and scholarship. The top portion of the page consists of calculations, in Latin, on motion in a resisting medium. The middle remarks in English are on Continental currencies. The bottom deals, in English and Greek, with the theological views of the Church Fathers.

Not all Newton's manuscripts carry material of deep intellectual import. Here he recorded his purchase of a chamber-pot, *a table to jot down ye number of my cloathes in the wash*, and other necessities of living.

legacy is now back in Cambridge and increasingly consulted by scholars from around the world. Much of this scholarly interest has hitherto remained confined to the pages of academic journals. It is important to make current insights more widely accessible. This book aims to make available the fascinating results of research over the past 20 or 30 years which has shown Newton to be an even more complex and ambivalent figure than was previously realized.

In a book devoted to explaining—and perhaps inevitably celebrating—the life and work of Britain's greatest scientist, we are tempted to adopt a style of history in which our hero is omnipresent and all-knowing, shining out so strongly that his contemporaries, predecessors, and successors all fade into his shadow. By the time of Newton's death, Voltaire had already noticed the tendency to attribute all knowledge and discovery to Newton:

> There are people who think that if we are no longer content with the abhorrence of a vacuum, if we know that the air has weight, if we use a telescope, it is all due to Newton. Here he is the Hercules of the fable, to whom the ignorant attributed all the deeds of the other heroes.

Some of his contemporaries started the trend of praising Newton so lavishly that the boundary line between mortal man and divinity seemed to dissolve. As the century progressed, the enthusiasm in some quarters increased. Indeed, as Derek Gjertsen recounts in Chapter 1, a French enthusiast proposed that the British properly recognize Newton's divinity by relocating the start of the calendar to Christmas Day 1642, the day on which the hero emerged into the world whose structure he would reveal.

Such enthusiasm was not universal. There were reactions to these unmeasured assessments of Newton through the eighteenth century and onwards, as explained by Geoffrey Cantor in Chapter 10. Indeed, despite the clear lead he seemed to give in the epitaph quoted earlier, Alexander Pope was perplexed by the near-divine adulation given to Newton, which he tried to temper in the gentle irony of *An essay on man*:

> Superior beings, when of late they saw
> A mortal Man unfold all Nature's law
> Admir'd such wisdom in an earthly shape,
> And shew'd a Newton as we shew an Ape.
> Could he, whose rules the rapid Comet bind,
> Describe or fix one movement of his Mind?

By the beginning of the nineteenth century, as Maureen McNeil shows in Chapter 11, some saw Newton as pre-eminently responsible for the

We see something of the early near-deification of Newton in this sketch by William Stukeley, a London physician who befriended him in his later years. It depicts the image of Newton being held by many-breasted Nature, sitting on a celestial globe.

brutal mechanistic world-view and the dehumanization of nature. William Blake wrote of seeing

> Bacon and Newton, sheath'd in dismal steel, their terrors hang
> Like iron scourges over Albion.

Such responses antagonistic to Newton are still tributes to his influence, for good or ill, and to the way he seems to tower as an intellectual force over his contemporaries, and indeed subsequent generations. An important trend in history-writing this century, however, has been to move away from the 'great man' or hero-worshipping school, towards setting historical figures more securely in their historical context. This has involved trying to see how any scientist's contribution depends on the knowledge of the time and on the work of many others. It has also prompted historians to consider the problems tackled by any historical figure in relation to the social and economic needs of the period. Such approaches to history have become increasingly popular within the past 30 years, and have done much to enhance the exciting and rewarding aspect of the subject.

The Newton revealed by modern scholarship is not the single-handed creator of the modern world-view; nor was his life, as a Victorian biographer put it:

> one continued course of labour, patience, charity, generosity, temperance, piety, goodness, and all other virtues, without a mixture of any vice whatever.

But Newton does remain one of the intellectually richest and most complicated figures of whom there is historical record. He is still capable of surprising the hardened historian, no less than the student of popular science, with the unexpected ways in which he transmuted ideas and drew upon a host of unfamiliar influences.

Style in science

To begin to understand Newton's legacy, we may need to revise our notion of science. All too often the scientist today is seen as a distant, supremely rational creature. The very name of *science* evokes an image, reinforced in films, newsprint, and advertisements, of detached beings wielding something called *the scientific method* like a hammer. The nineteenth-century essayist Charles Lamb gave voice to this still potent, if increasingly inappropriate, image when he tagged Newton as '*a fellow who believed nothing unless it was as clear as the three sides of a triangle*'. Lamb was here enjoying Newton's reputation as the first of modern scientists. But in the investigations of Keynes a century later, another image emerged. He saw Newton as:

> the last of the magicians, the last of the Babylonians and Sumerians, the last great mind which looked out on the visible and intellectual world with the

same eyes as those who began to build our intellectual inheritance rather less than 10,000 years ago ... the last wonder-child to whom the Magi could do sincere and appropriate homage.

First modern scientist? Last ancient magician? These judgements attest to the difficulty of grasping Newton in his totality. It is not really helpful to insist on considering Newton as one or the other. Nor is it sensible to consider a multiplicity of Newtons: one engaged in science, another dabbling in alchemy, a third devoted to theology, and so on. We need to appreciate that Newton could be *one and all* of these things, and not suffer a modern crisis of identity in the process. To embrace Newton as an archetypal scientist is to recognize that science itself is a much richer and more ambivalent activity than we may have been taught to believe.

Take, for instance, so apparently straightforward a task as establishing the nature and behaviour of light. It might be thought that one has only to set up the right bits of apparatus in the right way for the true results to become revealed, as in a school demonstration. Yet when we come to study the progress of Newton's optical researches, they turn out, as Casper Hakfoort shows in Chapter 4, to be vastly more complicated conceptually than we ever imagined they could be—science was never like this in our school textbooks!

Newton was certainly concerned to assert a new view about light and colours, the view that is now generally accepted—namely, that white light consists of a mixture of rays of different colours. But he was *also* propounding a new view about how such physical claims should be assessed. He was proposing by example a *new pattern* for science, one in which mathematics and experimentation both play a part—with the emphasis placed on description and prediction, rather than on guessing at the causes of things. But his ideas were put forward in a characteristically Newtonian style, with glancing hints and ambiguous remarks, and a far from full and open tale of what he had done and why. Further, as we learn from Penelope Gouk in Chapter 5, some of Newton's views—not least the influential claim that there are seven colours in the rainbow—derive from thoughts of musical harmony, barely at all from optical judgements. Newton clearly had to work hard to ensure that his beliefs on what experiments *should* show were in some degree consistent with the *actual* experimental results.

There is a wide gap between the public image of science, once it has reached the textbooks, and the behind-the-scenes work which brought that about. This gap is now quite familiar to the historians of science. Indeed, some have seen a widespread pattern of scientists *negotiating* with nature, trying to reach an accommodation between two conflicting tensions: on the one hand, preconceived notions and assump-

The traditional image of an alchemist, from a woodcut of about 1520. This is not how we usually think of Newton, yet we know that he had a chemical laboratory attached to his rooms in Trinity College, and that he laboured for years trying to reproduce processes described in alchemical books. He also had an assistant, Humphrey Newton, who understood as little of Newton's endeavours as did, apparently, the assistant in this picture.

tions about procedures, and on the other, the set of facts which cannot be tailored to one's theories indefinitely, and which arise from experiments which are done for a variety of reasons. The work of Isaac Newton is a striking example of this process, with the further fascinating feature that it is very clear how Newton conducted the *social* negotiations leading to the spread of Newtonian science.

Newtonian chemistry, for example, was a body of knowledge and belief which was constructed through Newton's disciples and their teaching and publications, as Jan Golinski shows in Chapter 7. In Newton's view, chemical effects could be explained by analogy with gravitation, as the result of forces acting between tiny particles of matter. He came to believe that these forces were real observable phenomena. Newton himself hinted at what he believed, while shrinking from any firm assertion for which he could be held responsible and criticized. Instead, he manoeuvred his young supporters into positions of influence, from which they could promulgate Newtonianism on his behalf.

What also emerges from Jan Golinski's analysis is how the Newtonian chemistry, openly proclaimed in the early eighteenth century by Newton's acolytes, was the presentable face of a secret thought-process which he never made public—his decades of alchemical investigation. Here again, we benefit from the modern historical researches which have revealed the strange concerns lying within Newton's public achievements.

It would, however, be a mistake to make too much of the 'strangeness' of Newton's concerns. If they appear that way to us, this is partly because we have lost the sense of what people in the seventeenth century thought, and how they viewed the world. In addition, we are still influenced by, or react against, the Victorian perception of Newton as a hero of rationality, progress, and moral virtue. So, as a background for understanding the chapters in this book, it will be helpful to recall some aspects of seventeenth-century England, and how Newton's life interacted with his times.

Newton's England

Isaac Newton was born in 1642, just after the Civil War had started, with the Stuart king Charles I on the throne. He died in 1727, at the end of the reign of the first Hanoverian king, George I. In between, there were great changes in English society and intellectual life, as well as in royal dynasties. To understand the intellectual atmosphere in which Newton grew up, we should start by recalling some of his contemporaries.

Francis Bacon advocated a blend of experimenting and theorizing for making progress in science, which was an inspiration to the members of the Royal Society later in the century. The title page of his *Great Instauration* (1620) shows a ship sailing between pillars into the wide ocean and new worlds beyond, with the slogan *Many shall pass through and knowledge will increase.*

The Royal Society was founded in the early years of Charles II's reign; this contemporary engraving, designed by the diarist John Evelyn, captures the spirit of Restoration science shortly before Newton's influence began to be felt. Francis Bacon (on the right), and the Society's first President, the mathematician William Brouncker (on the left), attend Fame's crowning of Charles II with a laurel wreath. The bookcase contains works by Copernicus, Harvey, and Bacon, which inspired the approach of the new science. The collection of scientific instruments attests to the practical and experimental interests of the Society's members.

Newton's birth occurred only a few months after the death of Galileo Galilei, the great Italian scientist whose work helped to lay the ground for Newton's studies of mechanics and astronomy. At the same time, the French polymath René Descartes was living in exile in Holland and, in his mid-forties, was preparing the *Principles of philosophy* which was to be so influential on Newton's *Principia*. Also in Holland, the painter Rembrandt was 36, and reaching a turning point in his career—1642 was the year of his great painting *The night watch*. In England William Harvey, the discoverer of the circulation of the blood and by now royal physician, was 64 and reaching the end of his professional life—in October 1642 he had attended Charles I at the battle of Edgehill. The poet John Milton was 34, and becoming known as the great pamphleteering champion of the Puritan Revolution.

Several of the men who would play important roles in Newton's life were born in the previous decade. The mathematician and architect Christopher Wren, later President of the Royal Society, was aged 10 in 1642, as was Newton's admirer, the philosopher John Locke. The diarist Samuel Pepys, President of the Royal Society when Newton's *Principia* was published, was a year younger. And Newton's arch-enemy Robert Hooke, the talented physicist who believed Newton to have stolen his insights, was seven years old at the time of Newton's birth.

Those of Newton's generation grew up and reached maturity during a time of rapid social change and conflict. The great public events—the capture and beheading of the king, the creation of the Commonwealth, the Protectorate of Oliver Cromwell, and the Restoration of the Monarchy within two years of Cromwell's death—were but the visible indications of deeper social forces. In the long term, England was in the process of changing from a traditional hierarchical society to a more recognizably modern one, in which commerce and the middle classes assumed a more powerful role. But at the time, it seemed as though the chaos and disruption of over-zealous fanatics was giving way to a more relaxed and peaceful order within society.

For the heavens had been in disarray. A writer in 1672 bemoaned the fact that any student of cosmology had four different world-systems from which to choose—some men even spoke of seven. Fifteen years later, Newton had brought unity and harmony to the heavens and the physical sciences. In a sense which his contemporaries recognized, Newton's imposing of order and reason upon the cosmos was all of a piece with the new social forces.

The flight of the Catholic king James II in 1688, and the 'Glorious Revolution' in which the crown was offered to the Protestant monarchs William and Mary, testify to the importance of religion in this age. Newton played a more prominent public part in these matters than he had done hitherto about anything. He was a member of the 1689–

90 parliament which enacted the Bill of Rights; this laid down, among other things, that no Catholic could again ascend to the British throne—although Newton's contribution to the proceedings was reputedly limited to a request that a draughty window be closed. He was more forceful on the issue of whether James II could force Cambridge University to admit a Benedictine monk. Newton set aside the final work on the *Principia* so as to support publicly the University's opposition. Newton's anti-Catholicism was thus a matter of public record. What has not been widely realized until recently, however, is that Newton's private religious beliefs were heretical in the eyes of the established church of his day—or indeed our day, although the concept of heresy has considerably less force now than it did then.

The details of Newton's beliefs are discussed more fully by John Brooke in Chapter 8. The essential thing to recognize at this stage is just how *important* were religious feelings, views, beliefs, and differences throughout that century. Little of Newton's work and approach can be understood without seeing the ramifications everywhere of religious impulses and preconceptions which are less fashionable today.

A life in five scenes

In order to have a perspective from which to explore the chapters which follow, it will be helpful to see Newton's life in outline. Outwardly, it was very uneventful by the standards of his age. The drama of his internal life took place against the backdrop of only three locations: Lincolnshire, Cambridge, and London. The man who is famous for comparing himself to a boy playing with pebbles on the seashore is unlikely ever to have seen the sea. We can think of Newton's earthly trajectory as a life in five scenes.

Lincolnshire, 1642–61

Isaac Newton was born on Christmas Day 1642—this is the date *old style* by the Julian calendar then in force in England; for the rest of Europe already using the modern Gregorian calendar, the date was 4 January 1643.

His father, an illiterate but fairly prosperous yeoman farmer, had died three months earlier. The baby was grievously premature, and given little hope of survival: it was said that he was so small that he could be fitted into a quart pot. When young Isaac was three, his mother Hannah—a strong, self-reliant woman—remarried and moved to the next village to live with her new husband, a wealthy elderly clergyman. But Isaac stayed behind, in the house where he was born. His grandmother cared for him until his stepfather's death eight years later, when his mother returned, together with the three children of her second marriage. All Newton's recent biographers have seen this separation from his mother, between the ages of three and ten, as

Woolsthorpe Manor, near Grantham, Lincolnshire—the birthplace of Isaac Newton.

The Free Grammar School of King Edward VI, Grantham, where Newton was a pupil.

crucial in helping to form the suspicious, neurotic, tortured personality of the adult Isaac Newton.

Mother and son were reunited only for a couple of years. At the age of 12, Isaac was sent to the Free Grammar School in Grantham, seven miles away. There he lodged with the local apothecary, and first met the chemicals to which he would later devote so much energy. We have less solid information than we would like about the details of the education Newton received at school; he would have learned mainly Latin grammar—which is what *grammar schools* were for—and more than a modicum of basic arithmetic. He was fortunate in his school, an old foundation with a tradition of good education, and in his master, Henry Stokes. In later years, many stories of Newton's school-days were put about, not least by the ageing Sir Isaac himself, about his mechanical inventiveness, his experimental ingenuity, and his uneasy relations with his fellow-pupils. However much we may doubt some of the details, it is not implausible that the teenage Newton was noticeably out of step with his class-mates, and showing early signs of the manual dexterity which later stood him in such good stead.

At 17, it was time for him to come home and learn to manage his estate. Apparently this was a total failure: the young man could not grasp the importance of watching sheep lest they stray, or conducting business in Grantham market. He seems to have preferred to read books and build models, which was no way to prosper the estate. Fortunately, both his schoolmaster and his uncle, Hannah's clergyman brother, persuaded Hannah that the attempt to make a yeoman farmer of Isaac Newton was futile. He returned to Grantham after nine months, to lodge with Stokes and be prepared for his uncle's old college at the University of Cambridge.

Boys will be boys! A solid memory of Newton's school-days, in the form of this name carved on a window-ledge of his school in Grantham.

Cambridge 1661-5

In June 1661, Newton joined Trinity College, Cambridge, the community of some 400 scholars and students which was his home for

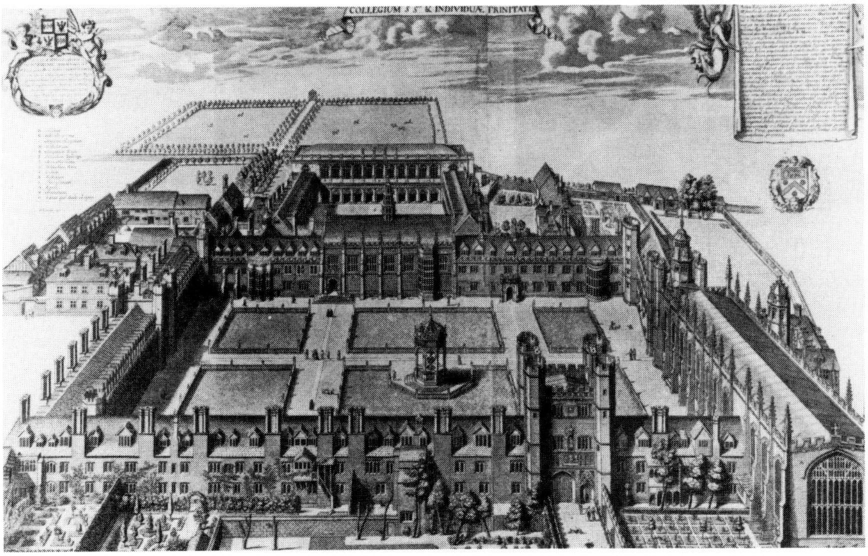

Trinity College, Cambridge, in about 1690.

most of the next 35 years. To begin with, he was a subsizar, which meant that he earned his keep by serving the Fellows and wealthier students—cleaning boots, waiting at table, emptying chamber-pots, and so forth. He seems to have supplemented his income by money lending, although perhaps with an uneasy conscience, since 'Setting my heart on money' figures in a list of his sins he drew up in 1662.

What did Newton learn as an undergraduate? The *official* curriculum was mainly devoted to teaching Aristotelian philosophy. He read through the logic, ethics, and rhetoric of the ancient Greek, together with more recent commentaries on these. Unnappetizing as this may sound (and was), it provided, if nothing else, a superb training in argument techniques and logical presentation—a training which showed itself throughout Newton's life in his formidable ability to marshal arguments and demolish anyone who crossed him. But the truly important content of his university studies was the *unofficial* curriculum which he read for himself. We can tell something of his range of reading from his notebooks; it appears that by about 1664, Newton began to explore voraciously the new intellectual world of the seventeenth century—the English philosophers Thomas Hobbes and Henry More, the Frenchman René Descartes, and many more. Then he moved to some prominent scientific works, Johannes Kepler on optics, Galileo Galilei, Pierre Gassendi, and more Descartes. At some stage, his lack of mathematical background became an obstacle, which he set about remedying with ferocious application. In short, Newton was essentially self-taught, in a wide range of current philosophical and scientific knowledge, by his own self-directed reading.

In early 1665, Newton became a Bachelor of Arts. But this was a formality, following automatically on four years having elapsed since he had come up to university. The more crucial academic milestone was passed the previous year, when he was elected a scholar of Trinity—somewhat surprisingly, since up until then there is no evidence of his having distinguished himself academically in the eyes of the University. With Newton's election as a scholar, in April 1664, his duties as subsizar ceased. He was now guaranteed at least four further years' residence in the college, to pursue his own interests. But after a year, in which his interest in and pursuit of mathematics grew ever more intense, the even tenor of life in Cambridge abruptly ceased. The dreaded plague reached Cambridge in the summer of 1665, and the University closed down until it was safe to reopen. Isaac Newton returned home, and carried on working and thinking in the rural calm where he had proved such a poor shepherd five years before.

Lincolnshire, 1665–7

We have Newton's own account, written over 50 years later, of his ideas at this period. Whether or not one appreciates its detailed references, the list is a remarkable one:

> In the beginning of the year 1665 I found the Method of approximating series & the Rule for reducing any dignity of any Binomial into such a series. The same year in May I found the method of Tangents of Gregory and Slusius, & in November had the direct method of fluxions & the next year in January had the Theory of Colours & in May following I had entrance into ye inverse method of fluxions. And the same year I began to think of gravity extending to ye orb of the Moon & (having found out how to estimate the force with w^{ch} [a] globe revolving within a sphere presses the surface of the sphere) from Keplers rule of the periodical times of the Planets being in sesquialterate proportion of their distances from the centers of their Orbs, I deduced that the forces wch keep the Planets in their Orbs must [be] reciprocally as the squares of their distances from the centres about wch they revolve: & thereby compared the force requisite to keep the Moon in her Orb with the force of gravity at the surface of the earth, & found them answer pretty nearly. All this was in the two plague years of 1665–1666. For in those days I was in the prime of my age for invention & minded Mathematicks & Philosophy more than at any time since.

Not all of these details can be corroborated by historians, but the spirit of the account seems to be quite right—in an extraordinarily short time, Newton laid the foundations for his epoch-making work in no fewer than three areas: mathematics, optics, and celestial dynamics. These ideas did not all fall off trees in the Woolsthorpe garden, nor indeed were they solely the product of meditation in rural Lincolnshire.

Newton had been investigating mathematics and dynamics in the months before he left Cambridge in the summer of 1665. It is clear that from his last undergraduate year he had been advancing at a phenomenal speed towards the frontiers of mathematical knowledge, which he was beginning to push forwards. He had also been stimulated to think about motion and forces, and began the train of thought which culminated in the *Principia* 20 years later, by reading Descartes' *Principles of philosophy* in the winter of 1664–5. How his interest in light started is not known for certain: it may be that he bought a prism at a fair, or perhaps the stimulus of Hooke's *Micrographia* (1665) started him thinking about how colours are produced and what their relationship is to white light.

At all events, the years 1665–6 with Newton reading, thinking, and writing, first in Cambridge and then in Lincolnshire, were those in which he became one of the leading mathematicians and natural philosophers of Europe.

How did he do it? Many different factors were involved, of course, but the judgement of John Maynard Keynes remains very plausible:

> I believe that the clue to his mind is to be found in his unusual powers of continuous concentrated introspection ... His peculiar gift was the power of holding in his mind a purely mental problem until he had seen straight through it. I fancy his pre-eminence is due to his muscles of intuition being the strongest and most enduring with which a man has ever been gifted. Anyone who has ever attempted pure scientific or philosophical thought knows how one can hold a problem momentarily in one's mind and apply all one's powers of concentration to piercing through it, and how it will dissolve and escape and you find that what you are surveying is a blank. I believe that Newton could hold a problem in his mind for hours and days and weeks until it surrendered to him its secret.

Cambridge, 1667–96

The University of Cambridge reopened in the spring of 1667, and Newton returned to Trinity College soon after. That autumn, he was elected to a fellowship of his college, and two years later he became, at the age of 26, Lucasian Professor of Mathematics, the position he held for the next 32 years. This rapid ascent up the academic ladder must have owed something to the results of his intense studies during the plague years—but in a somewhat roundabout way.

On his return, Newton seems to have dropped mathematics for a couple of years, to pursue his growing interest in alchemy. But in late 1668 there appeared a book, Nicolas Mercator's *Logarithmotechnia*, which described some of the techniques for infinite series which Newton had worked out—in far greater generality—three or four years earlier. Newton was horrified, seeing his private invention about to be rediscovered by others. Clearly he would have to claim his priority. There followed a typically Newtonian scene. He hastily composed a treatise, which we know as *De analysi*, to explain his ideas, which his friend Isaac Barrow communicated to a London mathematician. It was not for some weeks that Barrow was allowed to reveal the name of the author—Newton's reluctance to make his work known was always in uneasy contention with his reluctance to let anyone else be credited. This episode brought Newton's work to the private attention of mathematicians in London and abroad, through the letters between mathematicians which were then a prominent feature of mathematical communication.

Shortly afterwards, Isaac Barrow resigned from the Lucasian Chair to pursue his ecclesiastical career, and Isaac Newton was appointed, presumably on Barrow's recommendation. The duties were not onerous. The professor was supposed to lecture on 'some part of Geometry, Astronomy, Geography, Optics, Statics, or some other Mathematical discipline'. Newton's first lectures were on optics, as this subject was fascinating him more and more. But over the years, his lecturing does not seem to have been a great success. It is not as an aspiring lecturer that Newton is remembered. Later, his assistant Humphrey Newton (no relation) recorded that

> so few went to hear Him, & fewer y^t understood him, y^t oftimes he did in a manner, for want of Hearers, read to ye Walls.

Humphrey Newton it was who was privileged to be present the one time Newton is recorded as having laughed: it was when an acquaintance asked him what use studying Euclid's *Elements* would be.

The first optical work of Newton to become widely known was not his theoretical inquiries into the nature of colours, but his reflecting telescope. This caused a sensation when it reached London in late 1671 and ensured Newton's election to the Royal Society. Newton

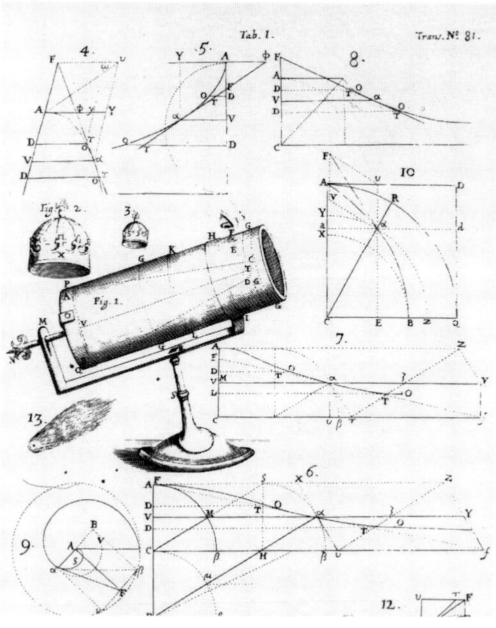

'*An Accompt of a New kind of Telescope, invented by Mr. Isaac Newton*' appeared in the March 1672 issue of the Royal Society's *Philosophical Transactions*. As well as the drawing of the telescope (*Fig. 1*), two crowns were pictured: an object on a weathercock 300 feet away as seen through Newton's instrument (*Fig. 2*) and through a 25-inch refracting telescope (*Fig. 3*). Other matters discussed that month were *Eggs to be found in all sorts of Females*, John Wallis's method of tangents (*Fig. 4* onwards), and a new comet seen at Dantzig (*Fig. 13*).

had great manual skills (not reflected in his drawing ability, it may be admitted)—he constructed the telescope himself, building the tube, grinding the mirror, and making all his own tools too. These skills came in very useful in another activity to which the Lucasian Professor increasingly devoted long hours, the study of alchemy and chemistry.

As the decade went on, he was also becoming more interested in theology. Newton was incapable of tackling anything superficially, and his manuscripts show a massive investment of effort in studying the Bible, the church fathers, the work of Hebrew scholars, and ancient and modern theologians. His growing private conviction was that the scriptures, and thus Christianity, had been deliberately corrupted in the fourth and fifth centuries. His beliefs were incompatible with the tenets of the Church of England, in which he was expected, as a Fellow of Trinity College, to become a clergyman. A crisis seemed imminent, when a *deus ex machina* arrived in the form of a royal decree, apparently at Barrow's intercession, that exempted the Lucasian Professor from needing to take holy orders.

During the 1670s, Newton's alchemical and theological investigations flourished, while his public career as a natural philosopher dwindled. In 1672, he had boldly allowed his *New theory about light and colours* to be made public. But the critical response involved Newton in seemingly endless defensive re-explanations and clarifications. Although he took his part in several vigorous correspondences, gradually he withdrew and carried on with his own interests, largely alchemy and theology, in private.

The 1680s we remember as the decade in which the *Principia* appeared (the story is told by John Roche in Chapter 2)—the decade in which Edmond Halley invaded the Cambridge lair of the sleeping giant and squeezed the work out of its reluctant author. A world which was beginning to forget about Isaac Newton, except in select scientific circles, awoke to find the world changed by him. Newton could never afterwards bury himself away, and within a decade chose to leave his Cambridge fastness for the hurly-burly of London life and a public role.

But there were tribulations to be overcome first. Notably, in autumn 1693 Newton suffered a mental breakdown of some kind. The first his friends learned of it was by receiving somewhat sad and strange letters. The philosopher John Locke one day opened a letter, to read:

> Sr
> Being of opinion that you endeavoured to embroil me wth woemen & by other means I was so much affected with it as that when one told me you were sickly & would not live I answered twere better if you were dead. I desire you to forgive me this uncharitableness. For I am now satisfied that what you have done is just & I beg your pardon for my having hard thoughts of you for it & for representing that you struck at ye root of morality in a principle you laid down in your book of Ideas & designed to pursue in another book &

that I took you for a Hobbist. I beg your pardon also for saying or thinking that there was a designe to sell me an office, or to embroile me. I am

your most humble & most
unfortunate Servant
Is. Newton

The news was soon all round European scientific circles, and gained greatly in the telling—Newton's laboratory and papers had been burned, it was said, and Newton gone mad through worry and locked up by his friends until he recovered. Newton himself gave a simpler explanation later: he said he had not been sleeping well. It is quite possible that decades of overwork were taking their toll—a colleague in the 1670s had expressed fears that Newton was killing himself through work. Other explanations have been offered, including mercury poisoning from his years of alchemy experiments.

One factor in Newton's life at that time was his relationship with Fatio de Duillier, which had ended a month or two before, in early summer 1693. Fatio was a young Swiss mathematician whom he had known since 1689, and this friendship was the closest Newton appears to have come in his life to having a warm human relationship (apart from with his mother). Fatio later became a religious zealot, involved in an obscure sect of millennial prophets—but not before he had published, in 1699, the treatise which more than any other set off the Newton–Leibniz priority dispute, through its somewhat intemperate claims for Newton's sole invention of the calculus.

Nicolas Fatio de Duillier (1664–1753).

In a decision which illustrates yet again the complexities of Isaac Newton's mind, he left Cambridge in 1696 to become Warden of the Mint, in London.

London, 1696–1727

The last 30 years of Newton's life are ones in which the secretive retiring scholar became an influential public figure, attaining and ruthlessly wielding power. He first put the Mint to rights. His appointment as Warden may have been intended as an agreeable sinecure, but Newton, who could do nothing half-heartedly, did not take it lightly. He took charge of the recoinage, which was needed to stabilize the monetary crisis in the economy. He turned out to be an extraordinarily efficient administrator and a shrewd political operator, accreting more powers and influence until in 1700 he was appointed Master of the Mint. His duties went further than simple administration—the Warden was responsible for prosecuting coiners (whose offence was punishable by death), a task which Newton took to with grisly assiduity.

In his early years in London, Newton paid little attention to the Royal Society, which was going through an unhappy and directionless phase. But the death of Robert Hooke in March 1703 removed a major

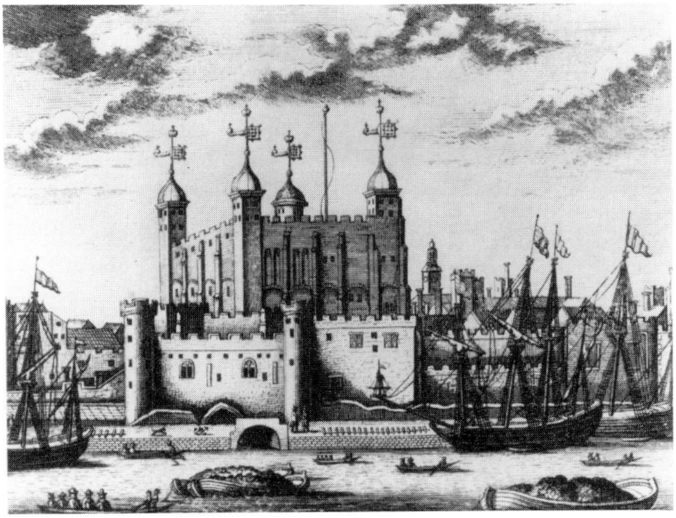

The Tower of London (where the Mint was situated), 1707. When Newton became Warden of the Mint, he lived at first in the Tower.

irritant, the man who for 30 years had criticized Newton and claimed priority in a number of areas (notably in the matter of the inverse-square law that was so important a part of *Principia*). In November of that year, Newton was elected to be President of the Society, and turned his formidable powers on pulling the Society together.

The following year, he brought out his *Opticks*, written long before; its publication at this stage was another event possibly not unconnected with the happy release of Robert Hooke, who had been so troublesome over the 1672 paper on light and colours. *Opticks* became a very popular book, its imagery resonating down through eighteenth-century poetry. The next year Newton was knighted by Queen Anne. Success and public recognition were coming fast. At the same time, Newton was working to ensure that the Newtonian philosophy would spread. An entourage of bright young men gathered around Newton, whom he would try to get appointed, usually with success, to positions in universities and schools where they could teach the Newtonian approach, and write textbooks to spread the word further afield.

As intellectual storm-troopers, the young Newtonians had to help fight his battles, too. Newton's capacity for taking offence and for implacable argument in no way diminished with the passing of years. The most notorious of his disputes is that with Leibniz over the invention of the calculus. Nasty tactics were used by the principals and their henchmen on both sides. This episode is a revealing one about the individuals involved, but also about the state of the social practice of knowledge. Political issues were involved too. The death of Queen Anne in 1714 was followed by the succession of the Hanoverian monarch George I, Leibniz' employer, so the question of who had influence at which court was a critical one.

Newton outlived Leibniz, as he outlived Hooke. When he eventually

Characteristic of the style of engravings celebrating Newton is this one, incorporating Sir Godfrey Kneller's 1702 portrait and various more-or-less appropriate mathematical and other references.

died, in his eighty-fifth year, it was the signal for a display of pomp and pageantry, and a wealth of poems, statues, medallions, and other commemorations. Those who visit his tomb in Westminster Abbey today can still find the exhortation upon it, *Let Mortals rejoice That there has existed such and so great an Ornament to the Human Race*. The man long celebrated as '*the greatest and rarest genius that ever rose*' may no longer be so exalted today, but his life and work still stand as the high point of a fertile age and a source of unending fascination and delight.

Date	*Age*		*Event*
1642			Birth of Isaac Newton
1655	12		Attends Grantham Grammar School
1661	18		Goes up to Trinity College, Cambridge
1665	22	Jan:	Graduates Bachelor of Arts at Cambridge
		Aug:	Moves back to Lincolnshire because of plague
1667	24		Return to Cambridge, elected Fellow of Trinity
1669	26		Elected Lucasian Professor of Mathematics
1672	29		Elected Fellow of the Royal Society
1684	41		Halley's visit leads to preparation of *Principia*
1687	44		Publication of *Principia*
1689	46		Member of Parliament for Cambridge University
1693	50		Mental breakdown
1696	53		Moves to London as Warden of the Mint
1700	57		Master of the Mint
1703	60		Elected President of the Royal Society
1704	61		Publication of *Opticks*
1705	62		Knighted by Queen Anne
1727	84		Death of Isaac Newton

Further reading

Readers of this book who wish to pursue some particular topic will find help in the 'Further reading' section at the end of each chapter. Detailed references to the quotations used in chapters are given at the end of this book, and the sources cited there may also be helpful. To follow up a general interest in Newton, and in what has recently been found out about him and his influence, the first three books in this list are especially helpful, while the last three are the major recent editions of Newton's work.

Never at rest: a biography of Isaac Newton, Richard S. Westfall, Cambridge University Press, Cambridge, 1980.

Newton and Newtoniana 1672–1975: a bibliography, Peter and Ruth Wallis, Dawson, Folkestone, 1977.

The Newton handbook, Derek Gjertsen, Routledge and Kegan Paul, London, 1986.

The correspondence of Isaac Newton, 7 volumes, edited by H. W. Turnbull, J. F. Scott, A. R. Hall, and L. Tilling, Cambridge University Press, Cambridge, 1959–77.

The mathematical papers of Isaac Newton, 8 volumes, edited by D. T. Whiteside, Cambridge University Press, Cambridge, 1967–84.

The optical papers of Isaac Newton, edited by Alan Shapiro, Cambridge University Press, Cambridge, 1984–.

CHAPTER ONE

Newton's success

DEREK GJERTSEN

Newton's success—both worldly and intellectual—was rather special. If not unique and unprecedented, it is sufficiently distinctive to deserve some description and analysis in its own right. One way to bring out the magnitude of Newton's achievements would be to make a list of his numerous discoveries and show that the list is larger and richer than any list compiled from the works of his rivals. Apart from revealing Newton's range and virtuosity, this exercise would illuminate little. Equally long lists could be drawn up for Newton's contemporaries, Edmond Halley and Christiaan Huygens, and indeed for many lesser scientists. Moreover, it is by no means clear that, in learning that Newton formulated a law of cooling as well as the inverse-square law, much light has been thrown on the special character of Newton's success. Nor does the insistence that Newton's discoveries were more fundamental or important than those of other scientists do anything more than invite further questions about *why* Newton's discoveries are so fundamental and important.

Historians of science have their own way of characterizing Newton's success, and this is not surprisingly expressed in terms of his broad position in the historical development of science. They conventionally adopt one of two general characterizations.

According to the first, Newton is seen as the great synthesizer. With his work, the scientific revolution reached its climax. The astronomical revolution, carried out by Copernicus and Kepler, was united by Newton with the new theories of motion proposed by Galileo and Descartes. In this manner, Newton succeeded in revealing nature's unity. For the first time, the same laws of nature and the same explanatory principles could be applied to both the heavens and the earth. Thus, for Toulmin and Goodfield, Newton's success lay in his 'imaginative integration of many ideas into a single picture', and in similar style, A. R. Hall has spoken of Newton's 'grand synthesis'.

The success of Newton at the time of his death may be gauged from this *Allegorical monument to Isaac Newton*, painted in 1727–30 by Giovanni Battista Pittoni. It is more noticeable for a mass of loose scientific–mathematical symbolism than for accurate Newtonian details. A version of his prism experiment is displayed, with light coming from above the *Urn, wherein is supposed to be deposited the Remains of the deceased Hero.*

Other historians of science, however, have seen Newton's success not so much in the assembly of already constructed units, but in the creation of something entirely novel. Thus, in *The Newtonian revolution* (1980), I. B. Cohen has rejected the notion of Newton as grand synthesizer, on the grounds that Newton had shown in the *Principia* that most elements of the supposed synthesis were false. Kepler, for example, had claimed that the solar force diminishes *directly* as the distance, while for Galileo the moon exercised no tidal influence. How, asked Cohen, could a true science be constructed from a mere amalgamation of false ideas and principles? For Cohen, therefore, the Newtonian revolution must have involved the creation of a new method, a distinctive Newtonian style, which he went on to identify with a significant new mode of using mathematics in natural philosophy.

Valuable as such historical analyses undoubtedly are, they can reveal no more than Newton's role in the internal development of science. Even if accurate, they are unlikely to account for the manner in which a technical treatise in mathematical physics came to influence such sciences as chemistry and physiology, and also served as a model for poets, philosophers, theologians, and scholars from many other fields. Others have initiated and completed scientific revolutions without finding their ideas a matter of common currency. Wherein, then, lies the source of Newton's distinctive success?

Some special features of Newton's success

Before considering the source of Newton's success, let me attempt to identify some of the distinctive features of that success.

Rapidity

The first feature of interest is the extraordinary rapidity with which success came Newton's way. Today we are used to the idea of instant scientific success. In 1956, Lee and Yang published a classic paper on the violation of parity in weak interactions, and in the following year they shared the Nobel physics prize.

In Newton's day, things were ordered somewhat differently. For example, Bernard de Fontenelle (author of the *Éloge* on Newton, delivered in Paris in 1727) was struck by Newton's 'peculiar happiness, to enjoy the reward of his merit in his life-time'. This was quite contrary, he noted, to Descartes who received no honours until well after his death. Voltaire, writing in 1734, was similarly struck by the manner in which Newton could live into his eighties, 'always tranquil, happy and honoured in his own country', whereas Galileo had ended his days persecuted by the Inquisition, and Descartes had died in exile in Stockholm surrounded by hostile scientists and tended by an unfriendly doctor.

According to Thomas Hobbes, the anatomist William Harvey had been the only man ever to see his own doctrines established in his own lifetime. One reason for the tardy acceptance of new ideas is that some men, like Copernicus and Galileo, published their work late in life: Copernicus' *De revolutionibus* (1543) came literally from his deathbed, while Galileo's *Two new sciences* (1638) was published just four years before his death. In other cases, the significance of the work eluded contemporaries. This point can be illustrated by reference to the fate of Kepler's laws, so basic to the development of modern astronomy, in the hands of seventeenth-century astronomers.

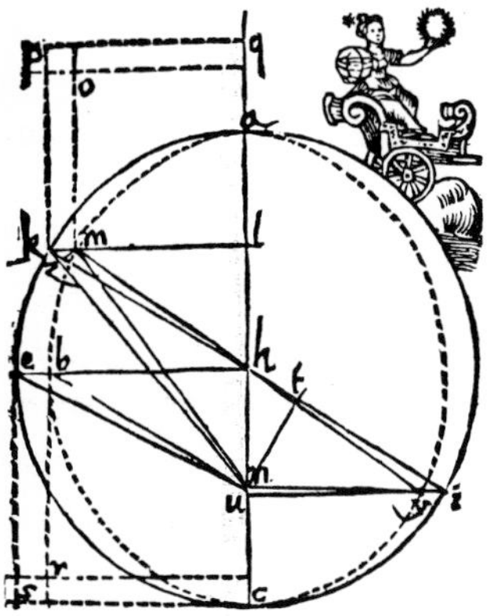

Kepler's diagram of the orbit of Mars, illustrating his *first law*, that planets travel around the Sun in elliptical orbits, with the Sun at one focus (labelled *n*) of the ellipse (the dotted oval within the circle).

Kepler's first law, that the planets move in elliptical orbits, and his second law, that a line joining a planet to the Sun sweeps out equal areas in equal times, both appeared in Kepler's *Astronomia nova* (1609). Kepler's third law, relating a planet's orbital period to its distance from the Sun, was published a decade later in his *Harmonice mundi*. Yet, as D. T. Whiteside noted to his surprise in 1964, only Kepler's third law was widely accepted by the astronomers of the period. The first law was accepted only tentatively, in need of further confirmation, while the second law was seldom even mentioned. This curious indifference to Kepler's work is apparent in the *Principia*. The first reference to Kepler's laws comes late in Book II (Proposition LIII), where they are perversely attributed to Copernicus! As Cohen has reminded us, '*there was no Keplerian revolution before 1687*'.

Newton's success, of course, was not instantaneous, nor was it universally acknowledged. There were many like Leibniz who resisted Newtonian dynamics on the grounds that to talk of attraction was to reintroduce into physics the occult qualities of the renaissance magi. Similarly, Newton's theories on light and colour, first publicly propounded in 1672, became widely accepted in France only after 1715. The reason for the delay was very simple: French attempts to replicate Newton's work had, for a variety of reasons, invariably failed. When a number of senior members of the Paris Académie des Sciences visited London in 1715 to observe a solar eclipse, Newton took the opportunity to have demonstrated before them some of his more important optical experiments. The French scientists were at last convinced, and returned to Paris in broad agreement with Newton's views. Thus, the point can still be maintained. Newton's success, although not immediate, was still widely recognized within his own lifetime. Furthermore, it was more durable than that attained by any of his predecessors.

Durability

On the third voyage of his travels, Gulliver visited Glubbdubdrib, the isle of magicians, where the Governor invited him to conjure the spirits of his choice. Aristotle was summoned, along with the two leading representatives of French mechanical philosophy, René Descartes and Pierre Gassendi. After admitting his own errors, Aristotle noted how their contemporaries had identified equally damaging mistakes in the theories of Gassendi and Descartes. He concluded by predicting a similar fate for *attraction*:

> whereof the present learned are such zealous asserters. He said, that new systems of nature were but new fashions, which would vary in every age; and even those who pretended to demonstrate them from mathematical

Mathematicians in the eighteenth century were not always treated with respect—this scene in Bedlam, from Hogarth's *The Rake's Progress* (1735), shows a mad astronomer who imagines his roll of paper is a telescope, and a mad mathematician scribbling a method for determining longitude. The method is taken from the works of William Whiston, Newton's successor at Cambridge.

principles would flourish but a short period of time, and be out of vogue when that was determined.

Swift's view of science as fashion, while not entirely groundless even today, must have looked much more plausible to an observer of the early eighteenth century. What hope could there be for the long-term survival of Newtonian science to someone who had already seen the rise and fall of numerous scientific reputations? The notion that science was a durable and universal creation had yet to emerge; its first and prime exemplar was to be Newton himself.

The most straightforward evidence of Newton's durability is clearly displayed in the pages of histories of science from the seventeenth century onwards. In the *Histoire des sciences* (1751) which Jean D'Alembert contributed to the monumental *Encyclopédie*, Cartesian vortices were dismissed as ridiculous, whereas Newton's work was judged to have given 'philosophy a form which apparently it is to keep'. Furthermore, no praise could be too great or could match 'his innumerable discoveries and genius'.

A century later, in his influential *History of the inductive sciences* (1837), William Whewell found Newton 'altogether without a rival or neighbour', and his work on universal gravitation, 'indisputably and incomparably the greatest scientific study ever made'. More recently still, and in more critical times, R. S. Westfall's *Construction of modern science* (1971) could still conclude that 'modern science continues to pursue its effective course within the framework established by Newton'.

It may be thought that such are the rather special views of historians of science, too attached to the past to recognize the present state of science. Have not Newton's theories, like those of Aristotle, Descartes, and Gassendi before him, been superseded by later work? Two contemporary scientists who think otherwise are the mathematical physicists Stephen Hawking, a twentieth-century successor of Newton as Lucasian Professor at Cambridge, and Werner Israel. Writing in *The Times*, they described Newton as '*a colossus without parallel in the history of science*', and went on to consider the precise question of whether Newton's work was now superseded:

> The answer is no. Newton's theory will never be outmoded. Designed to predict the motions of the heavenly bodies, it does its job with unbelievable accuracy—better than one part in a hundred million for the motion of the earth around the sun—and it remains in daily use to predict the orbits of moons and planets, comets and spacecraft.

Range

Newton's genius had many dimensions. Indeed, there are few scientists who have displayed their talents in quite so many ways. His powers as a mathematician, and his originality as a theoretical physicist, are well enough known. Less familiar is his skill as an *experimental physicist*.

Theoretical physicists often pride themselves on their inability to undertake even the simplest of experiments. Georg Gamow, a physicist himself, has made the not entirely frivolous claim that the standing of theoretical physicists can be measured by their power to break delicate devices merely by touching them. By this standard, he noted, the Nobel laureate Wolfgang Pauli, before whom 'apparatus would fall, break, shatter or burn when he merely walked into a laboratory', must have been an outstanding theoretician.

Whether serious or not, Gamow's theory breaks down completely when applied to Newton. Something of Newton's experimental skills may be gleaned from the following two examples. In 1672, a reflecting telescope designed by Newton was demonstrated at the Royal Society. Newton, however, was much more than the instrument's designer. He ground and polished the various lenses himself, and also built the instrument. Asked in later life where he had obtained the necessary tools, he replied that he had made them himself, and added:

> If I had staid for other people to make my tools and other things for me, I had never made anything of it.

The second example is taken from Newton's work on coloured rings. At one stage in his investigations he found an error of less than one hundredth of an inch. Westfall has described Newton's response:

> He refused to ignore it but stalked it relentlessly until he found that the two faces of his lens differed in curvature ... No one else in the seventeenth century would have paused for an error twice the size.

His reflecting telescope remains one of the best-known symbols of Newton's success, as we see on stamps from Ascension and Lesotho.

The bust of Isaac Newton in the Stowe *Temple of British Worthies* was by Michael Rysbrack (who was also the sculptor of Newton's tomb in Westminster Abbey). The inscription over Newton's bust, between those of John Locke and Francis Bacon, reads:

Sir Isaac Newton
Whom
the God of Nature made to comprehend his Works;
and from simple Principles, to discover the Laws never known before,
and to explain the Appearance never understood,
of this Stupendous Universe.

Reception

Newton's work was greeted enthusiastically by mathematicians and physicists. That is not surprising. But it was also, and less predictably, accepted with equal enthusiasm by scholars working in unrelated fields. Many poets of the eighteenth century, for example, went out of their way to celebrate in verse what they took to be Newton's main achievements. The verse itself may not have been of the highest quality, and often resorted to little more than nationalistic accounts of how Newton had finally triumphed over French obscurantism. Thus, Richard Oakley wrote of how, after Descartes had 'Fallacious led philosophy aside', Newton had appeared and:

> in orient beauty bright,
> He rose, and brought the world's dark laws to light.

Yet, despite its limitations, eighteenth-century verse frequently exhibited Newton as a *scientist*, and not simply as a national hero. For example, James Thomson, watching a rainbow from Greenwich Hill, was inspired enough to declare:

> How just, how beauteous the refractive law.

The poets of the nineteenth century seldom expressed such sentiments about the work of the eminent scientists of their own era.

A further feature was the level of the praise directed towards Newton. So special did his achievements seem, that even the most extravagant praise began to appear inadequate. To Locke he was 'incomparable', and to Hume 'the greatest and rarest genius that ever arose'. High

The *Temple of British Worthies* at Stowe, near Buckingham, was constructed in 1735 by William Kent. It was the first monument especially built to commemorate national genius, though also to make a political point about the decay of reason and liberties under the Tory government of Sir Robert Walpole. The worthies range from Alfred the Great, Queen Elizabeth I, and John Hampden, to Shakespeare and Milton.

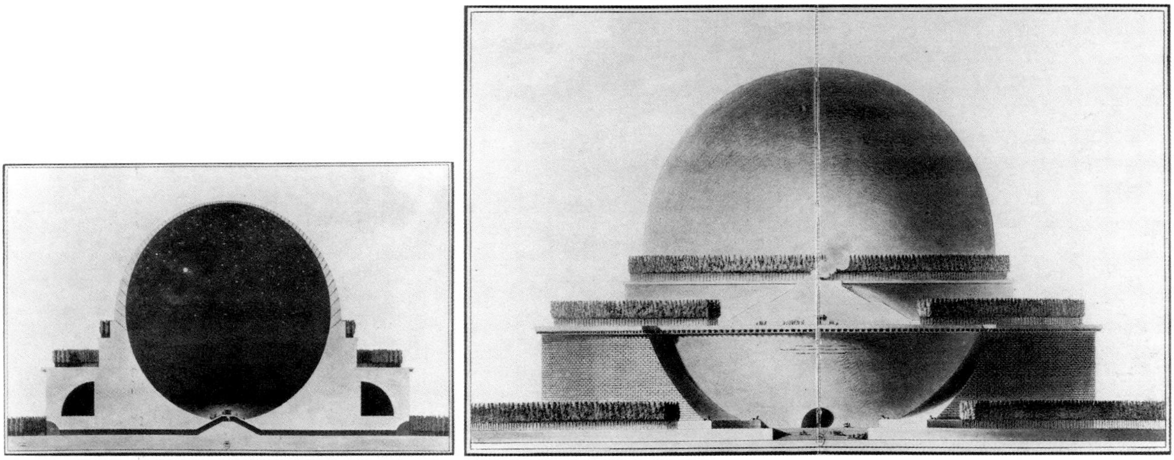

Boullée's *Cenotaph for Newton* (1784), external view and in cross-section. The cypress trees and the human figures give an idea of the scale of this conception. The effect was intended to be something like a vast planetarium. In his accompanying essay, Boullée wrote *O Newton! With the range of your intelligence and the sublime nature of your Genius, you have defined the shape of the earth; I have conceived the idea of enveloping you with your discovery.*

praise indeed, but clearly insufficient for those struggling to find a language appropriate to his unique genius.

Only one possibility beckoned, absurd as it might seem, and that was the language of apotheosis. It began with Halley, in the *Ode* he added to the *Principia*. If Newton was not divine, Halley mused, then

> Nearer the gods no mortal may approach.

Others, like Pope in his famous couplet, were content to suggest that Newton had been especially chosen by God. This view was echoed in the Temple of British Worthies at Stowe, in Buckinghamshire, where it was claimed that God had created Newton 'to comprehend his Works'. A third option, exercised by John Conduitt and Dr Johnson, was the recognition that had Newton flourished in ancient times he would certainly have been worshipped as a divinity.

Such comments are just within the bounds of reason. More extreme reactions came from revolutionary France. In 1796, Champlain de la Blancherie denounced the English for their failure to honour Newton's divinity properly. He proposed that the calendar should be restarted with 1642 (the year of Newton's birth) taken as year 1, and that Newton's home at Woolsthorpe should be turned into a sanctuary. At the same time, the architect Étienne-Louis Boullée was designing an enormous spherical cenotaph. The top would be pierced with holes through which the light could pass in daytime and stars be seen at night. It would carry the legend *Esprit sublime! Génie vaste et profond! Être divin!* Like so many other of Boullée's fantasies, it was never realized.

The source of Newton's success

How can we explain the wide-ranging influence of Newtonian ideas outside the relatively narrow areas of mathematics and physics? It is only occasionally that, as in this case, a scientific theory escapes from the confines of its own traditions and appeals to a much wider audience.

This process is far from common, and seems to be unconnected with the importance of the subject. Few scientific disciplines are as deep, and say as much about nature at its most general, as thermodynamics. When, however, the physicist and novelist C. P. Snow commented in 1959 that few of his educated friends could even state the second law of thermodynamics, the point was greeted with ridicule. For long afterwards, the mere mention of the second law, in certain circles, would be greeted with giggles and snorts of indignation. Again, one of the most important contemporary scientific breakthroughs is quantum theory. Yet, outside its strictly professional influence, and the common misuse of the term *quantum leap*, the subject seems to have filtered into the popular consciousness only through its rather dubious adoption by popular mystics and philosophers.

The contrast with Newtonian science is remarkable. The essential nature of Newton's approach is very simple, and was indicated by him very candidly and clearly in his *Preface* to the *Principia*. Having first derived gravitational forces, Newton described how he had gone on to show how they could be used to explain the motions of the planets, the Moon, and the tides. Further, he suspected that all other natural phenomena were caused by similar, but as yet unknown, forces of attraction and repulsion. 'Whatever reasoning holds for greater motions', Newton argued elsewhere, 'should hold for lesser ones as well'.

The moral was clear, and quickly seen by many contemporary scholars. If Newton could explain most celestial events using one simple kind of attractive force, perhaps others, given the right kind of force, could be equally successful in explaining hitherto mysterious domains of nature. Newton's own caution prevented him from public speculation on the character of these as-yet-unknown forces. Others were not as reticent, but were ambitious to become the Newtons of other less well-charted regions. Consequently, following the publication of the *Principia*, a number of scholars may be seen confidently setting out to become the Newtons of theology, philosophy, chemistry, medicine, and much more besides. Some of these less-than-successful programmes will be sketched below. Further discussion of theology and chemistry will be found in the chapters by John Brooke and Jan Golinski.

Theology

One of the first attempts to deploy Newtonian concepts in another field came from the mathematician John Craig, in his significantly titled

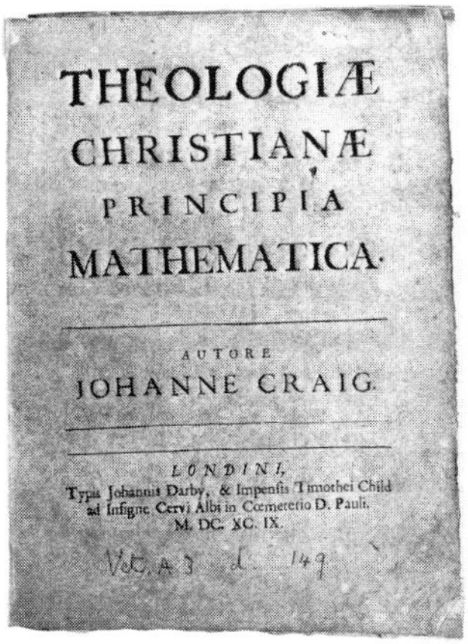

The title of this work, published only 12 years after Newton's *Philosophiae naturalis principia mathematica*, attests to the rapid spread of the Newtonian style to diverse fields.

Theologiae christianae principia mathematica (1699). Just as mathematical principles could illuminate the heavens, so too, Craig argued, could they throw light on Christian theology.

Like Newton, Craig began, with three laws. Compare the first law of each:

Newton: Every body continues in its state of rest or of uniform motion in a right line.

Craig: Every man endeavours to prolong pleasure in his mind, to increase it, or to persevere in a state of pleasure.

From his laws and definitions, Craig went on to derive such Newtonian-sounding theorems as:

Velocities of suspicion produced in equal periods of time increase in arithmetical progression.

Behind this apparent parody of Newton there lay a serious, if misguided, point. St Luke 18 : 8 declares:

Nevertheless when the Son of Man cometh, shall he find faith on earth.

From this verse, Craig inferred that Christ would be greeted by at least one believer on his return to Earth. He also held that belief in historical events diminished as they receded further into the past. If we could determine both the initial degree of belief Christ's disciples had in him, and the rate at which such beliefs diminish, then we should be able to establish an upper limit for the second coming. After much complex reasoning and calculation Craig concluded that, as the probability of the belief in Christ's return would have declined to zero by the year 3150, he must appear before that date.

The further history of Newton's impact on eighteenth-century theology can be seen at its clearest in the *Boyle lectures*. On his death in 1691, Robert Boyle endowed an annual set of lectures to be delivered by a cleric in defence of Christianity against the attacks of atheists and other critics. Richard Bentley, the first lecturer, approached Newton on the issue of the relevance of the *Principia* to God. In four remarkable letters, Newton went to some considerable length to show that many features of the universe require the 'counsel and contrivance of a voluntary Agent'. Why, for example, did the planets move in the same direction and in the same plane? No natural cause could account for such an effect as, Newton pointed out, comets could move in all manner of ways.

Bentley happily followed the Newtonian line, as did many of his fellow Boyle lecturers. Two of the better-known lecture series were William Derham's *Physico-theology* (1714) and *Astro-theology* (1715). The titles readily indicate the mode of reasoning. This tradition survived the eighteenth century, and could be found still flourishing in the 1830s when another patron, the Earl of Bridgewater, invited the

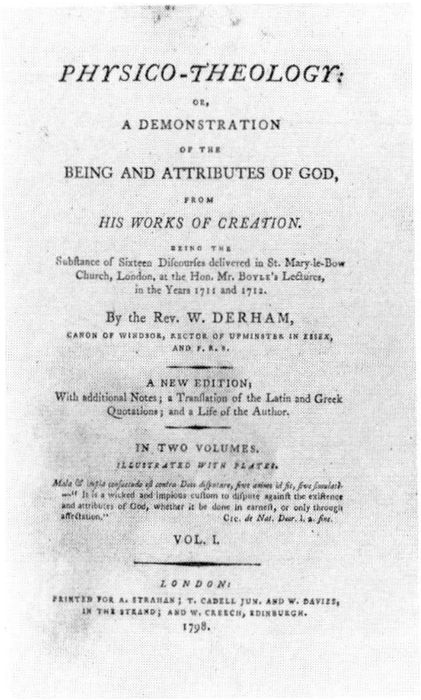
PHYSICO-THEOLOGY:

OR,

A DEMONSTRATION

OF THE

BEING AND ATTRIBUTES OF GOD,

FROM

HIS WORKS OF CREATION.

BEING THE

Subſtance of Sixteen Diſcourſes delivered in St. Mary-le-Bow Church, London, at the Hon. Mr. BOYLE's Lectures, in the Years 1711 and 1712.

By the Rev. W. DERHAM,

CANON OF WINDSOR, RECTOR OF UPMINSTER IN ESSEX, AND F. R. S.

A NEW EDITION;

With additional Notes; a Tranſlation of the Latin and Greek Quotations; and a Life of the Author.

IN TWO VOLUMES.

ILLUSTRATED WITH PLATES.

Mala & impia conſuetudo eſt contra Deos diſputare, ſive animo id fit, ſive ſimulatè.—"It is a wicked and impious cuſtom to diſpute againſt the exiſtence and attributes of God, whether it be done in earneſt, or only through affectation." CIC. *de Nat. Deor.* l. 2. *fine.*

VOL. I.

LONDON:

PRINTED FOR A. STRAHAN; T. CADELL JUN. AND W. DAVIES, IN THE STRAND; AND W. CREECH, EDINBURGH.

1798.

A characteristic work in the theological tradition sustained by Newtonian arguments. The appeal of such works lasted throughout the eighteenth century (and beyond), as the date of this 'new edition' indicates.

scientists of the day to show how God's power and wisdom could be seen in his creation.

Philosophy

David Hume began his *Treatise of human nature* (1738) by noting, like many before and since, 'the present imperfect condition of the sciences'. As it was clear to Hume that 'all the sciences have a relation . . . to the human mind', it followed that only by developing 'the science of Man' could these numerous imperfections be removed. Hume consequently sought in his *Treatise* to develop this important new science.

He began in a Lockean manner by dividing the contents of the mind into impressions and ideas. Ideas are faint images of the impressions met with in thinking and perceiving. All simple ideas, such as the memory of a colour, are merely copies of the corresponding simple impressions. There could therefore be nothing in the mind which could not be traced to a corresponding initial impression.

So far Hume had done no more than to list the contents of the mind; it remained to add a dynamics responsible for, and controlling, all mental operations. He began by noting:

> Were ideas entirely loose, chance alone would join them; and it is impossible the same simple ideas should fall regularly into complex ones (as they commonly do), without some bond of union among them.

What then was this 'bond of union'? What led ideas to associate in a regular way? Hume identified three principles of association amongst ideas: resemblance, contiguity, and cause and effect. He went on to illustrate their use:

> A picture naturally leads our thought to the original [resemblance]; the mention of one apartment in a building naturally introduces an enquiry . . . concerning the others [contiguity]; and if we think of a wound, we can scarcely forbear reflecting on the pain which follows it [cause and effect].

It may or may not have been a coincidence that Hume, like Newton, began with three laws. Of the source of Hume's approach, however, there can be no doubt. Following his account of the principles behind the association of ideas, Hume commented:

> Here is a kind of attraction, which in the mental world will be found to have as extraordinary effects as in the natural, and to show itself in as many and as various forms.

To an eighteenth-century reader, the term *attraction* could refer only to the physics of the *Principia*.

A century later, associationists could still be found formulating their laws. John Stuart Mill, for example, accepted the associationist programme in his *System of logic* (1843), and consequently proposed his own three laws of similarity, contiguity and intensity. Later in the century the last important associationist, Alexander Bain, in his *Mental and moral science* (1872), formulated yet another set of three laws on which the science of the mind must be based—namely, the laws of contiguous adhesion, similarity, and compound association.

The impact of Newton on Hume and the associationists is, of course, simply one example of his influence on philosophy. From a fertile source one further example can be taken. One distinctive style of thought to emerge in the eighteenth century, and known to historians as the *Scottish school of common sense philosophy*, was clearly based on Newton's methodology. It took Newton's claim that he feigned no hypotheses as seriously as it took the four 'Rules of reasoning in philosophy' which preface Book III of the *Principia*. In Rule I Newton had insisted that:

> We are to admit no more causes of natural things than such as are both true and sufficient to explain their appearances.

Thomas Reid, a leading member of the Scottish school, inferred from this that we should 'treat with contempt hypotheses in every branch of philosophy'—that is, postulated entities must really exist, and be demonstrated to exist, before they can be used in either science or philosophy. Given this stringent requirement, Reid and his followers also found it necessary to reject all forms of analogical reasoning.

On this basis, Reid was at last able to attack directly some of the fundamental assumptions of British empirical philosophy. For example, according to the empiricists, we never see the Sun directly; instead we have an *idea* or *impression* of the Sun. But, Reid responded, the existence of *ideas* and *impressions* is no more than an hypothesis:

> The authors who have treated of ideas have generally taken their existence for granted, as a thing that could not be called into question.

Furthermore, the reasoning involved was clearly analogical:

> Thought in the mind is conceived to have some analogy to motion in a body: and as a body is put in motion by being acted upon by some other body, so we are apt to think the mind is made to perceive by some impulse it receives from the object.

It is curious to note how varied Newton's influence could be. Some, like Hume, found it liberating, and a charter to develop new approaches to philosophy. Others, like Reid, used the same sources to suggest ways in which philosophy must be restricted, and thought curtailed. And so it would continue, with some thinkers responding to the strictness of Newton's methodological rules, and others allowing themselves to be more stimulated by Newtonian speculations on the role of forces in the system of the world.

Chemistry

Chemists of the period tended to adopt the latter strategy. Newton had written upon chemical matters in the *Queries* added to successive editions of his *Opticks*. Thus, in Query 31 he spoke of how attractive forces might hold between various common substances. Water and oil do not mix because they lack 'an attractive virtue'. But mercury and copper mix with difficulty because they share a weak attraction, while mercury and tin mix readily because of their strong attractive virtues for each other.

Passages like these, tentative though they may be, were more than enough to convince eighteenth-century chemists that they too could transform their subject if only they could find some way to measure and to calculate 'the attractive virtues', spoken of so enticingly by Newton.

One who took up the challenge was the Comte de Buffon, the 'Newton of France', in his monumental *Histoire naturelle* (1749–). The laws of chemical affinity, he argued with a staggering boldness and a total lack of evidence, are the same 'with that general law by which the celestial bodies act one upon another'. Consequently, all matter without exception was attracted 'in the inverse ratio of the square of the distance'. Attempts were indeed made to show that, just as the $1/r^2$ law controlled the motions of the planets, it was also responsible for the precise affinity between the various chemical elements.

An example of this approach can be seen in the work of the French chemist Guyton de Morveau, who floated discs of different metals on mercury and measured the force necessary to lift them. Thus, while 446 grains were needed to remove gold, zinc required 204 grains, and iron no more than 115. Guyton noted that the affinity of mercury for gold, zinc, and iron is governed by the same sequence. It followed that the force of attraction between two substances was a measure of their chemical affinity. Admittedly, although a typical claim that 'the affinity of mercury with gold is as the affinity of mercury with zinc as 446 : 204' lacked the simplicity of the $1/r^2$ law, it remained a possibility for Guyton that chemical reactions could become as predictable as the paths of the stars.

It would gradually become clear that affinity was a more complex phenomenon, dependent in part on such factors as temperature and concentration: it could not be expressed as a simple function of distance. When the chemical revolution did come, it was brought about by another Newtonian, John Dalton. By concentrating upon the weights of the ultimate particles, Dalton succeeded in creating a new chemistry.

Medicine and physiology

Newton was familiar with both the medicine and physiology of his

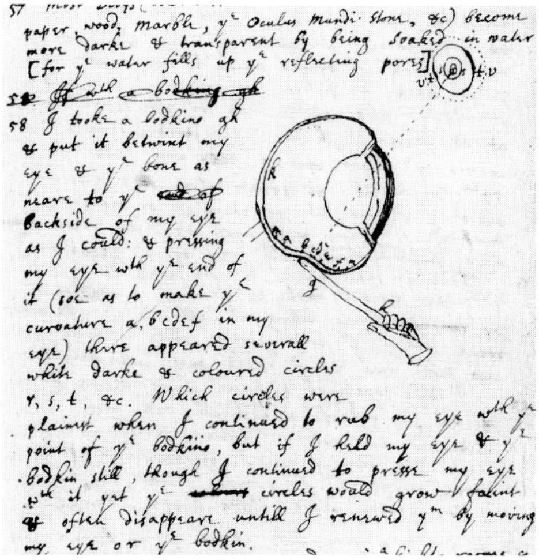

As part of his investigations of colour, Newton wanted to discover the effect of altering the curvature of his eyeball. He found coloured circles could be produced by pressure from a bodkin. The reader is urged not to attempt to replicate this experiment.

day, such as it was, and spent some time working on the anatomy of the eye and studying the visual process. He also saw himself as something of a medical expert, ever free with diagnosis and advice to his family and friends. On a memorable occasion, hearing that the Astronomer Royal John Flamsteed was suffering from prolonged and severe headaches, Newton offered him '*a certain cure*'. Flamsteed should 'bind his head strait with a garter till the crown of his head nummed'. In this way, Newton explained, the retarded circulation would cool his head and ease the pain.

Others took a more theoretical interest and sought to show how disease and health could be represented in terms of the familiar Newtonian notion of attractive forces. Richard Mead, Newton's own physician, saw health as a function of the state of a body's fluids. Like fluids moving through vessels, they possessed velocity and pressure. If the fluids moved with the right velocity at the right pressure, then all would be well; failing this, disease resulted. Once the physician had worked out ways to measure the velocity and pressure of body fluids, treating a patient would require little more than solving a set of hydrodynamic equations. For this reason, Mead declared, the distinguishing mark of a physician from a quack would soon be the possession of 'mathematical learning'.

Suspecting that such a time would be long in coming, many turned to the more convenient domain of mechanical models. Thus, in his *An account of animal secretion* (1708), James Keill attempted to show how the various secretions of the body, such as tears, bile, and semen, all arose initially from the blood. The attractive forces between the various fluids varied as the shapes of the particles composing the fluids varied:

A large particle attracts not more strongly than a small one of the same solidity, but a diversity of figures causes different degrees of attraction in particles, that are otherwise the same ... so that the attractive force varies according as the particles are cones, cylinders, cubes, or spheres, and ceteris paribus a spherical particle has the strongest attractive power.

With such assumptions, it required little ingenuity for Keill to construct a supposedly Newtonian physiology. It is unlikely, however, that Newton would have recognized in work of this kind anything but the wildest speculation.

Social science

Even eighteenth-century sociology had its Newtonian overtones. When the Baron de Montesquieu published *The spirit of the laws* (1748), he began, in the manner of Newton, by laying down fundamental principles from which he later derived a number of consequences. Furthermore, he readily adopted the language of Newtonian mechanics; for example, an efficient monarchy was described in terms of gravitational forces attracting bodies to a system's centre.

To conclude this section, it is natural to ask whether any other scientists have exercised a comparable influence over so many areas. One name which readily suggests itself is that of Charles Darwin. The publication of *The origin of species* (1859) was followed by many attempts to apply the key notions of evolution and natural selection to a wide range of disciplines. Consequently, the late nineteenth century saw the appearance of many books on the evolution of marriage, morals, incest, kingship, the state, monotheism, the lotus design, the swastika, language, capitalism, and virtually every other feature of thought and society. In more recent times, scientists have

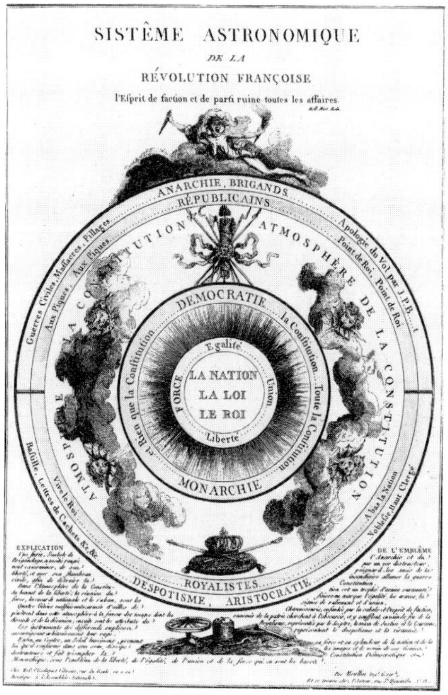

Like the Montesquieu work referred to in the text, this broadsheet of the French Revolution uses the imagery of a Newtonian universe for a political statement.

learnt how to extend Darwinian concepts to the more exact sciences, so that it is now perfectly legitimate to speak of molecular evolution, chemical evolution, and even cosmic evolution.

The Darwinian concepts of evolution and selection have proved as manipulable and as popular as the Newtonian concepts of force and attraction. Just as it can be said of most things that they attract each other, it can also be maintained that most things have evolved. The temptation to adapt Darwinian concepts to their own needs has proved as irresistible to scholars of the past 200 years as had Newton's work to the scientists of the eighteenth century.

How did Newton see his own success?

Bertrand Russell once described a dream. It was set in the distant future, in the Cambridge University Library. Russell was watching a library assistant going around shelves, taking down various books and after examining them, either returning them to the shelves or dumping them into an enormous bucket. Finally the assistant came to the last surviving copy of Russell's *magnum opus, Principia Mathematica*. He took down one of the volumes, turned over a few pages, and looked puzzled. He then closed the volume, balanced it in his hand, and hesitated...

Russell's nightmare reminds us that few people are immune from doubt about the ultimate value of their work. The twentieth-century mathematician Kurt Gödel, whose investigations into the foundations of mathematics are generally recognized as among the deepest results of modern science, was reported to be beset by 'a gnawing uncertainty that maybe all that he had discovered was another paradox'.

Did Newton fully appreciate the value of his own work? How, in fact, did he see his own success?

'On ye shoulders of Giants'

There is little doubt that Newton thoroughly enjoyed, and took some pride in, his worldly success. Knighted in April 1705 by Queen Anne, he rapidly established his pedigree and by November was in a position to apply to the College of Heralds for his coat of arms—Sable, two shin bones saltire-wise, the sinister surmounted of the dexter argent. Clearly, this was the behaviour of a very satisfied man.

What, though, of his intellectual triumphs? According to John Conduitt, his successor at the Mint and husband of his niece Catherine Barton, Newton's view of himself was so humble that:

> He had no relish of the applause that was deservedly paid him; and he was so little vain and desirous of glory from any of his works, that he ... would have let others run away with the glory of these inventions ... if his friends and countrymen had not been more jealous, than he, of his and their glory.

Conduitt's view of a humble Newton finds little documentary support. Although Newton's attitudes to his own work were undoubtedly strange and complex, indifference to it formed no part. A single example will suffice. In May 1686, Robert Hooke approached Edmond Halley, then busily preparing the *Principia* for publication, and requested that Hooke's contribution to Newton's work should be acknowledged. The request was far from baseless, and arose from a correspondence with Newton in 1679. Hooke, it must be emphasized, was asking for no more than an acknowledgement of his earlier help, but Newton's response was extreme. Far from allowing Hooke to 'run away with the glory of these inventions', Newton denounced him as 'a man of strange unsociable temper', and instructed Halley that, rather than acknowledge him in any way, he preferred to suppress Book III of the *Principia* entirely. Once his initial rage abated, Newton allowed Halley to proceed with the full text. He did, however, insist upon one change. In the original draft, Hooke had been granted the epithet *Clarissimus*; the published text referred to Hooke by name alone.

Further evidence of Newton's humility is sometimes gathered from his often quoted judgement;

> If I have seen further it is by standing on ye shoulders of Giants.

Many have found in this comment a remarkable expression of Newton's noble character. Sir David Brewster, Newton's first biographer, enthused in 1831 of Newton's modesty, 'What a lesson to the vanity and presumption of philosophers.'

Brewster's admiration was somewhat premature. In his remarkable book *On the shoulders of giants* (1965), Robert Merton has shown that by Newton's time the expression had achieved a conventional status. The expression has, in fact, been traced back to the twelfth century. It was precisely the kind of thing that the great and the good were expected to say in a certain context. So familiar was it that it can be found decorating the windows of the south transept of Chartres Cathedral, in the form of the evangelists sitting on the shoulders of the prophets. Indeed, before Newton some 26 earlier uses were recorded by Merton. Thereafter, it has continued in use and can be found glibly proclaimed by that most egregious of self-publicists, the editor and pornographer Frank Harris.

Newton as careerist

The ambitious scientist of today, forever moving between honorary degree ceremonies and prestigious government committees, is a familiar figure. It is natural to ask whether Newton used his scientific success to reap the appropriate worldly gains.

Once the *Principia* had been published, Newton began to tire of Cambridge and academic life. Friends were consulted on the suitability

The windows in the south transept of Chartres Cathedral were constructed in about 1227. The design is one of the earliest occurrences of the *On the shoulders of giants* theme: St Luke on the shoulders of Jeremiah, St Matthew on the shoulders of Isaiah, St John on the shoulders of Ezekiel, and St Mark on the shoulders of Daniel.

of a number of other positions. When the invitation came in 1696 to join the Royal Mint, Newton accepted without hesitation. Offered the post on 19 March, he had abandoned his Cambridge home of over 30 years and established himself in London by 20 April. Thereafter, Newton seems to have accepted without demur whatever offices and duties came his way.

The profile of Newton's career bears a superficial and uncomfortable resemblance to many a modern careerist, for whom promotion and worldly success are all-important. However, the resemblance remains no more than superficial. Any such account of Newton as careerist must face two seemingly fatal objections.

In the first place, much of Newton's career seems to have developed by accident, *despite* his intentions rather than *because of* them. If Halley had not visited Cambridge in 1684, would the *Principia* have been written? Even if it had been, would it have been published in Newton's lifetime? Many other important manuscripts remained unpublished. His first full account of fluxions, *De methodis fluxionum*, was composed in 1671, and was a work which would have revolutionized the mathematics of his day, but appeared only in 1736, after his death. Indeed, one of the most remarkable features of Newton the mathematician was his failure to publish any mathematics in the first 60 years of his life. The first mathematical texts that he actually published appeared as appendices to his *Opticks* (1704) when he was nearly 62. In this strange behaviour, there is little sign of the ambitious young scientist seeking to establish a reputation.

Secondly, for a careerist Newton took a number of quite unnecessary risks. In 1675 it seemed inevitable that he would have to abandon his academic career. Cambridge University regulations insisted that all Fellows be ordained clergymen of the Anglican Church, a regulation which was theologically unacceptable to Newton. He therefore began to prepare for his departure from Trinity College. In January he wrote to Henry Oldenburg, Secretary of the Royal Society, informing him that for financial reasons he would soon be unable to pay his membership fees. A special dispensation, granted by Charles II in April, preserved Newton's Fellowship, Chair, and presumably his public scientific career.

On another occasion, in February 1687, Newton seemed prepared to risk all. James II had instructed Cambridge University to admit a Catholic monk to the degree of Master of Arts. This was indisputably against statute. Newton temporarily abandoned the *Principia* and set about challenging the king's authority. In April he pleaded the University's case before Judge Jeffreys, best remembered to this day for his role in the 'bloody assize' of 1685. Jeffreys proffered the warning: 'Go your way, and sin no more lest a worse thing come unto you.'

The times were dangerous ones in which to stand against the king. Yet Newton seems to have gone out of his way to adopt a full public position of total opposition to the Court. This was hardly the behaviour of a careerist. As it happened, within two years James was in exile in France and Jeffreys was imprisoned in the Tower. Newton survived in Cambridge and the *Principia* eventually did appear. Things, however, could well have been different.

If things had gone otherwise, Newton would presumably have retired to Woolsthorpe to spend the rest of his life managing his estates and pursuing whatever area of scholarship appealed to him at the time. No doubt his scientific writings, in manuscript, would continue to grow, and would be shown to a few friends and colleagues. While a few might have suspected the full range of his genius, none could have been quite sure. His results would probably have leaked out piecemeal, or have been independently discovered over the years by other scholars. Eventually, long after his death, his papers would come to light and would show that Newton had anticipated much of the science of a later age.

Conclusion

Some might impatiently object that much of this argument is irrelevant. The essential nature of Newton's success is quite clear, and rests upon the manner in which Newton's account of the universe was confirmed repeatedly and publicly in all later experiments and observations. Other accounts of the universe were available to the scholars of the early eighteenth century. But it was Newton's account, and Newton's alone, which was confirmed by experience.

Parts of the argument are indeed persuasive. The *Principia* was subjected to a number of stringent tests and, for the most part, survived intact. The two best known concerned the shape of the Earth, and the return of Halley's comet. In Book III of the *Principia*, Newton had calculated that 'the diameter of the earth at the equator is to its diameter from pole to pole as 230 is to 229'. Such figures required the Earth to be slightly flattened at the poles, and elongated at the equator. Expeditions organized by the Paris Académie in the late 1730s confirmed Newton's prediction. The return of Halley's comet in 1759 offered further confirmation of some very precise predictions derived from the *Principia*.

Against this argument, however, there stands the powerful objection that the great public confirmations of Newtonian mechanics took place long after Newton's death, and long after poets had begun to sing his praises, and philosophers, chemists, and others had begun to adopt Newtonian pretensions. It was clearly the content of Newtonian science which proved so attractive, rather than the degree of support bestowed upon it by complex measurements and distant observations.

People did not turn to Newton's theories because they had been certified successful. It was because so many *did* turn to his theories that their success was ensured.

Further reading

The impact of Newton's thought on eighteenth-century science is surveyed most fully in two works by I. B. Cohen—*Franklin and Newton*, American Philosophical Society, Philadelphia, 1956, and *The Newtonian revolution*, Cambridge University Press, Cambridge, 1980. In a further work, *The birth of the new physics*, Penguin Books, Harmondsworth, 1987, Cohen has attempted to assess Newton's contribution to the scientific revolution.

The influence of Newton's thought on chemical theory is one of the main themes of Arnold Thackray's *Atoms and powers*, Harvard University Press, Cambridge, Mass., 1970. The fullest account of his influence on eighteenth-century verse is to be found in Marjorie Nicolson's *Newton demands the muse*, Princeton University Press, Princeton, 1966. Newton's theological influence can be followed in R. S. Westfall's *Science and religion in seventeenth-century England*, Yale University Press, New Haven, 1958; M. C. Jacob's *The Newtonians and the English Revolution 1687–1720*, Cornell University Press, Ithaca, 1976; and James Force's *William Whiston: honest Newtonian*, Cambridge University Press, Cambridge, 1985. Several of the papers in *The methodological heritage of Newton* (edited by R. E. Butts and J. W. Davis), Clarendon Press, Oxford, 1970, trace Newton's influence on philosophy.

Much of interest on the reception of Newton's work is to be found in Henry Guerlac's *Newton on the Continent*, Cornell University Press, Ithaca, 1981; while the emergence of the Newtonian legend is dealt with by Francis Haskell in 'The apotheosis of Newton in art', in *The annus mirabilis of Sir Isaac Newton* (edited by R. Palter), MIT Press, Cambridge, Mass., 1970. Many of Newton's achievements are described in Derek Gjertsen's *The Newton handbook*, Routledge and Kegan Paul, London, 1986.

PHILOSOPHIÆ NATURALIS PRINCIPIA MATHEMATICA.

Autore *IS. NEWTON*, *Trin. Coll. Cantab. Soc.* Matheseos Professore *Lucasiano*, & Societatis Regalis Sodali.

IMPRIMATUR.
S. PEPYS, *Reg. Soc.* PRÆSES.
Julii 5. 1686.

LONDINI,

Jussu *Societatis Regiæ* ac Typis *Josephi Streater*. Prostat apud plures Bibliopolas. *Anno* MDCLXXXVII.

CHAPTER TWO

Newton's Principia

JOHN ROCHE

There are signs everywhere that the great pioneering period of Western theoretical physics—a period which began in the early seventeenth century, and achieved mastery of method with Newton—is slowly drawing to a close. It may be superseded by centuries of equally exciting and equally innovative consolidation and reconstruction. The historical study of the foundations of physics will be of central importance to such an endeavour, and central to the history of physics stands the achievement of Isaac Newton.

Newton did not simply construct a theory: he created a method and a language, applied them superbly, and inspired others to follow his example. Any future programme which involves the clarification and reconstruction of mechanics, optics, astronomy and chemistry will surely turn to Newton's work for guidance.

Newton remains a rich resource for those of today's scientists who have mastered his idiom, appreciated his subtle distinction of fact and hypotheses, grasped the powerful explanatory techniques he applied, and recognized that his use of mathematical artefacts, both in exploration and proof, was rarely confused with the deployment of mathematics to describe physical nature.

That resource has been deepened and extended over the recent years by the work of historians of science such as D. T. Whiteside, I. B. Cohen, A. R. Hall, A. Shapiro, and others. Between them, they have published Newton's mathematical papers and his correspondence, and have launched the publication of his optical papers. Add to this Richard Westfall's exhaustive and definitive biography of Newton, which now establishes a starting point for all future Newtonian studies, and the comprehensive bibliography of Peter and Ruth Wallis, and there is available a treasure trove for scientist, scholar, and interested reader.

In the world of scientific literature, Newton's *Philosophiae naturalis principia mathematica* is the jewel in the crown. It may even be compared to a great cathedral soaring above the transitory and occasionally ramshackle constructions surrounding it. Indeed, Newton's masterpiece concludes with an exuberant prose hymn to God the Creator, for he saw the *Principia* not only as building afresh the foundations of natural philosophy, but also as contributing to theology. He regarded the *Principia* as his greatest achievement in print, a view echoed perhaps in the boldness of statement expressed in it. At the beginning of Book III, for example, he proudly declared '*I now demonstrate the frame of the System of the World*'. Coming from anyone else,

The title page of the first edition of the *Principia*, published in 1687.

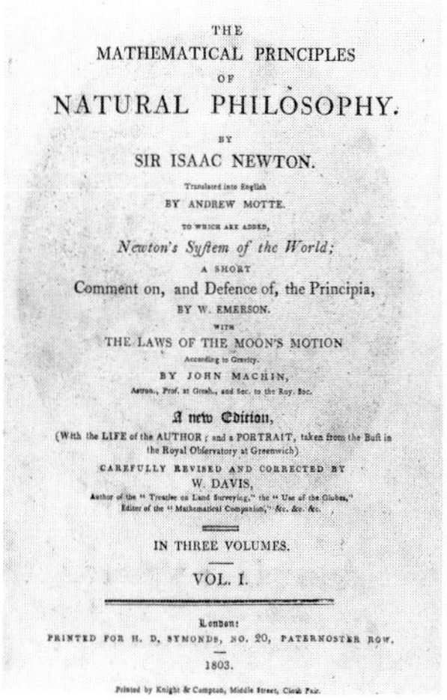
THE
MATHEMATICAL PRINCIPLES
OF
NATURAL PHILOSOPHY.
BY
SIR ISAAC NEWTON.
Translated into English
BY ANDREW MOTTE.
TO WHICH ARE ADDED,
Newton's Syſtem of the World;
A SHORT
Comment on, and Defence of, the Principia,
BY W. EMERSON.
WITH
THE LAWS OF THE MOON'S MOTION
According to Gravity.
BY JOHN MACHIN,
Astron., Prof. at Gresh., and Sec. to the Roy. Soc.
A new Edition,
(With the LIFE of the AUTHOR; and a PORTRAIT, taken from the Buſt in the Royal Obſervatory at Greenwich)
CAREFULLY REVISED AND CORRECTED BY
W. DAVIS,
Author of the "Treatise on Land Surveying," the "Use of the Globes," Editor of the "Mathematical Companion," &c. &c. &c.
IN THREE VOLUMES.
VOL. I.
London:
PRINTED FOR H. D. SYMONDS, NO. 20, PATERNOSTER ROW.
1803.
Printed by Knight & Compton, Middle Street, Cloth Fair.

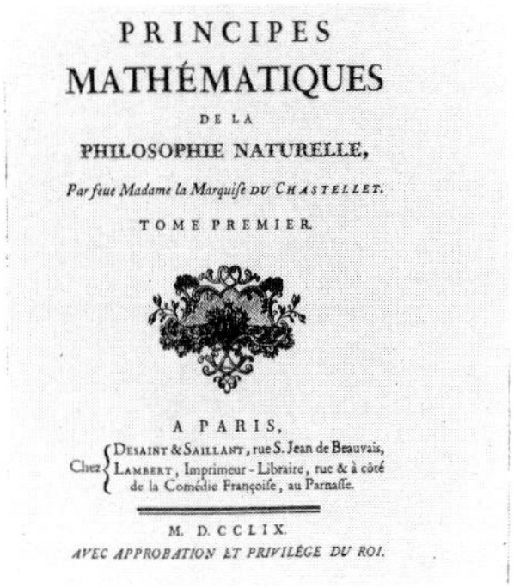
PRINCIPES
MATHÉMATIQUES
DE LA
PHILOSOPHIE NATURELLE,
Par feue Madame la Marquiſe DU CHASTELLET.
TOME PREMIER.
A PARIS,
Chez { DESAINT & SAILLANT, rue S. Jean de Beauvais, LAMBERT, Imprimeur-Libraire, rue & à côté de la Comédie Françoiſe, au Parnaſſe.
M. D. CCLIX.
AVEC APPROBATION ET PRIVILÉGE DU ROI.

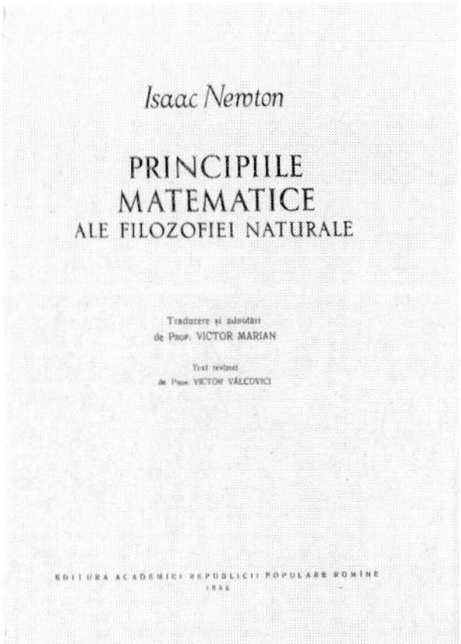
Isaac Newton
PRINCIPIILE
MATEMATICE
ALE FILOZOFIEI NATURALE
Traducere şi adnotări
de Prof. VICTOR MARIAN

English, French and Rumanian translations of the *Principia*.

this would be monumental presumption. Newton, however, was as good as his word. He did indeed demonstrate the structure of the universe, and did so to the satisfaction of his peers and subsequent natural philosophers.

The importance of the work can be gauged to some extent by the fact that it has gone through about one hundred editions since 1687, the year of its publication. There have appeared edited, annotated, condensed, popular, and school editions, along with translations into English, Russian, Romanian, Italian, Swedish, Dutch, and many other languages.

The origins of the *Principia*

Newton laid the mathematical and physical foundations of the *Principia* during a period of extraordinarily intense study in 1665 and 1666, while he was still in his early twenties.

Sometime during the summer of 1665, we know that the plague arrived in Cambridge, having moved north-eastwards from London where it wreaked great havoc. The University was closed down, and Newton set off to Lincolnshire where he remained until April 1667, with the exception of a short return to Cambridge in 1666. That year was immensely fertile for Newton; it may indeed be the most creative year any scientist has ever spent, although the months leading up to it also witnessed prodigious creativity on his part. Newton, in a remarkably brief period, laid the foundations for modern mathematics, optics, and mechanics.

By 1672 he had spent nearly eight years in a state of virtually uninterrupted creative exhilaration and exhaustion, studying and pondering so intensely that he took little recreation, begrudged sleep, and cared little about his appearance.

Even the pleasures of food he denied himself, and although some Victorians like to picture him, like Sherlock Holmes, pipe in hand, he took neither snuff nor tobacco, declaring to his amanuensis, Humphrey Newton, that *he would make no necessities to himself*.

Newton's largely private mathematical researches, and his equally private experimental and theoretical studies in mechanics and optics at Cambridge, had advanced him well beyond the best of his contemporaries anywhere in Europe. However, his desire to be allowed to pursue his studies without interruption or interference kept many of his discoveries hidden from the scientific world. His perfectionism, his intuition that maturity of thought takes time, and his temperamental revulsion against exposing his ideas to criticism, only added to the relative secrecy of many of his researches.

During the period leading up to the publication of the *Principia*, Newton also devoted himself passionately to alchemy, to theology

Newton, as pictured by the nineteenth-century cartoonist George Cruikshank. Newton did not in fact smoke, and is unlikely to have tamped down tobacco using his lady-friend's finger!

and critical religious history, as well as to mathematics and natural philosophy. These topics are discussed in later chapters of this book. Some of the conclusions which Newton drew from his alchemical studies, in particular those concerning the forces between particles, have become a permanent part of physical science, and shaped the *Principia* in various ways.

The immediate impetus for the writing and publication of the *Principia* was a visit by Edmond Halley to Newton in Cambridge in August 1684. Earlier that year, Sir Christopher Wren, Robert Hooke, and Halley had discussed at the Royal Society whether the elliptical form of the planetary orbits could be deduced from a force impressed upon the planets which varied with the inverse square of their distance from the Sun. According to Halley:

> Mr Hook said that he had it, but that he would conceale it for some time so that others, triing and failing might know how to value it, when he should make it publick.

When Halley put the problem to Newton in August, Newton declared that an inverse-square law of force would produce an elliptical orbit, a result which he claimed to have already demonstrated mathematically.

According to a later account of that meeting, the Doctor asked him what he thought the curve would be that would be described by the planets, supposing the force of attraction towards the Sun to be reciprocal to the square of their distance from it.

> Sr Isaac replied immediately that it would be an Ellipsis, the Doctor struck with joy & amazement asked him how he knew it, why, said he I have calculated it, whereupon Dr Halley asked him for his calculation without any

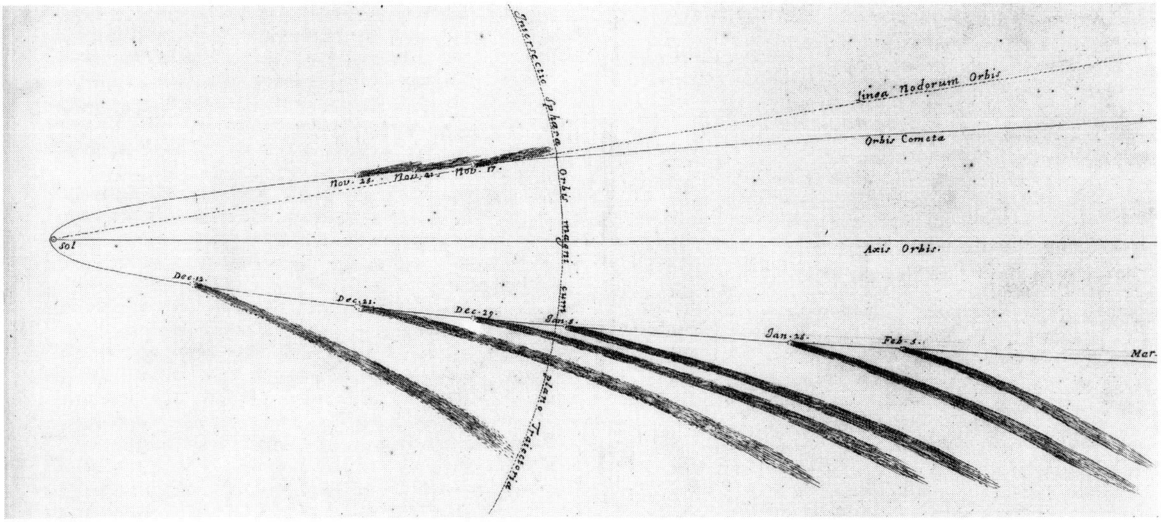

Calculations involving comets formed an important testing ground for Newton's theories. This *true representation of the orbit* of the great comet of 1680 is from Newton's *Principia*, Book III.

farther delay, Sr Isaac looked among his papers but could not find it, but he promised him to renew it, & then to send it him.

Newton had in fact arrived at this result in 1680, stimulated by an exchange of letters with the same Robert Hooke whom he came afterwards to detest so much.

Newton sent an improved version of his proof to Halley in November of 1684, in a short paper entitled *De motu corporum in gyrum* (*On the motion of bodies in an orbit*). Suddenly Newton recognized the magnitude and scope of his achievement, and a vast horizon of further possibilities opened out before him. He now became totally absorbed in developing and establishing his dynamical astronomy. In a brief period of two years, matching in intensity the years 1665–6, Newton transformed the nine-page *De motu* into his architectonic and magisterial *Principia*.

On 28 April 1686, Newton sent the first part of his Latin manuscript of the *Principia* to the Royal Society in London for publication, dedicating it to the Society. Halley, who was Clerk to the Society, committed them to its publication. The Society's finances, however, at this time were in poor condition due to their earlier publication of a very handsome and expensive *History of fishes*, which sold badly, so Halley promptly agreed to print the work at his own expense.

That was not the end of Halley's involvement for, in the course of the next year, he had to coax and flatter Newton into proceeding with the rest of the book. Newton had been incensed by the news that Hooke was claiming priority in discovering the inverse-square law. As a result, Newton announced that he would withdraw Book III altogether. He wrote to Halley:

The third I now designe to suppress. Philosophy is such an impertinently

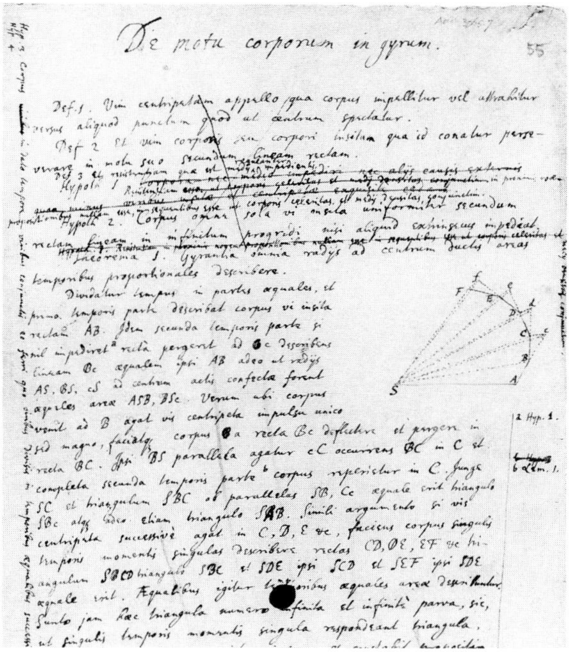
De motu corporum in gyrum.

Def. 1. Vim centripetam appello qua corpus impellitur vel attrahitur versus aliquod punctum quod ut centrum spectatur.

Newton's initial draft of *De motu corporum in gyrum* starts with the important result that became Theorem I of *Principia* (see p. 53).

litigious Lady that a man has as good be engaged in Law suits as have to do with her. I found it formerly so & now I no sooner come nearer her again but she gives me warning.

In a very limited sense, Hooke's claim that he had considered the inverse-square law prior to Newton was true. However, Hooke was unable to develop this idea, as Newton did, into a complete *System of the World* based on dynamical principles. As Derek Gjertsen has already mentioned, Newton never granted Hooke the acknowledgement he sought.

By early April 1687, Halley had received the complete work and by 5 July was able to write to Newton to say that he had 'at last brought your book to an end'. The first edition consisted of a quarto volume of 511 printed pages, at a cost of seven shillings unbound and nine shillings bound in leather. If the glory of writing the work is Newton's, much of the credit for publishing is surely Halley's.

The appearance of the *Principia* guaranteed Newton's status as a mathematician, and completely changed the nature of mathematical physics. There were many extravagant reactions to the book, some of which even queried whether the author was a mere mortal. The Marquis de l'Hôpital

cried out with admiration Good god what a fund of knowledge there is in that book? he then asked the D^r every particular about Sr I. even to the colour of his hair said does he eat & drink & sleep, is he like other men?

Newton brought out a substantially revised second edition of the

The detailed argument in Newton's *Principia* depended in part on a mass of observational data provided by the Royal Observatory at Greenwich, set up in 1675. This contemporary engraving is of the Octagon Room.

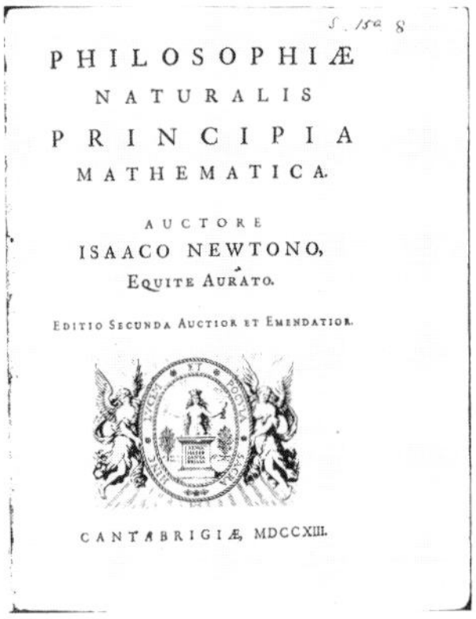
PHILOSOPHIÆ
NATURALIS
PRINCIPIA
MATHEMATICA.

AUCTORE
ISAACO NEWTONO,
EQUITE AURATO.

EDITIO SECUNDA AUCTIOR ET EMENDATIOR.

CANTABRIGIÆ, MDCCXIII.

The second edition of *Principia*.

Principia in 1713, under the inspired editorship of Roger Cotes of Trinity College. In this edition, Cotes provided an important preface which undertook to explain and defend Newton's account of gravity. Among other novelties, this edition contains Newton's famous *General Scholium* in which he addressed various criticisms of the first edition. In particular, it contains the famous declaration '*hypotheses non fingo*', which may be translated as '*I contrive (or feign) no hypotheses*'. What Newton seemed to mean by this is that he was not interested in speculation about the causes of gravity, but was concerned rather about strictly logical conclusions from established experimental relations.

The structure and content of the *Principia*

What is the structure and content of this much celebrated book? The *Principia* operates on many different levels. At the most obvious level, it is a mathematical investigation of the forces and motions of bodies, both on the Earth and in the heavens. In brief, Newton, for the first time in history, successfully united terrestrial and celestial mechanics into a single exact science.

The *Principia* was divided into an Introduction and three Books. The Introduction states the famous *laws of motion*, Books I and II consider various hypothetical forces and motions, and Book III applies the general theory of the previous books to particular cases of planetary and terrestrial motions.

Next after Euclid's Elements the Elements of y[e] Conic sections are to be understood. And for this end you may read either the first part of y[e] Elementa Curvarum of John De Witt, or De la Hire's late treatise of y[e] conick sections, or D[r] Barrow's epitome of Apollonius.

For Algebra read first Barth{ol}in's introduction & then peruse such Problems as you will find scattered up & down in y[e] Commentaries on Cartes's Geometry & other Alegraical {*sic*} writings of Francis Schooten. I do not mean y[t] you should read over all those Commentaries, but only y[e] solutions of such Problems as you will here & there meet with. You may meet with De Witt's Elementa curvarum & Bartholin's introduction bound up together wth Carte's Geometry & Schooten's commentaries.

For Astronomy read first y[e] short account of y[e] Copernican System in the end of Gassendus's Astronomy & then so much of Mercator's Astronomy as concerns y[e] same system & the new discoveries made in the heavens by Telescopes in the Appendix.

These are sufficient for understanding my book: but if you can procure Hugenius's Horologium oscillatorium, the perusal of that will make you much more ready.

At y[e] first perusal of my Book it's enough if you understand y[e] Propositions wth some of y[e] Demonstrations w[ch] are easier then the rest. For when you understand y[e] easier they will afterwards give you light into y[e] harder. When you have read y[e] first 60 pages, pass on to y[e] 3[d] Book & when you see the design of that you may turn back to such Propositions as you shall have a desire to know, or peruse the whole in order if you think fit.

In 1691, Richard Bentley asked Newton to advise on preparatory reading for studying the *Principia*. Newton's reply reveals the expectations he had of his readers.

The structure of the *Principia* may be described, in slightly more detail, as follows. In order to emphasize the quantitative character and the logical rigour of his text, Newton followed the model of Euclid's *Elements* which had long been a basis for the presentation of mathematical investigations. The *Principia* begins with definitions and axioms, and continues with propositions, theorems, problems, lemmas, corollaries, and scholia. At the end of most of his proofs, whether mathematical or physical, he wrote Q.E.D. (*quod erat demonstrandum*, 'which was to be proved') or Q.E.I. (*quod erat inveniendum*, 'which was to be found'). The Euclidean framework of the *Principia*, although occasionally forced, strikes home as a highly effective example of the use of *rhetoric*, the art of persuasion, in a scientific text.

There is very little algebra, recognizable as such, in the *Principia*. The mathematical language employed by Newton is in part the ancient language of geometry and proportion, and partly his own invented mathematics of vanishingly small quantities. Forces, velocities, accelerations, times, densities, and distances are all represented, in his extraordinarily complicated geometrical constructions, by lines and areas.

On reading the *Principia* again, I received a strong impression that Newton had done considerable violence to geometry. An ancient and venerable mathematical science had been pressed into service in a subject area for which it seems inappropriate. Newton's geometry seems to shriek and groan under the strain, but it works perfectly. Newton's mastery of his chosen mathematical idiom I find breathtaking.

In later years the belief grew, encouraged by Newton, that he had arrived at the results of the *Principia* by using calculus, but wrote them up in a traditional geometrical form for publication. D. T. Whiteside has argued convincingly, however, that Newton used the same mathematics in his discoveries as in their presentation in the *Principia*.

According to B. Goldstein, the mathematics of the *Principia* is the mathematics of a mathematical physicist, not that of a pure mathematician. It is mathematics designed to be a service subject, rather than a subject for abstract contemplation and logical rigour. Various aspects of Newton's mathematical arguments, in particular, his method of *analogy of nature* which is discussed later, inclines me to agree with this assessment.

Newton began the *Principia* by defining carefully those properties or aspects of natural bodies which he intended to deal with, in the course of his investigation. These include quantity of matter or *mass*, quantity of motion or *momentum*, passive force or *inertia*, and three kinds of active force—namely, *bulk force* and *distributed force*, both impressed upon a body from the outside, and *absolute force*, which is the external source of that impressed force. Newton asserted the existence of an immovable absolute space and an absolute time, which he distinguished carefully from the relative space and relative time of the senses.

Newton then stated the laws which the previously defined physical quantities must obey. The *first law*, derived from Galileo, Gassendi, and Descartes, declares that *a body will rigidly maintain its state of uniform motion in a straight line, or its state of rest, unless it is acted upon by an impressed force*. Today, this law is know as the *law of inertia*.

The germ of the *second law* of motion is also present in Galileo's writings. Galileo discovered that the effect of a force (such as weight)

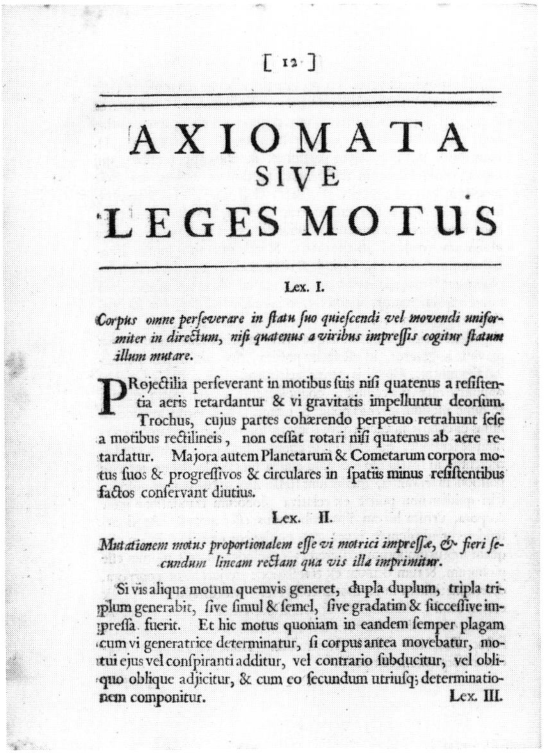

[12]

AXIOMATA SIVE LEGES MOTUS

Lex. I.

Corpus omne perſeverare in ſtatu ſuo quieſcendi vel movendi uniformiter in directum, niſi quatenus a viribus impreſſis cogitur ſtatum illum mutare.

PRojectilia perſeverant in motibus ſuis niſi quatenus a reſiſtentia aeris retardantur & vi gravitatis impelluntur deorſum. Trochus, cujus partes cohærendo perpetuo retrahunt ſeſe a motibus rectilineis, non ceſſat rotari niſi quatenus ab aere retardatur. Majora autem Planetarum & Cometarum corpora motus ſuos & progreſſivos & circulares in ſpatiis minus reſiſtentibus factos conſervant diutius.

Lex. II.

Mutationem motus proportionalem eſſe vi motrici impreſſæ, & fieri ſecundum lineam rectam qua vis illa imprimitur.

Si vis aliqua motum quemvis generet, dupla duplum, tripla triplum generabit, ſive ſimul & ſemel, ſive gradatim & ſucceſſive impreſſa fuerit. Et hic motus quoniam in eandem ſemper plagam cum vi generatrice determinatur, ſi corpus antea movebatur, motui ejus vel conſpiranti additur, vel contrario ſubducitur, vel oblique adjicitur, & cum eo ſecundum utriuſq; determinationem componitur.

Lex. III.

Newton's laws of motion, in the Latin wording in which they first appeared in print (1687).

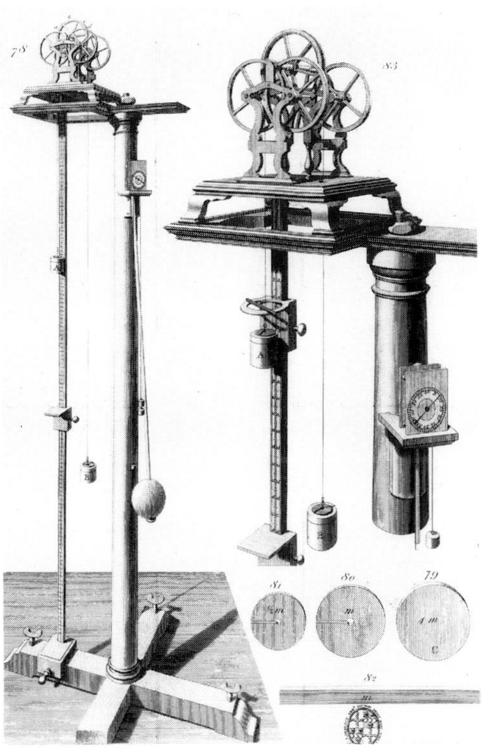

During the eighteenth century several experimental demonstrations of Newton's laws were devised. This apparatus, described by George Atwood in 1776, is for demonstrating *Newton's second law*. By timing the rate of fall of different weights, it can be shown that the rate of change of speed is proportional to the force producing it.

on a free body was not simply to cause it to move, but to *accelerate*. Newton recognized that all forces cause acceleration, and that if the force is doubled then so is the acceleration. His second law was not quite expressed like this; nevertheless, that is how he frequently employed it.

Newton apparently arrived at his famous *third law*—namely, that *to every action there is an equal and opposite reaction*—by studying colliding bodies. The seeds of this law can also be found in many earlier writings. So, what *was* Newton's contribution? It was to express these three laws definitively in an economical and quantitative form, and to gather them together as the foundation of theoretical mechanics.

Newton dealt with virtually the whole science of statics in the short space of the second corollary to his laws of motion. This is an astonishingly condensed piece of analysis which uses a single diagram with multiple interpretations. One is immediately struck by Newton's casual mastery of his medium, and by the density and economy of his style.

Newton concluded his introduction to the *Principia* by treating several general problems of motion, including the *law of conservation of momentum*. He ended with a Scholium where, among other things, he set out to demonstrate the equality of action and reaction using two suspended balls, the ancestor of the toy known today as *Newton's cradle*.

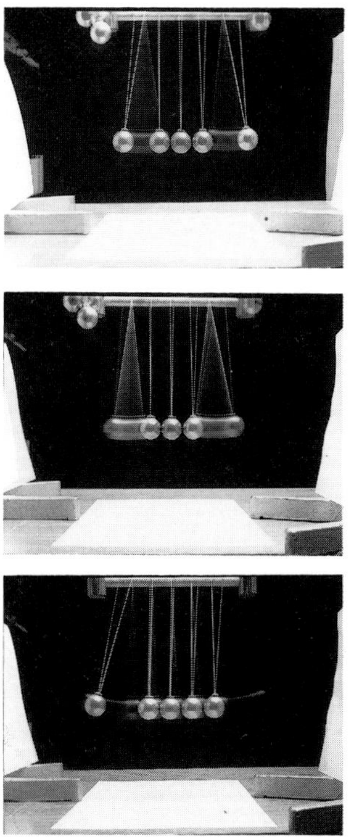

Newton's cradle is a device constructed to illustrate *Newton's third law*, following a hint in the *Principia*.

The remainder of the *Principia* is divided into three very long Books.

Book I

This begins with a mathematical introduction to elementary aspects of Newton's famous calculus of vanishingly small quantities, and the ratios of these quantities. Throughout the *Principia*, Newton used this powerful mathematical tool as an instrument of both discovery and proof.

Newton next carried out an investigation of the motion of a body under the action of a *centripetal force*, his term for a force directed towards a fixed point. His first result (Proposition I, Theorem I) was that *the imaginary line joining an orbiting body to a fixed point must sweep out areas proportional to the times, if the force acting on that body is directed towards that point*. He also proved the converse result in Proposition II—namely, that *if the line between a fixed point and the moving body always describes areas proportional to the times, then the force acting on the moving body is directed towards that point*. According to Kepler's second law of 1609, which was established by astronomical observation, the line joining a planet to the Sun does indeed sweep out equal areas in equal times. Newton was therefore able to draw the conclusion (which he did later at the beginning of Book III) that *the force acting on each planet points towards the Sun*.

PROPOSITION I. THEOREM I

The areas which revolving bodies describe by radii drawn to an immovable centre of force do lie in the same immovable planes, and are proportional to the times in which they are described.

For suppose the time to be divided into equal parts, and in the first part of that time let the body by its innate force describe the right line AB. In the second part of that time, the same would (by Law I), if not hindered, proceed directly to *c*, along the line B*c* equal to AB; so that by the radii AS, BS, *c*S, drawn to the centre, the equal areas ASB, BS*c*, would be described. But when the body is arrived at B, suppose that a centripetal force acts at once with a great impulse, and, turning aside the body from the right line B*c*, compels it afterwards to continue its motion along the right line BC. Draw *c*C parallel to BS, meeting BC in C; and at the end of the second part of the time, the body (by Cor. I of the Laws) will be found in C, in the same plane with the triangle ASB. Join SC, and, because SB and C*c* are parallel, the triangle SBC will be equal to the triangle SB*c*, and therefore also to the triangle SAB. By the like argument, if the centripetal force acts successively in C, D, E, &c., and makes the body, in each single particle of time, to describe the right lines CD, DE, EF, &c., they will all lie in the same plane; and the triangle SCD will be equal to the triangle SBC, and SDE to SCD, and SEF to SDE. And therefore, in equal times, equal areas are described in one immovable plane: and, by composition, any sums SADS, SAFS, of those areas, are to each other as the times in which they are described. Now let the number of those triangles be augmented, and their breadth diminished *in infinitum;* and (by Cor. IV, Lem. III) their ultimate perimeter ADF will be a curved line: and therefore the centripetal force, by which the body is continually drawn back from the tangent of this curve, will act continually; and any described areas SADS, SAFS, which are always proportional to the times of description, will, in this case also, be proportional to those times. Q.E.D.

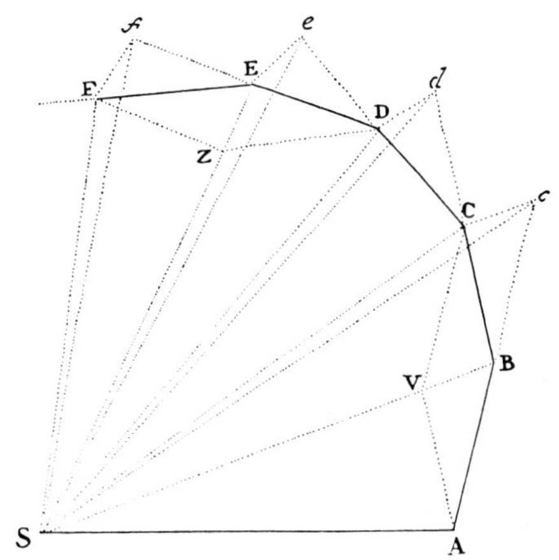

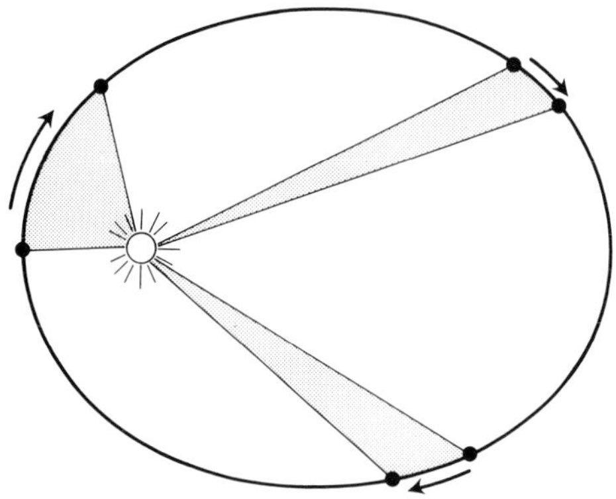

Kepler's second law states that the line joining a planet to the Sun sweeps out equal areas in equal times—essentially, this is a way of quantifying the notion that planets move faster when they are nearer to the Sun, and slower at the far extremities of their orbits.

He then considered the following problem:

Given the shape of the orbit and the fixed centre towards which the force responsible for the shape of that orbit points, how does the magnitude of that force vary with the distance from that centre?

Newton considered a variety of cases; one of these is of particular importance since it has immediate practical application in astronomy. This is the famous Proposition XI, problem VI:

If a body revolves in an ellipse; it is required to find the law of a centripetal force tending to the focus of the ellipse.

Newton proved that *the force must obey an inverse-square law*. As can be seen, his proof involves geometry, proportions, ratios of evanescent quantities, and the laws of motion. The proof is certainly difficult and non-intuitive, and it seems hard to understand how he arrived at it. Nevertheless, Newton was able to draw from it the concrete consequence in Book III that:

since the planets revolve in ellipses, and with centripetal forces directed to the Sun at the focus of each ellipse, the forces acting on each planet must obey an inverse-square law.

He went on to argue that *an inverse-square law force must give rise only to an ellipse, a parabola, or an hyperbola*, but this does not seem to be proved explicitly. Its validity has been disputed, but careful study by mathematicians has shown that Newton's proof is indeed valid. He had thus resolved, and generalized, the problem put to him by Halley in 1684.

Newton went much further in Book III, where he showed that Kepler's famous third law, relating the periods of the planets to their orbital radii, can also be deduced from the same principles. *Here was a dramatic unification of the known celestial laws of motion.*

As yet, however, Newton was not logically equipped to prove that the force which deflects the planets from rectilinear inertial paths into elliptic orbits about the Sun was the familiar force of terrestrial gravity.

PROPOSITION XI. PROBLEM VI

If a body revolves in an ellipse; it is required to find the law of the centripetal force tending to the focus of the ellipse.

Let S be the focus of the ellipse. Draw SP cutting the diameter DK of the ellipse in E, and the ordinate Qv in x; and complete the parallelogram $QxPR$. It is evident that EP is equal to the greater semiaxis AC: for drawing HI from the other focus H of the ellipse parallel to EC, because CS, CH are equal, ES, EI will be also equal; so that EP is the half-sum of PS, PI that is (because of the parallels HI, PR, and the equal angles IPR, HPZ), of PS, PH, which taken together are equal to the whole axis 2AC. Draw QT perpendicular to SP, and putting L for the principal latus rectum of the ellipse (or for $\frac{2BC^2}{AC}$), we shall have

$$L \cdot QR : L \cdot Pv = QR : Pv = PE : PC = AC : PC,$$

$$\text{also, } L \cdot Pv : Gv \cdot Pv = L : Gv, \text{ and, } Gv \cdot Pv : Qv^2 = PC^2 : CD^2.$$

By Cor. II, Lem. VII, when the points P and Q coincide, $Qv^2 = Qx^2$, and Qx^2 or $Qv^2 : QT^2 = EP^2 : PF^2 = CA^2 : PF^2$, and (by Lem. XII) $= CD^2 : CB^2$. Multiplying together corresponding terms of the four proportions, and simplifying, we shall have

$$L \cdot QR : QT^2 = AC \cdot L \cdot PC^2 \cdot CD^2 : PC \cdot Gv : CD^2 \cdot CB^2 = 2PC : Gv,$$

since $AC \cdot L = 2BC^2$. But the points Q and P coinciding, 2PC and Gv are equal. And therefore the quantities $L \cdot QR$ and QT^2, proportional to these, will be also equal. Let those equals be multiplied by $\frac{SP^2}{QR}$, and $L \cdot SP^2$ will become equal to $\frac{SP^2 \cdot QT^2}{QR}$. And therefore (by Cor. I and V, Prop. VI) the centripetal force is inversely as $L \cdot SP^2$, that is, inversely as the square of the distance SP. Q.E.I.

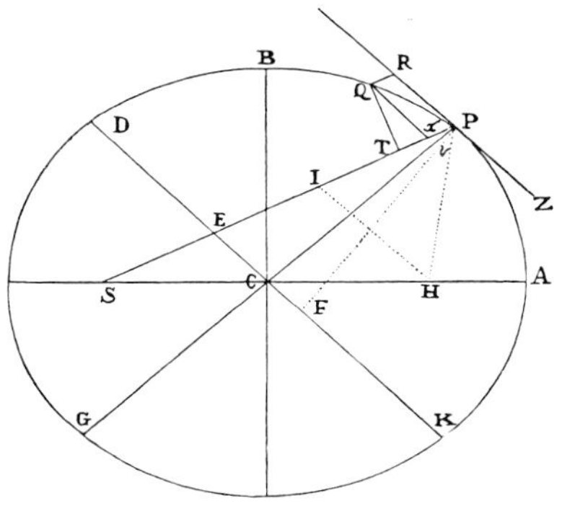

Let us now see how he built up his attack on this question in Book I.

Newton considered a large variety of cases, showing how to deduce orbital dimensions when given observational data of various sorts. He proceeded to consider the motion of orbits themselves. The elliptical figure described by a planet in space may itself revolve around the Sun. When applied to the movement of the Moon's apogee (its furthest point from the Earth), Newton's mathematical theory was of crucial importance, because he was able to deduce that *the orbital force acting on the Moon also obeys an inverse-square law*. Armed with this proof, Newton was able to advance his theory of universal gravitation in Book III. His argument in Book III is developed as follows.

Having established that the Moon obeys an inverse-square law, Newton calculated the acceleration towards the Earth which the 'lunar apple' would experience if it was very near to the Earth's surface. This turned out to be exactly the same as the acceleration of ordinary falling bodies near the Earth's surface. Therefore, Newton was able to conclude:

> the force by which the Moon is retained in its orbit is that very same force which we commonly call *gravity*, for were gravity another force differing from that, then bodies falling to the Earth with the joint impulse of both forces would fall with double that velocity which we actually experience.

Newton then argued that *the economy of nature requires us to make gravity responsible for the orbital force acting on each of the planets*. Finally, he contended that *gravity acts on all of the bodies in the universe*.

Today we take the notion of universal gravitation so much for granted that we find it hard to imagine a period when gravity was thought of as confined to the Earth's surface only. This is the measure of Newton's success.

Book II

Book II is chiefly devoted to a detailed study of the motions of bodies in resisting media, in a large variety of hypothetical cases. There are discussions of the motion of bodies subject to various forms of air resistance, of the density and pressure of liquids, and of a pendulum oscillating in resisting media. The extent of this section is surprising, since it receives little attention in standard textbooks today. However, there was, before Newton, a long tradition in physics which assigned central importance to motions in resisting media.

Every great mind presents to itself a model which it is determined to equal or to excel. The young Newton seems to have regarded Descartes as such a model. By the end of his career, however, he seems to have so far surpassed Cartesian physics that he found it intellectually offensive.

Earlier in the century, Descartes had described real motions in our

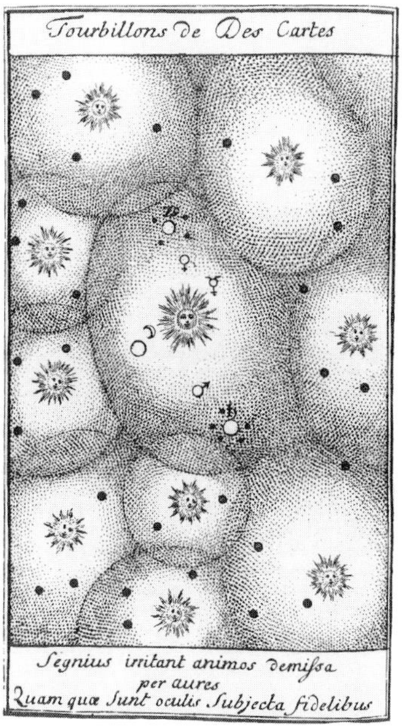

Tourbillons de Des Cartes
Segnius irritant animos demissa per aures
Quam quæ sunt oculis subjecta fidelibus

The Cartesian view that planets are swept round in material vortices, like corks in a whirlpool, was dealt a decisive blow by Newton's argument in Book II of the *Principia*. This picture from an eighteenth-century text—showing many solar systems, with ours prominent in the centre—illustrates Descartes' conception.

atmosphere, and had argued that the planets are carried around by material vortices. At the end of Book II, Newton produced a powerful argument, based on his studies of fluid media, which he regarded as a conclusive refutation of the existence of these vortices. Newton considered this refutation to be one of the great triumphs of the *Principia*. Indeed, he went further and argued that the persistence of the orbits of the planets proved that they moved in a near vacuum.

Book II also includes a mathematical study of wave motion. What we today call the wavelength, Newton called the *breadth* of the wave. Newton worked out his laws of water waves and of sound waves, using a method which he later called the *analogy of nature*. He discovered a mathematical and physical resemblance between the motion of a pendulum and the rocking up and down of water in a U-shaped tube. This rocking motion is in turn made analogous to wave motion. Newton was thereby able to apply the well-known theory of the pendulum to the analysis of waves.

Before I read his theory, I was quite unable to imagine how Newton could possibly have worked out the complicated mathematics of wave motion. I was quite unprepared for his method of analogy—it is breathtakingly simple and effective. From his study of the manner in which pulses and waves in material media spread out after passing through gaps, Newton argued that since light travels straight on through such gaps, its nature cannot be understood using wave theory alone. Newton thereby refuted by implication the theories of light of Descartes and Hooke. Here Newton's reasoning was sound, but his evidence was inadequate.

Book III

As we have seen, Book III, *The system of the world*, applies the general theory of Book I to moons, planets, and comets. I have already dealt with the origins of Newton's universal law of gravity. He then proceeded to apply his gravitational theory to explain the tides, account for the motion of comets, and begin to predict lunar and other motions. Also included in Book III are accounts of the variation in gravity at different places on the Earth's surface, the flattening of the Earth's surface at the poles (due to the rotation of the Earth), and the precession of the equinoxes.

Unfortunately, there is no space to discuss such topics in this very brief survey of the *Principia*. I have inevitably had to omit some important topics and over-simplify others, but I hope to have given at least a flavour of its style and content.

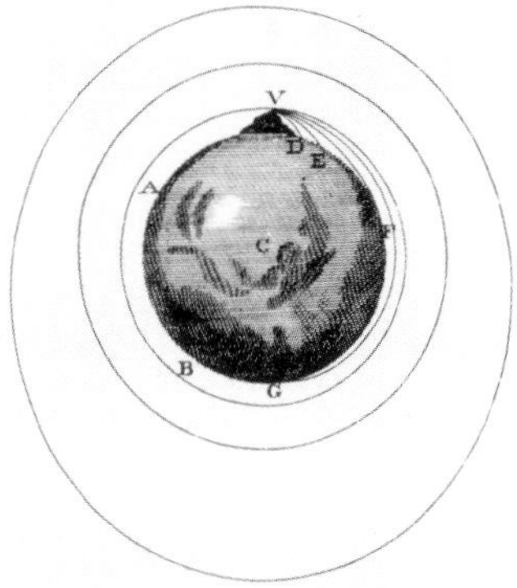

If a projectile is fired with enough force, it will remain in orbit around the Earth, in much the same way as the Moon is in orbit (rather further away). This plausible thought-demonstration of Newton's ideas about universal gravitation is from *A treatise of the system of the world*. This was a more popular, less mathematical account of Book III of the *Principia*, which Newton wrote in the 1680s but was not published until after his death.

The *Principia* today

The Russian mathematician Vladimir Igorevich Arnol'd has recently found a theorem that seems to have been previously unnoticed by mathematicians, because Newton was centuries ahead of his time in the ideas that he used. The result is technical, but is concerned with

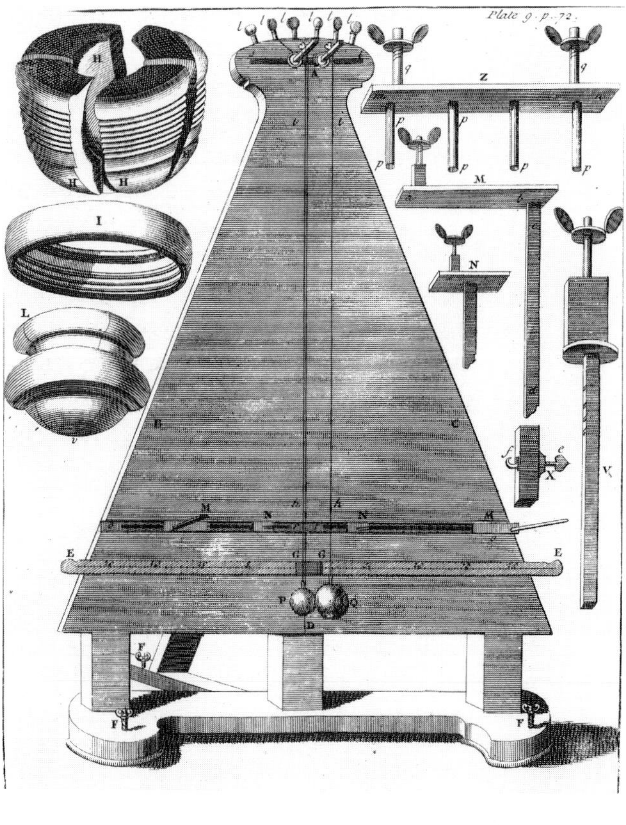

Newtonian physics was taught as an experimental science, with many demonstrations devised to illustrate Newtonian conceptions and laws. This apparatus, for displaying the laws of collision, was pictured in a work of 1725 by a prominent Newtonian teacher, Willem 'sGravesande.

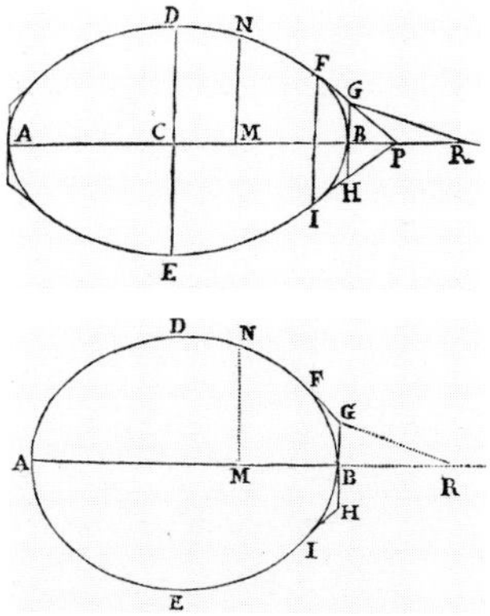

Different editions of the *Principia* have had significantly different diagrams. In Newton's surprising result that a smooth ellipsoid offers *more* resistance to motion through a fluid than a body of more angular section, the diagram in the first two editions (*above*) was simplified for the third edition (*below*).

how the area of the piece cut out from an oval by a straight line depends upon the line. Arnol'd also mentions another problem. It concerns

> the solid of revolution which has least resistance under motion along its axis in a very rarified medium. Here Newton was 300 years ahead of his time: the extremum is not smooth but has a break and Newton knew about it. As V.M. Tikhomirov has informed me this break appears in Newton's picture but is absent from the picture in some later editions of the *Principia* because until now, when the problem has become topical in connection with astronautics, the mathematicians did not understand Newton.

What flaws are there in the *Principia*? For one thing, as Westfall has argued, Newton was not averse to adjusting his calculations to fit his theories. For another, there are certainly some inadequacies in the presentation of Newton's arguments. According to Whiteside:

> the logical structure [of the *Principia*] is slipshod, its level of verbal fluency none too high, its arguments unnecessarily diffuse and repetitive and its very content on occasion markedly irrelevant to its professed theme ... but these faults ... can largely be excused by the very rapidity with which the *Principia* was written.

To conclude this chapter, let me raise a few points which seem not to have been made the subject of scholarly investigation.

I have always been puzzled by the strange wording of the definitions of mass, momentum, and force, at the beginning of the *Principia*. For example, Definition I states '*the quantity of matter is the measure of the same, arising from its density and its bulk conjointly*'. Why does Newton again and again identify a physical property or quantity with its measure? There is surely more to a physical quantity than a statement of how it is measured?

The answer is possibly to be found in Newton's early Scholium on absolute space and time. Since, according to Newton, we can only measure *relative* space and time, and not *absolute* space and time, all we can know about physical quantities are not the absolute quantities themselves but merely their relative substitutes—that is, their measures. This argument is not well worked out by Newton. If it were pushed to extremes, it could lead to scepticism about our access to true knowledge about the world. Newton, however, does not follow that well-trodden path to cognitive perdition.

Like all great thinkers, Newton used language as an instrument to articulate, clarify, and promote his own views. It seems that he was strongly influenced here by Descartes' well-known commitment to clear and distinct ideas. Newton coined various terms, or re-defined others, so effectively that they have become part of our language. For example, Newton invented the term *centripetal force*. His definition of inertia is that now generally adopted, as is his concept of *gravity*. He wrote that the meanings of words are to be determined by their use, and warned against violating the accuracy of language which ought to be kept precise.

In the course of the *Principia*, Newton laboured to use words with razor-sharp precision. An interesting example of this concern for verbal accuracy was the manner in which he apologized several times for using certain expressions. For example, on one occasion, when he multiplied the mass of a body by its velocity to obtain the quantity of motion or momentum, he politely remarked '*If I may so say*'. Why was this? Because, like all great innovators, the conservative in Newton struggled against the revolutionary. In ancient mathematics, and right up to Newton's day, quantities of different species were never multiplied directly together, or divided into one another. Even today, school-children sometimes object when they are told that 'density is mass divided by volume'. 'You cannot divide different physical things by each other', they complain, 'it is like dividing eggs by apples'.

They are, of course, quite right. Strictly speaking, physical things whether similar or different cannot be divided or multiplied together at all. Mass cannot be meaningfully multiplied by velocity. What *can* be multiplied together, however, are the measuring number of mass and the measuring number of velocity. Similarly, the numerical value of mass may be divided by the numerical value of volume. The new number which results from such manipulations may, in certain circumstances, be a numerical measure of some *third* physical quantity, as in the case of momentum or density. In Newton's day, heterogenous multiplication was just becoming acceptable, and Newton clearly felt that it was still bad mathematical grammar to use it in a respectable book.

In conclusion, my judgement is that there may have been minds gifted with greater powers and vision than Newton outside the exact sciences. But, within those sciences, from antiquity to the present, no greater mind is surely to be found.

Further reading

For an excellent introductory account of the *Principia*, see Chapter 10 of R. S. Westfall, *Never at rest: A biography of Isaac Newton*, Cambridge University Press, Cambridge, 1980.

More specialized studies of the *Principia* and its origins include J. Herivel, *The background to Newton's Principia, Clarendon Press, Oxford, 1965; and I. B. Cohen, Introduction to Newton's 'Principia'*, Cambridge University Press, Cambridge, 1971. An exhaustive study of the mathematical astronomy and mechanics in the manuscripts of the *Principia* can be found in Volume 6 of D. T. Whiteside, *The mathematical papers of Isaac Newton*, Cambridge University Press, Cambridge, 1967–80. Much light is also shed on the *Principia* by Volumes 2 and 3 of *The correspondence of Isaac Newton* (edited by H. W.

Turnbull, J.F. Scott, A.R. Hall, and L. Tilling), Cambridge University Press, Cambridge, 1959–77.

A very authoritative and readable analysis of the origin and content of many of Newton's dynamical and methodological concepts will be found in A. Koyré, *Newtonian studies*, Chapman and Hall, London, 1965.

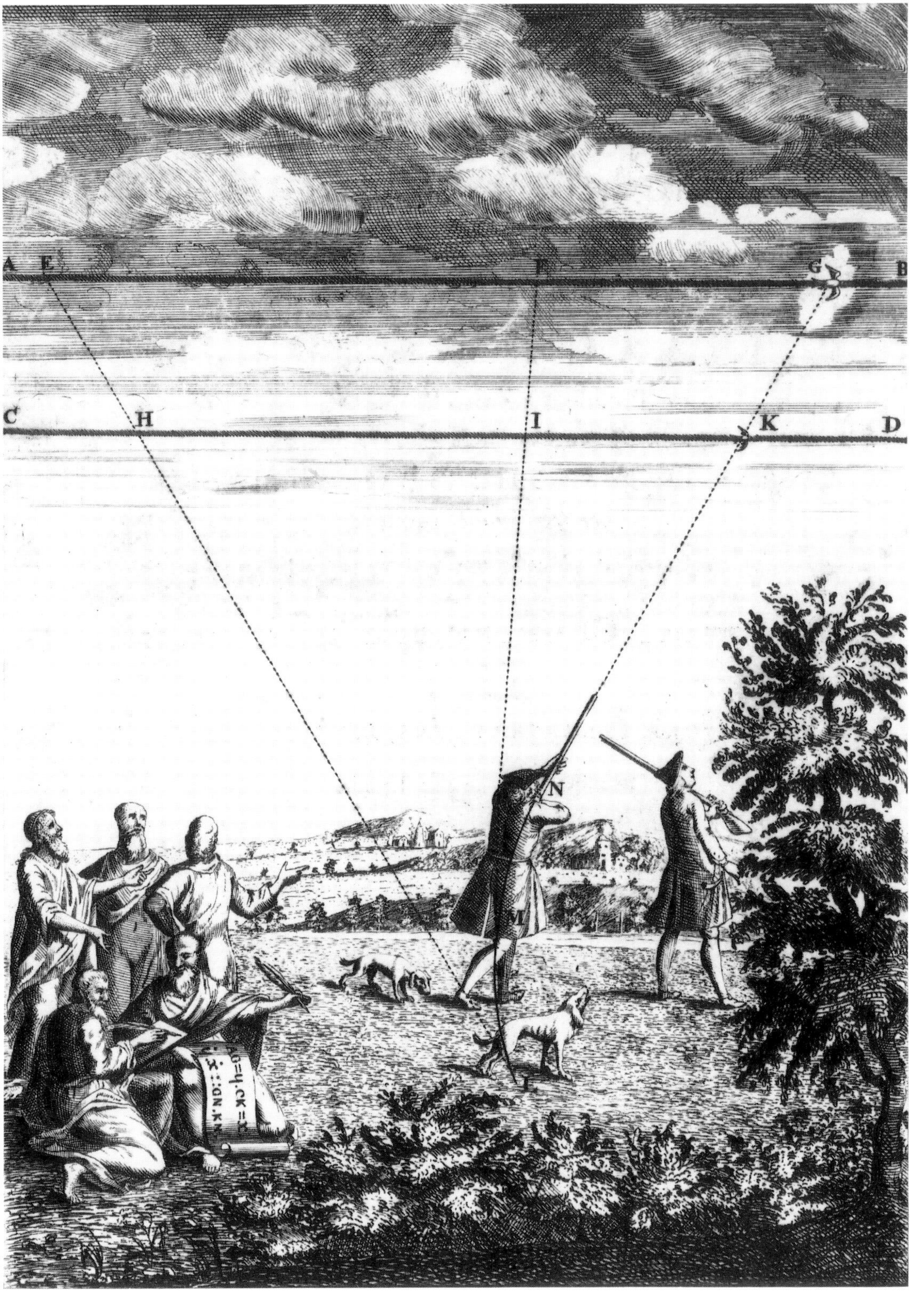
A
E
F
G
B
C
H
I
K
D
N
M

CHAPTER THREE

Newton's mathematical work

JON PEPPER

Little is known about the details of Newton's education before he entered Trinity College, Cambridge, in the summer of 1661, aged 18. However, it is unlikely that he was quite as dull as popular legend has suggested; very high intelligence is not always recognized as such by ordinary folk. As for what he was taught at school, the headmaster of King's School in Grantham provided a pretty thorough course, both in the elementary surveying necessary for the local farmers' sons, and in more abstract trigonometry. As we may infer from Newton's still surviving school notebook, this seems to have included the calculation of sine tables, and approximate constructions for geometrical figures, such as a seven-sided regular polygon.

Newton later claimed that Euclid's work caused him some difficulties, and surviving notes seem to confirm this. In fact, Euclidean geometry was never much of an attraction to Newton, nor did it influence his work very much—he always preferred moving into newer abstractions.

In this chapter, I can give only a flavour of Newton's mathematical work. In addition to the mathematical contributions in the *Principia*, discussed in the previous chapter, recent editions of Newton's mathematical writings comprise two full volumes of work published in (or shortly after) his lifetime, and a further eight very thick volumes of the surviving mathematical manuscripts. Much of his mathematical work was not actually published during his lifetime—many works were started, but abandoned when the immediate impetus which led to their creation was spent.

The direction of Newton's work was set in his early twenties. It was then that he developed his ideas about algebra and infinite series. These, with his fluxions—the approach to calculus which he alone began to develop single handedly at that time—continued to be his main mathematical interests as long as he was involved in creative writing. Later he wrote, or rewrote, the history of his own mathematical development, an exercise perhaps not free from its own creative element.

A significant benefit of Newton's invention of *fluxions* was the ease with which problems involving motion could now be handled. The frontispiece to his *Method of fluxions* shows the benefit to traditional English country pursuits, while some ancient Greeks look on admiringly.

The mathematical renaissance

Newton's work grew out of the renaissance of mathematics in Western Europe over the previous two centuries. This followed the introduction of printing, and the publication of the great fifteenth and sixteenth

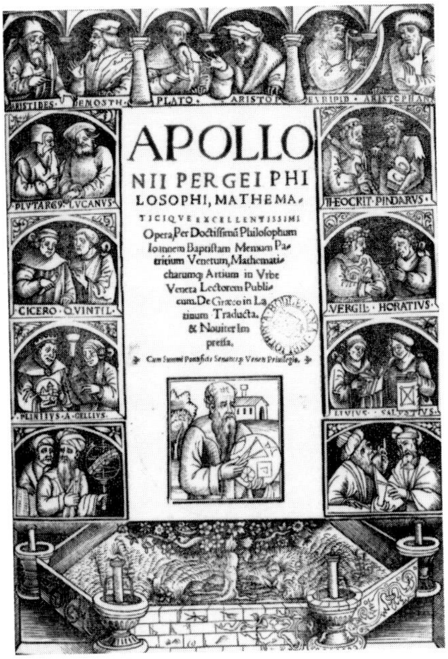

Newton was heir to several generations of scholars who had produced magnificent editions of the great Greek mathematicians, such as this Apollonius edition of 1537. Most of the classical worthies pictured have no bearing on mathematics.

century editions of Euclid, Archimedes, Apollonius, Pappus, and others. There was a good deal of what might now be called 'pre-calculus' work in the first half of the seventeenth century—work which formed the transition from particular results to the more general methods of Newton and Leibniz. The 'transitionalists' included Pierre Fermat, Francesco Cavalieri, Blaise Pascal, and John Wallis. Although some general principles had been enunciated, each individual problem was still usually solved in its own particular way.

One such problem was the determination of the area under the

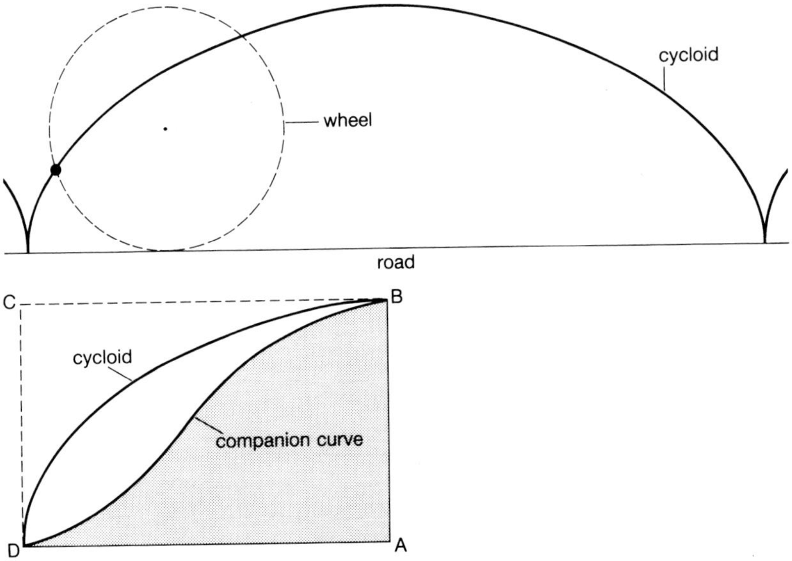

The *cycloid*, or *cycloidal curve*, is the curve traced by a point on the rim of a wheel rolling along a straight road. The *companion curve*, shown on the right, encloses an area equal to half that of the rectangle *ABCD*. The area between the two curves turns out to be the area of the semicircle with diameter *AB*. Thus the area under the cycloid can be deduced.

cycloidal curve. This problem was solved by the French mathematician Gilles de Roberval, who associated with this cycloid a so-called 'companion curve' which depends on the geometry of the original curve. Since the area of the companion curve can be calculated by a simple argument, the area under the cycloidal curve can be deduced. (Christopher Wren, who, but for his work in architecture, would still be known for his work in astronomy and mathematics, similarly used an ingenious transformation to determine the length of the cycloidal curve.)

Specific methods such as these are delightful and ingenious in themselves, but leave one with little detailed guidance for the next problem. The *general* methods of Newton and Leibniz were to change all that. That is the great force of their unified approach to calculus.

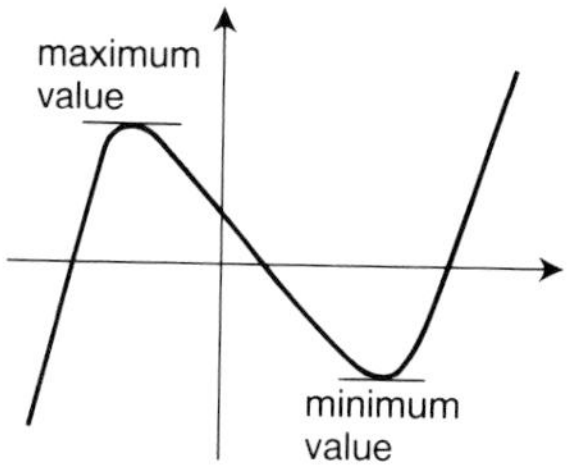

An example of *maximum and minimum values*. In general, the problem is: given some conditions on a varying quantity, how can you calculate its maximum and minimum values?

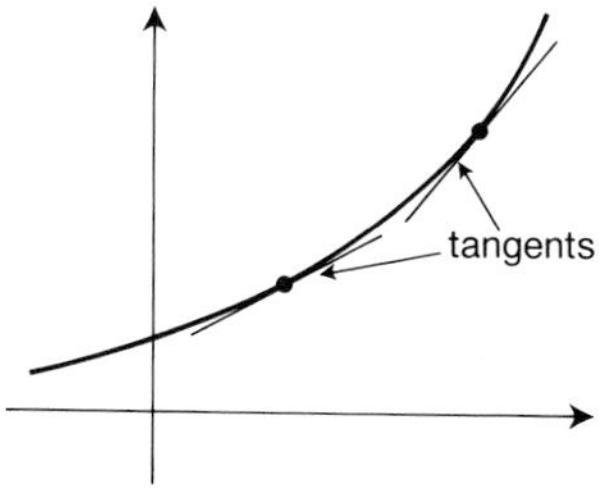

A *tangent* is a line touching a curve at just one point. In general, the problem is: how do you determine which line is the tangent at any given point on the curve?

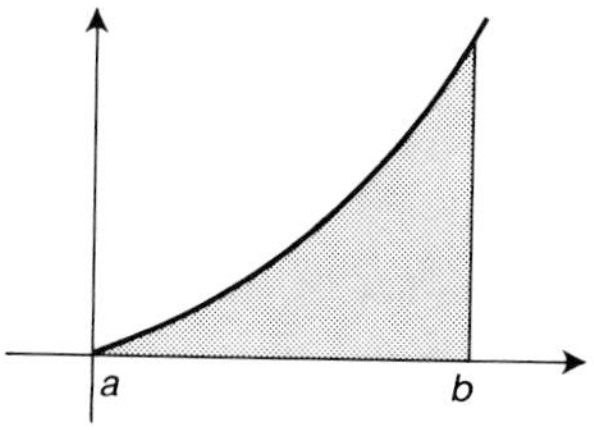

An example of an *area under a curve*—that is, the area between the curve and the horizontal axis. In general, the problem is: how do you determine the area under a given curve between any two given points *a* and *b* on the horizontal axis?

Near contemporaries

Descartes, Fermat, and others had worked on how to determine maximum and minimum values of functions represented by curves and other geometrical quantities. At the same time, independent work was going ahead on the theoretical construction of tangents on various curved lines. Able mathematicians closer in time to Newton, such as James Gregory and Isaac Barrow, were coming to realize that the problems of tangents to curves and the areas under the same curves were in some way related—that they were 'inverse', as we should now say. This fact is now termed the *fundamental theorem of calculus*, known to Isaac Barrow who published something like it in 1670, and perhaps also to Evangelista Torricelli in the 1640s. Newton's own realization of this result came in papers conjecturally dated to the middle of 1665. Indeed, as we see later in this chapter, it was thanks to Newton that all these earlier strands were effectively pulled and woven together.

It is sometimes claimed that Newton developed his mathematics virtually from scratch, but it is clear from his surviving notes and annotations, that in his early Cambridge years he studied the work of many earlier writers. In particular, he studied topics in algebra, geometry, trigonometry, and probability in the writings of William Oughtred, François Viète, Frans van Schooten, and Christiaan Huygens. In Wallis' *Arithmetica infinitorum* (1655), he found rules for the areas of various parabolas. He also read other authors who are less well known today, except perhaps for their part in his development. These included Jan Hudde and Hendrick van Heurat of Leiden, whose writings he studied in the period 1664–6, the *anni mirabili* in which he became a creative mathematician.

In the mid-1660s, Newton began to explore the ideas of *coordinate geometry*, originated by Descartes and Fermat some 30 years previously. He calculated subnormals, as well as investigating the

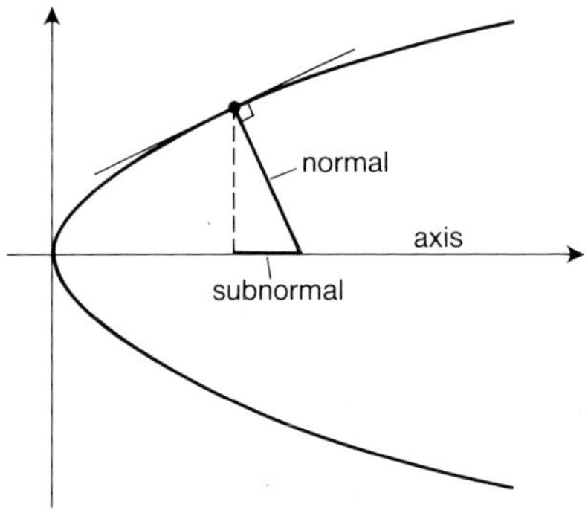

A *normal* is a line perpendicular to a curve at a given point. The corresponding *subnormal* is obtained by projecting that portion of the normal between the curve and the horizontal axis onto the axis.

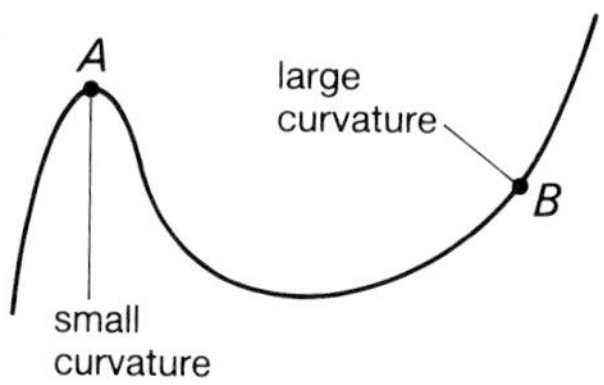

Curvature is a numerical measure of 'how curved' a line is at a given point. Here, the curvature at *A* is much smaller than the curvature at *B*.

curvature of a curve, and soon turned his attention to the inverse problems of finding the area under, and tangents to, a given curve.

Descartes' influence on Newton's development should not be underestimated, although, characteristically, Newton later tried to minimize its importance. D. T. Whiteside has argued persuasively that what made Newton into the mathematician he became was his reading, in the summer of 1664, of van Schooten's Latin translation of Descartes' *La géométrie*. Certainly, Descartes' use of algebraic structures and symbolism are apparent in much of Newton's later work.

Descartes' geometry was not developed systematically. He gave examples of what his ideas could achieve, and left it to his readers to go on from there—a good approach for readers of the greatest potential, but less helpful for others. He was thus important for giving methods which Newton could see were capable of further development.

Calculus

While it is difficult to summarize Newton's work in a few words, we must say something about the effect of his work on the part of mathematics for which he is best known—the *calculus*. Over the years of working and reworking his earliest ideas, Newton systematized the rules for dealing with the problems of the infinitesimal calculus. Not all of these rules were new, but the unification was his. To *define* differentiation (finding tangents to curves) and integration (finding areas under curves) as inverse processes is an example of this unification, although later mathematicians were to revert to regarding an integration as a type of summation.

As we shall see, Newton's *algebraic* symbolism was developed from Descartes, and was particularly powerful. However, his *calculus* notation was perhaps none too successful—although it was no hindrance to Newton himself, who worked largely in isolation. Ironically, it was Leibniz' misconceptions of differentials which gave us his more fruitful notation, the one most commonly in use today.

The Newton–Leibniz dispute has been equably resolved on this stamp from Paraguay, in attributing to Newton the integration symbol devised by Leibniz.

Newton's aims were seemingly more specific and concrete than those of Leibniz, who was more interested in broad philosophical principles. Newton's patterns of thought were more *physical*. His variable quantities varied with *time*—they were flowing quantities (*fluents*) with a velocity, or rate of change (a *fluxion*)—as opposed to Leibniz' more formal and static *infinitesimals*. Although Newton was not a geometer in the Greek tradition, as a glance at the *Principia* might suggest, he nevertheless relied more on ideas which could be expressed as pictures than did his great contemporary.

The priority dispute between Newton and Leibniz over the invention of the calculus dragged on for many years. Whole books have been written about this dispute, and the lines still seem to be drawn on a national basis. No one now doubts that much of Leibniz' work was independent, but it is hard to say to what extent it was influenced by a knowledge, however imprecise, of Newton's interests and successes. Leibniz' aims, too, were somewhat different—he was probably looking for a more abstract and general approach to a wider range of problems than Newton, whose interests seem more specific and 'mathematical'.

Infinite series

Descartes' algebra involved finite expressions such as $x - \frac{1}{2}x^2 + \frac{1}{3}x^3$, called *polynomials*. An *infinite series* resembles a polynomial, except that it 'goes on for ever', such as

$$x - \tfrac{1}{2}x^2 + \tfrac{1}{3}x^3 - \tfrac{1}{4}x^4 + \ldots.$$

Newton's realization of the importance of infinite series was one of his most influential contributions to mathematics. It turned out that many mathematical functions could be expressed as infinite series, and learning how to handle them was a major advance.

Foremost among these were the *binomial series*. It had been known for a long time that, if k is a positive integer, then the expression $(1+x)^k$ can be 'multiplied out' as a polynomial—for example:

$$(1+x)^2 = 1 + 2x + x^2;$$

$$(1+x)^3 = 1 + 3x + 3x^2 + x^3;$$

$$(1+x)^4 = 1 + 4x + 6x^2 + 4x^3 + x^4;$$

and so on. Newton extended this idea to the case when k is a fraction, such as $\frac{1}{2}$ or $\frac{2}{3}$, where the result is no longer a polynomial, but an infinite series—for example:

$$(1+x)^{1/2} = 1 + \tfrac{1}{2}x - \tfrac{1}{8}x^2 + \tfrac{1}{16}x^3 + \ldots.$$

Newton, in fact, had a general rule for handling any expression of the form $(1+x)^{m/n}$, where m and n are integers.

According to a letter (the *Epistola posterior*) that he sent to Leibniz in 1676, Newton's method for dealing with infinite series arose from an attempt to extend Wallis' investigation of curves of the form

$$y = (1-x^2)^n, \text{ where } n = 0, 1, 2, \ldots.$$

Newton went far beyond any existing work, by taking the known values of y when n is an integer, and 'interpolating' between these values to find the corresponding values when n is a fraction, such as $\frac{1}{2}$. This leads to infinite series, such as the above series for $(1+x)^{1/2}$.

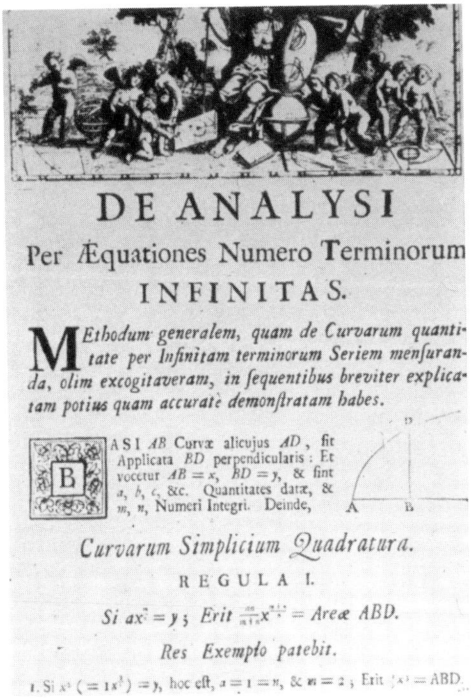

DE ANALYSI

Per Æquationes Numero Terminorum

INFINITAS.

Methodum generalem, quam de Curvarum quantitate per Infinitam terminorum Seriem mensuranda, olim excogitaveram, in sequentibus breviter explicatam potius quam accuratè demonstratam habes.

BASI *AB* Curvæ alicujus *AD*, sit Applicata *BD* perpendicularis: Et vocetur $AB = x$, $BD = y$, & sint a, b, c, &c. Quantitates datæ, & m, n, Numeri Integri. Deinde,

Curvarum Simplicium Quadratura.

REGULA I.

Si $ax^{\frac{m}{n}} = y$; *Erit* $\frac{an}{m+n}x^{\frac{m+n}{n}} =$ *Areæ ABD.*

Res Exemplo patebit.

1. Si x^2 $(= 1x^{\frac{2}{1}}) = y$, hoc est, $a = 1 = n$, & $m = 2$; Erit $\frac{1}{3}x^3 =$ ABD.

It is fairly typical of the efficiency with which Newton let his work be published that *De analysi*, written in 1669, first appeared in print in 1711. On the opening page the familiar rule for integrating a power of x may be seen (*Regula I*, or Rule I).

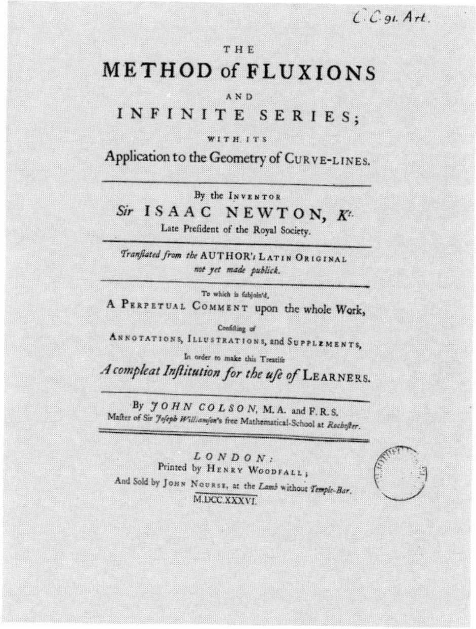
C. C. 91. Art.

THE

METHOD of FLUXIONS

AND

INFINITE SERIES;

WITH ITS

Application to the Geometry of CURVE-LINES.

By the INVENTOR

Sir ISAAC NEWTON, *K^t.*

Late Prefident of the Royal Society.

Tranflated from the AUTHOR'*s* LATIN ORIGINAL *not yet made publick.*

To which is fubjoin'd,

A PERPETUAL COMMENT upon the whole Work,

Confifting of

ANNOTATIONS, ILLUSTRATIONS, and SUPPLEMENTS,

In order to make this Treatife

A compleat Inftitution for the ufe of LEARNERS.

By *JOHN COLSON*, M.A. and F.R.S.

Mafter of Sir *Jofeph Williamfon*'s free Mathematical-School at *Rochefter*.

LONDON:

Printed by HENRY WOODFALL;

And Sold by JOHN NOURSE, at the *Lamb* without *Temple-Bar*.

M.DCC.XXXVI.

The manuscript of this tract of the early 1670s was made widely available to Newton's friends, but was not printed until 1736. By this time its content, although crucial to the development of mathematics in the 1670s–1690s, was mainly of historic interest—more up-to-date books incorporating Newton's ideas had been produced.

Newton described this in the throwaway phrase '*I put* $n = \frac{1}{2}$'—a momentous advance then, although it may seem just a little step to us over three centuries later.

In the years 1664–6, Newton was developing into the leading mathematician of his time, surpassing even Christiaan Huygens and James Gregory, although his labours would have been known only to himself and his few close associates. Many threads of his work at this time were drawn together in a paper on fluxions of 1666, written after he had returned to Cambridge following the closure of the University in 1665–6. A little later, spurred on by the publication of Nicolaus Mercator's *Logarithmotechnia* (1668), which contained the infinite series for $\log(1 + x)$—namely,

$$\log(1 + x) = x - \tfrac{1}{2}x^2 + \tfrac{1}{3}x^3 - \tfrac{1}{4}x^4 + \ldots$$

—Newton wrote down his own more general methods in *De analysi* (1669). His work on fluxions was extended in *De methodis fluxionum* (1670–1), which was not published until 1736.

Cubic curves

By about 1667, Newton was working on the classification of *cubic curves*—that is, curves given by an equation in two variables x and y, in which each term has degree 3 or less—for example:

$$y = x^3 + x^2 + x + 1, \text{ or } y^3 = xy^2 - 2x^2y + y - 3.$$

This is an intricate problem which had not previously been considered.

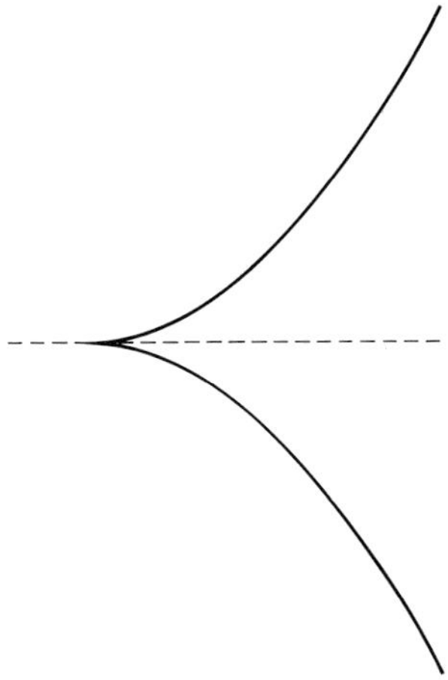

The *cissoid of Diocles*, a curve known since the second century BC, is a celebrated example of a cubic curve. Its equation is

$$x^3 + xy^2 = y^2$$

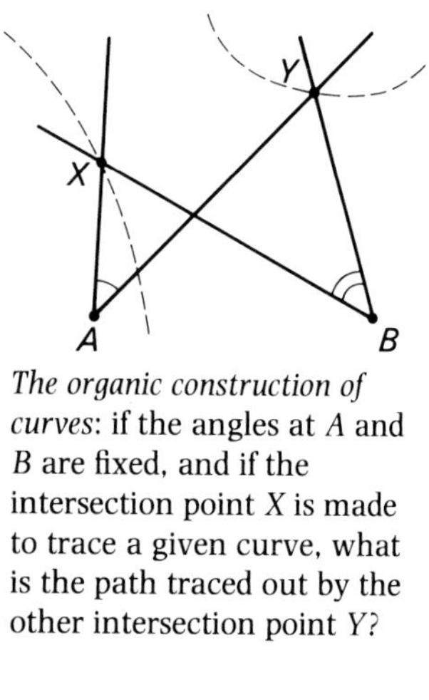

The organic construction of curves: if the angles at A and B are fixed, and if the intersection point X is made to trace a given curve, what is the path traced out by the other intersection point Y?

In fact, very few individual cubic curves had been described, and it is not known whether all those that had been were understood to be cubic curves, since in some cases they arose from quite different formulations. Such curves included the *cissoid of Diocles*, used for duplicating the cube in antiquity, and a handful of other curves discovered during the seventeenth century.

The classification of *quadratic curves* was well known—they are the conic sections, and are essentially of three different types (ellipses, hyperbolas, and parabolas). The classification of cubic curves is of a different order of difficulty. Newton reduced the general cubic equation to five standard forms (which he called *divergent parabolas*). Just as the three types of conic section can all be obtained by projecting a circle on to a plane, so all non-trivial cubic curves could be obtained by projection from one of these five standard forms.

By considering all the various cases, he ended up with no fewer than 72 species of cubic curve, which he published as an appendix to his *Opticks* (1704). Six further types, which Newton knew of, but omitted from his text, were rediscovered in the eighteenth century, yielding a final total of 78 different types of cubic curve.

When this appendix on cubics came out in 1704, it was poorly understood by Newton's contemporaries. Even some of its sound passages were thought to be incorrect. Despite this, and the fact that it was unrelated to any immediately preceding or subsequent work, versions of Newton's writings on cubics were published at least seven times during the eighteenth century.

Related to his work on cubics is an account of the *organic construction of curves*. This arises when two fixed angles rotate about two fixed points A and B, in such a way that one intersection traces a known curve. What is the path of the other intersection?

Newton obtained a number of general results dealing with the cases when the known curve is a straight line, a conic section, or a cubic curve, as well as a curve of higher order. In 1672 he sent his results to the mathematical correspondent John Collins, and Leibniz knew about them in 1676. If the given curve is a straight line, then the

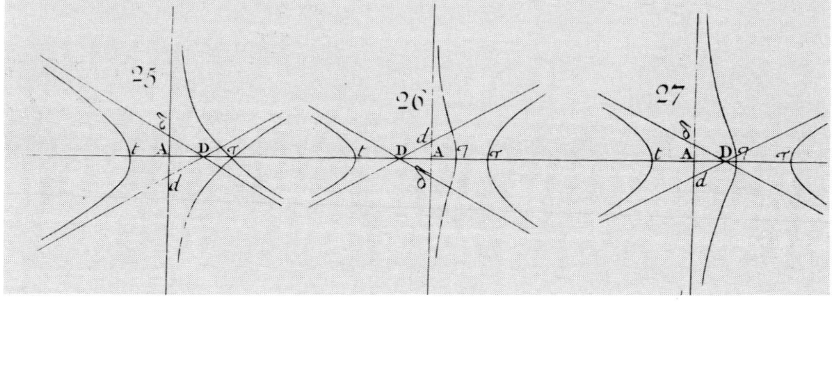

Newton made a spectacular contribution to pure geometry in his classification of cubic curves. These are some of them, as they first appeared in 1704—in an appendix to his *Opticks*.

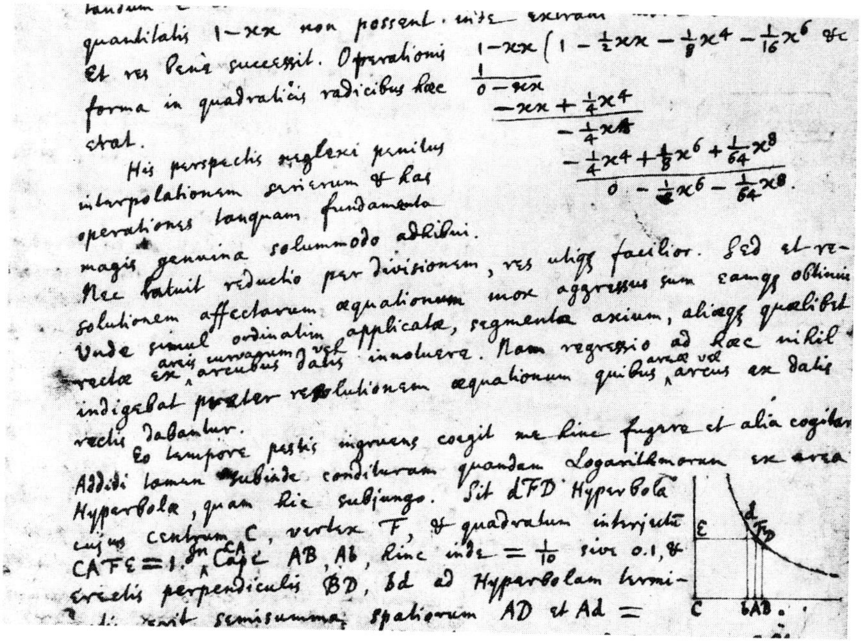

quantitatis $1-xx$ non possent ... Et res bene successit. Operationis forma in quadraticis radicibus haec erat.

$1-xx\,(1-\frac{1}{2}xx-\frac{1}{8}x^4-\frac{1}{16}x^6$ &c

His perspectis neglexi penitus interpolationem serierum & has operationes tanquam fundamenta magis genuina solummodo adhibui. Nec latuit reductio per divisionem, res utique facilior. Sed et resolutionem affectarum aequationum mox aggressus sum eamque obtinui. Unde simul ordinatim applicatae, segmenta axium, aliaeque quaelibet rectae ex areis curvarum vel arcubus datis innotuere. Nam regressio ad haec nihil indigebat praeter resolutionem aequationum quibus areae vel arcus ex datis rectis dabantur.

Eo tempore pestis ingruens coegit me hinc fugere et alia cogitare. Addidi tamen ... constructionem quandam Logarithmorum ex area Hyperbolae, quam hic subjungo. Sit dFD Hyperbola cujus centrum C, vertex F, & quadratum inscriptum CAFE = 1. In CA cape AB, Ab, hinc inde = $\frac{1}{10}$ sive 0.1, & erectis perpendiculis BD, bd ad Hyperbolam terminatis; semisumma spatiorum AD et Ad =

On this page from the *Epistola posterior*, Newton recounted for Leibniz how he came to realize that expressions such as $(1-x^2)^{1/2}$ could be handled in terms of infinite series.

transformed curve is generally a conic (ellipse, hyperbola, or parabola), whereas conics similarly transform to equations of degree 3 and 4. Newton applied his methods to the construction of a conic when five points on it are known, and to the construction from seven points of a cubic curve with a cross-over point.

Analysis

Two important sources for Newton's earlier work are the letters known as the *Epistola prior* and the *Epistola posterior*. They are both dated 1676, and were sent to Leibniz via Henry Oldenburg, Secretary of the Royal Society. They were published in the 1699 edition of Wallis' *Algebra*, and describe Newton's work on the binomial theorem and on infinite series. Newton was fairly open in what he said, sounding formal but friendly.

In addition to its discussion on infinite series, the second letter was notable for its references to maxima and minima, the quadrature of curves (finding areas), and the construction of tangents. He concealed the fact that he had obtained methods for this last topic, by using an exceedingly difficult anagram. Another anagram dealt with the ability to solve 'fluxional equations' (or 'differential equations', as they are now known). In 1693, Newton gave Leibniz a solution to the first anagram, and in 1699 Wallis published them both. The anagrams were quite lengthy and, with the usual accidental errors, totally secure. Newton was not keen to continue a correspondence with Leibniz, for he had other interests arousing his attention in the late 1670s—

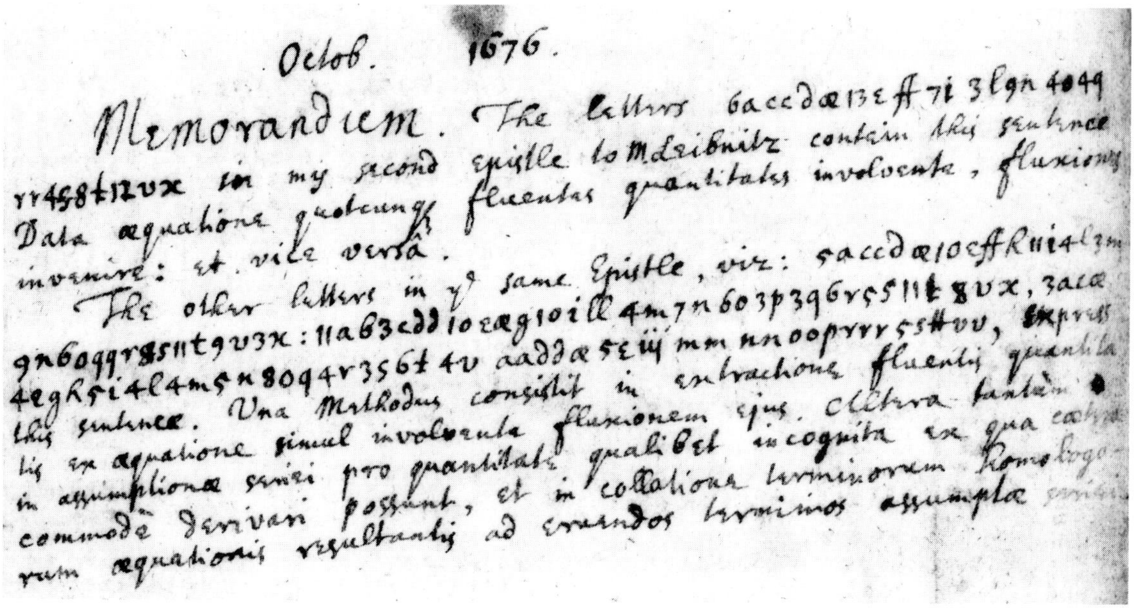

Octob. 1676.

Memorandum. The letters 6accdae13eff7i3l9n4o4qrr4s8t12vx in my second epistle to Mr Leibnitz contain this sentence Data aequatione quotcunque fluentes quantitates involvente, fluxiones invenire: et vice versa.

The other letters in ye same Epistle, viz: 5accdae10effh11i4l3m9n6oqqr8s11t9v3x: 11ab3cdd10eaeg10ill4m7n6o3p3q6r5s11t8vx, 3acae4egh5i4l4m5n8oq4r3s6t4v aaddaeeeeiijmmnnooprrrsssssttuu, express this sentence. Una Methodus consistit in extractione fluentis quantitatis ex aequatione simul involvente fluxionem ejus. altera tantum in assumptione seriei pro quantitate qualibet incognita ex qua caetera commode derivari possunt, et in collatione terminorum homologorum aequationis resultantis ad eruendos terminos assumptae seriei

We gain insight into seventeenth-century academic practices from this entry in Newton's notebook. It gives the key to the anagrams in which he communicated to Leibniz that he had made significant discoveries in the calculus—but without telling him what these discoveries were. The first anagram concealed a statement of the fundamental theorem of calculus.

notably, alchemy and chemistry (as described by Jan Golinski in Chapter 7). Nevertheless, Newton's protégé, Joseph Raphson, felt able to claim in 1715 that Leibniz had solved the anagrams—a sign of the hysteria of the priority dispute which arose between Leibniz and Newton.

The first of Newton's major manuscripts to make his name outside Cambridge was *De analysi per aequationes numero terminorum infinitas* (1669), or *De analysi* for short, which we have already met in connection with infinite series. This work gives rules for finding areas under curves of the form $y^n = x^m$, and expanding as infinite series simple quotients and square roots, which can then be analysed a term at a time. (This is now called 'term-by-term integration'.) For example, knowing that

$$\frac{1}{1+x} = 1 - x + x^2 - x^3 + \ldots,$$

we can integrate this series term by term to give the infinite series for $\log(1+x)$:

$$\log(1+x) = x - \tfrac{1}{2}x + \tfrac{1}{3}x^3 - \tfrac{1}{4}x^4 + \ldots.$$

Newton's manuscript was the first to give infinite series for functions such as $\sin^{-1}x$ (that is, the number whose sine is x). It is probably Newton's use of the word *analysis* in this context that has carried through to the use of the term for infinite processes in mathematics ever since. His use of the integration rule depends on small increments which were divided out and then allowed to diminish to zero. This idea had occurred earlier, in a different and cruder form, to Fermat and Wallis. In *De analysi*, Newton may be claimed finally to have 'invented the calculus', in the sense of recognizing and using the inverse natures of differentiation and integration, and of formalizing the rules involved.

Another topic discussed in *De analysi* was the approximation to solutions of polynomial equations such as $x^3 + 2x^2 + 10x = 20$, which cannot be solved exactly. This was a subject which already had a long history, and which had more recently been investigated by Viète, the leading French mathematician of the sixteenth century. Newton made a major breakthrough by introducing what is now known as the *Newton–Raphson method* for the numerical solution of such equations.

Newton continued his researches into fluxions and infinite series. One of his main contributions was *De methodis fluxionum et serierum infinitorum* (1671), which treated such important problems as finding the fluxional derivative of an equation—that is, the term-by-term rates of change of the elements of the equation. It also dealt with the inverse problem—that of determining the tangents to curves defined in various coordinate or reference systems, as well as finding the curvature, area, and arc-length.

The sheer quantity of Newton's writings, even on comparatively slight matters, is overwhelming. For example, the picture below shows some of his detailed calculations on the infinite series associated with the logarithm function. But, during his 30 years in Cambridge, he had

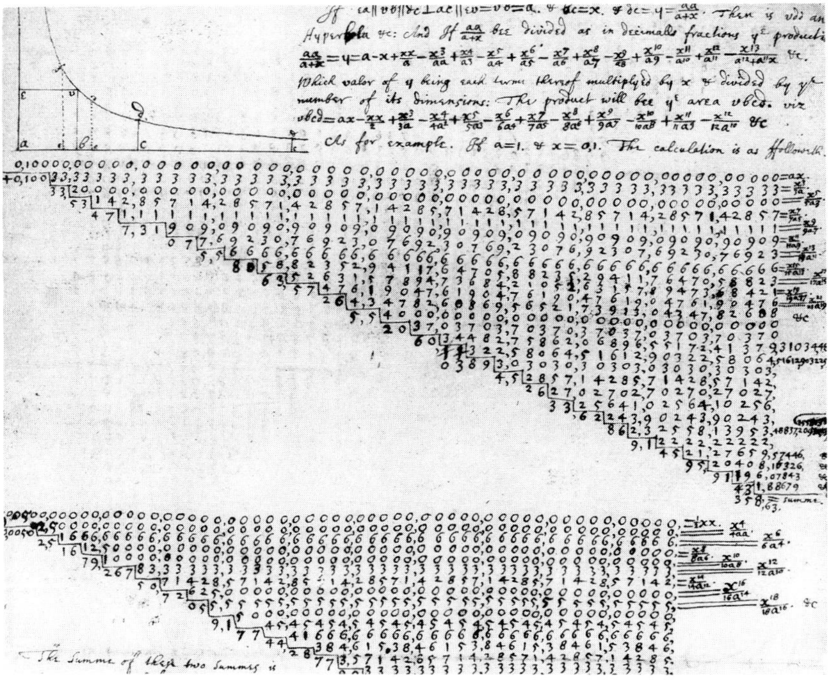

Newton's remarkable ability to take pains is very evident from this manuscript page of about 1665. He was calculating the area under a hyperbola—a logarithm, in effect—to no less than 55 places, by adding the values from each term of an infinite series.

little else to occupy his time. He had few pupils or collaborators, although later on there were followers—even his lectures seem to have been rather a formality. True, he had *colleagues* in London (such as Edmond Halley) and opponents (such as John Flamsteed), but he had little in the way of close academic or personal relationships.

During the years 1674–84, Newton produced several less well-known, but interesting, results. Of these, the most important deals with the problem of calculating tables of logarithms or other functions. If you can calculate certain key values, how do you find the values in between? Newton worked on this interpolation problem using a technique known as the *method of finite differences*, a technique already used by Thomas Harriot and Henry Briggs. This idea surfaces again in the *Principia*, where he gave a more general method which is needed when the key values are not equally spaced.

We also find work in elementary number theory, and plane and spherical trigonometry, and the Latin draft of a splendidly named *Specimen of a universal system of mathematics*, dating from about 1684. This last was a response to a work of David Gregory on a construction by his uncle (James Gregory) of the area of a general conic section, and on other questions relating to the geometry of curves. David Gregory's writings looked increasingly like Newton's own unpublished work on how mathematical quantities can be treated as infinite series. The *Specimen* was intended as a response to this—that is, to publicize Newton's own contributions. But it became more than this: it was a response, albeit brief, to Leibniz' work. Then it became yet more—a treatise on the computation of series. This was enough for Newton. The response made, the work was never finished. It was not published until very recently, in Whiteside's edition of the mathematical papers.

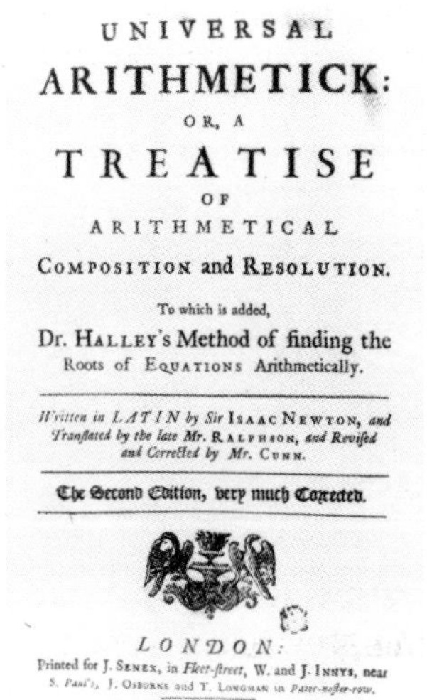
UNIVERSAL
ARITHMETICK:
OR, A
TREATISE
OF
ARITHMETICAL
COMPOSITION and RESOLUTION.
To which is added,
Dr. HALLEY's Method of finding the
Roots of EQUATIONS Arithmetically.

Written in LATIN by Sir ISAAC NEWTON, *and Translated by the late Mr.* RALPHSON, *and Revised and Corrected by Mr.* CUNN.

The Second Edition, very much Corrected.

LONDON:
Printed for J. SENEX, in *Fleet-street*, W. and J. INNYS, near *S. Paul's*, J. OSBORNE and T. LONGMAN in *Pater-noster-row*,
M.DCC.XXVIII.

Arithmetica universalis, first published in 1707, was an algebra text written by Newton in the early 1680s. The content ranged from elementary operations and problems to sophisticated new results in the theory of equations. This is the second English edition, of 1728.

Algebra

In the decade up to 1684, Newton may have delivered lectures on algebra as part of his professorial duties. He was obliged to deposit with the University a fair copy of the 97 lectures given, but for some time did not do so. He was eventually prevailed upon to fulfil this task, even if the lectures themselves may have been fictitious, and he was helped in this by his young amenuensis Humphrey Newton, who later wrote out the *Principia* and *The system of the world*. These lectures have been known, since their eventual publication in 1707, as the *Arithmetica universalis*.

As always, it is difficult to convey the richness of Newton's extensive and detailed work. Although the *Arithmetica universalis* contains some fairly trivial stuff, there are many matters of consequence, too. In particular, Newton dealt with sums of powers of the roots of algebraic equations, and his results are now known as *Newton's equations*, or

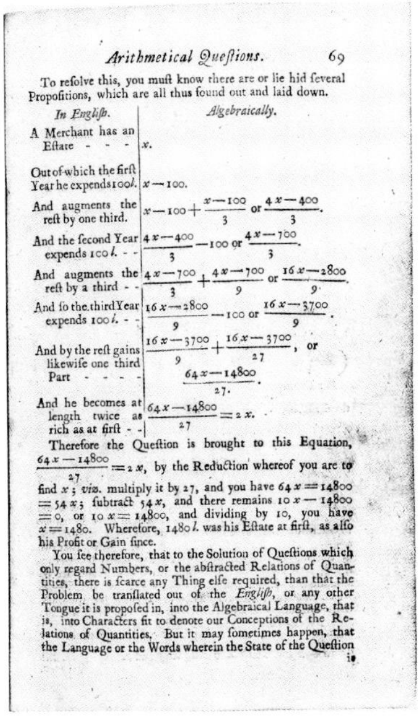

Arithmetical Questions. 69

To resolve this, you must know there are or lie hid several Propositions, which are all thus found out and laid down.

In English.	*Algebraically.*
A Merchant has an Estate - - -	x.
Out of which the first Year he expends 100*l*.	$x - 100$.
And augments the rest by one third.	$x - 100 + \frac{x-100}{3}$ or $\frac{4x-400}{3}$.
And the second Year expends 100*l*. - -	$\frac{4x-400}{3} - 100$ or $\frac{4x-700}{3}$.
And augments the rest by a third - -	$\frac{4x-700}{3} + \frac{4x-700}{9}$ or $\frac{16x-2800}{9}$.
And so the third Year expends 100*l*. - -	$\frac{16x-2800}{9} - 100$ or $\frac{16x-3700}{9}$.
And by the rest gains likewise one third Part - - - -	$\frac{16x-3700}{9} + \frac{16x-3700}{27}$, or $\frac{64x-14800}{27}$.
And he becomes at length twice as rich as at first - -	$\frac{64x-14800}{27} = 2x$.

Therefore the Question is brought to this Equation, $\frac{64x-14800}{27} = 2x$, by the Reduction whereof you are to find x; *viz.* multiply it by 27, and you have $64x = 14800 = 54x$; subtract $54x$, and there remains $10x - 14800 = 0$, or $10x = 14800$, and dividing by 10, you have $x = 1480$. Wherefore, 1480*l*. was his Estate at first, as also his Profit or Gain since.

You see therefore, that to the Solution of Questions which only regard Numbers, or the abstracted Relations of Quantities, there is scarce any Thing else required, than that the Problem be translated out of the *English*, or any other Tongue it is proposed in, into the Algebraical Language, that is, into Characters fit to denote our Conceptions of the Relations of Quantities. But it may sometimes happen, that the Language or the Words wherein the State of the Question is

In a choice of topic that was doubtless helpful in the future careers of any students attending his lectures, Newton explained on this page of his *Universal arithmetic* how to translate into algebraic language the problem: *A certain Merchant encreases his Estate yearly by a third Part, abating 100l. which he spends yearly in his Family; and after three Years he finds his Estate doubled.* Query, *What was he worth?*

Newton's identities. In a more old-fashioned vein, he solved polynomial equations of degree 3 and 4 using intersections of conics. Most important of all, perhaps, he extended *Descartes' rule of signs*, which can be used to find bounds for the numbers of positive and negative roots of an algebraic equation:

there are as many positive roots as there are changes of sign among consecutive coefficients;

there are as many negative roots as there are like signs among consecutive coefficients.

For example, the algebraic equation

$$x^4 - x^3 - 19x^2 + 49x - 30 = 0$$

has three changes of sign, and so three positive roots, and has one pair of like signs, and so just one negative root. Newton's rule was more complicated, and could be used to determine the number of imaginary roots of an algebraic equation; it was not proved until 1865, by J. J. Sylvester.

Dynamics

Immediately after this, in late 1684, Newton's interests changed rather dramatically to the area of dynamics, the mathematics of forces and motions. As John Roche observed in the previous chapter, he started work on *De motu*, Book I of the *Principia*. This work, and the following two Books, occupied him fully and with great intensity for the next three years.

Newton's dynamics properly belongs to the *Principia*, so I shall mention a few items only. For example, there is his famous result that Kepler's second law of planetary motion (*equal areas are swept out in equal times*) is true for *any* body attracted towards a central point, and not just for one moving in an elliptical orbit.

A key result of Newton's dynamics (although not really quite so crucial as is often made out) is that under an inverse-square law, *the gravitational attraction at any point inside a thin spherical shell is zero.* Coupled with the inverse-square result for an external point, one deduces that the attraction on an external point by a solid sphere varies inversely as the square of the distance from the point to the *centre* of the sphere—in other words, *the sphere behaves as though all of its mass is concentrated at the centre.*

There were, of course, many other results. For example, Newton gave a useful method for solving Kepler's equation for the position of a planet at a given time. This method was a forerunner of the now standard Newton–Raphson technique for the numerical solution of equations, mentioned earlier in connection with *De analysi*. And there were numerous results on the pure geometry of conics, such as the organic construction, mentioned above.

Later work

After the *Principia* years, Newton continued to revise and refine many of his early results. In the early 1690s, before leaving Cambridge for the Royal Mint, he carried out further work on the classification of

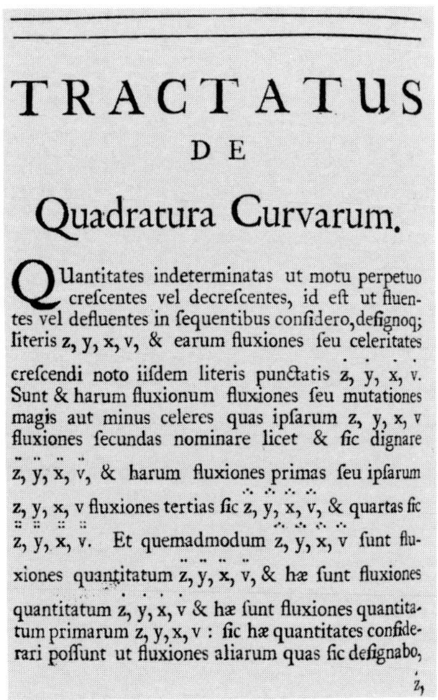

TRACTATUS

DE

Quadratura Curvarum.

QUantitates indeterminatas ut motu perpetuo creſcentes vel decreſcentes, id eſt ut fluentes vel defluentes in ſequentibus conſidero, deſignoq; literis z, y, x, v, & earum fluxiones ſeu celeritates creſcendi noto iiſdem literis punctatis $\dot{z}, \dot{y}, \dot{x}, \dot{v}$. Sunt & harum fluxionum fluxiones ſeu mutationes magis aut minus celeres quas ipſarum $\dot{z}, \dot{y}, \dot{x}, \dot{v}$ fluxiones ſecundas nominare licet & ſic dignare $\ddot{z}, \ddot{y}, \ddot{x}, \ddot{v}$, & harum fluxiones primas ſeu ipſarum $\ddot{z}, \ddot{y}, \ddot{x}, \ddot{v}$ fluxiones tertias ſic $\dddot{z}, \dddot{y}, \dddot{x}, \dddot{v}$, & quartas ſic $\ddddot{z}, \ddddot{y}, \ddddot{x}, \ddddot{v}$. Et quemadmodum $\dddot{z}, \dddot{y}, \dddot{x}, \dddot{v}$ ſunt fluxiones quantitatum $\ddot{z}, \ddot{y}, \ddot{x}, \ddot{v}$, & hæ ſunt fluxiones quantitatum $\dot{z}, \dot{y}, \dot{x}, \dot{v}$ & hæ ſunt fluxiones quantitatum primarum z, y, x, v : ſic hæ quantitates conſiderari poſſunt ut fluxiones aliarum quas ſic deſignabo,

$\acute{z}$,

Newton's mathematics first appeared in print (the *Principia* aside) as an appendix to his *Opticks* of 1704. On this opening page he indicated his fluxional notation: where he wrote $\dot{z}$, $\ddot{y}$, etc., we now generally follow Leibniz' notation, $\frac{dz}{dt}$, $\frac{d^2y}{dt^2}$, etc.

cubic curves, and wrote his *Tractatus de quadratura curvarum*. He later claimed that the *De quadratura* really dated from 1676, a claim most charitably described as 'unhistorical'.

In this work may be found a form of the *Taylor expansion* of a quantity—the expression of a function as an infinite series. For example, the logarithmic function leads to the infinite series

$$\log(1+x) = x - \tfrac{1}{2}x^2 + \tfrac{1}{3}x - \tfrac{1}{4}x^4 + \ldots .$$

Characteristically, Newton did not complete or publish *De quadratura* at that time, but it appeared eventually as an appendix to his *Opticks* (1704). It is sometimes claimed that this was the first of Newton's mathematical work to be published, but this is to overlook the *Principia* itself. The appendix to the *Opticks* also contained the first published version of his binomial theorem of some 40 years earlier. After this lengthy delay, the *De quadratura* was reissued many times.

In the 1690s, too, he looked more closely into Greek higher geometry. Viète earlier, and Halley a few years later, were among those who attempted to reconstruct classical geometrical works which had survived in fragmentary form, and Newton joined their number. He was interested in geometrical *methods* as well as *results*. Thre had come down from antiquity the notion of an *analysis* of a problem or configuration being a prerequisite to the *synthesis* of a solution or proof. Newton believed that there had once been *esoteric* methods for finding mathematical results—methods of analysis which were not commonly known, but were available only to a few. (It is interesting to see this attitude of Newton's reflected in other areas of his work, such as are discussed by Piyo Rattansi in Chapter 9.) He was not alone in such beliefs, but they had been commoner in the previous century; mathematicians of the seventeenth century had long turned to devising their own mathematical methods.

Interestingly, some confirmation of the views of Newton, and others who saw an ancient wisdom about geometrical methods as having been lost, came in the early years of the twentieth century. In 1906, a text of Archimedes' *Method*—missing for over a millennium—was found in Constantinople. Archimedes' method, which was used for finding areas, volumes, and centres of gravity, is more closely related to discovery techniques than any of his other known works. The method can be interpreted as the use of infinitesimals and mechanical transformations, not unlike those of Cavalieri and others in the early seventeenth century.

After his short period of mental disturbance in 1693, for which many explanations have been offered, Newton still pursued mathematics for a while. Notably, he looked to Cartesian methods for analyzing high plane curves. But, probably recognizing the decline of his creative powers, he left his research life at Cambridge in 1696 for that of a

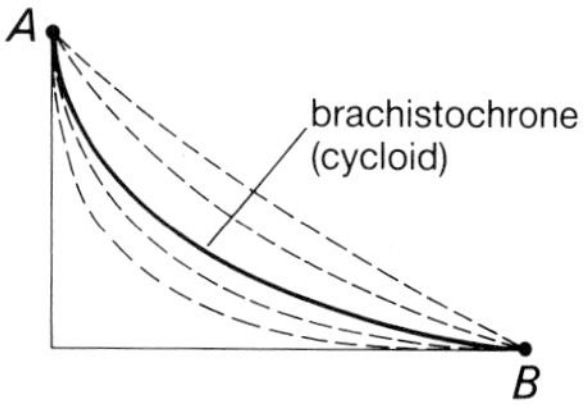

Given two points *A* and *B*, which curve joining them has the property that a weighted particle dropped from *A* reaches the point *B* in shortest time? The solution to this problem, the *brachistochrone problem*, is that the particle always moves along a cycloidal curve.

court servant at the Royal Mint, although he did not resign his Lucasian Chair for another five years. His powers had not yet faded, though, for he was still able to respond fully to a challenge from the Continental mathematician Johann Bernoulli in 1697. The challenge was to find what curve had the property of quickest descent, the so-called *brachistochrone problem*. Although Newton replied anonymously with the solution—which turns out to be a cycloid—Bernoulli was not fooled for an instant: 'I recognize the lion by his claws', he said.

Later, when he was settled in London and developing his public roles as Master of the Mint and President of the Royal Society, Newton became involved in revisions of the *Principia*. Most of the substantive work for the second edition of 1713 was done by a young Cambridge scholar, Roger Cotes, who encouraged Newton to agree to many clarifications and improvements. Apart from responding to Cotes, Newton in these years revised earlier mathematical works, and tried to ensure that his views of the history of his own work should prevail. His discreditable involvement in the affair of the *Commercium epistolicum* (1713) is sad, but deserves mention here.

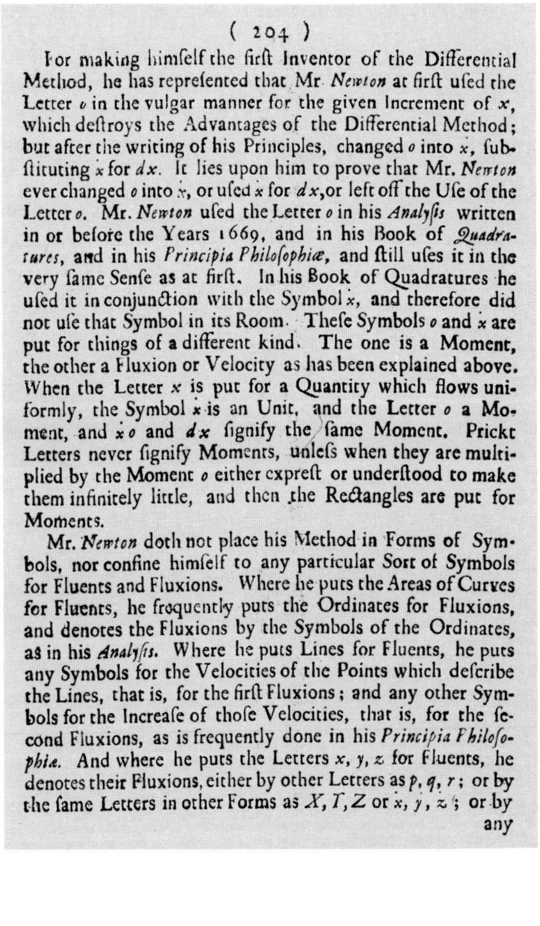
(204)

For making himſelf the firſt Inventor of the Differential Method, he has repreſented that Mr. *Newton* at firſt uſed the Letter *o* in the vulgar manner for the given Increment of *x*, which deſtroys the Advantages of the Differential Method; but after the writing of his Principles, changed *o* into $\dot{x}$, ſubſtituting $\dot{x}$ for *dx*. It lies upon him to prove that Mr. *Newton* ever changed *o* into $\dot{x}$, or uſed $\dot{x}$ for *dx*, or left off the Uſe of the Letter *o*. Mr. *Newton* uſed the Letter *o* in his *Analyſis* written in or before the Years 1669, and in his Book of *Quadratures*, and in his *Principia Philoſophiæ*, and ſtill uſes it in the very ſame Senſe as at firſt. In his Book of Quadratures he uſed it in conjunction with the Symbol $\dot{x}$, and therefore did not uſe that Symbol in its Room. Theſe Symbols *o* and $\dot{x}$ are put for things of a different kind. The one is a Moment, the other a Fluxion or Velocity as has been explained above. When the Letter *x* is put for a Quantity which flows uniformly, the Symbol $\dot{x}$ is an Unit, and the Letter *o* a Moment, and $\dot{x}o$ and *dx* ſignify the ſame Moment. Prickt Letters never ſignify Moments, unleſs when they are multiplied by the Moment *o* either expreſt or underſtood to make them infinitely little, and then the Rectangles are put for Moments.

Mr. *Newton* doth not place his Method in Forms of Symbols, nor confine himſelf to any particular Sort of Symbols for Fluents and Fluxions. Where he puts the Areas of Curves for Fluents, he frequently puts the Ordinates for Fluxions, and denotes the Fluxions by the Symbols of the Ordinates, as in his *Analyſis*. Where he puts Lines for Fluents, he puts any Symbols for the Velocities of the Points which deſcribe the Lines, that is, for the firſt Fluxions; and any other Symbols for the Increaſe of thoſe Velocities, that is, for the ſecond Fluxions, as is frequently done in his *Principia Philoſophiæ*. And where he puts the Letters *x*, *y*, *z* for Fluents, he denotes their Fluxions, either by other Letters as *p*, *q*, *r*; or by the ſame Letters in other Forms as *X*, *Y*, *Z* or $\dot{x}$, $\dot{y}$, $\dot{z}$; or by any

The President of the Royal Society in full flow, in the *Philosophical Transactions* for February 1715—an anonymous witness in his own cause. This typical page of his ruthless diatribe against Leibniz concerns their use of symbolism.

The priority dispute on the origins of the calculus had continued to fester since the turn of the century. In 1711 Leibniz went so far as to complain to the Royal Society about the accusations, and in 1712 the Royal Society set up a committee whose report was published the following year as the *Commercium epistolicum*. This apparently impartial account and adjudication of the dispute found in Newton's favour, and against Leibniz. Not until many years later did it become clear that Newton himself—the President of the Society—had written part of the *Commercium epistolicum*, and also the subsequent anonymous account of it published in 1715 in the Royal Society's *Philosophical Transactions*. But then, Newton had written that 'Leibniz could not be a witness in his own cause'.

It would be wrong to end this chapter on such an ungracious note. I hope that this outline of Newton's work has given an indication of the breadth, depth, and richness of Newton's contributions to the mathematical sciences. However interesting his personality—and it is one which has fascinated both his contemporaries, and many since—the reason for our interest must be very largely a realization, backed by some measure of understanding, of the importance of his contributions to mathematics and natural philosophy.

Further reading

General descriptions of Newton's mathematical writings can be found in Derek Gjertsen, *The Newton handbook*, Routledge and Kegan Paul, London, 1986. Full details are given in the eight volumes of *The mathematical papers of Isaac Newton* (edited by D. T. Whiteside), Cambridge University Press, Cambridge, 1967–84.

Also recommended are the still useful book by H. W. Turnbull, *The mathematical discoveries of Newton*, Blackie and Son, London, 1945; and Chapter 12 of John Fauvel and Jeremy Gray, *The history of mathematics: a reader*, Macmillan, London, 1987.

CHAPTER FOUR

Newton's optics: the changing spectrum of science

CASPER HAKFOORT

In 1699, the French philosopher and theologian Nicolas Malebranche gave a lecture to the assembled members of the Paris Académie des Sciences on the theory of light and colours. The theory he expounded was a medium or wave theory. According to Malebranche, light consists of pressure waves travelling in an etherial medium filling space. A relative novelty in his otherwise traditional exposition was the proposition that colours are related to the frequency of light waves, just as the frequency of sound waves determines musical tones. Although Malebranche admitted that he did not have a method to measure the number of vibrations corresponding to each colour, he claimed to know the order of the colours from high to low frequencies. The colour white had the highest frequency, and the other colours were arranged in descending order of brightness—first yellow, then red, followed by blue, and finally black, which was supposed to have frequency zero (no vibrations, no light). His postulated relationship between the frequency of light waves and colours turned out to be a major contribution to the developing tradition of medium theories of light. However, Malebranche's suggestion did not come out of the blue, and still had a long way to go before it was a mature and acknowledged element of this medium tradition.

In 1712, Malebranche publicly changed his mind as a result of his reading of Newton's *Opticks*, which had been published in 1704. He was greatly impressed by the

> experiments which Mr Newton, this learned mathematician who is so renowned in England and everywhere, has made with such an exactness that I cannot doubt the truth any more.

Malebranche accepted Newton's major proposition that the light of the Sun is a mixture of the simple or homogenous colours of the rainbow. So white light was not homogenous, as he had thought earlier. Malebranche also accepted Newton's musical division of the spectrum into seven colour bands (as Penelope Gouk explains in the next chapter), but in his view the reason for the harmonies in the spectrum was the harmonic ratios of the ether vibrations.

Newton's most famous optical experiment, to determine the composition of white light, was celebrated in this imaginative reconstruction by John-Adam Houston, 1870. The development of Newton's optical ideas is rather more complex than the traditional account suggests.

The change in Malebranche's ideas had occurred at least as early as 1707. In a letter written in that year, he not only praised Newton's *Opticks*, but also seemed to strike quite a different note:

Although Mr Newton is not at all a *physicist*, his book is very curious and very useful to those who have good physical principles, he is for that matter an excellent *mathematician*. Everything I believe concerning the properties of light fit all his *experiments*.

The first thought that crossed your mind while reading this comment might well have been: was a Continental philosophically inclined scholar qualified to give a fair judgement of Newton's physics and optics? Something else which might have caught your attention is the scent of paradox. Why did Malebranche praise Newton's experimental and mathematical skills, while at the same time disqualifying him as a physicist? Are not good mathematics and good experiments necessary, or perhaps even sufficient, conditions for the practice of good physics? Irritation and paradox are often symptoms of complex, as well as fundamental, problems. That is true in this case, too. The development and reception of Newton's optical work was full of confusion and controversy, but it also revealed fundamental changes in early modern science.

I should like to clarify the historical complexity by providing an outline of some of the more significant episodes from Newton's early work in 1664–6 until the reception of his mature work in the eighteenth century. In so doing, I shall query the widely-held opinion that Newton's optical work is *straightforward, clear, and accessible*.

In my view, his optical work is even more complex than the *Principia* (1687), which is generally taken to be sophisticated, opaque, and inaccessible. The main reasons for this are simple. First, Newton wanted not only to contribute to the science of optics, but also to advocate a particular view of science. Although the latter objective was present in the *Principia* too, the methodological reconstruction of optics and colour theory was conceived earlier than its counterpart in astronomy and mechanics. Therefore, although published earlier, the *Principia* was modelled after the spirit of the *Opticks*, and not the other way round as one might expect. Secondly, the reconstructional problems in the *Principia* were tremendous, but nevertheless more easily solved than those in optics. Thus, although Newton reached his goals in mechanics and astronomy almost completely, he had to admit that the ends he had set himself for optics were only partly achieved. This is not to deny Newton's great successes in the science of light and colours. Newton invested a lot of his talent in the *Opticks*, but maybe he reserved his genius for the *Principia*.

Descartes and the mechanization of colours

The French philosopher and scientist René Descartes was Newton's main partner in revolution. In optics, as in celestial mechanics, Newton framed much of his approach by learning what to reject and what to keep from Descartes' legacy. By doing this, Newton came to terms with mechanistic natural philosophy, which was the most prominent of early modern philosophies in the mid-seventeenth century, as John Henry shows in Chapter 6.

Descartes' global world picture, as presented in his *Principles of philosophy* (1644), was a full-blown mechanistic alternative to the still dominant Aristotelian natural philosophy. Like others, Descartes did not accept the fundamental Aristotelian distinction between *terrestrial* and *celestial* physics. In Aristotelian natural philosophy, the heavens and the planets were supposed to consist of a special substance or element, the *quintessence*, which did not exist in the sublunary sphere. Because it was part of the nature of this substance to go around in circles, the planets were moving in eternal circles. On Earth, the natural movements were rectilinear and temporary. In contrast to the Aristotelian distinction between two fundamentally different regions, Descartes used the same, mechanical principles in both areas. In Descartes' world-view, matter was the same in heaven as on Earth. The properties of matter were strictly limited to mathematical aspects, as considered in the science of mechanics—size, form, and movement. Qualitative properties of matter like inherent forces, smells, sounds, and colours, had no place in this mechanistic philosophy.

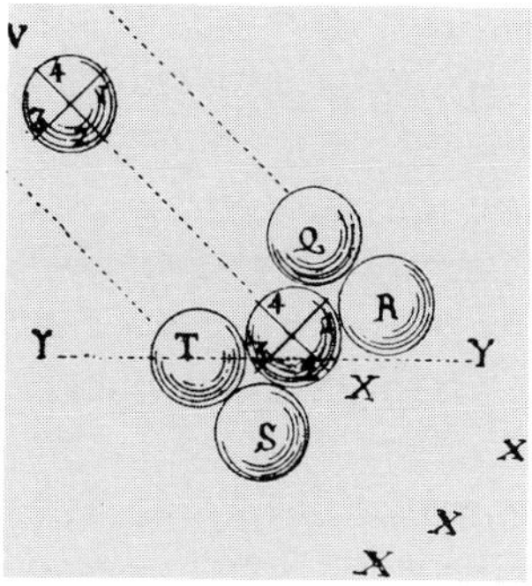

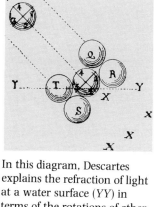

In this diagram, Descartes explains the refraction of light at a water surface (*YY*) in terms of the rotations of ether particles. This kind of explanation is the epitome of the *mechanical philosophy*.

The older qualitative view of matter was at the basis of another fundamental distinction in Aristotelian natural philosophy. This distinction was between *real* and *apparent* colours. Examples of the first class were the colours of apples and trees. According to early seventeenth-century Aristotelian theory, real colours are properties of the

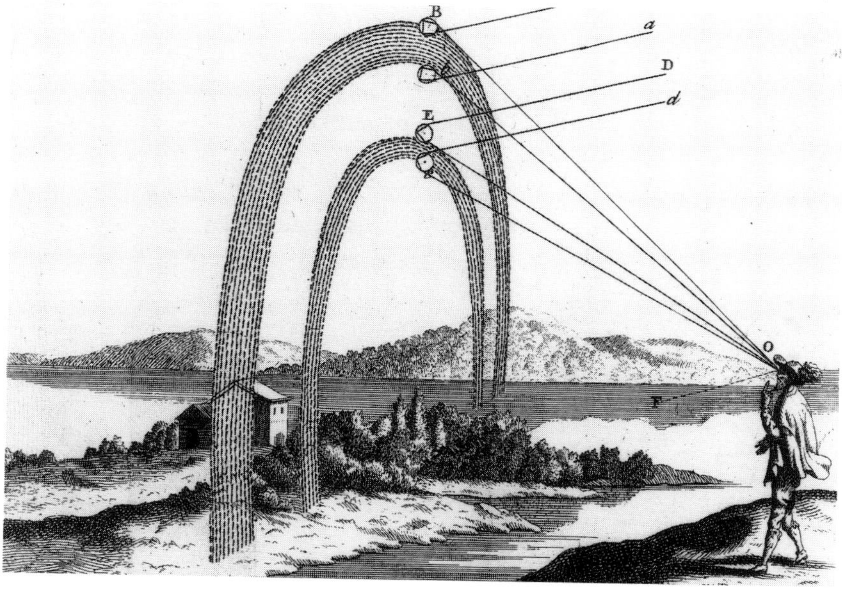

Descartes' account of the positioning of primary and secondary rainbows continues to be plausible, although he could not explain as helpfully as Newton could why they are coloured.

surface of bodies. These colours are visible when light is present, and do not disappear when it becomes dark, because they are inherent properties of bodies. Apparent colours, by contrast, do *not* exist in the dark. The colours of the rainbow are an example of this: they are produced by mixing light and darkness (in this case, clouds), and therefore cannot exist once light, one of its constituents, is absent. This view of the production of apparent colours has been called the *modification hypothesis*, and according to it, colours are produced by a modification of (white) light.

Descartes could not accept real colours as inherent qualitative properties of matter. He therefore rejected the Aristotelian distinction between real and apparent colours, and explained the colours of apples and rainbows using the same concepts. However, as I will show in a moment, this explanation was a *mechanistic* adaptation of the modification hypothesis for apparent colours. So this hypothesis, grounded in Aristotelian philosophy, was not only accepted by Descartes, but also extended by him to *all* colours.

In Descartes' view, light consists in the pressure (or, more correctly, the tendency to move) of an ubiquitous *ether*. *Colours* are the effect of an additional tendency of the ether particles, the tendency to *rotate*. For example, in the middle of a beam of white light falling on a glass prism, the rotational tendency is as great as the linear tendency, and therefore the colour is white. At the edges of the beam, contact with ether particles in the shadow, having no rotational tendency, leads to an increase or decrease of the rotational tendency of the beam particles. This change of rotational tendency, as contrasted with the linear tendency, results in colours—red and blue, respectively. In the case of an apple or another coloured body, colours are produced, because the surface of the body changes the rotational tendency of incoming light. In this way, white light is changed into red light or into light of some other colour, depending on the texture of the body.

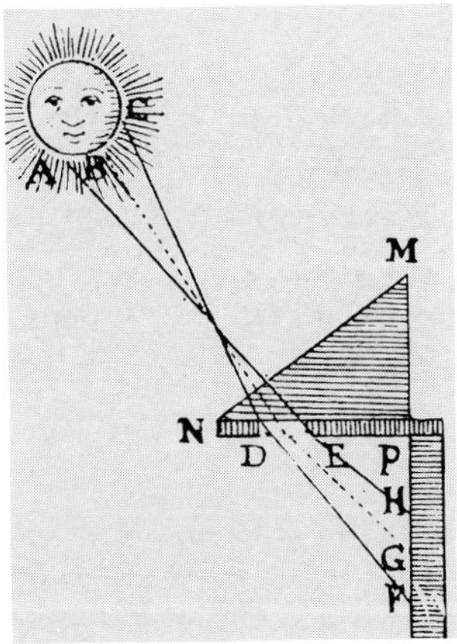

A diagram from Descartes' *Les météores*, the essay in which he explained the formation of rainbows. This shows a prism experiment which supposedly explains why colours are formed when white light is refracted.

So, according to Descartes, the colours produced by a prism or by the surface of an apple are *modifications of white light*. It was this common element of Aristotelian philosophy and Cartesian mechanistic philosophy, and indeed all theorizing about colours since ancient times, that Newton was to question, to attack, and finally to replace by a new theory of light and colours.

Newton's early optical research

Newton's first article, known as the *New theory about light and colours*, was published in the Royal Society's *Philosophical Transactions* in 1672, and met with considerable opposition. During the next four years, 10 criticisms by half a dozen different authors appeared in the *Transactions*, together with 11 replies by Newton. Whether or not this sets a record, it is certainly an indication of the contentious, if not the revolutionary, character of Newton's views. Why was this article such a provocation to the learned world?

Newton certainly invited a lot of criticism by attacking the universally held modification hypothesis. But this was not all. Intertwined with the exposition of a new optical theory, Newton became an increasingly zealous advocate of a particular methodology. This was not an invention of his, although he became one of its most able and influential users. The study of light and colours was the first field where Newton practised the new *style* of science. In the first dozen years of his scientific life this new style was formulated, developed, and defended against attacks. In the course of this process, it hardened into a sacred conviction, which Newton obeyed in his published work with an unrelenting rigour, only to be relaxed on the rarest of occasions.

Newton's work, undertaken during the years 1664 to 1672, was not published during his lifetime, but can be studied from his manuscripts. In his notebooks, Newton reported his reading of Aristotelian colour theory and of modern expositions by authors like Robert Boyle, Robert Hooke and, most prominently, Descartes. He read the latter's *Principles of philosophy* (1644), as well as his optical views contained in the *Dioptrics* (1637), *Les météores* (1637), and *La géométrie*.

Meanwhile, he started performing carefully planned experiments. From very early on, Newton seems to have held an emission hypothesis of light, conceiving light rays as streams of corpuscles, emitted by shining substances. This conviction formed part of his language to describe his earliest experiments on colours. Hypothesizing and experimenting, he gradually arrived at the concept of the different refrangibility of rays (or corpuscles). This was a very fruitful concept for Newton's emerging theory of colours. One of the major ideas it led him

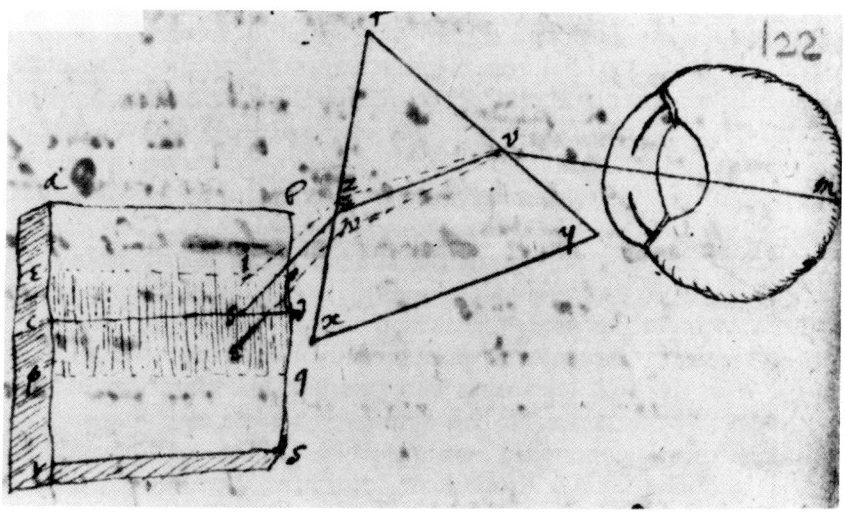

In 1665–6, Newton drew this eye viewing a shaded band through a prism. Three rays of light from the band are shown being bent through different degrees. Newton had the idea that rays could have different speeds, and that the slow ones were bent more than the fast ones.

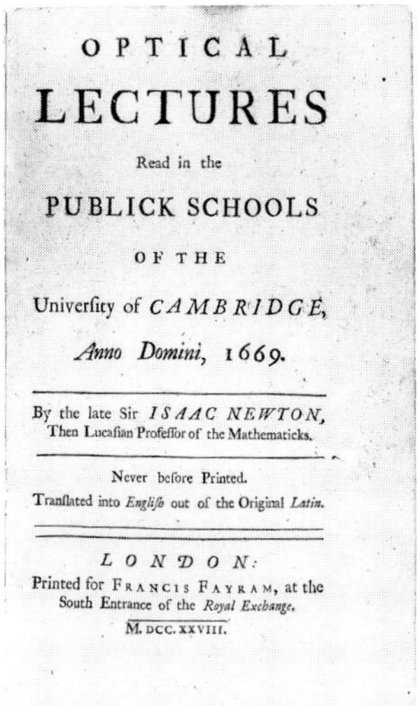

OPTICAL
LECTURES
Read in the
PUBLICK SCHOOLS
OF THE
Univerſity of *CAMBRIDGE*,
Anno Domini, 1669.

By the late Sir *ISAAC NEWTON*,
Then Lucaſian Profeſſor of the Mathematicks.

Never before Printed.
Tranſlated into *Engliſh* out of the Original *Latin*.

LONDON:
Printed for FRANCIS FAYRAM, at the
South Entrance of the *Royal Exchange*.
M.DCC.XXVIII.

Newton lectured on optics as part of his duties as Lucasian professor. Typically, his lectures for 1669 were first published in 1728, after his death.

to, in 1666, was the concept of *white light* as being an *aggregate of different homogenous rays*.

This kind of work was not very different from the marriage of theoretical natural philosophy, based on a global world picture (often atomism or another variant of mechanistic philosophy), and experimental philosophy, which was characteristic of the work of Hooke. But Newton gradually divorced himself from this widespread and acknowledged style of early modern science. To be sure, he continued to take a great interest in it, and to practise it, but he was sceptical about the certainty of the results produced by this approach. He preferred the certainty of a different style, in which descriptive mathematical laws and descriptive experimental conclusions were combined.

In his *Optical lectures*, he clearly expressed himself on his favourite style of science. He wrote:

It is affirmed that these propositions [on colours] are to be treated not hypothetically and probably, but by experiments or demonstratively.

He apologized for treating colours in a book on geometrical optics, a 'truly mathematical science', whereas the nature of colours was commonly treated in works of physics or natural philosophy:

although colours may belong to physics, the science of them must nevertheless be considered mathematical, insofar as they are treated by mathematical reasoning. Indeed, since an exact science of them seems to be one of the most difficult that philosophy is in need of, I hope to show—as it were, by my example—how valuable mathematics is in natural philosophy.

He urged mathematicians to investigate nature and natural philosophers to learn mathematics:

Hence the former shall not entirely spend their time in speculations of no value to human life, nor shall the latter, while working assiduously with an absurd method, perpetually fail to reach their goal. But truly with the help of philosophical geometers and geometrical philosophers, instead of the conjectures and probabilities that are being blazoned about everywhere, we shall finally achieve a natural science supported by the greatest evidence.

In this passage Newton made clear that he wanted a drastic change of method in science, making it *more* mathematical and experimental and, at the same time, *less* hypothetical. This method implied a new hierarchy between the traditional fields of mathematical science and theoretical natural philosophy, as well as the young, still-emerging field of experimental philosophy.

Newton's *New theory* reflected this general methodological shift. Take, for example, his central and most controversial proposition that the light of the Sun is not pure and homogenous, but consists of a mixture of rays that are bent by different amounts. What status did

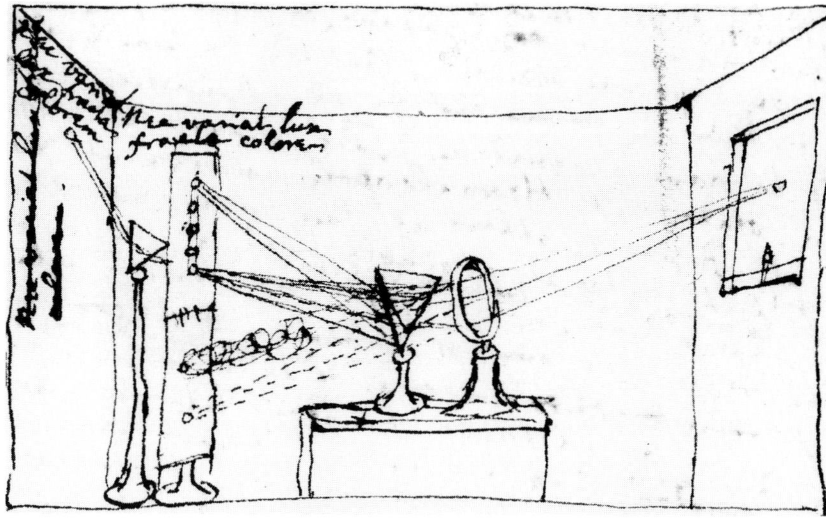

A drawing by Newton of the so-called crucial experiment (*experimentum crucis*) in which light from the sun is refracted through a prism, and one colour refracted through a second prism to show that it undergoes no further change.

this proposition have, and what kind of arguments were brought forward in its favour?

According to Newton, it was *not* a hypothetical proposition with the same status as, for example, the rotation hypothesis of Descartes. *It was a direct conclusion from experiments*. It was therefore not dependent on any hypothesis about the nature of light and could be attacked only on the basis of other experiments. So much for the emphasis on experiments, and the rejection of hypothetical reasoning!

Newton's emphasis on quantification and mathematics is less pronounced, partly for reasons I shall discuss in the next section. Nevertheless, the crucial role of the mathematical component in the new style becomes evident if we consider Newton's novel way of using glass prisms in his experiments.

Many others before him had seen the colours at the edges of a light beam which had passed through a prism, but they had usually asked for the general cause of the colours, without paying attention to the quantitative features of the experiment. Starting from a qualitative effect and asking for its cause, they ended with a qualitative theoretical account, or at best an unfruitful quasi-quantitative one, as in the case of Descartes. Newton, however, was struck by a quantitative anomaly—the fact that the length of the spectrum was about five times as great as its breadth; this contradicted the known law of refraction, which predicted a circular image. From this logical starting point, Newton proceeded to his famous *experimentum crucis* or 'crucial experiment' which, according to him, proved that '*Light* consists of *Rays differently refrangible*'.

Newton's views about the 'philosophical' nature of light and colours were not treated explicitly in the 1672 paper. He made one exception, however. In a paragraph which caused some confusion for his readers, he concluded from his experiments that

> it can no longer be disputed, whether there be colours in the dark, nor whether they be the qualities of the objects we see, no nor perhaps, whether Light be a Body.

In the first part of this statement, Newton obviously rejects Aristotelian colour theory. The second part is more ambiguous. Some of his critics (Hooke, for example) saw in it an assertion of the corpuscular, or emission, concept of light. This was a quite natural thing to do, as a corpuscular interpretation of Newton's propositions on rays and colours made them easier to understand. In addition, it was common practice to state one's hypothesis on the nature of light in reporting experiments, so Newton's readers expected him to follow suit. Newton, however, later denied that he had proposed an emission hypothesis of light. He had merely stated the *probable* conclusion that one or another mechanistic hypothesis of light was correct: light was probably some action or movement of a material substance. In his view, questions about the correct hypothesis of light could not be resolved at this stage by experimental or mathematical means and, indeed, were irrelevant to the kind of propositions he had put forward.

This methodological background to Newton's experiments and propositions was not spelled out in the *New theory*. As we now know, some of it had been written down in the (unpublished) *Optical lectures*. To others, and partly also to Newton himself, it gradually became clear during the discussion of the *New theory*.

If we try to put ourselves in the position of a competent scientist in 1672 who was confronted with Newton's paper, we are liable to experience the same irritation and confusion that were felt by renowned figures like Hooke, or Christiaan Huygens, the '*doyen of European science*'. What they observed was a young unknown scholar from Cambridge, who boasted of refuting the age-old modification theory of colours by a handful of sketchily described experiments, while his argument apparently rested on an emission hypothesis of light which was considered to be as much a conjecture as their own pet hypotheses.

Newton defended himself against these criticisms by giving a more detailed and complete description of his *experimentum crucis* (the original description was indeed wanting), and by disclosing the style of his reasoning and experimentation. Now, he believed, the critics could respond to what he really wanted to bring forward. They could assert whether they found his experimental evidence concerning the heterogenous nature of white light convincing, and whether they subscribed to his view on science. However, his hope proved to be in vain. The judgement of Huygens illustrates the inter-connectedness of

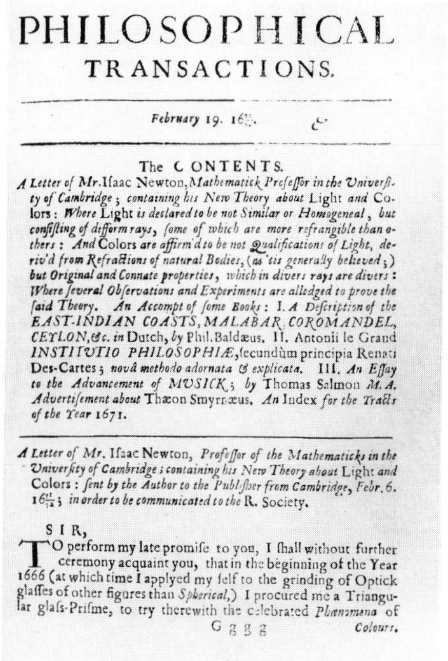

PHILOSOPHICAL TRANSACTIONS.

February 19. 16$\frac{71}{72}$.

The CONTENTS.

A Letter of Mr. Isaac Newton, *Mathematick Professor in the University of Cambridge; containing his New Theory about* Light *and* Colors: *Where* Light *is declared to be not Similar or Homogeneal, but consisting of difform rays, some of which are more refrangible than others: And* Colors *are affirm'd to be not Qualifications of Light, deriv'd from Refractions of natural Bodies, (as 'tis generally believed;) but Original and Connate properties, which in divers rays are divers: Where several Observations and Experiments are alledged to prove the said Theory. An Accompt of some Books:* I. *A Description of the EAST-INDIAN COASTS, MALABAR, COROMANDEL, CEYLON, &c. in* Dutch, *by* Phil. Baldæus. II. Antonii le Grand *INSTITUTIO PHILOSOPHIÆ*, secundùm principia Renati Des-Cartes; *novâ methodo adornata & explicata.* III. *An Essay to the Advancement of MUSICK; by* Thomas Salmon *M. A. Advertisement about* Thæon Smyrnæus. *An* Index *for the Tracts of the Year* 1671.

A Letter of Mr. Isaac Newton, *Professor of the Mathematicks in the University of Cambridge; containing his New Theory about* Light *and* Colors: *sent by the Author to the Publisher from Cambridge, Febr.* 6. 16$\frac{71}{72}$; *in order to be communicated to the* R. Society.

SIR,

TO perform my late promise to you, I shall without further ceremony acquaint you, that in the beginning of the Year 1666 (at which time I applyed my self to the grinding of Optick glasses of other figures than *Spherical*,) I procured me a Triangular glass-Prisme, to try therewith the celebrated *Phænomena* of

Gggg *Colours.*

The opening page of the 19 February 1672 issue of the *Philosophical Transactions*.

optical and methodological matters. In Huygens' view, the doctrine of differently coloured rays was *only* a hypothesis, although a very plausible one. It was more important to him that Newton had not solved 'the great difficulty of explaining by mechanical physics wherein this diversity of colours consists'. Newton's theory of colours was accepted by some of his opponents; at this stage his style of science was accepted by nobody.

Mathematics and natural philosophy in Newton's optics

In spite of its richness, the discussion about the *New theory* had failed to disclose all the themes in Newton's optical work.

One of these featured in Newton's original letter to Henry Oldenburg, which came to be published as the *New theory*, but Oldenburg suppressed the relevant passage when he edited the letter for the press. In the deleted passage, Newton expressed his hope of arriving at a mathematical science of colours:

> [a] naturalist would scearce expect to see ye science of those [colours] become mathematicall, & yet I dare affirm that there is as much certainty in it as in any other part of Opticks.

In the same year, Newton returned to his mathematical dream in an answer to Hooke's criticisms, but again this part was left out in the printed version. Newton was perhaps content about Oldenburg's interventions (which he even might have invited), because he was already less confident that his programme for a mathematical science of colours would advance beyond its first promising successes. The main stumbling block was the *law of dispersion*—namely, the regularity in the distribution of colours in the spectrum. Around 1675, he finally decided not to publish the mathematical part of the *Optical lectures*, and made his first plan of the later *Opticks*, in which no systematic mathematical treatment of colours would be given.

Hypothesizing on the nature of light and colours is another theme which was almost absent from the *New theory* and Newton's contributions to the discussion. As we saw earlier, it was present in his work before 1672, and hypotheses did indeed appear again and again in Newton's published and unpublished work after that year. One must admit, however, that these were always accompanied in print by a disclaimer. Such disclaimers should not be interpreted as absolute rejections of hypotheses; Newton did not believe that hypotheses were useless and should not be framed. However, he did assign a special place to them, and stressed that they should not be mingled with demonstrated mathematical or experimental propositions.

In 1675, as the discussion in the pages of the *Philosophical Transactions* was reaching its end, Newton sent a long paper to the Royal Society which he wished to be read out at one of their meetings, but not to be published. It was entitled *An hypothesis explaining the properties of light, discoursed of in my several papers*. In an introduction to this paper, he claimed to propose this hypothesis as an 'illustration' for the

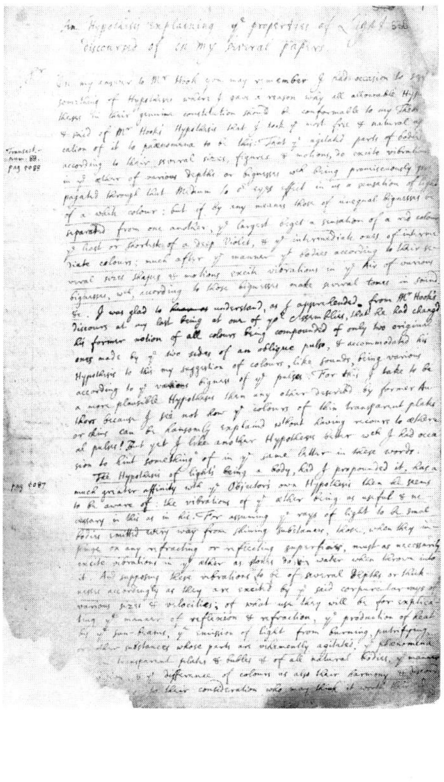

The manuscript of Newton's *An hypothesis explaining the properties of light*, 1675.

convenience of those who did not understand his work when he talked 'abstractedly' about light and colours.

After this disclaimer, Newton conjectured freely about the nature of light. Very prominent in the paper were his speculations about the existence of an all-pervading ether from which all things in the universe probably originated. These speculations have been taken as Newton's most complete expression of a global natural philosophy in the tradition of mechanistic philosophy. This is correct, but two qualifications should be made.

First, the context of Newton's mechanistic world hypothesis was quite different from Descartes'. For Newton, the hypothesis was a plausible, but uncertain conjecture about causes, developed *after* the experimental facts had been established. The main features of Descartes' mechanistic world picture shared the certainty he attributed to his metaphysics, and were considered to be the *starting-points* for experimental research. Secondly, Newton explicitly denied that he subscribed to an ether or medium hypothesis of light. He said:

> I suppose light is neither aether, nor its vibrating motion, but something of a different kind propagated from lucid bodies.

Somewhat hidden between other suggestions, he expounded the hypothesis he liked best—that light consists of:

> multitudes of unimaginable small and swift corpuscles of various sizes, springing from shining bodies at great distances one after another.

An example of Newton's use of the general ether hypothesis in combination with the emission hypothesis of light, is his explanation of *refraction*. He supposed that a ray of light moving through an ether of uneven density 'received a continual impulse or ply ... towards the rarer [part of the ether], and so is accelerated, if it move that way, or retarded, if the contrary'. He also supposed that the ether was rarer in glass than in air, so that a ray of light going from glass to air moved from a region of rare ether to a region of dense ether and was therefore decelerated. This deceleration caused the ray to move away from the perpendicular to the surface. If the incoming ray was too oblique, this resulted in (internal) reflection. Given some natural conditions about the details of the process, this ether density hypothesis leads to the laws of refraction and reflection.

In the period between the *New theory* and the *Opticks*, Newton published a somewhat more sophisticated use of his emission hypothesis of light in the *Principia*. By then, his general outlook in natural philosophical matters had changed. He now attributed a prominent place to *forces*. This was also reflected in a few optical propositions in the *Principia*, accompanied by a somewhat different disclaimer than he had given in *An hypothesis*. In the *Principia* he did not present his model of light as a guess about physical reality, but as a mathematical analogy. His hypothesis had no possible relation to reality whatsoever, as far as the corpuscularity of light was concerned. The paths travelled by little corpuscles in a force field were described by the same *mathematics* as the light rays in a field of refracting forces, but *physically*, he contended, there was no analogy at all between corpuscles and rays. Apart from the changed disclaimer, the same ideas as in *An hypothesis* were presented; the variable ether density was merely changed into a short-distance force, attracting the ray into a denser medium like glass. Some experimental evidence was given for the existence of an attracting force, but Newton explicitly stated that he was 'not at all considering the nature of the rays of light, or inquiring whether they are bodies or not'.

The *Opticks*, the *Queries*, and their reception

If Newton changed in the 30-odd years after the publication of the *New theory*, the scientific world around him changed more. What amounted to a double heresy to almost everyone in 1672 was accepted by many in 1704 as a model of experimental science. The first edition of Newton's *Opticks* was a careful reworking of material contained in the *Optical lectures*, the *New theory*, and *An hypothesis*. Neither the ether or the emission hypothesis was included, but there were additional experiments and observations—for example, on Newton's rings. But, for all its differences from the *New theory*, the methodological message

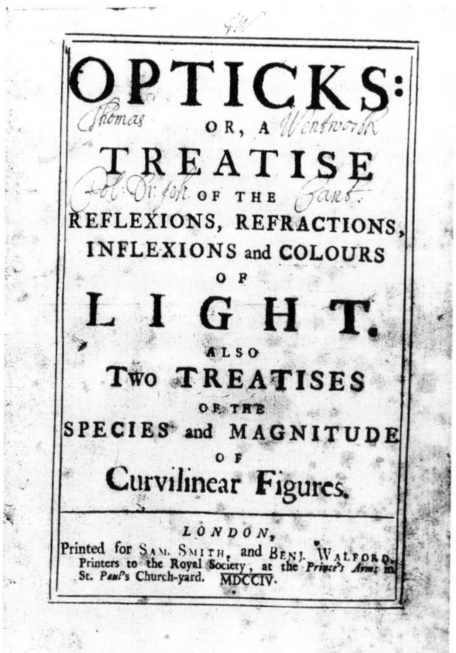

OPTICKS:
OR, A
TREATISE
OF THE
REFLEXIONS, REFRACTIONS, INFLEXIONS and COLOURS
OF
LIGHT.
ALSO
Two TREATISES
OF THE
SPECIES and MAGNITUDE
OF
Curvilinear Figures.

LONDON,
Printed for SAM. SMITH, and BENJ. WALFORD, Printers to the Royal Society, at the Prince's Arms in St. Paul's Church-yard. MDCCIV.

The title page of Newton's *Opticks* (1704).

was not significantly different from the one that emerged during the 1672 discussion. Nevertheless, the *Opticks* was received much more favourably than the *New theory*.

Of course, there were critical remarks in the early eighteenth century, but Newton's new critics more or less accepted his *style* of science. No one misunderstood Newton for advocating an emission hypothesis of light, as Hooke had done. And no one belittled the importance of his experimental discoveries because Newton had failed to give a satisfactory mechanistic explanation, as Huygens had argued.

The dominant kind of criticism was experimental, in line with Newton's scientific style. And, no doubt, being critical about Newton's experiments was reasonable enough. After all, the experiments on the unequal refrangibility of rays and the composite nature of white light had to provide the foundations for a controversial theory of colours. It was only natural to apply the recently established standards of experimental science and to ascertain whether these experiments could be replicated by others. We know of some nine occasions where repetition experiments were made in the two decades after 1704—in France, England, and Italy.

There had also been an earlier replication experiment by the French experimental scientist Edmé Mariotte, which was published in 1681, who claimed to have refuted Newton's *experimentum crucis*. A beam of violet light, produced by refraction in a prism, was refracted again in a second prism. According to Newton, the colour should not change. Mariotte, however, spotted yellow and red light in the final spectrum, in addition to the original violet light. Mariotte's claim was influential, and triggered at least two of the early eighteenth-century replication experiments.

Partly as a result of the success of most of the later trials, the mainstream of science came to accept Newton's colour theory about 20 years after the publication of the *Opticks*. Even before these experiments were made, authoritative scholars like Malebranche in France and Christian Wolff in Germany had accepted Newton's conclusions, solely on the basis of the experimental evidence provided by Newton in the *Opticks*.

The *Opticks*-induced acceptance of Newton's colour theory, the experimental character of the criticisms, and the general acceptance of the theory after a decade or two, all point to a general change in scientific style.

By the early eighteenth century, mechanistic philosophy had become somewhat less powerful, while experimental science had gained in self-confidence as well as authority since its programmatic emergence in the early seventeenth century, under the influence of philosophers like Francis Bacon. Mechanistic natural philosophers now acknowledged the truth claims of experimental scientists, independent of whether or not these claims were sustained by mechanistic explanations. The words of Malebranche, quoted in the first section of this chapter, signalled this change. By denying Newton the title of 'physicist', Malebranche had not offended him, but had correctly asserted that Newton had not mingled his experimental propositions with elements from a global world picture.

If the structure of the *Opticks* and its reception were really as simple as this, then one might certainly become suspicious. However, Newton could not resist the temptation to make matters somewhat more complicated. He did this by including, at the end of his text, 'some Queries, in order to a farther search to be made by others'. There were 16 Queries in the first edition of 1704, but in the subsequent editions their number was enlarged gradually to 31 (thereby expanding from 9 to 67 pages). An extra complicating factor is that their contents also changed.

The original 16 Queries were relatively limited in scope, but in the process of being rewritten and added to, they turned into a speculative programme for the study of the physical sciences. Even Newton's early speculations in *An hypothesis* reappeared, albeit in a significantly modified form. This presentation was in line with Newton's methodology, because the natural philosophical speculations were strictly separated from the undoubtable experimental propositions in the main text.

Newton chose to disclose his speculations little by little. From the original *Queries* in the 1704 edition of the *Opticks*, it was difficult to tell what Newton's speculative views were, even on the subject of the nature of light. However, in some new *Queries* added to the Latin edition of 1706, he stated his basic assumption quite clearly: '[a]re not the rays of light very small particles emitted from shining substances...?' He also gave his views on how prisms disperse light, simply by asserting that the production of colours in refraction could be explained by assigning different sizes to the light particles.

On the subject of refraction, Newton wrote in a way that was more elaborate—and more confusing. In the main text of the *Opticks*, he argued for the existence of an attractive force which made the light ray accelerate towards the denser medium. In that context, the concept of force was a descriptive concept. No claim was made about the nature or causes of the refractive force. In the *Queries* of 1706 however, Newton suggested that attractive forces were not merely responsible for refraction, but also (partly) for the phenomenon of *inflection*—or diffraction, as we now call it. This certainly made the impression on his readers that these forces were inherent to matter and were to be regarded as ultimate causes. Admittedly, Newton did assert that:

> [w]hat I call Attraction may be performed by impulse, or by some other means unknown to me. I use that Word here to signify only in general any

Force by which Bodies tend towards one another, whatsoever be the Cause.

However, this disclaimer was given at the very end of his additional queries, and it could therefore be ignored, overlooked, or misunderstood by friend and foe alike, in the same way as his famous disclaimer '*I feign no hypotheses*' in the General Scholium (added to the 1713 edition of the *Principia*) on the cause of gravitational force was often ignored or misread.

Whatever the interpretation of the refractive force, the hypothesis of a light ray as a stream of small particles was made without any qualification in the 1706 *Queries*, apart from the obligatory question mark. And so the refraction model in the *Principia* was transformed from a mathematical game into a serious hypothesis about reality.

In the 1717 edition of the *Opticks*, Newton made his refraction model still more complicated, by introducing an ubiquitous ether which he thought to be responsible for such diverse phenomena as refraction, diffraction, and Newton's rings. At first sight, this ether seems to be a reincarnation of the mechanistic ether of *An hypothesis*. On closer inspection, however, one realises that the two notions could not be more different. The ether of 1717 was composed of very small particles which had repulsive short-range forces. The elasticity of the ether was caused by the mutual repulsion of the ether particles. These inherent micro-forces flatly contradicted the mechanistic dogma that the natural world has to be explained only by matter and motion. Apart from this fundamental difference between Newton's mechanistic ether of 1675 and his microforce ether of 1717, the mathematics involved did not change. The law of refraction could be derived on the basis of either ether. The example of refraction makes it clear that a reader of Newton's suggestions on the nature of light had difficult choices to make. The task of selecting, elaborating, and systematizing Newton's sketchy and (in some cases) contradictory suggestions, was one of making a complete theory out of a basic hypothesis, along with some hints. This task was mainly carried out by textbook writers in the 1720s and 1730s. An influential one, on the Continent as in Britain, was the Dutch scientist Willem Jacob 's Gravesande. When treating refraction, he ignored Newton's suggestions about the cause of the refractive force and conceived it as Newton himself had done in the main text of the *Opticks*: the refractive force really existed, but still had to be explained. A second influential Dutch textbook writer, Petrus van Musschenbroek, considered the refractive force as an inherent property of matter, an interpretation of Newton's *Queries* which was free, but quite understandable. Newton's final and most complicated account of refraction—a genuine force, caused by a density distribution of an ether, whose elasticity is caused by inherent microforces between the ether particles—is rarely found in the eighteenth century. It is an irony of history that the most 'Newtonian' interpretation of Newton's suggestions is found in the works of only six of the 67 British and Irish optical writers who accepted an emission theory of light between 1700 and 1840.

Debates on the nature of light

On many occasions, and often without being asked, Newton had given methodological advice to the opponents of his colour theory during the discussion following his 1672 paper. To attack his descriptive theory, he had proclaimed, his opponents had to perform exact experiments—nothing less would do. Newton certainly did not accept arguments based on any specific hypothesis on the nature of light. But, Newton notwithstanding, how should one evaluate such hypotheses? What rules ought one to follow? What kind of evidence was acceptable, or desirable, in a discussion on the 'philosophical' nature of light? Newton did not address these methodological questions explicitly in his style of science. However, we can infer his attitude on the basis of some other arguments he actually used.

A typical example is Newton's main argument against the medium hypothesis of light, which he propounded on several occasions, and which became very popular during the eighteenth century. In the *Queries*, its basic structure was as follows. Light travels in straight lines; waves do not; they bend around corners, as has been observed for sound and water waves; therefore, light cannot consist in (ether) waves.

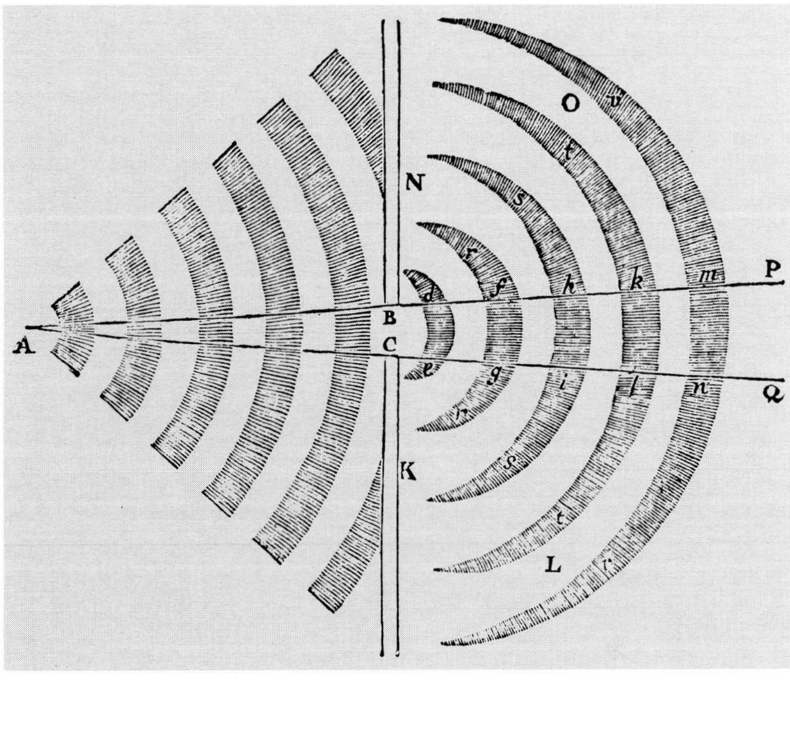

A diagram from Book II of the *Principia*, showing the fresh wavefront which is created when waves in a fluid come to a hole in an obstacle. Light seems not to behave like this, which for Newton was a strong reason why a medium hypothesis for light must be wrong.

The first thing that is striking about this argument is its lack of mathematical precision. For example, no quantitative measure of the bending was provided. The absence of mathematical detail was not only typical for Newton's arguments in the light debate, but was also found in the (counter-)arguments of his opponents.

A second feature of Newton's argument is related to the kind of empirical evidence he offered for the proposition that sound bends around corners. This evidence is given in one sentence:

> [f]or a Bell or a Cannon may be heard beyond a Hill which intercepts the sight of the sounding Body, and Sounds are propagated as readily through crooked Pipes as through straight ones.

Noticeable here is the lack of detail in describing the experimental situation. What was the size of the hill? What kind of pipe was used? What kind of sounds were made? What variations were made in the experiment? Obviously Newton reported only experiences of a general kind—just the kind of everyday experience which was typical of Aristotle's style of science. In the debate on the nature of light, Newton used no controlled experiments, such as he had performed to support his colour theory.

To avoid misunderstanding, I must add that Newton's conduct in the debate on the nature of light was not unusual in the context of eighteenth-century science. The example of the main opponent of the emission theory of light during the period bears this out. In 1746, the Swiss-born mathematician and physicist Leonhard Euler published a mathematically intricate and fairly complete wave theory of light, which was soon accepted as a major expression of the wave theory. From a twentieth-century vantage point, we might expect him to support his wave theory, and to attack the emission theory by arguments based on exact and refined experiments. In fact, nothing of the kind happened. Although Euler's arguments soon became the *locus classicus* for opponents of the emission theory, they were of a general nature. They did not rely on any detailed experiments and were, in addition, almost unconnected with the mathematical details of either his own theory or the theories he attacked.

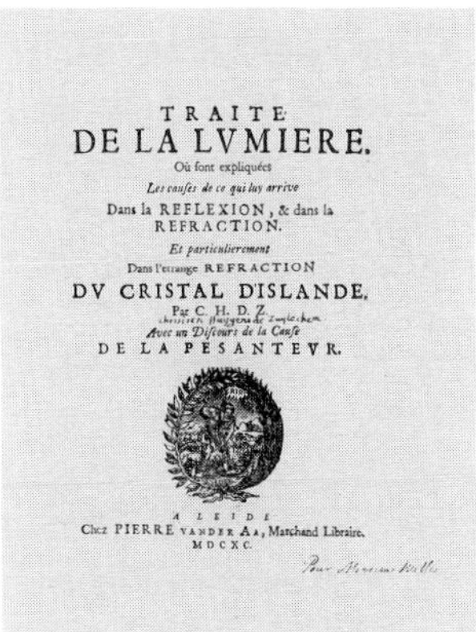
TRAITE
DE LA LVMIERE.
Où sont expliquées
Les causes de ce qui luy arrive
Dans la REFLEXION, & dans la REFRACTION.
Et particulierement
Dans l'etrange REFRACTION
DV CRISTAL D'ISLANDE.
Par C. H. D. Z.
Avec un Discours de la Cause
DE LA PESANTEVR.

A LEIDE
Chez PIERRE VANDER AA, Marchand Libraire.
MDCXC.

Huygens' *Treatise of Light* (1690).

A great many similar examples could easily be given, and this leads to the general observation that *in early modern science there was no strong research tradition in which there were integrated refined experiments, mathematical exactness, and natural philosophical hypotheses.* Two of these three elements could be found in combination—in Newton's work on colours, for instance—but a fruitful synthesis of all three was reached only on very rare occasions.

In optics, one such instance is to be found in the work of Huygens. In his *Treatise on Light* (1690), he offered a theory of the mathematical laws of double refraction in a crystal of Iceland spar, which he had established through a number of experiments. His theoretical account was based on his medium hypothesis of light. Huygens himself called this result a '*crucial experiment*' on the nature of light.

With hindsight, we can add that his method, as well as his theory, turned out to be crucial for the development of modern science.

From separation to integration

From the very beginning of his public career, Newton separated the experimental–mathematical description of rays and colours from the explanation of the 'philosophical' nature of light. Based on this relatively new style of science, he published a revolutionary descriptive theory of colours in 1672. Half a century or so later, he eventually succeeded in getting his colour theory accepted. Even in his own eyes, Newton failed to develop a complete mathematical account of colours. Moreover, his style of science was only partially accepted.

Newton's separation of certainty and uncertainty in his method was violated by many professedly Newtonian textbook writers. They systematized and reified Newton's hypothetical suggestions regarding the corpuscular nature of light, and combined them with mathematical and experimental laws. In addition, a good deal of fresh optical research was undertaken in the eighteenth century, but in many cases this research was purely experimental, or purely mathematical, or purely 'philosophical'. In some instances a combination of two of these approaches was adopted, but integrated research which combined all three ingredients was very seldom to be found.

There is nothing surprising in this. After all, Newton had failed to supply examples of such integrated research, and examples from other sources were few and far between. Huygens' treatment of double refraction might have been one such, but it had little impact since his version of the medium theory of light was soon rejected both by emission theorists and by medium theorists. Interestingly enough, it was Newton himself who supplied the main line of argument against Huygens' theory, when he claimed that it was unable to explain the rectilinear propagation of light.

Towards the start of the nineteenth century, a new style of scientific research was established, particularly in France. This style advocated a deliberate and explicit integration of natural philosophical theories with mathematics and experiments. One of the first fields to be reworked in this style was optics, particularly by such scientists as Pierre-Simon Laplace and Jean Baptiste Biot. Underpinning this new work was the old emission theory. But from about 1815, this theory was challenged by a new generation of wave theorists, among whom Augustin-Jean Fresnel and Dominique Arago figured prominently. Although the wave theorists employed a different model, they used essentially the same integrated style of research. Fresnel's account of the rectilinear propagation and diffraction of light synthesized the wave model with mathematically exact descriptions and carefully constructed experiments. Fresnel was able to destroy Newton's main argument against the wave theory, not by invoking some general everyday experiences, but by using refined experiments, mathematical deductions, and key notions of his theory.

During the exciting opening decades of the nineteenth century in France, Newton's colour theory remained unchallenged. But his style of science, which was strongly linked to that theory, was rejected. French scientists took the decision to integrate what Newton had tried to separate. I wonder how Newton would have reacted to the establishment of this new style of science. It is speculation of course, but I suspect he would have thought it a scandal. Fancy the French throwing together what he had laboured so hard to keep apart!

Further reading

Newton's mature views on optics are readily available in the 1952 edition of his *Opticks*, Dover, New York. His *New theory* of 1672 and the ensuing discussion papers are conveniently collected together in *Isaac Newton's papers and letters on natural philosophy and related documents* (edited by I. B. Cohen), Harvard University Press, Cambridge, Mass., 1978.

The best monograph on seventeenth-century optics is A. I. Sabra, *Theories of light from Descartes to Newton*, Cambridge University Press, Cambridge, 1981. A recent analysis of Newton's optical work prior to 1672 is the Introduction to *The optical papers of Isaac Newton*, Vol. I (edited by A. E. Shapiro), Cambridge University Press, Cambridge, 1984. H. Guerlac, *Newton on the Continent*, Cornell University Press, Ithaca, New York, 1981, describes the reception of Newton's colour theory in France. The development of theories of light after Newton's *Opticks*, especially in Britain and Ireland, is analysed in G. N. Cantor, *Optics after Newton: theories of light in Britain and Ireland 1704–1840*, Manchester University Press, Manchester, 1983.

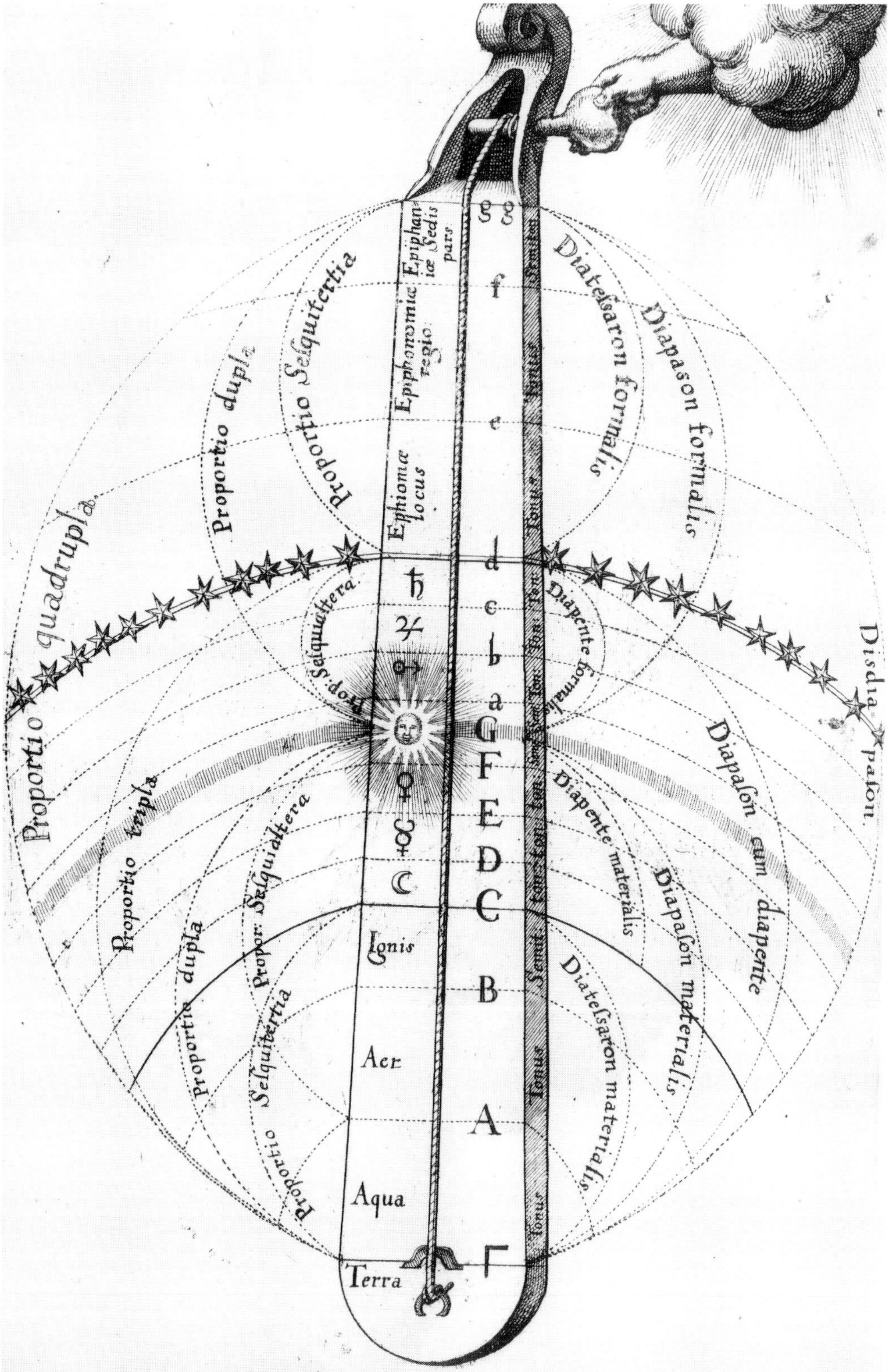
Proportio quadrupla
Proportio dupla
Proportio Sesquitertia
Epiphaniæ Sedis pars
Epiphonomiæ regio
Ephiomæ locus
Diatessaron formalis
Diapason formalis
Disdiapason
Diapente formalis
Prop. Sesquialtera
Proportio tripla
Proportio dupla
Propor. Sesquialtera
Proportio Sesquitertia
Proportio dupla
Proportio Sesquitertia
Diapente materialis
Diapason materialis
Diapason cum diapente
Diatessaron materialis
Ignis
Aer
Aqua
Terra
Γ
A
B
C
D
E
F
G
a
b
c
d
e
f
g
gg
Tonus
Semit.
Semiton.

CHAPTER
FIVE

The harmonic roots of Newtonian science

PENELOPE GOUK

Despite the immense outpourings by the so-called 'Newton industry' on all aspects of his life and works, Newton's interest in harmonics and musical science has gone unrecognized and almost entirely ignored. There is no reference to either, for example, in the index of Westfall's comprehensive biography, and aspects of Newton's musical studies are found only in specialist works.

Reasons for this neglect are not hard to find. The first is the problem of modern academic specialization, which leads to a rigid compartmentalization of knowledge. Music is an arts subject, and as such does not constitute part of the sciences or the history of science.

Another reason is the fact that Newton seems to have had little or no interest in the performance of music himself. For example, he 'never was at more than one Opera. The first Act, he heard with pleasure, the 2nd strech'd his patience, at the 3rd he ran away'. On another occasion 'Newton, hearing Handel play upon the harpsichord, could find nothing worthy to remark but the elasticity of his fingers'. It is hardly surprising that Newton and music are not normally associated with each other. However, it is our modern understanding of music which prevents us from recognizing its ancient and fundamental links with philosophy and mathematics, a connection familiar to Newton and his contemporaries.

There is a long tradition of seeing the universe as constructed on harmonic principles. This *Cosmic monochord* from Robert Fludd's *History of the macrocosm and microcosm* (1617) shows the region between Earth and Heaven as divided into intervals along two octaves of a musical string. The hand of God tunes the string which stretches down through the region of angels, then through the solar system with the Sun at its centre, and finally through the four elements to Earth. The whole is bound together by mathematical proportions and musical intervals.

The older idea of music can be more easily understood if we replace the word 'music' by 'harmony'. *Harmony* can be used simply to refer to the combination of musical chords which sound pleasing together. More generally, *it can signify agreement, balance, and proportion in things or ideas*. In the seventeenth century, the connection between these different senses of harmony was much more real than it is today.

In this chapter we shall see that harmonic science—notably, aspects of Pythagorean doctrine—played a significant role in Newton's natural philosophy. We look at three distinct but related topics: his earliest notes on the division of the musical scale, his work on light and the colour spectrum, and some important features of the law of universal gravitation. First, however, it is necessary to define the term *harmonic science* and outline those aspects of Pythagorean doctrine which are relevant to Newton's physics and metaphysics.

Harmonic science: background and definitions

In order to appreciate the scope and breadth of harmonic science, or *harmonics*, we have to go back to its Greek origins and later development in the Middle Ages. Since harmonics included the study of ratios corresponding to musical intervals, it was defined as a mathematical science. In the sixth century AD the term *quadrivium* was coined by Boethius to designate the four mathematical sciences dealing with numbers and magnitude: astronomy, geometry, arithmetic, and music. Together with grammar, rhetoric, and dialectic, the *trivium*, these subjcts consituted the *seven liberal arts and sciences* of the encylopaedia, the foundation of Western learning and education for over 1000 years. It was as a part of the quadrivium that Newton first encountered musical doctrine.

Like all Greek sciences, harmonics was both practical and speculative in orientation. *Practical harmonics* included the study of melody and singing as well as the physical and mathematical foundations of music. While such doctrine might be learned by the musician simply as a basis for performance, its other function was to provide an introduction to speculative music, the philosophical study of the proportion and structure of the cosmos. *Speculative music* was concerned with the harmony of all parts of creation, the structure of the physical, moral and spiritual worlds.

During the Middle Ages the chief authority on ancient harmonic theory was Boethius, who codified three divisions of speculative music in ascending order of perfection. The least perfect was *musica instru-*

In the traditional arrangement of knowledge and teaching in universities, music was one of the *seven liberal arts*, along with the other *quadrivium* subjects of arithmetic, geometry and astronomy. This woodcut dates from 1504.

mentalis, the audible music of voices and instruments. Next in order was *musica humana* (human music), the harmony in the body and soul of man, and the balance of the humours. The most perfect type of harmony was that of *musica mundana* (world music), including the motion of the heavenly bodies, the mixture of the elements, and the cycle of the seasons. Harmonic doctrine thus merged not only with the other mathematical sciences, but was absorbed into many other branches of knowledge, including medicine and theology.

Pythagorean doctrine

A substantial part of Greek harmonic science was based on the teachings of Pythagoras, who flourished in the sixth century BC. Pythagoras left no writings himself, but his ideas were preserved by later followers and critics. The most important sources for Pythagorean doctrine were the writings of Plato, particularly the *Timaeus*, and later commentaries on this by Neoplatonic authors such as Proclus.

At first this material was known only indirectly in the West through the Latin writings of Boethius and other medieval authorities. Fresh stimulus was given to the subject in the Renaissance by the discovery, translation, and eventual publication of original Platonic and Neoplatonic texts. Newton, in particular, was able to read these works for himself, which made their teachings seem exciting and relevant to him.

There are several key features of Pythagorean doctrine which can throw light on various facets of Newton's harmonic science. Pythagoreanism was a secret cult; its underlying orientation was religious, mystical, and philosophical. Philosophy was a means of spiritual purification, and the scientific study of mathematics offered a path towards beatific vision and knowledge of the deity. Such truths, known only to initiates, were to be hidden from public view by means of symbolism and allegorical language.

Great importance was attached to the names and numbers of things. According to the Pythagoreans, *numbers were the ultimate essence of reality*. They were a means of rendering perceptible what might otherwise remain beyond the grasp of human knowledge and sense experience. As powerful entities, numbers were endowed with mystic qualities. The most important numbers were the integers 1, 2, 3, and 4, whose sum is 10, the *tetraktys*.

Harmony, expressed in mathematical ratios and means, was the

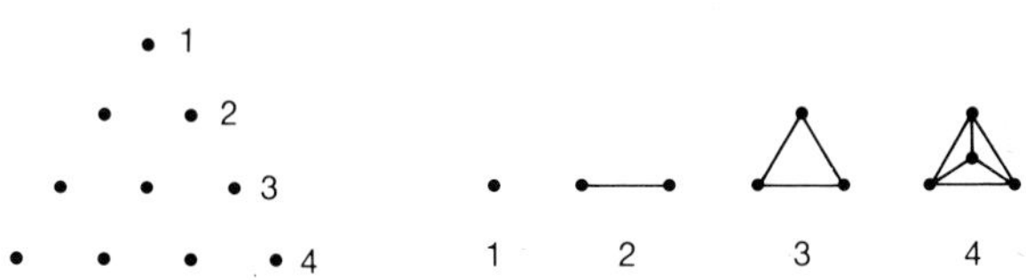

(*left*) The *tetraktys* 10, represented as 1 + 2 + 3 + 4; (*right*) Numbers were also used to build solids:

1 = point, 2 = line, 3 = plane, 4 = solid.

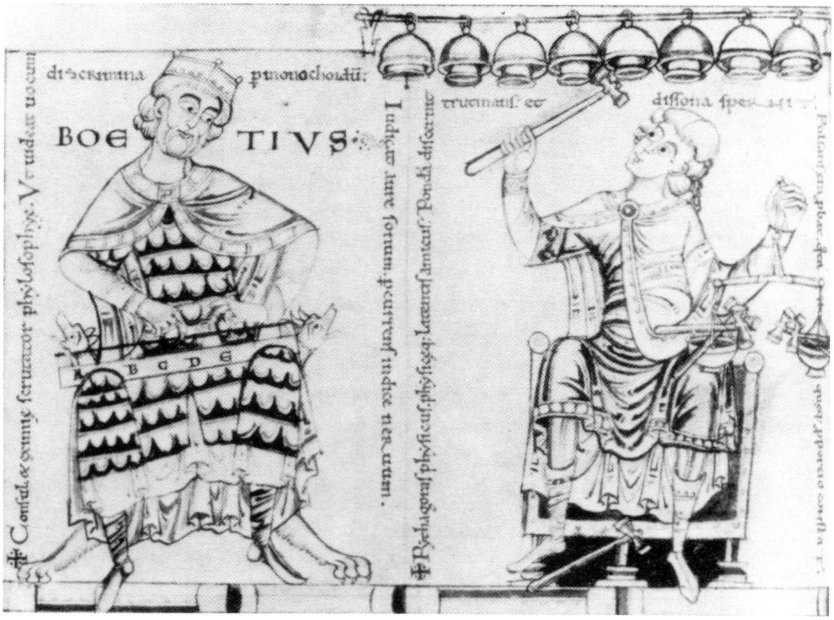

The legend of Pythagoras' discovery of a relation between musical notes and hammer weights, as portrayed in a twelfth-century manuscript. (Note the hammers whose weights are being ascertained on the balance in his left hand.) Boethius, meanwhile, is strumming a monochord.

controlling force of the cosmos. Arithmetic and music dealt with numbers as *multitude*, while geometry and astronomy dealt with numbers as *magnitude*. These interlocking disciplines provided a means of comprehending the true nature of the physical and metaphysical universe. Why was this so?

The archetypal story of Pythagoras is his discovery of the correspondence between musical consonances and simple numerical ratios. These were 2 to 1, corresponding to the *octave*; 3 to 2, corresponding to the *perfect fifth*; and 4 to 3 corresponding to the *perfect fourth*. The *double octave* (4 to 1), and the *twelfth* (3 to 1), were also considered perfect; note that the numerical ratio (3 to 1) corresponding to the twelfth (an octave plus a perfect fifth) is obtained by *multiplying* the ratios corresponding to an octave (2 to 1) and a fifth (3 to 2).

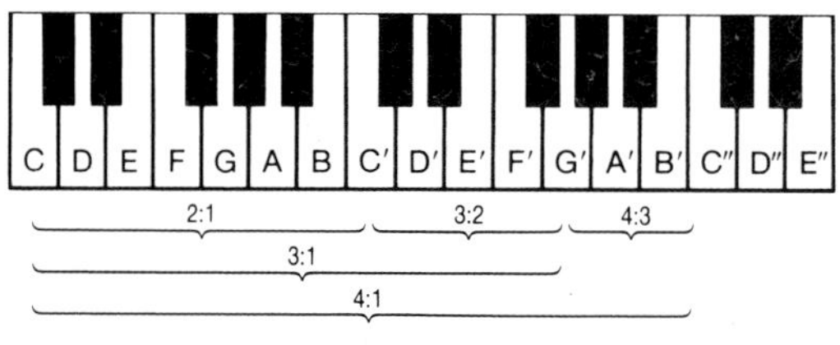

According to tradition, Pythagoras came to this discovery in the following manner. One day he was walking past a blacksmith's forge, where he heard the hammers giving off harmonious sounds as they beat out iron on the anvil. Curious to discover the reasons for the consonant sounds, he compared the weights of the five hammers. As Boethius described in his *De musica* (On music):

those two which gave the consonance of an octave were found to weigh in the ratio 2 to 1. He took that one which was double the other and found that its weight was four-thirds the weight of a hammer with which it gave the consonance of a fourth. Again he found that this same hammer was three-halves the weight of a hammer with which it gave the consonance of a fifth. Now the two hammers to which the aforesaid hammers had been shown to bear the ratio of 4 to 3 and 3 to 2, respectively, were found to bear each other the ratio of 9 to 8. The fifth hammer was rejected, for it made no consonance with the others.

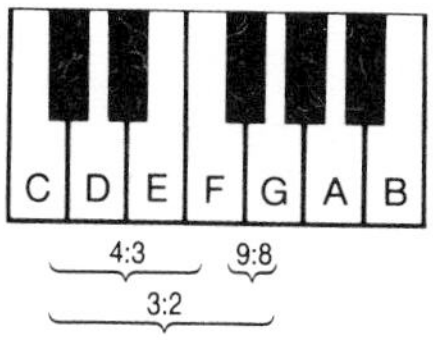

In other words, the various weights were in the ratios of 2 to 1, 3 to 2, 4 to 3, and 9 to 8. This last ratio corresponds to the *tone*, the difference between the perfect fifth and the perfect fourth; note that this ratio is obtained by *dividing* the ratios corresponding to a fifth (3 to 2) and a fourth (4 to 3).

Pythagoras apparently went on to discover that the same ratios could be found between different weights required to stretch strings of an equal length to produce the intervals of an octave, fifth, or fourth; between the different lengths of strings stretched by an equal weight; between the lengths of different pipes, the diameter of their bores, and so on. In the process of these experiments he developed the *monochord*, an instrument which could demonstrate the proportions. In fact, *most of these observations could not have been made*. The only part which *is* true is that the ratios correspond to the length of strings. This error was to be important in Newton's interpretation of the story.

What was important to the Pythagoreans was the arithmetical

Ancient harmonic discoveries are portrayed in this woodcut from Gafurio's *Theorica musice* (1492). Mathematical ratios are emphasized in the experiments attributed to Pythagoras.

relationship between the pitches, which can be expressed as 12:9:8:6. The double octave can similarly be expressed as 16:12:9:8:6:4, as shown in the illustration of Gafurio. This particular combination of proportions contains the *arithmetic, harmonic,* and *geometric means* bounded by the double octave—namely, for any two numbers a and b, we have

the arithmetic mean $\frac{1}{2}(a+b)$:	for example, $\frac{1}{2}(12+6)=9$;
the harmonic mean $2ab/(a+b)$:	for example, $2\cdot 12\cdot 6/(12+6)=8$;
the geometric mean $\sqrt{(ab)}$:	for example, $\sqrt{(12\cdot 6)}=\sqrt{(9\cdot 8)}$.

These numerical relationships were thought to provide a key to the structure of the entire universe. Indeed, the same ratios were thought to be found in the distances between the planets, and it was taught by the later Pythagoreans that the planets, or the spheres which carried them around a central fire, also produced sounds—the famous *harmony of the spheres*. It was claimed that among mortals only Pythagoras could hear this music. In this system, the consonances used in musical practice were naturally determined by the same numbers and ratios as those found in the heavens. Yet cosmic harmony was infinitely superior to sounding music, which was part of the changing and imperfect world of sense perception.

Newton's approach towards harmonics appears more intelligible when seen in the context of Pythagorean principles. He believed in a simple, harmonious structure of nature and spent his life attempting to discover a deeper spiritual reality which lay beyond the range of human sense experience. The study of numbers and the names of things would reveal this hidden truth.

As we can see from the other chapters, his work on mathematical physics formed only part of Newton's lifelong search, a religious and philosophical quest which embraced alchemy, chronology, and biblical exegesis, using various methods of experimentation, numerology, and hermeneutics. By the time Newton reached maturity, he was irrevocably committed to the belief that his own world-system represented the restoration of the original natural philosophy revealed by God to the ancients, including Pythagoras, in the tradition of the *prisca sapientia*, or ancient wisdom; this is discussed in detail in Piyo Rattansi's chapter. Yet, *even at the beginning of his scholarly career, harmonics appeared in Newton's studies*.

Newton's early notebooks

Newton's initial interest in harmonic science seems to have begun, conventionally enough, in practical harmonics. Most of his early notes on the subject are found in a student notebook which he used between 1664 and 1666, while he was an undergraduate at Trinity College,

Cambridge. At this time, the mathematical sciences of the quadrivium were an established part of the curricula of both English universities. It was therefore natural for undergraduates to devote some time to the study of musical ratios, not necessarily related to performance.

The central topic in Newton's musico-mathematical calculations was the *division of the octave* and the proportions of the musical scale. His work seems to have been based extensively on the mathematician William Brouncker's translation of, and commentary on, Descartes' *Compendium musicae* (1653). This book provided an introduction to some of the basic conceptual problems in practical harmonics which were directly related to wider developments in the mathematical and physical sciences. Commenting on Descartes' account of the scale and its proportions, Brouncker was the first English theorist to employ logarithms for dividing the octave. Before turning to Newton's own ideas and response to those of Descartes and Brouncker, let us see what the problem was.

The division of the scale: challenges to Pythagoras

Until the Renaissance, the *Pythagorean scale* was accepted as the correct ideal for practical tuning by most music theorists, who relied on Boethius as their authority. The consonances were limited to ratios using the numbers 1 to 4—namely, the octave (2 to 1), the perfect fifth (3 to 2), the perfect fourth (4 to 3), the twelfth (3 to 1), and the double octave (4 to 1); all other intervals were defined as dissonant. The ratio corresponding to the major tone is determined by dividing the ratios corresponding to a fifth and a fourth, giving 9 to 8, as seen earlier. The major third consisted of two tones added together, and had a ratio of 81 to 64, a *dissonance*. In Pythagorean tuning, the *diatonic scale* (corresponding to the 'white notes' of the piano) comprised five tones and two 'diatonic semitones'; the ratio corresponding to each semitone is determined by dividing the ratios corresponding to a fourth (4 to 3) and a third (81 to 64), giving 256 to 243.

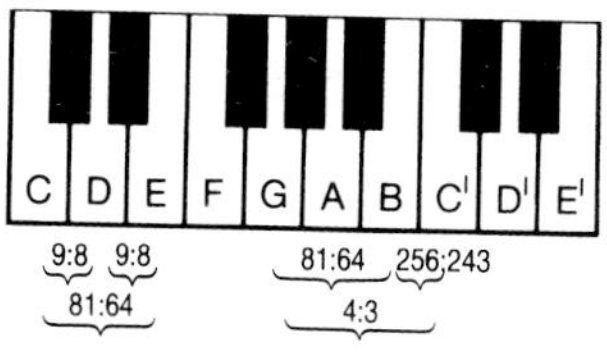

Unfortunately, *the Pythagorean scale has a fundamental flaw, which arises as a direct consequence of the mutual incompatibility of the pure consonances*. To see this, try to match up a series of seven octaves (C to C) with a series of 12 perfect fifths:

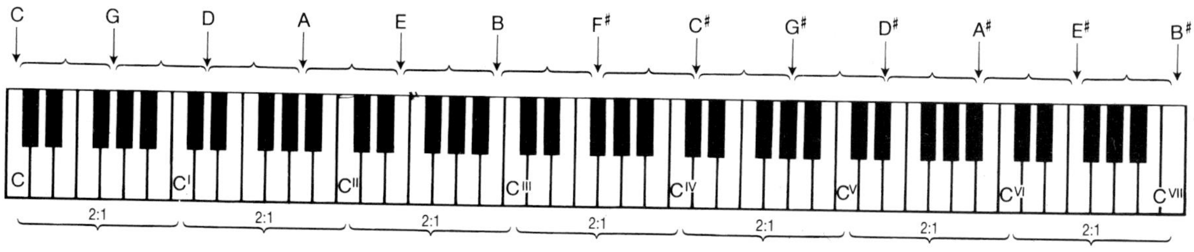

Note that, although they correspond to the same note on the piano, the last note of the second series (B sharp) is *not the same* as the last C of the first series, but is fractionally higher in pitch; the tiny interval between them is known as the *Pythagorean comma*. The corresponding ratios $(\frac{3}{2})^{12}$ and 2^7 agree to within 1 per cent, *but are not equal.*

In spite of this flaw, the Pythagorean scale proved suitable in practice, as long as music was homophonic and predominantly vocal as in ecclesiastical chant; such music featured on one line sung at a time, or voices moving in exact parallel an octave, perfect fifth, or perfect fourth apart. Styles of music gradually changed, however, and instruments were used more frequently from the fifteenth century. With the development of vocal and instrumental *polyphony* (multi-part music which also uses thirds and sixths in its harmony), Pythagorean theory did not seem so appropriate. It seemed to many musicians that when they sang major thirds (such as C and E, or F and A), the interval sounded sweet and consonant, and yet the theorists said this was impossible. An alternative system that reconciled theory and practice was now urgently required.

The problem appeared to be resolved by the mid-sixteenth century. In 1558, the Italian music theorist Gioseffo Zarlino offered an alternative system of *just intonation* as the correct theoretical scale. He claimed that the scale was first invented by Ptolemy in the second century AD, and therefore had ancient authority. This system was still based on the ratios of simple integers, but these now included the numbers 5 and 6. He called the numbers 1 to 6 the *senario*; 6 was the 'harmonic' or 'perfect number' which could generate all musical consonances. The addition of 5 and 6 meant that *thirds and sixths could*

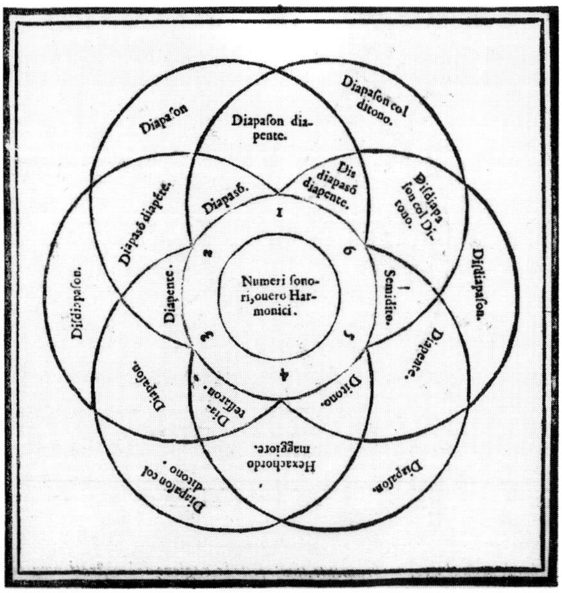

Gioseffo Zarlino's *senario* from *Istitutione harmoniche* (1558). The numbers 1 to 6 are joined by curved lines indicating the corresponding intervals: diapason = octave (2 to 1, or 6 to 3, &c), diapente = perfect fifth (3 to 2), ditono = major third (5 to 4), and so on.

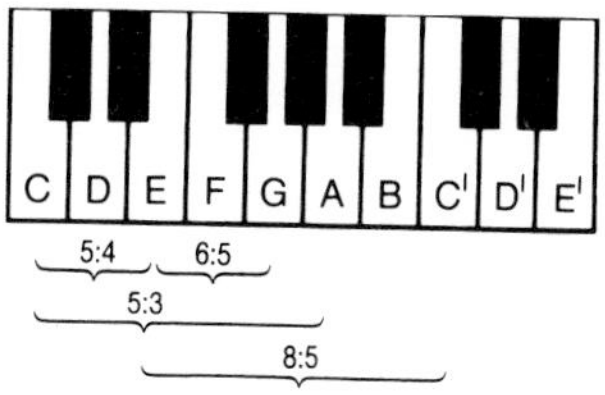

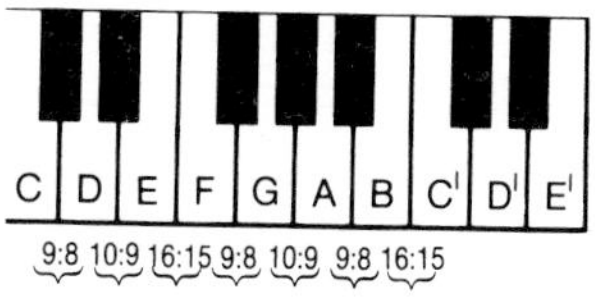

now be defined as consonances rather than dissonances, since they were now also expressed with simple ratios. The consonances corresponded to the following ratios: octave (2 to 1); perfect fifth (3 to 2); perfect fourth (4 to 3); major third, such as C to E (5 to 4); minor third, such as E to G (6 to 5); and major sixth, such as C to A (5 to 3). Also included was the minor sixth, such as E to C′, with ratio 8 to 5—the '8' was thought of as 2×4, and was therefore permissible.

The *just intonation scale* was made up from two sizes of tone and a semitone. Note that the ratio corresponding to the tones from D to E, and G to A, is 10 to 9, and not 9 to 8; it is determined by dividing the ratio corresponding to a major third (5 to 4) by the ratio corresponding to the tone from C to D, or F to G (9 to 8).

Zarlino's system worked well; if each consonance is taken *individually* and tested on a monochord, the string lengths correspond to the ratio given above. The just scale was widely adopted as the new theoretical basis of musical science in the seventeenth century.

Yet there is also a fundamental flaw in the just intonation scale: it cannot be used in actual practice when two or more parts are sung or played *at the same time*. That this is so is particularly evident in the case of instruments with fixed pitches—namely, keyboards, or fretted instruments such as the lute and viol. The difficulty arises from the fact that there are two different sizes of tone (9 to 8, and 10 to 9), the difference between them represented by a ratio of 81 to 80, the so-called *syntonic comma*. This means, for example, that the fifth D to A falls short of the fifth C to G by this ratio, and the minor third D to F falls short of the minor third E to G by the same ratio. The scale is inherently unstable.

In short, when the keys or frets of an instrument are tuned chromatically—that is, with 12 pitches to the octave, like the black and white keys on the piano—then *some form of compromise, or temperament, has to be made*. Temperament is based on the empirical observation that the ear is willing to tolerate *small* deviations from absolute purity, in all the consonances except the octave. By the sixteenth century, there were two main types of temperament which had been established by practitioners. *Equal temperament* was used in fretted instruments, while keyboards used a system called *mean-tone temperament*. Since Newton did not mention mean-tone temperament, we do not consider it here.

While temperament was accepted as a necessary part of musical practice, philosophers and mathematicians at first found it hard to provide an adequate theoretical basis for such a process, which went against established authority. In the Pythagorean–Boethian tradition, musical intervals were treated as multitudes, or discontinuous quantities, expressed in terms of whole number ratios. Using this arithmetical approach, it was impossible to accept that the octave or any other musical interval could be divided into *equal* parts. For example, the tone (with ratio 9 to 8) could not be split into two equal semitones, since each semitone would then correspond to a ratio of $\sqrt{9}$ to $\sqrt{8}$, or 3 to $2\sqrt{2}$, which is not a whole number ratio.

The old view was initially challenged in the late fifteenth century, when mathematicians began to rediscover Greek geometry and approached the problem of magnitudes, or continuous quantities. (The first Latin translation of Euclid's *Elements* was published in 1482.) Mechanical methods of dividing strings geometrically were now understood.

The invention of decimal fractions in the 1590s, and the development of logarithms around 1614, also enabled geometric divisions to be calculated arithmetically. It was only in the seventeenth century, then, that the theoretical tools required to divide the musical continuum into any number of parts (*multiple division*) became easily available. The search for elegant solutions to the problem of the division of the octave was one which appealed to mathematicians such as Newton, even if they were not concerned at all with practical reality.

Two major types of approach to dividing the octave are thus found in theoretical writings on music in the seventeenth century. These are *arithmetic methods* for calculating musical intervals using only whole number ratios, and *geometric methods* for calculating equal divisions of a scale with 12 or more pitches to the octave. How did Newton deal with the problem?

Newton's approaches to the problem

Newton's early musical calculations reveal his familiarity with both methods of dividing the musical scale. This familiarity did not require any direct knowledge of singing or playing. He clearly accepted the consonances of just intonation as the correct *ideal* basis for tuning, following the authority of Descartes and other natural philosophers of the time.

Even if these ratios are adopted, however, the fact remains that there is no single 'correct' distribution of the major and minor tones and semitones in each part of the just scale. For example, the perfect fifth with ratio 3 to 2 (such as C to G) is made up of a major third with ratio 4 to 3 (C to E) and a minor third with ratio 5 to 4 (E to G). But is the major third *followed* by the minor third, or is it the other way around? Again, the major third consists of a major tone (with ratio 9 to 8), *either preceded or followed* by a minor tone (with ratio 10 to 9). Each major tone consists of a major semitone and a minor semitone ... and so on.

Newton spent some considerable time working out all the possible combinations of these ratios in both the diatonic scale of seven notes and the chromatic scale of 12 notes. He also tried to establish which of these arrangements was objectively the best.

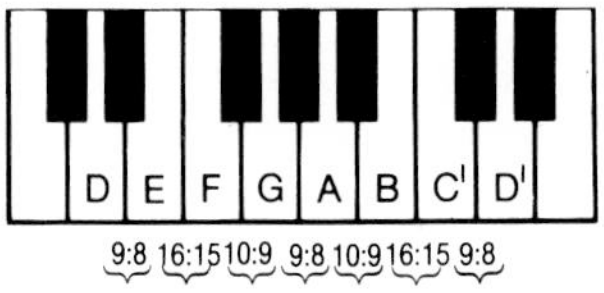

As can be seen here, his final selection of the correct ratios for just intonation was deductive. It was guided more by the desire to establish a pleasing symmetry than by any aural criteria. The various ratios are in the form of a *palindrome*: starting at D′, and moving down towards the D below, yields the same order of ratios as the other direction. We will see that the idea of a *symmetrical* division of the scale was one which Newton later applied to his work on optics and the colour spectrum.

Of particular interest in Newton's early calculations is his invention of a *standard unit* for measuring the sizes of various musical intervals determined by different methods. He adopted a system which used as a basic logarithmic unit the 'equal half-note', or *equal-tempered semitone*. This equal semitone was assigned a value of 1, which represented a ratio of $\sqrt[12]{2}$ to 1. This artificial division, or *common measure*, anticipated the modern system of *cents* in which the octave is divided into 1200 units, each equal semitone containing 100 cents. Newton used this method to compare the relative sizes of intervals in just intonation, equal temperament, and different types of multiple division.

Multiple division offered a simple theoretical solution to the problem of dividing the octave. It was possible to divide the octave into any fixed number of tiny acoustically equal parts, today called *microtones*. These small steps could build up the correct intervals for any key.

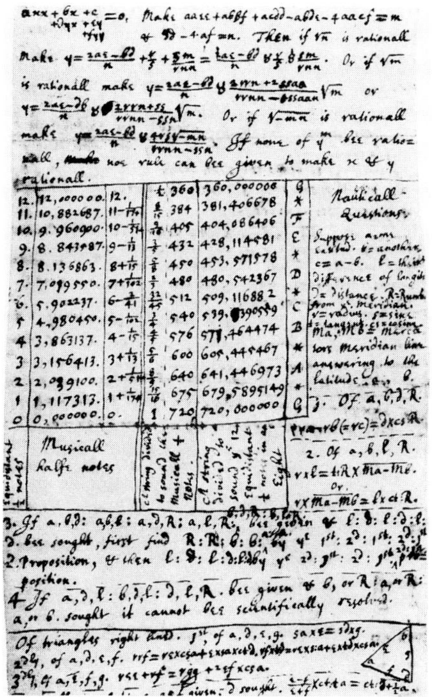

A characteristic page from an early Newton manuscript of about 1665, showing calculations on the 12-note scale (with *equidistant* $\frac{1}{2}$ *notes*), sandwiched between remarks on number theory and some trigonometrical questions with bearing on navigation.

Using his 'common measure', Newton compared the ideal semitones of the just scale with those produced by dividing the octave into 12, 20, 24, 25, 29, 36, 41, 51, 53, 100, 120, and 612 equal parts. He concluded that, of all these varieties, the 53-note division of the octave was the best. This was because, in this division, five microtones correspond almost exactly to a just semitone, eight microtones make up a minor tone, and nine microtones make up a major tone. All the different intervals of the just scale can be made up in a similar manner.

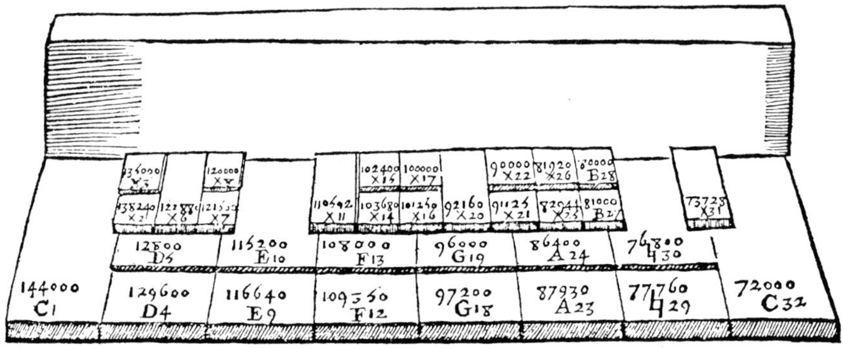

Multiple division of the octave was not just a theoretical device. This diagram from Marin Mersenne's *Harmonie universelle* (1636–7) shows an organ keyboard with 31 notes to the octave.

The analogy betwen microtones and the minute atomic particles which were thought to constitute matter in the mechanical philosophy is notable.

So these are the features of Newton's early musical calculations that we should notice especially. His approach to music was entirely deductive, based on *a priori* principles. It was also abstract and detached from actual music. Far more important to him than any aural interests were a fascination with ratios, permutations and combinations of the elements of the scale, its division into atomic particles, a preference for symmetrical arrangements, and the desire to manipulate musical space by means of number. Yet the problem of the division of the octave had already alerted him to the discrepancy between the ideal proportions of music and the intervals used in practice.

Colour, light, and harmony

It would be a mistake to assume that this early study of practical harmonics was merely an interesting, but ultimately irrelevant, part of Newton's work. On the contrary, the topic encapsulates some of the most important philosophical issues with which he and his contemporaries had to deal. Can there be a real correspondence between numbers and physical entities? If so, how is it possible to determine this relationship? Newton's work on light and colour, and his attempts to deduce mathematical laws for their physical properties, were obviously linked to contemporary developments in harmonic theory.

From the very beginning of his interest in optics around 1665–6, Newton simply assumed that colours, like sounds, were perceptions produced by motion communicated via the sense organs to the brain. This was not surprising since, as John Henry points out in the following chapter, this was a standard feature of all the various mechanical philosophies (such as those of Descartes and Hobbes) that were current at the time.

Newton himself always made a clear distinction between the propagations of sound and light. Sound, he thought, consists of an undulatory motion transmitted through an elastic medium. Light, on the other hand, consists of minute particles emanating from luminous bodies. How such corpuscles move, what properties they have, and why they produce sensations of colour when they strike the retina, were important and related problems. Newton was primarily interested in trying to find mathematical laws which accurately describe this motion, and which agree with observation and experience. Over many years he sought in vain for a single mathematical theory which would satisfactorily account for diverse phenomena such as refraction and diffraction.

Newton's first theory of light (1672)

In his earliest experimental work, which he began around 1666, Newton discovered that white light could be made to separate into a series of different colours, by means of a special prism. There seemed to be a direct connection between the way that light rays were refracted at different angles through the prism, and the different colours that were produced in the spectrum.

On the strength of this connection between colour and refrangibility, Newton tried to develop a mathematical theory in which colours of bodies were reduced to laws of elastic collision. This theory (which we will call *theory A*) assumed that light particles are of identical size, but travel at different velocities, so that when they pass through the prism they change direction at different angles. The mechanism by which these light particles and their motion give rise to the sensation of

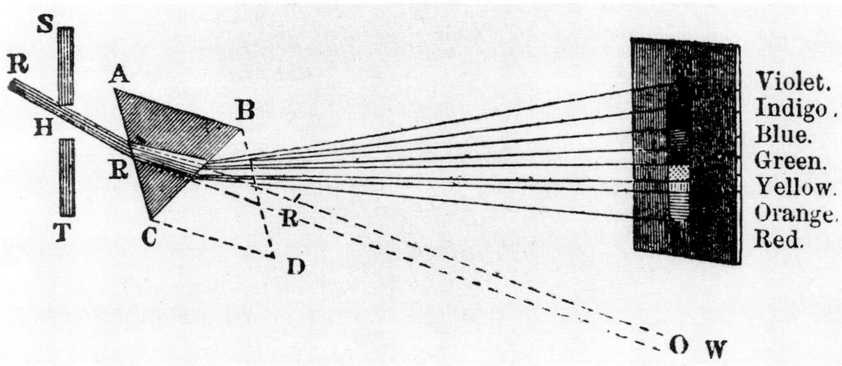

In Newton's prism experiment, a beam of white light (*RR*) was split up into a spectrum on passing through a prism. It is fascinating to trace how Newton reached the conclusion that there are *seven* colours in the spectrum.

different colours does not seem to have worried him at that stage. Newton sent a description of his discovery of the composite nature of white light to the Secretary of the Royal Society in early 1672, together with a brief account of his mathematical theory.

Robert Hooke, the Curator of Experiments to the Society, was the first natural philosopher to criticize Newton's theory. This was because he had a different explanation of the motion of light. Hooke thought that light is not corpuscular, but is a motion propagated through a very fine medium, or *ether*, and that colours are produced by a disturbance of vibrations in the ether and not by the action of different light particles. Hooke believed that his theory corresponded more closely to observation, because it could account both for diffraction and for the apparent periodicity of light, which Newton had not mentioned. Hooke also suggested in his letter that there was an analogy between musical harmonies and pleasing mixtures of colours.

Hooke's ideas were not suddenly invented to contradict Newton's theories. In his *Micrographia* (1665), he had already observed that thin plates or films of transparent materials such as mica appear to be coloured, and that the colours vary periodically with the thickness of the plates. Similarly, the analogy between musical tones and colours which he suggested in his 1672 letter was based on a comprehensive theory of matter which he first outlined in the *Micrographia*.

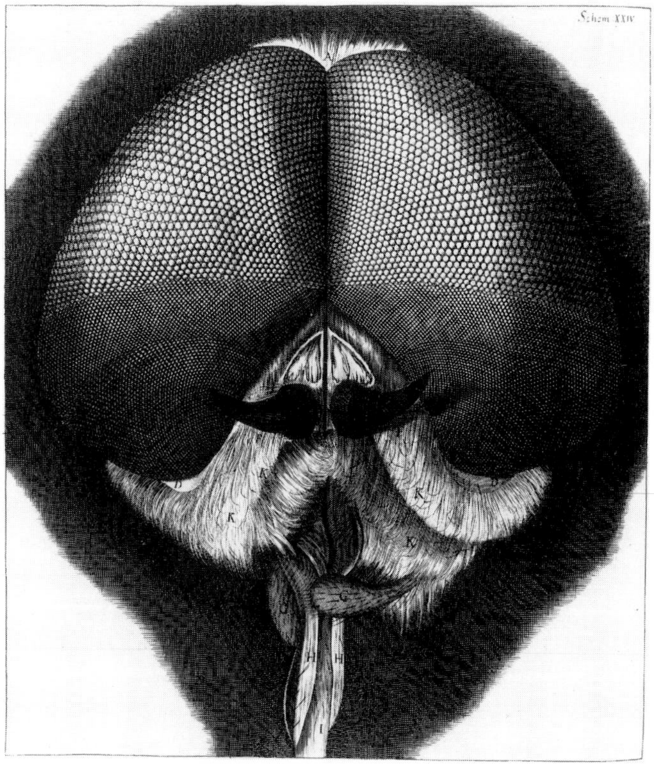

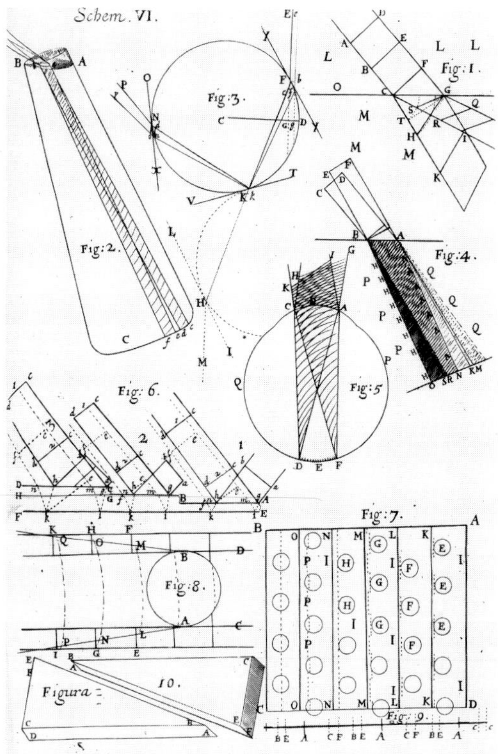

Robert Hooke's *Micrographia* (1665) was the first great work devoted to images seen under the microscope, as well as containing some of Hooke's thoughts about light and colours.

Hooke's musical theory of matter

Hooke's matter theory was based on the physical laws of musical strings and vibrating pendulums. Why did Hooke, and subsequently Newton, find musical ideas to be helpful in understanding the properties of light and other physical phenomena? To answer this, we have to go back to the long-established correspondence between numerical ratios and the musical consonances.

The arithmetic relationship between string length and pitch had been known since the time of Pythagoras. However, it was not until the end of the sixteenth century that anyone took this further, and actually began to experiment with strings and pendulums in the manner ascribed to Pythagoras. It was Vincenzo Galilei—musician, and father of the more famous Galileo—who first discovered that most of the experimental discoveries attributed to Pythagoras were wrong. This discovery led to further investigations by his son Galileo and other natural philosophers in the seventeenth century. The most systematic experiments were undertaken by the French friar Marin Mersenne, who published his results in his *Harmonie universelle* (1636–7).

Mersenne established that the pitch of a string is due to the *frequency* of its vibrations, which are always periodic or *isochronous*. He also demonstrated that this frequency is determined by the length, tension, and thickness of the string, and that the relationships between these physical variables can be expressed as mathematical laws. For example, a string vibrates twice as quickly as another of identical thickness and tension, if it is of half its length. Moreover, if it is the same length and thickness, then the tension must be increased fourfold to produce the same effect, and similarly with the other variables. Mersenne's laws can be summarized mathematically in the following law:

$$\text{pitch} \propto \frac{\sqrt{(\text{tension})}}{\text{length} \times (\text{diameter})^2}.$$

But this was not all that Mersenne established. Since the sound of a single note was obviously made up of a regular succession of vibrations striking the ear-drum, he thought that consonance must be due to the vibrations of two notes coinciding relatively frequently. The more often the vibrations coincide, the more pleasing the consonance. This is now known as the *coincidence theory* of consonance. There seemed to be a real, empirically verifiable relationship between regular motion and pleasing ideas of harmony in the mind. Many physical properties of musical sound could be expressed quantitatively with great success.

Since so few physical laws of this kind had been established by the mid-seventeenth century, it is not surprising to find that natural philosophers tried to relate their knowledge of the properties of strings and pendulums to other branches of mechanics, including optics and

Frontispiece of Marin Mersenne's *Harmonie universelle* (1636–7).

astronomy. It was assumed that the same harmonic or proportional relationships could be found in other forms of motion. Harmonics offered a *paradigm* of a mathematico-experimental science that might be applied to phenomena such as light and gravity. Hooke's theory of matter shows just how fruitful an analogy of this sort could be.

As he explained in his *Micrographia*, Hooke thought that all matter consists of invisible, inherently vibrating particles. The different frequencies of bodies are determined by the matter, shape, and bulk of their particles, like the length, tension, and thickness of strings:

for particles that are all similar, will, like so many equal musical strings equally stretcht, vibrate together in a kind of harmony or unison, whereas others that are dissimilar, upon what account soever, unless the disproportion be otherwise counter-ballanc'd, will, like so many strings out of tune to those unisons, though they have the same agitating pulse, yet make quite differing kinds of vibrations and repercussions, so that thought they may be both mov'd, yet are their vibrations so different, and so untun'd, as 'twere to each other, that they cross and jar agains each other and consequently cannot agree together, but fly back from each other to their similar particles.

The difference between solid bodies, fluids, and gases arises from the different frequencies at which such particles vibrate. It was this musical theory which led Hooke, in his critique of Newton's letter of 1672, to comment that:

> as there are produced in sounds several harmonies by proportionate vibrations, so there are produced in light several curious and pleasant colours, by the proportionate and harmonious motions of vibrations intermingled.

Just as certain periodic vibrations generated by bodies and communicated through the ether are responsible for producing the sensation of musical sounds in the ear, which are judged as pleasing by the mind, so it is assumed that more rapid vibrations of the ether produce the sensation of light and colours in the eye. Hooke extended this principle by analogy, to infer that there are other types of periodic vibration in matter which account for forces such as gravity and magnetism.

Newton's second theory of light (1675)

Hooke's criticisms influenced Newton more radically than has generally been recognized. First, it seems that Newton now began to experiment systematically with the colours in thin films, which were to become known as *Newton's rings*. Secondly, he began to develop an alternative physical model of light, *theory B*, based on an analogy with musical sound. This analogy, together with an entirely new comparison between the spectrum and the scale, was first made public in *An hypothesis explaining the properties of light* that Newton sent to the Royal Society in 1675. This document was not only concerned with light, however. Newton here outlined a general theory of ether which might explain light, gravity, magnetism, the processes of alchemical change, and even animal motion.

Newton still thought that light was corpuscular. In *An hypothesis*, all optical phenomena were explained by the interaction between light corpuscles of varying size or mass and an extremely fine material ether. Reflection and refraction of light were explained by the observation that, when light particles pass through this ether, the direction of their motion is altered according to its density. The perception of colour was explained by the analogy with musical sound.

According to their magnitude, strength, or vigour, light particles excite vibrations of differing 'bigness' (or *wavelength*) in the ether. These set up corresponding vibrations in the optic nerves and affect the sense of sight 'with various colours, according to their bigness or mixture'. The phenomena of thin films was similarly explained: at the surface of the film the density of the ether is successively condensed

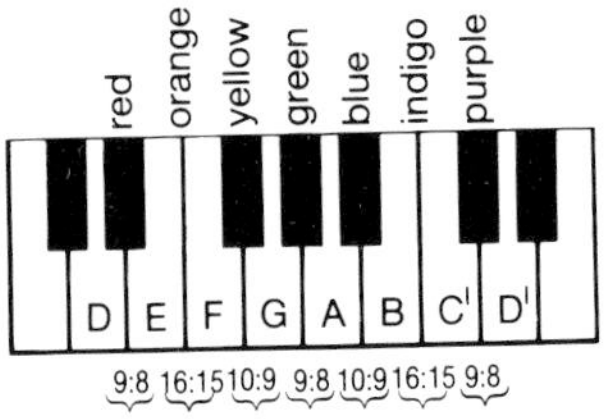

and rarefied by the wave motion excited by the light particles. When the particles themselves arrive at the surface, the ether is either rare enough to let them through, or dense enough to reflect them. The mass of each light particle determines its refrangibility.

This new theory allowed Newton to have light particles, and to explain their wave-like properties. Pursuing the *Analogy of nature*, as he described it, Newton went on to suggest that:

> as the harmony and discord of sounds proceed from the proportion of the aereal vibrations, so may the harmony of some colours . . . and the discord of others . . . proceed from the proportions of the aethereal. And possibly colour may be distinguished into its principal degrees, Red, Orange, Green, Blew, Indigo and deep Violet on the same ground, that sound within an eighth is graduated into tones.

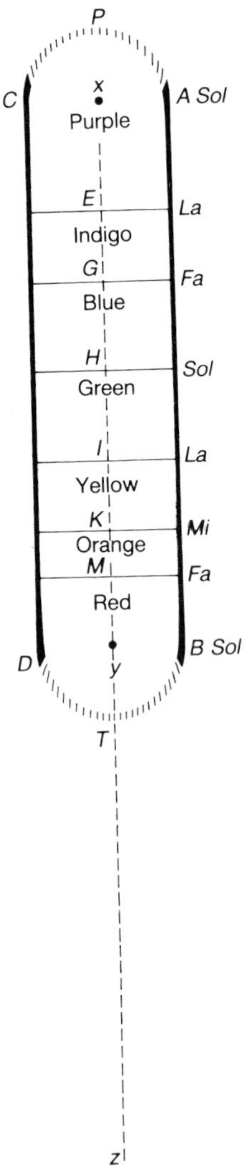

Newton's musical division of the spectrum, with the seven colours of the spectrum corresponding to the seven notes of the diatonic scale.

The spectrum-scale

At this point in *An hypothesis*, Newton introduced his 'discovery' that the spectrum can be divided up into ratios corresponding to those of a musical scale. He described how he asked an assistant to divide the spectrum into the strongest colours, and then found that this corresponded to a musical division. The same division of the spectrum was later presented by Newton in the *Opticks* (1704). Note that the proportions of the scale can be distributed symmetrically in the form of a palindrome.

Seven notes in the musical scale, seven colours in the spectrum! This indeed appears a most pleasing discovery. In both *An hypothesis* and the *Opticks*, this seven-fold division was presented as one objectively determined by experiment. Only in the second draft of his *Optical lectures* (written in 1672, but not published until after his death), did Newton offer a more candid reconstruction of his experiments.

First, he tried to measure distances between five main colours to see what might be deduced from this. *Then* he tried to divide it into seven colours, adding indigo and orange to the main colours 'in order to divide the image into parts more elegantly proportioned to one another'. He found that the proportions of one arrangement of the just intonation scale corresponded nearly exactly with this selection of colours. Yet he also found that a geometrical division of the spectrum, equivalent to equal temperament in a musical scale, was nearly as exact: it produced errors 'hardly visible to the keenest judge'. There was only approximate agreement here between theory and practice.

The difficulty that Newton found in making theory and observation agree is hinted at elsewhere in the *Opticks*. He applied the musical division to his colour-mixing circle, to the air films producing the principal colours in 'Newton's rings', and to the colours of thick plates. Newton was forced to carry out a series of *ad hoc* mathematical calculations, in order to make his experimental data fit the mathematical theory. Different arrangements of the just intonation ratios were therefore given in order to make the musical division approximately correct in each case.

There were more fundamental problems in the *Opticks*. The two mathematical laws of colour that Newton gave there were implicitly based on incompatible physical models, the theories A and B which he had developed in the 1670s. These can be summarized as follows:

- *Theory A* assumed that particles of light were the same size, and were reflected or refracted according to their velocity. Colours were reduced to laws of elastic collision. This theory underpinned the first section of the book.

- *Theory B* required that particles of light were of different masses and excited condensations and rarefactions in the medium which alternately reflected and transmitted the particles. This *ad hoc* theory was introduced in Book II as 'fits of easy reflexion and easy transmission' to explain the periodic properties of light.

Newton was keenly aware of the contradictions of the two physical models. In the *Opticks*, the mathematical laws were detached from any physical basis and were presented as though they were derived from

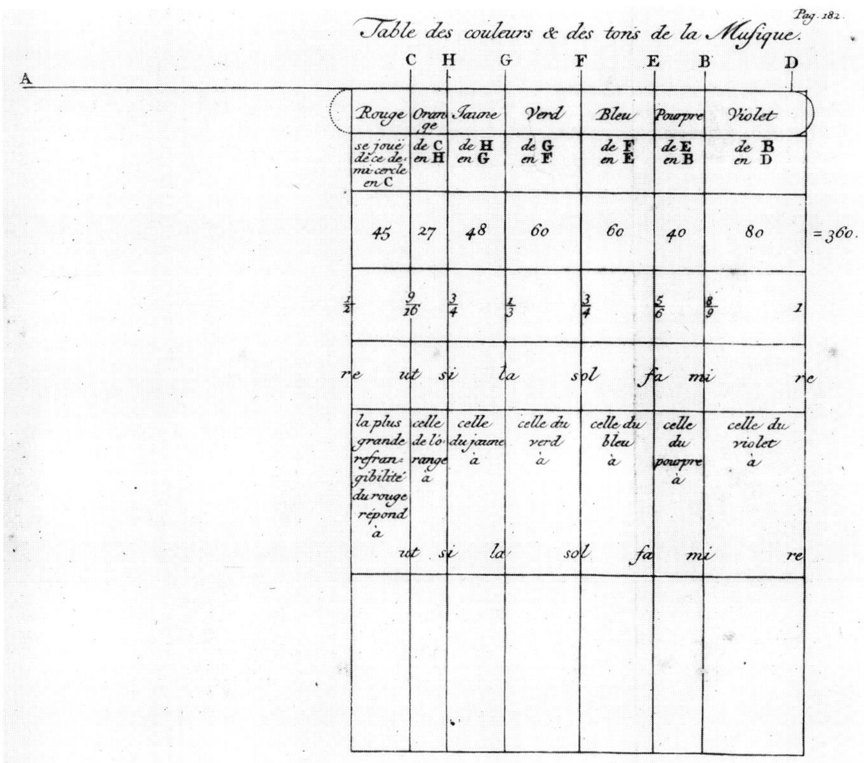

Pag. 182.

Table des couleurs & des tons de la Musique.

A — C H G F E B D

Rouge	Orange	Jaune	Verd	Bleu	Pourpre	Violet	
se jouë dé ce demi-cercle en C	de C en H	de H en G	de G en F	de F en E	de E en B	de B en D	
45	27	48	60	60	40	80	= 360.
la plus grande refrangibilité du rouge répond à	celle de l'orange à	celle du jaune à	celle du verd à	celle du bleu à	celle du pourpre à	celle du violet à	

1/2 9/16 3/4 1/3 3/4 5/6 8/9 1

re ut si la sol fa mi re

ut si la sol fa mi re

Newton's spectrum-scale was warmly received by his eighteenth-century admirers; for example, in Voltaire's *Elémens de la philosophie de Neuton* (1738).

experiment alone. Unpublished draft material reveals that, during the 1690s, Newton unsuccessfully tried to establish a connection between the various velocities and masses of light corpuscles and the frequencies of the ethereal vibrations they produced. In view of this, he eventually confined his remarks about the perception of colour and the analogies between colour harmonies and musical sound to the speculative section in Book III, Queries 12–14. Further conjectures about the vibrating ether and its role in the transmission of light and gravity were added to the second English edition of the *Opticks* (1717), especially in Queries 17–31.

Despite all attempts, Newton's quest for a single harmonic theory of light and colour met with failure. Nevertheless, it seems that, even at the end of his life, he remained convinced that there was a very real correspondence waiting to be discovered, between ratios and the perception of colour. This is perhaps not surprising. His search for the harmony of nature had already met with the most spectacular success in his laws of celestial dynamics.

The harmony of the spheres

The last aspect of Newton's harmonic science to be considered is his own unique interpretation of the ancient concept of the *harmony of the spheres*. Here the importance of Pythagorean doctrine in Newton's work is particularly apparent. The *Principia* itself, and particularly the theory of universal gravitation, publicly testified to Newton's belief in the underlying mathematical structure of the cosmos. As Piyo Rattansi points out in Chapter 9, it is only with the recent discovery of his theological and chronological writings, that it can be shown how Newton regarded his natural philosophy as an integral part of a radical and comprehensive recovery of the true ancient religion, which had been revealed directly to man by God. This apparently bizarre idea, and its significance for Newton's approach to celestial mechanics, can be shown in the context of the universal law of gravitation.

One of the problems in dealing with Newton's voluminous manuscripts is the impossibility of establishing precise dates for most texts. Any topic in which Newton was particularly interested went through numerous drafts, and it is very difficult to state their order with any certainty. What is clear, however, is that Newton began his theological studies in earnest during the early 1670s.

As is now well known, and as John Brooke describes in Chapter 8, it was not long before Newton had come to an extremely heterodox standpoint. By the mid-1670s he was convinced that the entire Christian church had become corrupted by Trinitarianism from the fourth century AD. This apostasy had been foretold, he thought, in the Book of Revelation. Newton became an Arian and regarded Catholicism and Anglicanism alike as corrupt religions. His desire to establish the exact correlation between prophecy and later events also led him to an intensive study of patristic texts and pagan mythologies, as sources of historical and allegorical truths. At the same period, he was engaged in alchemy, as described by Jan Golinski in Chapter 7. This involved a search for the ultimate nature of matter, a process which required both textual analysis and experiment.

Newton read systematically and exhaustively in all these fields, driven by the certainty that he could discover their hidden truths and the syncretism between them, if only the correct inductive method were applied. His search for the correct harmonic foundation of light and colours was part of the same process.

The development of Newton's theological ideas and their connection with his natural philosophy can perhaps be understood more clearly in the context of contemporary political and religious events. The Popish Plot of 1679, and the imminent threat of a Catholic succession, seem to have been linked in Newton's mind with the apostasy of the fourth century. In 1683, he began writing a work which he called the *Philosophical origins of gentile philosophy*. Here he explicitly associated popery, idolatry, and the worship of false kings with a corrupt geocentric natural philosophy. These were corruptions of a pristine truth revealed by God to man through Noah and his sons. It seems that Newton now regarded Cartesian mechanics, with its theory of interplanetary vortices, as an integral part of this gentile, popish tradition. In contrast, his own heliocentric vacuist system could be recognized as a recovery of the true natural philosophy and theology.

According to Newton's interpretation, the true world-system had been known to the ancients. This was expressed symbolically in Vestal temple ceremonies, where a central fire represented the Sun at the centre of the universe. The same symbol was found in the Jewish tabernacle, in which a central fire was surrounded by seven lamps, symbolizing the seven planets. The seven tones of the musical scale and seven colours of the spectrum had a similar numerological significance. The Pythagorean doctrine of the harmony of the spheres expressed this truth in symbolic form. Corruption set in when such symbols were misinterpreted.

Newton does not seem to have completed a final version of the *Philosophical origins*. However, many of its doctrines were worked into later writings. These include the drafts for the additional corollaries and Scholia that Newton wrote around 1694 for a projected second edition of the *Principia*. This material was intended to support the philosophical assertions on which the *Principia*'s demonstrations rest. Ultimately, however, most of it remained unpublished. Nevertheless, it is clear that Newton regarded such ideas as an essential justification for his system of celestial mechanics, together with its theories of matter, space, and gravitation.

In the Scholia on Proposition VIII of Book III, the section on universal gravitation, Newton asserted that Pythagoras had known the inverse-square law theory. He argued that Pythagoras had discovered by experiment the inverse-square relationship in the vibrations of strings. For two strings to be in unison, their tensions were reciprocally as the square of their lengths—thus, in order to produce the musical ratios 2 to 1, 3 to 2, and 4 to 3, the weights have to be in the ratio of 1 to 4, 4 to 9, and 9 to 16, an inverse-square relation. From this discovery, he said, Pythagoras went on to apply the same principle to the heavens:

> and consequently by comparing those weights with the weights of the planets, and the lengths of the strings with the distances of the planets, he understood by means of the harmony of the heavens that the weights of the planets towards the Sun were reciprocally as the squares of their distances from the Sun.

Why had this knowledge been lost until Newton rediscovered it? Newton thought this was because the Pythagoreans, like most ancient philosophers, wished to hide their mystic knowledge from the vulgar, by means of allegory and symbol. Pythagoras hid his secret in a number of ways. He expressed the musical ratios arithmetically, in terms of simple reciprocals, which was in fact true only for string lengths, and not weights. These arithmetic ratios were then applied to the ratios of the distances between the planets. To make things even more confusing, as Newton remarked:

> Pythagoras numbered the musical tones from the Earth, as though from here to the Moon were a tone, and thence to Mercury a semitone, and from thence to the rest of the planets other musical intervals.

In the *Philosophical origins*, Newton assumed that the proportions of this planetary scale correspond to the proportions of his own spectrum scale—that is, of just intonation. In this respect, he misrepresented the ancient tradition that had been transmitted by Plato in the *Timaeus*, where the planetary distances corresponded to the ratios of Pythagorean intonation. It was Johannes Kepler, in his *Harmonices mundi libri V* (1619), who was first to attempt to discover the proportions of the just intonation scale in planetary harmony.

The other part of Pythagoras' musical doctrine, which Newton thought had successfully obscured the laws of gravity, was the idea that the planets themselves produce musical sounds in their orbits. Taking this literally, later Gentile astronomers from Eudoxus and Ptolemy onwards had thought that these sounds were produced by the solid crystalline spheres, which carried the planets around, rubbing

Robert Fludd's *Temple of music* (1618), a complex amalgam of musical references, shows Pythagoras entering the blacksmith's forge in the basement. The numbers displayed above that scene testify to the Pythagorean relationship between numbers and harmony to which Newton attached such significance.

against each other. The ratios of the speeds of these spheres also corresponded to the musical intervals.

What had been poetic truths were thus made concrete and enshrined in Ptolemaic astronomy. However, the essential truths were not entirely lost to mankind. Taking the idea from Macrobius' commentary on the *Timaeus*, Newton remarked that 'Apollo's lyre of seven strings provides understanding of the motions of all the celestial spheres over which nature has set the Sun as moderator'. The fables of Apollo, Pan, and Orpheus, and the story of Pythagoras weighing the blacksmiths' hammers, all provided (with correct exegesis) the key to the true harmony of the heavens that only initiates such as Newton could penetrate.

Conclusion

This chapter has shown how aspects of harmonic science were directly related to the central topics of Newton's work, the nature of light and gravity. His understanding of harmonics matured and developed along with the rest of his studies. He became familiar with the basic elements of practical harmonics through his early reading of Descartes and other authors. Practical harmonics was traditionally regarded as providing an introduction to the proportions and harmonies which existed throughout nature. Newton subsequently applied his knowledge of musical ratios and theories of musical perception to the construction of his optics and theories of the nature of light and colour. In this respect, he was certainly influenced by Hooke, who claimed that the vibration of musical strings and the principles of consonance and dissonance could be used to understand the structure and properties of the physical world. Thanks to Hooke, Newton made a fruitful association between the periodicity of musical sound and that of light. The apparently 'natural' idea that there are seven colours in the rainbow, or spectrum, owes its popular acceptance today to the *a priori* connection that Newton made between musical and colour harmonies.

The most important feature of Pythagorean harmonic science was its religious and metaphysical dimension. Similar priorities, which are all too easily lost sight of, are found in the case of Newton. The existence of many pages of writings and commentaries on chronology and religion provides ample evidence that Newton regarded the development of the mathematical principles of natural philosophy as only one part of a much broader programme embracing moral philosophy and a true knowledge of God, the realm of speculative harmonics. His reading of patristic and Neoplatonic texts, all of which focused on spiritual harmonies of the cosmos, underpinned his search for, and his ultimate discovery of, the principles of celestial mechanics.

Newton's public achievement was his ability to express the motions of the heavens in the language of mathematics. In his own eyes, he had also succeeded in tearing aside the veil of allusion in ancient myths and prophecies, in deciphering secret words and numbers. He had thereby arrived at the original learning which God had given to man, the true ancient theology. Newton might well be regarded as a seventeenth-century Pythagorean, his life being devoted to the study of universal harmony.

Further reading

Information about the science of the Greeks can be found in W. Burkert, *Lore and science in ancient Pythagoreanism* (translated by E. L. Minar, Jr.), Cambridge University Press, Cambridge, 1972; and in M. R. Cohen and I. E. Drabkin, *A source book in Greek science*, Cambridge, Mass., 1972.

Excellent accounts of the history and theory of musical scales are given in J. M. Barbour, *Tuning and temperament, a historical survey*, East Lansing, Mich., 1951; and in M. Lindley, *Lutes, viols and temperaments*, Cambridge University Press, Cambridge, 1984.

References for Newton's work on optics and alchemy can be found in the 'Further reading' sections of Chapters 4 and 7.

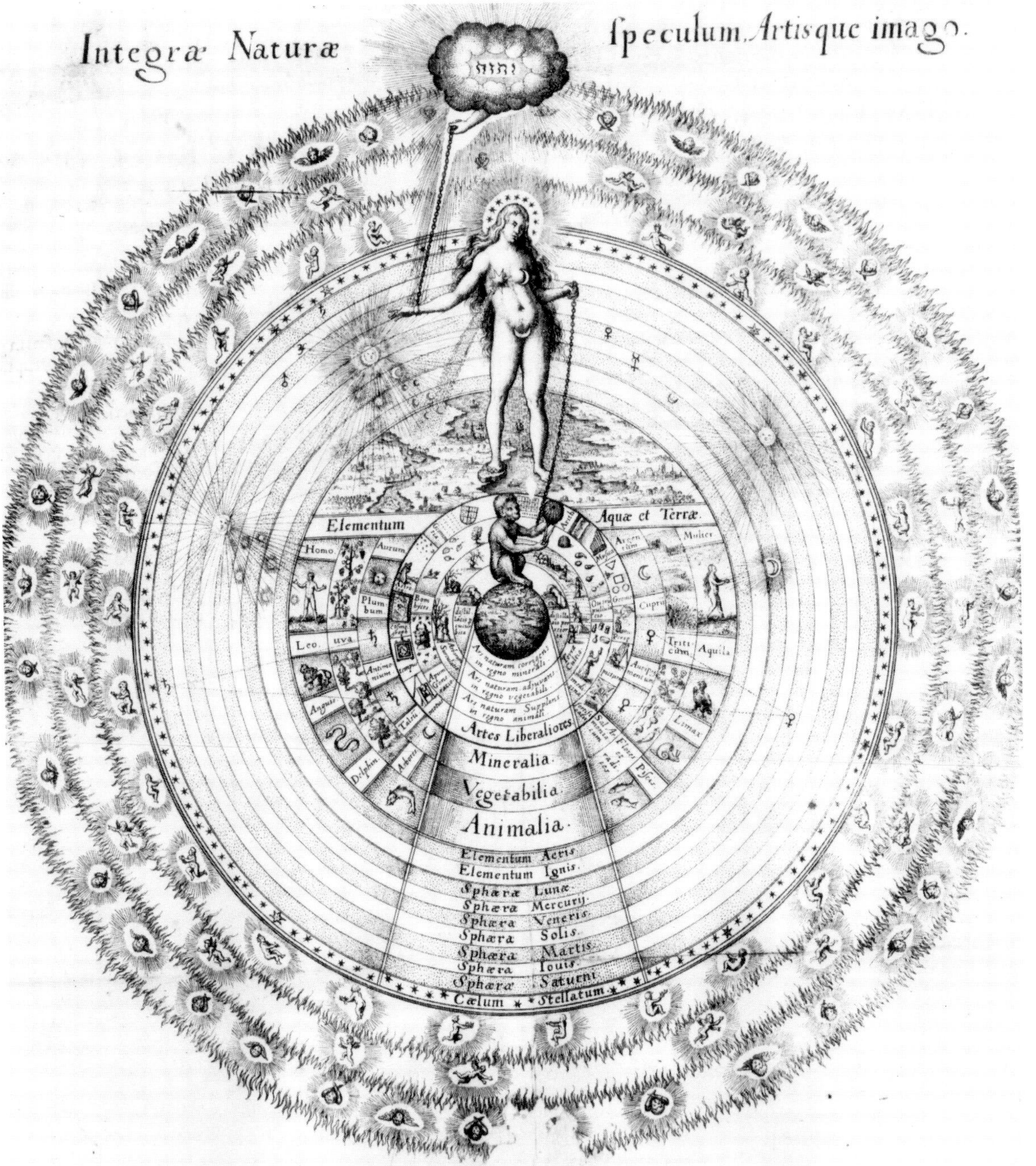
Integræ Naturæ
speculum Artisque imago.
Elementum
Aquæ et Terræ
Homo
Aurum
Plumbum
Leo.
uva
Argentum
Mulier
Cupro
Triticum
Aquila
Limax
Delphin
Arbores
Artes Liberaliores
Mineralia.
Vegetabilia.
Animalia.
Elementum Aeris
Elementum Ignis.
Sphæræ Lunæ.
Sphæra Mercurij.
Sphæra Veneris.
Sphæra Solis.
Sphæra Martis.
Sphæra Iouis.
Sphæræ Saturni
Cælum Stellatum.

CHAPTER
SIX

Newton, matter, and magic

JOHN HENRY

Theories of matter have always been of major importance in attempts to understand the workings of the physical world. Such theories are about what the world around us is made of, how it behaves, and how one piece or parcel of matter interacts with another. Even today, it is the matter theorist who is most easily seen as the embodiment of the leading edge of scientific advance—today's matter theorists, of course, are the high-energy physicists who use accelerators and cyclotrons to search for new sub-atomic particles with names such as *quarks*, *upsilons*, *charmed lambdas*, and *gluons*. But this is not a recent phenomenon. In the seventeenth century, the attempt to understand matter and its interactions was a major concern (if not *the* major concern) of Isaac Newton in his *Principia*.

In the Preface to the first edition of the *Principia* (1687), Newton went so far as to say that, although he concentrated here on 'gravity, . . . , elastic force, the resistance of fluids, and the like', in some ways this was only a preliminary sortie. He went on to intimate the wider design:

> I wish we could derive the rest of the phenomena of Nature by the same kind of reasoning from mechanical principles, for I am induced by many reasons to suspect that they may all depend upon certain forces by which the particles of bodies, by some causes hitherto unknown, are either mutually impelled toward one another and cohere in regular figures, or are repelled and recede from one another. These forces being unknown, philosophers have hitherto attempted the search of Nature in vain.

This statement is a quite outrageous piece of bravado on Newton's part, and can be seen as succinctly summarizing how different Newton's ideas were from the views prevailing at the time. It can therefore be used as a key to understanding just how innovatory Newton's views were. His suggestion was that all the phenomena of nature can be explained on two assumptions: that all bodies are made up of particles, and that there are *forces* operating between these bodies and particles.

It is the second of these presuppositions which distinguishes Newton's statement of scientific faith from those of his contemporaries. By this time, virtually all leading natural philosophers subscribed to the *corpuscular*, or *atomic*, theory of matter. Matter was thought to be made up of small indivisible atoms, but all interactions between them were explained solely in terms of contact action. The only allowable notion of force, therefore, was *force of impact*; all other concepts of force,

Robert Fludd's *Mirror of the whole of nature and the image of art* (1617) is one of the finest examples of what was once a common pictorial genre—schemes of the structure and order of the universe. The right hand of Mother Nature is directly controlled by the hand of God, while she herself guides the hand of human ingenuity, depicted in the centre as the *Ape of Nature*. The ape was traditionally held to be a clever mimic, and all human powers and achievements are here seen to derive from the imitation of natural processes. The concentric circles indicate some of the correspondences between different parts of creation, which gave power to those who understood them.

such as attraction and repulsion, were regarded by these natural philosophers as *occult*. The use of occult forces or powers in scientific explanations was regarded by Newton's contemporaries as an abdication of the main duty of the natural philosopher—namely, to *explain the causes* of all physical phenomena. As we see from the above quotation, however, Newton himself had no scruples against discussing forces which operate by *unknown causes*.

In 1687, most of Newton's readers would have found this approach puzzling, and many thought that it was utterly misconceived. Nevertheless, Newton persevered with these views in his subsequent publications, seeking to back them up experimentally in the Queries appended to the *Opticks*, and defending them on theoretical and methodological grounds in subsequent editions of the *Principia*. As we now know, his faith in forces was justified to such an extent that it is widely regarded as Newton's most important scientific innovation. His assertion, that there do exist forces of attraction and repulsion between particles of matter which are not in contact, was a major revision in seventeenth-century natural philosophy and a crucial influence on all subsequent physical science.

Why did Newton's ideas about forces between particles seem to many contemporary readers so outlandish and misconceived? And from where could Newton have drawn his revisionist ideas?

Aristotelianism and occult qualities

In Newton's day the prevailing natural philosophy was still that of Aristotle. Aristotelian philosophy had become established in the universities of Europe by the thirteenth century, and its domination in Arts Faculties was thereafter virtually complete. What was taught in natural philosophy was not how the world is constructed and how it works, but rather what Aristotle *said* about how the world is constructed and how it works. The focus was not on nature itself, but on Aristotle's system of natural philosophy. By the seventeenth century, Aristotelianism was so closely identified with academic training that it was frequently referred to as *Scholasticism*, or as the philosophy of *The Schoolmen*. (It is also sometimes called *Peripatetic* philosophy, after an old name for followers of Aristotle.)

Newton regarded himself as working within the tradition of what was called the *mechanical philosophy*. This is what he meant, in the Preface quoted above, by 'reasoning from mechanical principles'. The mechanical philosophy was a comparatively new movement, which had rapidly established itself among natural philosophers as superior to the approach of Aristotle. One of the major claims of mechanical philosophers was that their philosophy *explained* physical change in a way which was much more immediately comprehensible than the

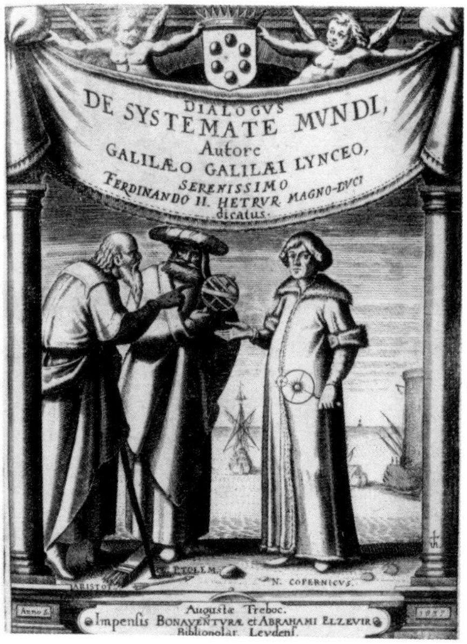

The title page of Galileo's *Dialogue on the great world systems* (1632) shows Aristotle, Ptolemy and Copernicus in discussion, while the ship in the harbour behind them prepares to sail into the unknown. Aristotle is evidently still a powerful teacher, after nearly 2000 years.

Aristotelian account. This claim seems undeniable, from our post-mechanical perspective. To understand its force, we need to see how people with a traditional scholastic education viewed the world.

Aristotelian natural philosophy was based on animate, frequently human, models and exemplars. Thus, Aristotle's accounts of how one thing *causes* another are almost exclusively based on the examples of sculptors creating sculptures, potters making pots, and—in the best traditions of Greek satire—doctors causing people to regain health. The general message of these discussions was that *the agent in any causal chain has the power to perform what is attributed to it, and the thing acted upon has the ability to be changed in the requisite way.* A potter has the power to cause pots to be made out of clay, but only because clay has the potential to be made into pots.

This theory of causation was not helpful when translated into the inanimate realm: impacts between moving bodies, interactions between chemicals, the operation of poisons on the human body—none of these was made any clearer by the Aristotelian account. An analysis claiming, for example, that substance A has the power to dissolve substance B *because* substance B has the potential to dissolve in substance A does not get very far.

Alternative attempts were made by scholastics to explain causation, centring on the notion of *specific forms*. According to Aristotle, all things are made up of a universal undifferentiated matter principle and a specific form; the latter is what gives a particular parcel of matter its peculiar characteristics. So, lead differs from gold because they each have their own specific form. Aristotle tried to reduce all the properties of a body to four elementary qualities: hot, cold, dry and wet. (These

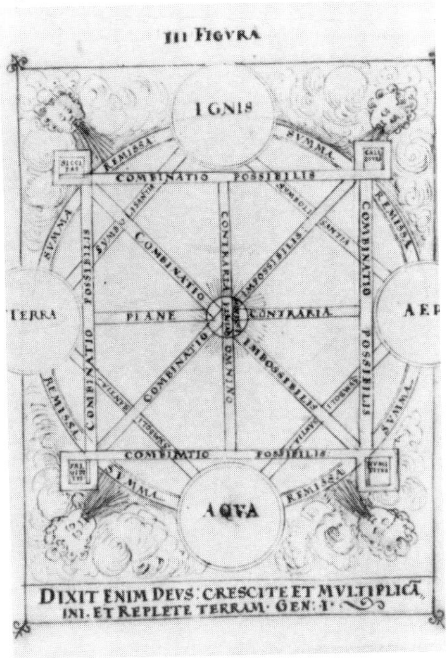

This diagram from a treatise by *Cornelius Petraeus, student of hermetic philosophy*, shows the four Aristotelian elements (in the circles) as combinations of the elementary qualities (in the small square at each corner). The biblical quotation at the foot (Genesis: 28) is a reminder of how thoroughly Aristotelian and Christian ideas were interwoven by the seventeenth century.

properties appeared combined in pairs as the qualities of the four elements, Earth, Water, Air, and Fire—fire is hot and dry, Earth is cold and dry, and so on.)

The ability of a substance to affect another seemed unproblematic for Aristotelians, provided that it could be attributed to *manifest qualities* such as heat or coldness. It was easy to see that a hot body, for example, affected other bodies by warming them up, transferring the quality of heat so that their specific forms were thereby changed. But unfortunately there were many interactions between bodies which defied the most ingenious attempts to analyse them in terms of the four elemental or manifest qualities. (Such interactions were things like dissolving, magnetic attraction, and the effect of poisons.) To account for these there was a somewhat embarrassing proliferation of *non-manifest* or *occult qualities*, powers, virtues, faculties, or forces (these terms were frequently used interchangeably).

In such cases, the specific form of a body was simply said to endow that body with the *occult power* of affecting other bodies in particular ways. Once again, the Aristotelian had returned to the notion that A has the power to affect B, and B has the potentiality to be affected by A. These conceptions provide the background to Molière's famous attack on academic medicine in *Le malade imaginaire* (1673). Asked why opium puts people to sleep, a doctor in the play replies, 'because it has a dormitive virtue'—that is, it has a sleep-making power!

By the beginning of the seventeenth century, the inability of Aristotelian natural philosophy to explain even very common everyday phenomena had become something of a scandal. This alerted some thinkers to the fact that even causal accounts based on the manifest

A good example of explaining things by occult powers is found in Athanasius Kircher's *Magnetic kingdom of nature* (1667). Kircher saw the world as bound together by magnetic power—the flying scrolls tell us that *The world is bound by secret knots*. The three medallions show magnetism's responsibility for the steadfastness of things (the compass needle), the resurgence of the oppressed (a plant), and natural correspondences between things (the cock and the stag). All these qualities are supported by the hand of God.

qualities (such as heat and cold) were unsatisfactory. As Daniel Sennert, a leading chemical philosopher, pointed out in 1618:

> the natural philosopher knows no more of heat but that it heats and that it flows from and depends upon the form of fire; but this form is as unknown to man as those forms from which the occult qualities arise.

The stage was set, therefore, for the mechanical philosophy to come in and set the philosophical world to rights.

Rejecting scholastic occult qualities: the mechanical philosophy

The mechanical philosophy was based on the assumption that all physical phenomena can be explained in terms of the motions, combinations, and configurations of vanishingly small particles of matter. Physical change was brought about when one set of particles affected another set, by dissipating it, combining with it, or altering its motions. Clues to understanding these microscopic interactions were provided by analogy with physical interactions on the macro-level, or by imaginative reconstruction.

Why does acid have such a sharp astringent taste? Because it is made up of particles which are like tiny knives or needles which prick the tongue. How does liquid A dissolve powder B? The fast-moving free-flowing particles of A bombard the powder and divide it still smaller, into its constituent particles; these particles are then small enough to fit in between the particles of the liquid, and so remain in solution. With a little ingenuity, this became an easy game to play in order to account for most physical phenomena.

According to its proponents, the strength of the mechanical philosophy lay in its ability to give easily-intelligible explanations of complex physical phenomena, including all those which had previously been explicable only by recourse to occult qualities. The point was that, even if certain operations remained inscrutable for now, they could in principle be explained in micromechanical terms. Indeed, it no longer made sense to distinguish between phenomena which could be explained by *manifest* qualities and those which could only be explained by *occult* qualities, once all phenomena were explicable in terms of the behaviour of invisible particles.

A famous example of an occult phenomenon being explained in mechanistic terms is Descartes' account of the magnet. Magnetic

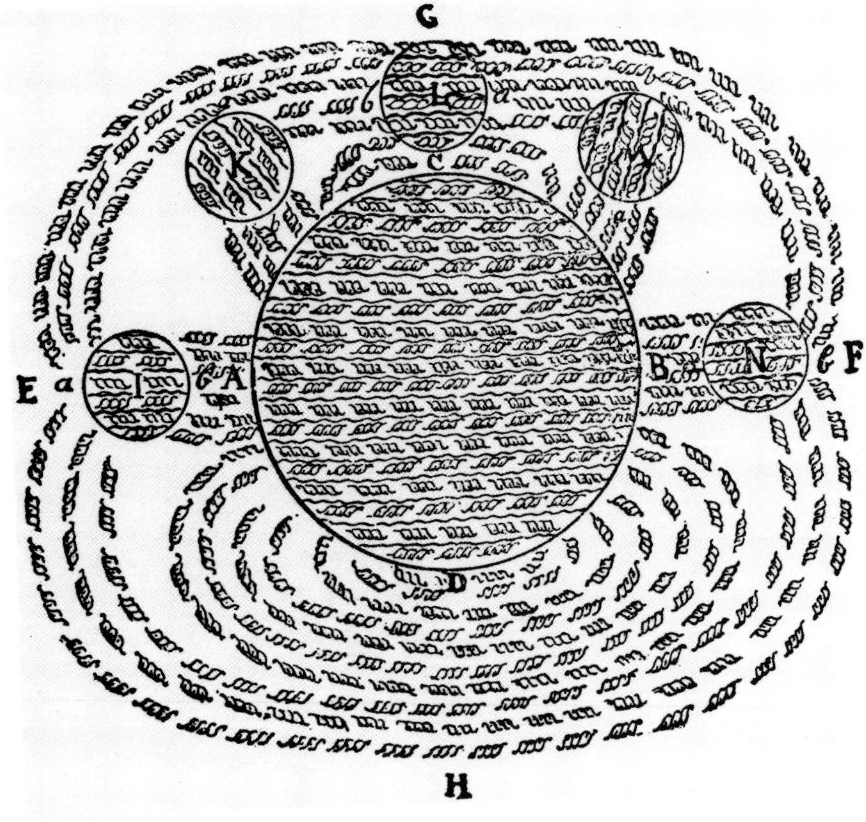

Descartes' mechanical explanation of how a magnet works.

attraction and repulsion were perhaps the most striking examples of occult powers, and yet Descartes explained them simply in terms of the actions of streams of particles emitted by the magnet. He assumed that magnets were pervaded with continuous pores, through which there was a continually circulating stream of invisibly small particles. In order to account for the attraction and repulsion of magnets, he supposed that the particles were screw-shaped, some with left-hand and some with right-hand threads. When two streams of oppositely threaded particles met, repulsion would ensue; attraction took place when the particles from a magnet could enter into the (correctly threaded) pores of another magnet or a piece of iron and, operating like tiny corkscrews, draw it towards the source magnet.

In Descartes' natural philosophy, nothing was left unexplained. As he wrote at the end of his *Principles of philosophy* (1644):

> And thus by simple enumeration, it is concluded that no phenomena of nature have been omitted by me in this treatise. For nothing is to be numbered among the phenomena of nature, except what is perceived by the senses ... thus ... there is nothing visible or perceptible in this world that I have not explained.

This means that, in trying to account for all things in terms of the shape, size, and motion of the constituent particles, he also had to offer explanations of *how* different parts of matter acquired their shapes, sizes, and motions. Shape, size, and motion were, after all, the foundations on which the rest of Descartes' system was based. Unfortunately, as a number of his contemporaries insisted, these foundations were by no means secure.

Consider the example of *motion*. We can see all around us that new motions are continually being initiated, while other things come to rest. But why do things move? Why isn't the whole universe one vast fixed stationary mass? Why do some parts of the universe suddenly begin to move, and maybe as suddenly cease to move? Do we not have to admit that there is some occult principle of movement operating in the world?

In order to avoid such notions of occult powers of motion, much of Descartes' *Principles of philosophy* was devoted to an explanation of how or why matter moves, and what keeps it in motion. Bound up with this was his clear statement of rectilinear inertia—that moving bodies tend to carry on moving, and in straight lines—and other *laws of motion*:

> *The first law of nature*: that each thing, as far as is in its power, always remains in the same state; and that consequently, when it is once moved, it always continues to move.
>
> *The second law of nature*: that all movement is, of itself, along straight lines; and consequently, bodies which are moving in a circle always tend to move

away from the centre of the circle which they are describing.

The third law: that a body, upon coming into contact with a stronger one, loses none of its motion; but that, upon coming into contact with a weaker one, it loses as much as it transfers to that weaker body.

Descartes insisted that the amount of motion in the universe is constant. At the Creation God gave the universe a cosmic push to set the ball rolling and, *because matter is completely passive and inert*, it cannot stop itself or even slow down. If the motion of some body decreases, we have to ask what made it do so—it cannot slow down of its own accord. The only change in motion that can occur is transference from one part of matter to another, according to the laws of motion and the seven *rules of impact* which Descartes also expounded. All the movements in the universe, in short, are one vast chain reaction initiated at the Creation by God.

As might have been expected, there were a number of mechanical philosophers who could not accept this. Newton was one of them:

If you think that the *vis inertiae* [force of inertia] is sufficient for conserving motion, pray tell me the experiments from whence you gather thy conclusion. Do you learn by any experiment that the beating of heart gives no new motion to the blood, that the explosion of gunpowder gives us no new motion to a bullet or that a man by his will can give no new motion to his body? Do you learn by experiment that the beating of your heart takes away as much motion from something else as it gives to the blood or that explosion takes away as much motion from something else as it gives to the bullet or that a man by his will takes away as much motion from something else as he gives to his body? If so, tell me your experiments; if not your opinion is precarious.

Newton's insistence that the natural world cannot be explained solely in terms of the arrangement and inertial movements of totally passive particles of matter is now regarded as one of the initial premisses upon which his subsequent great achievements were built. Older contemporaries of Newton, including great scientists such as Robert Boyle and Robert Hooke, had recognized that it was impossible to account satisfactorily for many natural phenomena (particularly chemical and biological phenomena) on Cartesian assumptions—but they were unable to improve matters. It was Newton who transformed the mechanical philosophy by introducing into it his notion of *active principles*. These principles were to be called upon to account for those spontaneous workings of nature which could not be explained according to the principles of strict mechanism:

Seeing therefore the variety of motion which we find in the world is always decreasing, there is a necessity of conserving and recruiting it by active Principles, such as are the cause of gravity, by which Planets and Comets keep their Motions in their Orbs, and Bodies acquire great Motion in falling; and the cause of Fermentation, by which the Heart and Blood of Animals are kept in perpetual Motion and Heat . . . For we meet with very little Motion in the World, besides what is owing to the active Principles.

Newton went on to argue that, without these active principles, the world would be dead, barren, lifeless, and unmoving. So, for Newton, it was obvious that:

Particles have not only a *vis inertiae*, accompanied with such passive Laws of Motion as naturally result from that Force, but also that they are moved by certain Active Principles.

With the benefit of hindsight, we know that Newton's ideas were to lead to the triumph and the apotheosis of the mechanical philosophy. However, during Newton's own lifetime, a number of leading natural philosophers were dismayed and appalled by Newton's notions of active principles, because they saw them as a betrayal of the principles of the mechanical philosophy. Newton's active principles seemed to represent a return to the lazy and slipshod occult qualities of Aristotelianism. As Leibniz, Newton's most implacable rival, said:

Gravity [and, by implication, any of his active principles] must be a scholastic occult quality or the effect of a miracle.

Newton was quick to rebut these charges. Significantly, however, in his different attempts to deny the validity of Leibniz' criticism, he did not deny the *occult* nature of his active principles. What Newton took exception to was the charge that they were *scholastic* or *Aristotelian*:

These Principles I consider, not as occult Qualities, *supposed to result from the specifick Forms of Things*, but as general Laws of Nature, by which the Things themselves are form'd; their Truth appearing to us by Phaenomena, though their Causes be not yet discover'd. For these are manifest Qualities, and their Causes only are occult. And the *Aristotelians* gave the name of occult Qualities, not to manifest Qualities, but to such Qualities only as they supposed to lie hid in Bodies, and to be the unknown Causes of manifest Effects: Such as would be the Causes of Gravity, and of magnetick and electrick Attractions, and of Fermentations, if we should suppose that these Forces or Actions arose from Qualities unknown to us, and *uncapable of being discovered and made manifest*.

The nub of the matter is that Aristotelian occult qualities were held to be 'uncapable of being discovered and made manifest'. As Newton freely admitted, 'Such occult Qualities put a stop to the Improvement of natural philosophy, and therefore of late Years have been rejected'.

The suggestion that occult qualities were invoked by Aristotelians as a refuge from, or an excuse for, ignorance was a common charge, and it was one of the major elements in mechanical philosophers' efforts to discredit Aristotelianism. Newton certainly did not want to defend this notion of occult quality, but equally he did not feel that occult qualities should be dismissed out of hand. As Newton insisted defensively:

> occult qualities are decried *not because their causes are unknown* but because the Schoolmen believed that those things wch were unknown to their Master Aristotel, *could never be known*.

Newton fully accepted, then, the notion of occult qualities and powers, as qualities whose 'causes are unknown'; but he rejected the Aristotelian conception of such qualities as unknowable even in principle, which would indeed be an end to all 'Improvement of natural philosophy'.

What are we to make of this? Newton refused to make any capitulation to Aristotelianism, and yet he accepted the use of occult qualities and powers. This seeming paradox is easily explained, in fact. Newton was drawing his notion of occult qualities not from scholastic traditions but from a completely separate tradition—the tradition of natural magic.

When the Hermetic writings were discovered by Renaissance scholars they were taken to be the work of the deified Egyptian sage known as Thoth to the Egyptians, Hermes to the Greeks, and Mercury to the Romans. He was called *Hermes Trismegistus*—Thrice-great—because he was held to be philosopher, priest, and king, and he began to be regarded as a spiritual father of Christianity, as on this mosaic pavement in Siena Cathedral (1480s).

Occult qualities in the natural magic tradition

The various magical arts have a continuous history from ancient times right through to the seventeenth century and beyond, but during the Renaissance they enjoyed a considerable rise in their fortunes when they came to be embraced by a significant number of leading intellectuals. The reasons for this new vogue are complex, but one very important stimulus was the rediscovery of a number of ancient magical texts. These texts were purportedly written by ancient sages by the names of Hermes Trismegistus (the *Hermetic* texts), Zoroaster, Orpheus, and other magi, who were all held to be near-contemporaries of Moses. In fact, we now know that these texts were not as old as that, but were written by various unknown mystical thinkers in the Near East during the first and second centuries AD, or even later.

Other traditions too were available to the Renaissance intellectual. One such was the *Cabbala*, a Jewish spiritual magic supposed to have been handed down by oral tradition from Moses himself. *Alchemy* was a Hermetic science—some alchemical texts were attributed to Hermes Trismegistus. And in the late Renaissance some of these traditions are found mingled in shadowy secret societies, of which the *Rosicrucian* brotherhood is one that has been studied by historians in recent years.

Throughout the Middle Ages and Renaissance, one of the most prominent of the magical arts was *natural magic*. This was a rich and complex tradition, based upon the assumption that there are various

Hermes Trismegistus was also regarded as the founder of alchemy. In this picture from a 1617 alchemy text, Hermes indicates the importance in alchemy of mercury (the Moon) and gold (the Sun), and the mediating role of fire. Newton's alchemical work made extensive use of mercury, gold, and fire.

The symbolism embedded in Hermetic images such as this *Alchemical microcosm and macrocosm* can be overwhelming: here the rich blend of Christian, astrological, and alchemical symbols testifies to the perception of cosmic correspondences in the natural magic tradition. Newton's library contained two editions of the book from which this picture comes, *Museum hermeticum* (1625).

occult but *natural* powers suffused throughout the world. These could be harnessed by the adept, either for the benefit of himself, his patron or client, or (if he was very enlightened) for the benefit of mankind. Virtually everything in the world, from stars to herbs and stones, was endowed with some kind of occult virtue which could be used by the adept to achieve certain ends. The trick was to discover what these powers were: what things had what powers over what other things.

There were three main methods of learning about the occult powers of things in the magical tradition. First, you could summon a demon, an angel, or even a dead magus, and ask or command him to tell you how to achieve the desired outcome. Needless to say, this method was fraught with dangers to your immortal soul. Alternatively, you could scrutinize the natural world and hope to discover the *signatures* of things—the signs which God incorporated into his creatures to indicate the connections between them: the *mandrake root*, which looked like a little man, seemed to indicate a cure for impotence, whereas the *walnut*, which looked like the brain, seemed to suggest a power of curing headaches. The drawback of this method was its inherent subjectivity, which made it prone to uncertainty and error. The safest and most successful way to discover the secret powers of nature was empirically, by careful observation of the effects of one thing on another, where possible by experimental trial.

A leading Renaissance magician gave this account of the nature of natural magic:

Natural magic is that which having contemplated the virtues of all natural and celestial things and carefully studied their order proceeds to make known the hidden and secret powers of nature in such a way that inferior and superior things are joined by an interchanging application of each to each; thus incredible miracles are often accomplished not so much by art as by nature, to whom this art is a servant when working at these things. For this reason magicians are careful explorers of nature, only directing what nature has formerly prepared, uniting actives to passives and often succeeding in anticipating results; so that these things are popularly held to be miracles when they are really no more than anticipations of natural operations ... therefore those who believe the operations of magic to be above or against

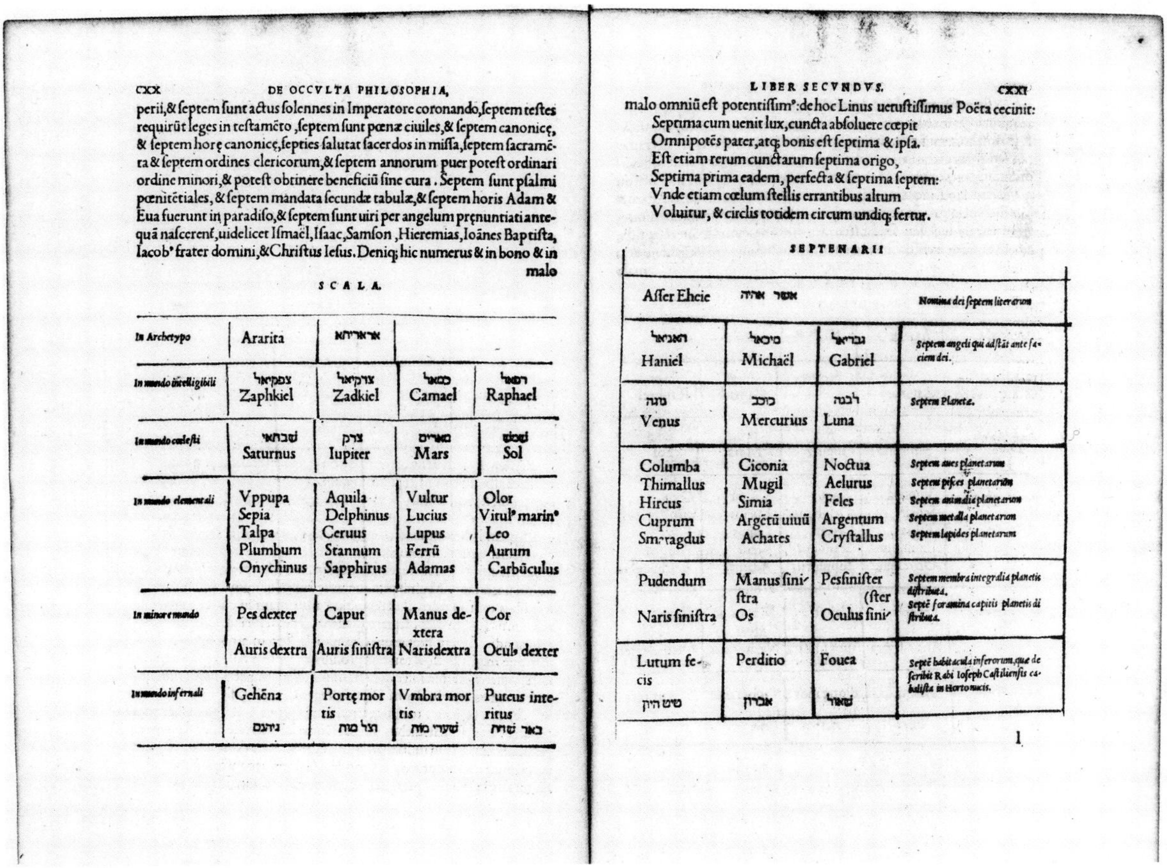

CXX DE OCCVLTA PHILOSOPHIA,

perii,& ſeptem ſunt actus ſolennes in Imperatore coronando,ſeptem teſtes requirũt leges in teſtamẽto ,ſeptem ſunt pœnæ ciuiles,& ſeptem canonicę, & ſeptem horę canonicę,ſepties ſalutat ſacerdos in miſſa,ſeptem ſacramẽta & ſeptem ordines clericorum,& ſeptem annorum puer poteſt ordinari ordine minori,& poteſt obtinere beneficiũ ſine cura . Septem ſunt pſalmi pœnitẽtiales, & ſeptem mandata ſecundæ tabulæ,& ſeptem horis Adam & Eua fuerunt in paradiſo,& ſeptem ſunt uiri per angelum pręnuntiati antequã naſcerenť,uidelicet Iſmaël,Iſaac,Samſon ,Hieremias,Ioãnes Baptiſta, Iacob' frater domini,&Chriſtus Ieſus. Deniq; hic numerus & in bono & in malo

SCALA.

In Archetypo	Ararita	אראריתא		
In mundo intelligibili	צפקיאל Zaphkiel	צדקיאל Zadkiel	כמאל Camael	רפאל Raphael
In mundo coelesti	שבתאי Saturnus	צדק Iupiter	מאדים Mars	שמש Sol
In mundo elementali	Vppupa Sepia Talpa Plumbum Onychinus	Aquila Delphinus Ceruus Stannum Sapphirus	Vultur Lucius Lupus Ferrũ Adamas	Olor Vitul' marin' Leo Aurum Carbũculus
In minore mundo	Pes dexter Auris dextra	Caput Auris ſiniſtra	Manus dextera Narisdextra	Cor Ocul' dexter
In mundo infernali	Gehẽna גיהנם	Portę mortis צלמות	Vmbra mortis שערי מות	Puteus interitus באר שחת

LIBER SECVNDVS. CXXI

malo omniũ eſt potentiſſim':de hoc Linus uetuſtiſſimus Poëta cecinit:

Septima cum uenit lux,cuncta abſoluere cœpit
Omnipotẽs pater,atq; bonis eſt ſeptima & ipſa.
Eſt etiam rerum cunctarum ſeptima origo,
Septima prima eadem, perfecta & ſeptima ſeptem:
Vnde etiam cœlum ſtellis errantibus altum
Voluitur, & circlis totidem circum undiq; fertur.

SEPTENARII

Aſſer Ehcie אשר אהיה			Nomina dei ſeptem literarum
האניאל Haniel	מיכאל Michaël	גבריאל Gabriel	Septem angeli qui adſtãt ante faciem dei.
נוגה Venus	כוכב Mercurius	לבנה Luna	Septem Planetæ.
Columba Thimallus Hircus Cuprum Smaragdus	Ciconia Mugil Simia Argẽtũ uiuũ Achates	Noctua Aelurus Feles Argentum Cryſtallus	Septem aues planetarum Septem piſces planetarum Septem animalia planetarum Septem metalla planetarum Septem lapides planetarum
Pudendum Naris ſiniſtra	Manus ſiniſtra Os	Pesſiniſter Oculus ſiniſter	Septem membra integralia planetis diſtributa. Septẽ foramina capitis planetis diſtributa.
Lutum fecis טיט היון	Perditio אבדון	Fouea שאול	Septẽ habitacula inferorum,quæ deſcribit Rabi Ioſeph Caſtilienſis cabaliſta in Horto nucis.

1

Agrippa's *Of occult philosophy* (1531–3) earned him the reputation of the foremost magician of the age. It included a series of 'correspondences' based on different numbers. Newton's own copy of this book is now lost, but we may suppose he took great interest in *The scale of the number seven*, which shows correspondences of seven-ness in the various worlds. Newton's belief in numerological correspondences led him to suppose that there must be seven colours in the rainbow, to correspond with the seven-sounding harmony of the music of the spheres (the seven planets) and the seven notes of the musical octave.

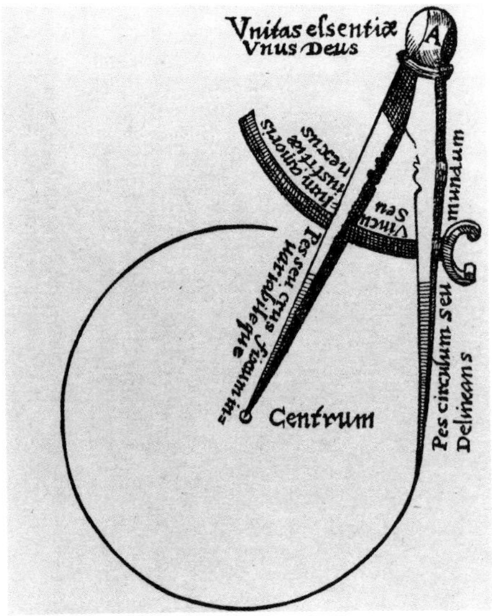

In Newton's time, the assumption that the world was constructed according to a mathematical or geometrical pattern was still widely associated with the magical tradition. The supposed founder of this view was Pythagoras (sixth century BC), who was allegedly taught mathematics and magic by Hermes Trismegistus himself. Here are two early seventeenth-century images (from the works of Michael Maier and Robert Fludd) showing how the drawing of geometrical diagrams was believed to have creative cosmic significance.

nature are mistaken because they are only derived from nature and in harmony with it.

This defence of natural magic appeared in an otherwise sceptical account *Of the vanity and uncertainty of the sciences*, written in 1531 by Henry Cornelius Agrippa von Nettesheim. Similarly, for Giovanni Baptista della Porta, author of the leading manual of *Natural magick* (1658):

Magick is nothing else but the knowledge of the whole course of Nature. For, whilst we consider the Heavens, the Stars, the Elements, how they are moved, and how they are changed, by this means we find out the hidden secrecies of living creatures, of plants, of metals, and of their generation and corruption; so that this whole science seems merely to depend upon the view of Nature ... This Art, I say, is full of much vertue, of many secret mysteries; it openeth unto us the properties and qualities of hidden things, and the knowledge of the whole course of Nature; and it teacheth us by the agreement and the disagreement of things, either so to sunder them, or else to lay them so together by the mutual and fit applying of one thing to another, as thereby we do strange works, such as the vulgar sort call miracles, and such as men can neither well conceive, nor sufficiently admire ... Wherefore, as many of you as come to behold Magic, must be perswaded that the works of Magick are nothing else but the works of Nature, whose dutiful hand-maid magick is.

As can be seen from these quotations, the emphasis in natural magic is all on the empirical discovery of what *actives* act on what *passives* in order to bring about a desired result. These operations must be known to be reliable, repeatable, and predictable (notice Agrippa's 'anticipating results'). There is no concern, however, with knowing *how* these effects are brought about. The causes are expected to remain inscrutable because they cannot be discovered by experimental means. It is because of this last point that magicians referred to their subject as an art and not a science. *Science*, according to philosophers, was concerned with knowledge of causes, *art* was merely a knowledge of techniques and practices for producing various effects.

The logic underlying the magicians' approach to the discovery of natural phenomena was *inductive logic*—formulating general laws from specific observations. By the time Newton came to publish his *Principia*, inductive logic had been established as the most fruitful and reliable method for discovering the secrets of nature, thanks to the influence of Francis Bacon at the beginning of the century, and to the Royal Society at the end. Bacon himself was profoundly affected in his opinions by magical traditions, and it is this tradition, and Bacon's endorsement of it, which underwrites Newton's famous denial, 'hypotheses non fingo':

> But hitherto I have not been able to discover the cause of those properties of gravity from phenomena, and I feign no hypotheses; for whatever is not deduced from the phenomena is to be called a hypothesis, and hypotheses, whether metaphysical or physical, whether of occult qualities or mechanical, have no place in experimental philosophy. In this philosophy particular propositions are inferred from the phenomena and afterward rendered general by induction ... And to us it is enough that gravity does really exist and act according to the laws which we have explained, and abundantly serves to account for all the motions of the celestial bodies and of our sea.

The magician too feigned no hypotheses to explain the operation of the occult qualities he dealt with. He simply affirmed from his experience that they did 'really exist'.

Thus, the crucial difference between the occult qualities of the Scholastics and the occult qualities of the magical tradition was that in Aristotelian philosophy they were simply empty attempts to leave the concept of specific forms intact, with no further attempt to understand the workings of nature. In the magical tradition, however, the putative existence of an active power, an occult principle, was the cue for a series of experimental investigations. Even if these investigations could not determine the precise causal pathway by which those powers worked, they could make *manifest* not only that it did work but also all the different ways in which it worked, the particular circumstances of its efficient operation, and so on.

Newton, the natural magician

In a famous essay, published in 1947, John Maynard Keynes used his extensive knowledge of Newton's unpublished papers to argue that

Newton was the last of the great Renaissance magicians, 'the last wonder-child to whom the Magi could do sincere and appropriate homage'. Since then, research into the contents of Newton's personal library has revealed that, out of 1752 books, 170 were concerned with what we would consider to be magical subjects, and only 369 were scientific books. Most of these were alchemical works, but also included were Hermetic and Rosicrucian writings, a famous compendium of cabbalistic teachings, della Porta's encyclopaedic *Natural magick*, Cornelius Agrippa's *Occult philosophy*, and a number of lesser known magical texts including *The art of magic, or natural and artificial magic showing the effects, virtues and secrets in the elements, gems, stones, herbs and animals, according to certain figures of the stars and positions of the planets* (1631), and *An essay on the ancient and modern use ... of physical necklaces for distempers in children ...* (1719).

Lord Keynes was the first scholar to pay serious attention to Newton's marked obsession with alchemy, but he was clearly puzzled by it. Newton's alchemy was, according to Keynes, 'wholly devoid of scientific value'. From our stance today, Keynes here allowed the prejudices of his own time to cloud his judgement. Believing that alchemy was simply nonsense, Keynes assumed that Newton's obsession with it was an aberration—'Geniuses *are* very peculiar', Keynes wrote apologetically. When he discovered Newton's interest in alchemy, Keynes might have realized that our current perception of this ancient art has lost sight of what made it significant in seven-

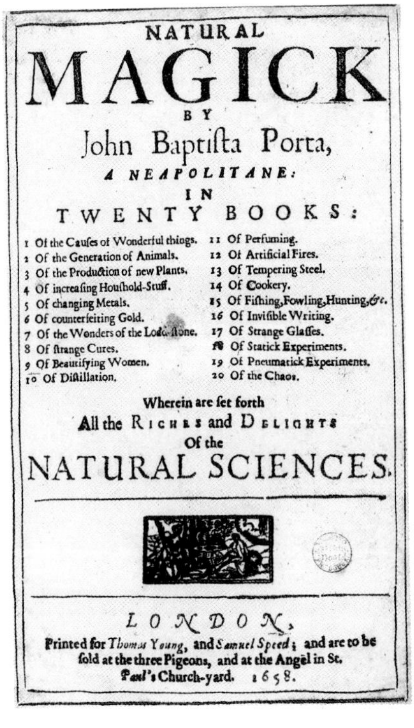
NATURAL
MAGICK
BY
John Baptiſta Porta,
A NEAPOLITANE:
IN
TWENTY BOOKS:

1 Of the Cauſes of Wonderful things.	11 Of Perfuming.
2 Of the Generation of Animals.	12 Of Artificial Fires.
3 Of the Production of new Plants.	13 Of Tempering Steel.
4 Of increaſing Houſhold-Stuff.	14 Of Cookery.
5 Of changing Metals.	15 Of Fiſhing, Fowling, Hunting, *&c.*
6 Of counterfeiting Gold.	16 Of Inviſible Writing.
7 Of the Wonders of the Lodeſtone.	17 Of Strange Glaſſes.
8 Of ſtrange Cures.	18 Of Statick Experiments.
9 Of Beautifying Women.	19 Of Pneumatick Experiments.
10 Of Diſtillation.	20 Of the Chaos.

Wherein are ſet forth
All the RICHES and DELIGHTS
Of the
NATURAL SCIENCES.

LONDON,
Printed for *Thomas Young*, and *Samuel Speed*; and are to be ſold at the three Pigeons, and at the Angel in St. Paul's Church-yard. 1658.

Della Porta's *Natural magick*, first published in Latin in 1558, was one of the most successful compendia of magic for over a century. Newton owned a copy of the 1651 Leiden edition. The book's subtitle spoke, revealingly, of *All the riches and delights of the natural sciences*, and its contents interpreted the word 'magic' liberally—the chapters ranged from discussions of *Strange Glasses* and *counterfeiting Gold* to *Beautifying Women* and *Cookery*.

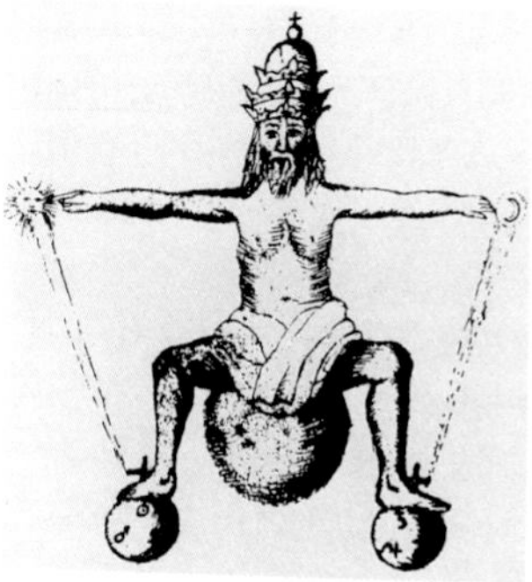

This drawing by Newton of *Jupiter enthroned* accompanies the copy, in his hand, of an unpublished alchemical work. The rays of influence from the Sun and Moon at Jupiter's hands to the orbs beneath his feet are reminiscent of the chains in Fludd's *Mirror of nature* (p. 126). Certainly, Newton's belief in alchemy testifies to his acceptance of the general idea of 'correspondences'. During the 1690s he wrote a commentary on *The emerald tablet*, a famous alchemical text attributed to Hermes Trismegistus himself, which included the important principle *The things below are as the things above.*

teenth-century eyes. Newton may have been very peculiar indeed, but he was no fool. If he felt that there was something worthwhile in alchemy then, from the perspective of his own time, he was probably right.

As we have seen above, Newton's concept of force, the major innovation of his scientific work, derived from concepts of occult powers in the natural magic tradition. There can be no doubt that the most important part of this tradition, for Newton's purposes, was *alchemy*. This is most easily seen, for example, by comparing Newton's *An hypothesis explaining the properties of light*, which was read to the Royal Society in 1675, with an alchemical work written by Newton sometime in the early 1670s. In *An hypothesis*, Newton suggested that all bodies may be composed of 'certain aethereal spirits, or vapours' condensed in different degrees and 'wrought into various forms'. This power of concretion and formation in nature was initiated by God with the command 'increase and multiply', so that nature 'became a complete imitator of the copies set her by the protoplast'. One of these putative spirits, the *ether*, is referred to variously as a 'humid active matter' and the '*succus nutritius* of the earth, or primary substance'. The second of these spirits, disseminated throughout the first, is *light*. 'Light and aether mutually act upon one another' we are told, 'generating fluids out of solids, and solids out of fluids' and much more besides. The incessant mutual interactions of these two spirits ensure that 'nature is a perpetual worker'.

All these ideas can be found in Newton's alchemical account *Of nature's obvious laws and processes in vegetation* (*c.* 1674). For example:

> ye aether is but a vehicle to some more active sp[iri]t. & ye bodys may bee concreted of both together, they may imbibe aether as well as air in gen-[er]ation & in y^t aether ye spt is intangled. This spt perhaps is ye body of light becaus both have a prodigious active principle, both are perpetuall workers.

Even Newton's mature pronouncements on the nature of light, published in the various editions of the *Opticks*, included the same kind of speculations about the chemical interaction of light and matter. In the influential *Queries* at the end of the *Opticks*, Query 5 asks, 'Do not Bodies and Light act mutually upon one another ...?', while Query 30 begins, 'Are not gross Bodies and Light convertible into one another, and may not Bodies receive much of their Activity from the Particles of Light which enter their composition?' Newton's train of speculations culminated in the final query, Query 31:

> Have not the small particles of Bodies certain Powers, Virtues, or Forces, by which they act at a distance, not only upon the Rays of Light ... but also upon one another for producing a great Part of the Phaenomena of Nature?

The ideas expressed in Query 31 show clear signs of descent from *An hypothesis* of 1675 and the alchemical speculations which preceded it, but they also can be seen as a reiteration of Newton's wish, in the Preface to the *Principia* which was quoted at the beginning of this chapter. The continuity is clear and undeniable. When, in 1687, Newton wrote 'I am induced by many reasons to suspect that [the phenomena of nature] may all depend upon certain forces', the reasons he had in mind were seemingly those which occurred to him during his alchemical investigations of the 1670s.

Newton's belief in the value of alchemy, and his willingness to defend and make use of occult qualities in his published work, clearly confirm Keynes' judgement that he was the last of the great magicians. Unlike Keynes, however, we must not fall into the trap of picturing Newton at the alchemical furnace with a wizard's cap on—a cap which he would doff as he stepped out of the elaboratory, in order to don the garb of the sober scientist. To see Newton, as Keynes did, 'with one foot in the Middle Ages and one foot treading a path for modern science', or as a great scientist who managed to keep his unfortunate obsession with alchemy from contaminating his scientific theories, is to miss the point entirely. We have every reason to suppose that, had Newton *not* been steeped in alchemical and other magical learning, he would never have proposed forces of attraction and repulsion between bodies as the major feature of his physical system. In Newton's day it was perfectly possible to believe that the key to understanding the universe was more likely to be found through the experimental investigations and inductive method of natural magicians than in the traditional natural philosophy of the Scholastics. We should not regard Newton as a split personality simply because *we* regard science and magic as incompatible approaches to the understanding of the world. Rather, we should recognize that *magic*, and even *science*, mean different things to different cultures.

Further reading

Those who remain unconvinced that the origins of the experimental method are to be found in the magical tradition should read, for penance, the eight volumes of evidence presented with the most meticulous scholarship by Lynn Thorndike, *A history of magic and experimental science*, Columbia University Press, New York, 1923–58. There is a recent general survey of the role of magic in the formation of modern science by Charles Webster, *From Paracelsus to Newton: magic and the making of modern science*, Cambridge University Press, Cambridge, 1982. The article by Lord Keynes which is discussed above is entitled 'Newton, the man', and was published in The Royal Society *Newton Tercentenary Celebrations*, Cambridge University Press, Cambridge, 1947, pp. 27–34. All that is known about Newton's library has been brought together in John Harrison, *The library of Isaac Newton*, Cambridge University Press, Cambridge, 1978. For an excellent summary of the role of Newton's alchemy in his development of the concept of force, see R. S. Westfall's paper 'Newton and alchemy' in *Occult and scientific mentalities in the Renaissance* (edited by Brian Vickers), Cambridge University Press, Cambridge, 1984, pp. 315–35.

At ye end of ye 4th Key 10

Although full many Artists still
At me their aim direct
Yet very few have had ye skill
My true force to detect.

In ye Manuall operations at ye end of ch 4.

Unable's wit all times to comprehend
Each thing wch Venus doth attain
No man soon finds it in his brain
Vain reason it exiles & far doth send.
Sure by its spirit onely all shall speed
So Mercury his office duely keep.

At ye end of chap 5

If me alone thou dost not know
Then a meet help on me bestow
Judge then & hearken to my lore
So shalt thou find what's in my powr.

At ye end of ye Microcosm.

Venus a hunting here you now do see
But if a hound should catch a hare then she
Here will much older grow affirm I dare
Whereof Don Mercury is well aware.
For Venus once begining to grow proud
Makes many hares grow monstrous fierce & wood
Wherefore o Mars draw out thy killing sword
That thy much loved Venus be not whoor'd.

CHAPTER SEVEN

The secret life of an alchemist

JAN GOLINSKI

Of all the subjects to which Isaac Newton devoted attention during his long and incessantly active intellectual career, his work on chemistry and alchemy is the least well understood. The image of Newton as chemist, still more of Newton as alchemist, is one that we find troubling and anomalous, in relation to his more familiar image as the pioneer of modern mechanics, cosmology, and optics. The picture of Newton which appeared on the English pound note (see p. 232), with the apple sprig at his shoulder, the prism and the reflecting telescope on a table at his elbow, and the *Principia* open on his knee, gives no hint of his lengthy labours at the furnace, or his intensive reading of the works of alchemists.

There are both good and bad reasons for this comparative neglect of Newton's alchemy and chemistry. The good reasons concern the sheer difficulty of interpreting the evidence. Newton published no complete work on chemistry, only fragmentary texts. Towards the end of his life, aspects of his chemical work did assume the form of a public doctrine, but for most of his career he kept his interest in this field strictly private. So the evidence that the historian has to use takes the form of manuscript notes. Very large quantities of these survive—it has been estimated that they amount to over one million words—although they are widely dispersed and only partially catalogued.

One of the most important of these manuscripts is a notebook in the library of Cambridge University, known affectionately to specialists by its call-number, *Additional MS* 3975. It contains Newton's record of a lengthy series of chemical experiments, apparently begun at the end of the 1660s, and continuing until the mid-1690s. This notebook has become the object of fairly intensive investigation by historians. As a result, we have gained some understanding of what Newton was doing, even if little is yet clear as to why he did it. The experiments remain difficult to decipher, since Newton gave few clues as to their rationale, and because they concern little-known reactions of metals such as gold, mercury, and lead, and of complex alloys that are not familiar to modern chemists.

Newton has here copied out the verse epigrams from an English alchemical manuscript, *Basil Valentine's mystery of the microcosm*, including a picture of hounds chasing hares which illustrates the symbolism of the final verse.

In addition to this notebook, and a few loose sheets on which Newton recorded the results of experiments, there are many hundreds of pages of Newton's non-experimental notes. Most of these are notes taken from his voluminous reading, including complete transcriptions of some short works, and numerous collections of extracts. There are also occasions (all too rare, from the historian's point of view) when

Newton attempted to synthesize some of his ideas. The largest collection of notes of this kind is presently in King's College, Cambridge. It returned to Cambridge through the generosity of Lord Keynes, half a century after the University had declined to accept them from Lord Portsmouth on the grounds that they were of *no scientific interest.*

It is easy to understand why this stern Victorian judgement was made, when one takes a look at what are now known as the Keynes Manuscripts. They pose all the normal problems of interpreting Newton's manuscripts, compounded by particular difficulties stemming from our ignorance of seventeenth-century alchemy. Newton had a number of bad habits which make his manuscript notes difficult to read—he revised and corrected them obsessively, writing on top of an existing text or upside down on the same sheet of paper; he made frequent transitions from Latin to English and back again; and he reused old scraps of paper for new notes, so that comments from widely separated periods of his career ended up in close proximity.

In the case of the alchemical manuscripts, there is the additional difficulty that we know very little about the writers from whom he was copying, and on whom he was commenting. This makes it hazardous to try to decide when Newton was being original, and when he was echoing a remark from one of the writers he had read. When historians read Newton's notes to find out what he thought of Robert Boyle and René Descartes, they can build on the fact that these philosophers are fairly well known. But faced with notes on figures such as Michael Maier, Michael Sendivogius, 'Eirenaeus Philalethes', and 'Basil Valentine', we start with an added disadvantage. *Basil Valentine* apparently did not exist; the writings attributed to this supposed fifteenth-century Benedictine monk actually date from the beginning of the seventeenth century. *Eirenaeus Philalethes* was a pseudonym, probably for the mid-seventeenth centurey writer George Starkey. Maier and Sendivogius are among the better-known of those alchemical writers whose works Newton read, although even they have received little scholarly attention. In many cases, Newton was commenting on works which were not even printed, but which he acquired as manuscripts, a fact which further hampers their identification.

Michael Maier (1568–1622) was a physician and a courtier of the Emperor Rudolph II in Prague. He wrote a number of books of alchemical emblems—drawings containing symbolic representations of the secrets of nature. Newton read Maier's works extensively, and took detailed notes from many of them.

So there are significant and genuine difficulties which confront us in trying to understand Newton's alchemy. Newton was probably better acquainted with the whole body of alchemical writing than anyone before him, and certainly than anyone since, and he interpreted those writings in conjunction with experimental investigations of a kind which modern chemistry has never repeated. Since the 1970s, when the subject was put on the historians' agenda by P. M. Rattansi and R. S. Westfall, serious scholarly attention has begun to be devoted to Newton's alchemy. As a result, some of his aims and preconceptions, and the motives for some of his experimental inves-

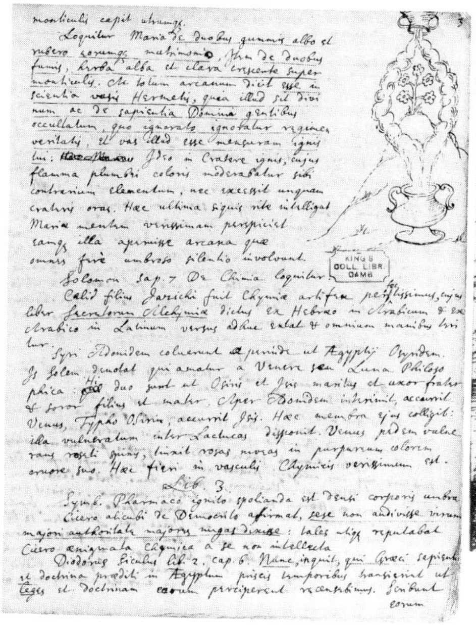

Newton's summary of Book II of Maier's *Symbolae aureae mensae* (1617), with his copy of part of an illustration. The original Maier illustration shows Maria the Jewess, a legendary figure in the history of alchemy (and the eponymous originator of the *Bain Marie*). The device on the right, which Newton copied, represents Maria's basic doctrine: *One becomes two, two becomes three, and by means of the third and fourth achieves unity; thus two are but one.*

tigations, are beginning to become clear. In particular, Betty Jo Dobbs has broken entirely new ground in this respect in her book *The foundations of Newton's alchemy* (1975) and in subsequent articles. Much of what appears here is strongly indebted to her work.

Faced with these very real difficulties, it seems unnecessary to add to them the kind of confused embarrassment which has sometimes surrounded discussion of Newton's alchemical interests. The classical expression of this was by his nineteenth-century biographer, Sir David Brewster, who announced:

> There is no problem of more difficult solution than that which relates to the belief in alchemy ... by men of high character and lofty attainments.

For Brewster, the disparity between the baseness of alchemy and the nobility of mathematics was so stark and so self evident that he could only conclude that Newton's interest in the former reflected a 'peculiar bent of his mind', that same mind which was otherwise 'of such power, and so nobly occupied with the abstractions of geometry'.

Brewster's awkward inability to face the implications of the fact that Newton was interested in alchemy has been shared by some historians nearer to our own time. In their 1958 survey of what they were careful to call 'Newton's *chemical* experiments', Marie Boas and A. R. Hall appeared excessively anxious not to admit that Newton was any kind of alchemist. He was at all times, they insisted, *a rational, experimental scientist*, concerned only with the experimental study of the structure of matter, and preserving a decent scepticism towards the alchemists whose texts he read. Unfortunately for their thesis, more recent research has made some of these claims untenable. It is now clear that Newton's intensive reading of alchemical authors did not follow after 'the epoch of [his] great discoveries' (as Boas and Hall had claimed), but was contemporaneous with them. It is also apparent that this reading was an active interpretative process, one which would have made no sense at all if Newton had believed that 'many alchemical writers were at best but dupes of themselves or of others, and at worst brazen liars and cheats'.

For Boas and Hall, even to describe what Newton was doing as *alchemy* would be to invoke undesirable and embarrassing connotations. They insisted that Newton was not 'in any admissible sense of the word an alchemist', implying that the admissible senses of the term should be those which would exclude Newton. Their remark highlighted the difficulty of defining what we mean by 'alchemy', and deciding whether the term is an appropriate one to apply to Newton's work. Historians have still not achieved any degree of consensus as to how this difficulty should be resolved. Disagreements as to whether Newton was really an 'alchemist' continue, and depend very largely upon the chosen definition of the term.

To define *alchemy*, and to distinguish it from *chemistry* in this period, may in fact be inappropriate. The seventeenth century saw very extensive changes in all aspects of the conceptual and practical manipulation of matter. Prolonged debates occurred about the realm of phenomena which it was proper for chemists to study, the relationship of their studies to religion and natural philosophy, the achievability of the technological aims which they espoused (in such fields as medicine, agriculture, and metallurgy), and the way in which chemical experience should be conveyed in writing. Newton's work raised all of these issues at a time when little agreement existed as to how they should be resolved. It therefore seems advisable not to reduce him either to an *alchemist* or to a *chemist*, but rather to try to grasp the full complexity of his work and the historical context in which he operated.

Alchemy as secret work

In trying to do justice to Newton's work in this field, there is one distinction which seems more relevant and more fertile than that between 'alchemy' and 'chemistry', and it is upon this that the following argument will be based. It is the distinction between chemical work as *private pursuit*, and as *public doctrine*.

When Newton began his interest in alchemy, and for the 30 years that he pursued it in his study and laboratory in Trinity College, it was a private passion. For thousands of hours, he laboured with his furnace or pored over alchemical books, but he communicated virtually

Alchemy as theory and practice. The three alchemists in Maier's *Tripus aureus* (1618) discuss the theory of the art in a book-lined alcove, while an operative stokes the laboratory furnace.

nothing of what he was doing, except perhaps in intimate conversations with fellow devotees. In the mid-1690s, he moved to London and assumed a role on the public stage, becoming successively Warden and Master of the Royal Mint, and President of the Royal Society. At this important transition point in his life, he abandoned his laboratory experiments in chemistry, and apparently ceased to take an interest in alchemical books. As Newton became a man of authority, the patron of the nation's science, a public image of his scientific achievements was constructed and widely diffused. His alchemical interests were transmuted into the form of a public doctrine. Through the Royal Society, and Newton's growing network of disciples, a Newtonian chemical doctrine was fabricated, which was strongly influenced by his private investigations, but which concealed the circumstances of its origin.

This distinction between public and private in Newton's chemistry is related to one he himself made, in an important manuscript of the early 1670s, now preserved in the Smithsonian Institution in Washington, DC. In this manuscript, entitled *Of nature's obvious laws and processes in vegetation*, Newton distinguished 'vulgar chymistry' from a more sublime interest in the processes of vegetation—in other words, the processes of growth and life, which were thought to occur among metals as well as among plants and animals. 'Nature's actions are either vegetable or purely mechanical', he wrote. Art could imitate nature in either type of operation. The imitation of mechanical changes in nature would be common, or vulgar, chemistry, whereas the art of inducing vegetation was 'a more subtile secret & noble way of working'.

Newton's rooms at Trinity College, Cambridge, were to the right of the gatehouse, on the first floor. His laboratory was probably the shed that can be seen, in this contemporary engraving, at the end of the garden against the wall of the chapel.

It was that subtle, secret, and noble way of working that Newton was seeking to master in the course of his intensive chemical investigations. Each of these three terms was crucial to Newton's conception of his task. The work was subtle because it used nature's own agent of vegetation—a 'vegetable spirit', described as 'an exceeding subtile & unimaginably small portion of matter diffused through the masse wch if it were separated there would remain but a dead & inactive earth'. To bring this spirit under the control of human art was potentially to attain mastery of the processes of growth and maturation in the material world. This was a noble aim, because if it succeeded man would come to share in the power of God, who had created the spirit, and whose agent it was. But precisely because it was so sacred and potentially so powerful, this way of working also had to be kept secret; it could not be exposed to the eyes of 'the vulgar'.

This was the belief which motivated Newton's careful drawing of a veil of secrecy around his chemical investigations. His laboratory, in the garden attached to his rooms at the front of Trinity College, was a private place. In contrast with Robert Boyle, who kept a virtual open house and frequently admitted spectators to his laboratory, Newton allowed almost no one to visit him at the site of his chemical work. He mostly laboured alone, building his furnaces himself (without even the aid of a bricklayer), and teaching himself the basic chemical operations from scratch. This was a rare achievement in the seventeenth century, when most gentlemen who were interested in chemistry attended lectures on the subject, or hired an 'operator' to teach them. The only person whom Newton appears to have admitted to his laboratory was young Humphrey Newton, his assistant and amanuensis between 1685 and 1690. Writing to John Conduitt after Newton's death, Humphrey gave a memorable description of his master's chemical work. He related how 'About 6 weeks at Spring & 6 at ye fall ye fire in ye Elaboratory scarcely went out', with the two men taking turns to sit up overnight minding the furnaces. But it is apparent that Newton told Humphrey nothing about what the aims of the work were. 'What his Aim might be, I was not able to penetrate into', Humphrey confessed, adding, 'Nothing extraordinary, as I can Remember, happen'd in making his Experiments, wch if there did . . . I could not in ye least discern it'. Newton's chemical labours were a self-motivated, largely self-sustained, and almost entirely private activity.

Of course, Newton did occasionally share his chemical interests with others. But the striking thing about these few known instances of communication is how constrained they were. Newton received advice from a number of other chemists, but seems to have passed information to them only on a confidential basis. We know of a number of chemists from whom he received manuscripts of alchemical writings, and of an incident in 1696, when an anonymous Londoner, a contact of Robert Boyle, visited Newton in Cambridge to give him details of an alchemical process. The usual practice between alchemists was to trade secrets on a reciprocal basis, or (as it was put by Oswald Croll, an alchemical writer of the early seventeenth century) to 'Give something, and take something'. But if Newton did reciprocate the secrets he received on these occasions, what he said remained confidential. Newton shared with the chemists with whom he dealt a keen sense of the necessary privacy of chemical discourse.

On a number of occasions during his career, Newton expressed a reluctance to communicate speculative ideas about chemistry. The thoughts about an alchemical spirit which he shared with Boyle, in a letter written on 28 February 1679, were said to be not 'fit to be communicated to others'. Newton had been severely taken aback a few years earlier, when his paper *A new theory about light and colours* (1672) generated a prolonged and intense dispute, in which his claims had been subjected to sustained attack from six other natural philosophers. When he subsequently sent *An hypothesis explaining the properties of light* (1675) to Henry Oldenburg (the Secretary of the Royal Society), he insisted that he wished to avoid 'such troublesome,

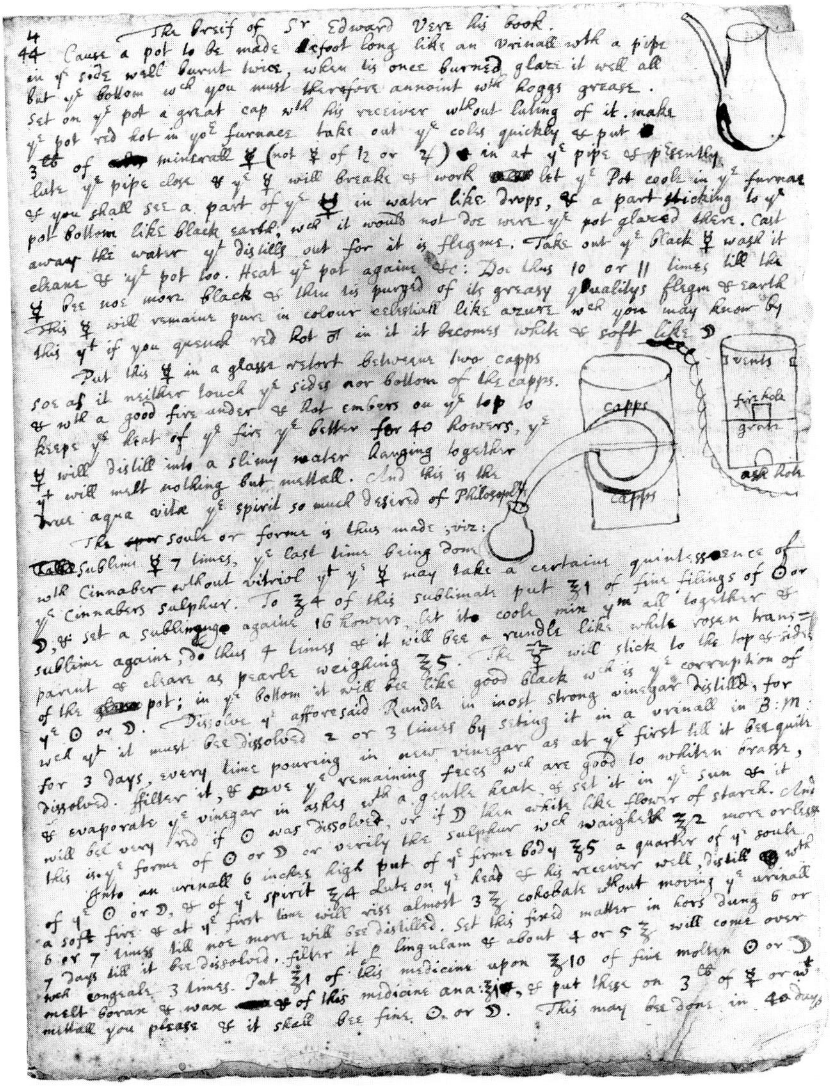
The Breif of Sr Edward Vere his book.
4
44 Cause a pot to be made a foot long like an Vrinall wth a pipe
in ye side well burnt twice, when tis once burned glaze it well all
but ye bottom wch you must therefore annoint wth hoggs grease.
Set on ye pot a great cap wth his receiver without luting of it. make
ye pot red hot in ye furnace take out ye coles quickly & put
3 lb of [illegible] minerall ☿ (not ☿ of ♄ or ♃) in at ye pipe & presently
lute ye pipe close & ye ☿ will breake & work let ye Pot coole in ye furnace
& you shall see a part of ye ☿ in water like drops, & a part sticking to ye
pot bottom like black earth, wch it would not doe were ye pot glazed there. Cast
away the water yt distills out for it is flegme. Take out ye black ☿ wash it
cleane & ye pot too. Heat ye pot againe &c: Doe thus 10 or 11 times till the
☿ bee noe more black & then tis purged of its greasy qualitys flegm & earth
this ☿ will remaine pure in colour celestiall like azure wch you may know by
this yt if you quench red hot ♂ in it it becomes white & soft like ☽
Put this ☿ in a glasse retort betweene two capps
soe as it neither touch ye sides nor bottom of the capps.
& wth a good fire under & hot embers on ye top to
keepe ye heat of ye fire ye better for 40 howers, ye
☿ will distill into a slimy water hanging together
yt will melt nothing but mettall. And this is the
true aqua vitæ ye spirit so much desired of Philosophers
The soule or forme is thus made; viz:
Sublime ☿ 7 times, ye last time being done
wth Cinnaber without vitriol yt ye ☿ may take a certaine quintessence of
ye Cinnabers sulphur. To ℥4 of this sublimate put ℥1 of fine filings of ☉ or
☽, & set a sublimeing againe 16 howers, let it coole mix ym all together &
sublime againe, do thus 4 times & it will bee a rundle like white rosen trans=
parent & cleare as pearle weighing ℥5. The ☿ will stick to the top & sides
of the pot; in ye bottom it will bee like good black wch is ye corruption of
ye ☉ or ☽. Dissolve ye afforesaid Rundle in most strong vinegar distilld, for
wch yt it must bee dissolved 2 or 3 times by setting it in a vrinall in B:M:
for 3 days, every time pouring in new vinegar as at ye first till it bee quite
dissolved. ffilter it, & save ye remaining feces wch are good to whiten brasse,
& evaporate ye vinegar in ashes wth a gentle heat, & set it in ye sun & it
will bee very red if ☉ was dissolved, or if ☽ then white like flower of starch. And
this is ye forme of ☉ or ☽ or verily the sulphur wch waigheth ℥2 more or less
Into an urinall 6 inches high put of ye firme body ℥5 a quarter of ye soule
of ye ☉ or ☽, & of ye spirit ℥4 lute on ye head & his receiver well, distill wth
a soft fire & at ye first time will rise almost 3℥ cohobate without moving ye urinall
6 or 7 times till noe more will bee distilled. Set this fixed matter in hors dung 6 or
7 days till it bee dissolved, filter it p lingulam & about 4 or 5℥ will come over
wch congeale 3 times. Put ℥1 of this medicine upon ℥10 of fine molten ☉ or ☽
melt borax & wax & of this medicine ana ℥1, & put these on 3 lb of ☿ or wt
mettall you please & it shall bee fine ☉ or ☽. This may bee done in 40 days

In this page of Newton's alchemical notes, he has copied instructions for operations from a manuscript, *The work of an old priest*.

insignificant disputes', a stipulation that did not save him from further criticism at the hands of Robert Hooke.

So a general aversion to controversy could be part of the reason for Newton's reluctance to publish his chemical speculations. But there was probably also a more specific reason. Newton held the conviction, which he apparently shared with Boyle, that it was proper that certain secret and 'noble' subjects should not be discussed too publicly. When Boyle published a paper in the Royal Society's *Philosophical Transactions* in 1676, describing a preparation of mercury which generated heat when mixed with gold, Newton dispatched a letter to Oldenburg recalling Boyle to his obligation to preserve discretion:

The noble author, since he has thought fit to reveal himself so far, does prudently in being reserved in the rest ... But yet because the [subject] ...

> has been thought fit to be concealed by others that have known it, and therefore may possibly be an inlet to something more noble, not to be communicated without immense damage to the world . . . therefore I question not, but that the great wisdom of the noble author will sway him to high silence, till he shall be resolved of what consequence the thing may be.

This has sometimes been read as indicating a disparity between Newton and Boyle as to the proper extent of communication in chemistry; however, it was probably more like a reminder to Boyle of the value of 'high silence', which both men respected. In the paper Newton referred to, Boyle had admitted to having concealed some details of the preparation, and had mentioned the 'political inconveniences that may ensue', if fuller information were freely revealed. The correspondence between Newton and John Locke that followed Boyle's death in 1691 reveals that Newton and Boyle had entered into a pact to share knowledge about the mercury preparation, and not to communicate it to others. Practices of privacy and confidentiality, particularly where 'noble' information was concerned, were among the norms and proprieties of chemical discourse, which Newton and Boyle to a large extent shared. For Newton, privacy was both a necessary condition for his laboratory researches, and an accepted constraint on the extent of chemical communication. Knowledge of the 'subtle' and 'noble' powers of matter was legitimately to be withheld from the vulgar gaze; it was not proper to discuss such sacred topics in full public view.

Techniques of interpretation

The cultivation of secrecy had a further importance for Newton in relation to his method of interpreting the tradition of alchemical texts,

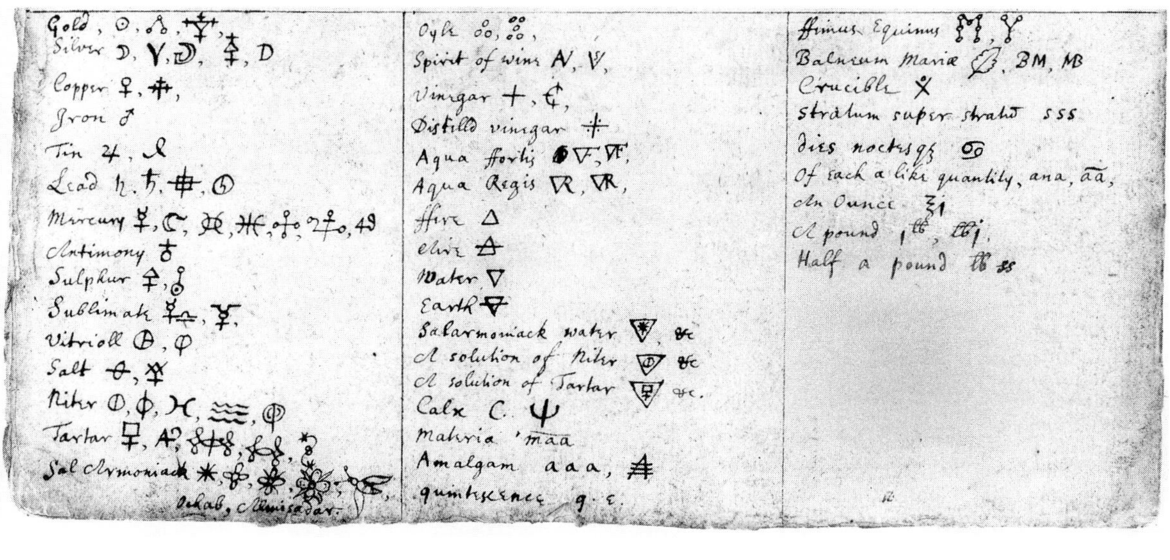

As part of his efforts to plumb the alchemical literature, Newton made this list of alchemical symbols.

and of orienting himself to them. In doing this, Newton believed that he was penetrating a secret tradition of knowledge, which had hitherto been protected from the scrutiny of the vulgar by its deliberately arcane language. By decoding this symbolic language, he sought to enrol himself among the ranks of the initiates of the ancient alchemical tradition.

As already indicated, Newton's acquaintance with the works of alchemical authors was of unparalleled extent and intimacy. What can be called 'intensive' and 'extensive' practices of reading both had a role in his strategy of interpretation of these writings. *Intensive* reading was necessary to penetrate the symbolic vocabulary of the texts, to 'open' them, as chemical substances were to be 'opened', and to expose their inner core of meaning. *Extensive* reading was required to collate together accounts from many different texts, in order to approach what Newton conceived as a single underlying truth.

A clear example of Newton's practice of extensive reading was his compilation of a series of lexicons or dictionaries, as a way of making sense of alchemical language. The first of these was the *Chemical dictionary* of the late 1660s, in which he attempted to grasp the basic terminology of chemical substances and operations. At a more advanced stage of his studies, between the early 1680s and the early 1690s, he drafted three successive versions of a more extensive *Index chemicus*. Each version was an expansion of the previous one, incorporating more headings of alchemical terms, and bringing to bear on each a larger number of references from an ever-expanding programme of reading. The final version cites at least 100 authors and 150 works, giving more than 5000 page-references under nearly 900 headings. Such an enormous undertaking testifies to Newton's strong conviction that a coherent system of terminology could be constructed out of the

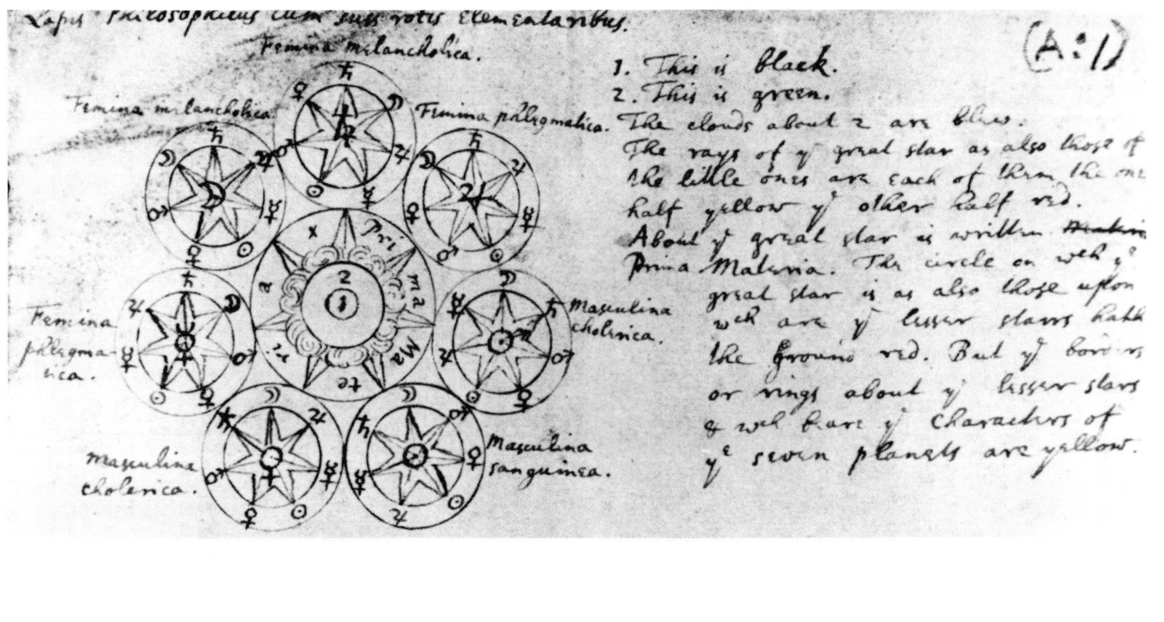

Newton copied a diagram of the *Philosopher's Stone*, the active principle of alchemy, together with a set of colouring instructions.

alchemical textual tradition, and that each writer had presented an aspect of a single fundamental doctrine.

Newton's intensive reading was governed by the same conviction. He devoted sustained efforts over many years to decoding the obscure descriptions of writers such as Philalethes, Sir George Ripley, and Nicholas Flamel—descriptions which used phrases like *the green lion, the doves of Diana*, and *Jove's eagle*. He also tried to decipher the emblematic illustrations of Michael Maier, which portrayed mythological characters in dramatic situations, and which Newton was convinced were complex allegories of alchemical processes. His delight when he felt he had cracked part of the code overflowed in passages like the following, from his annotations in his copy of Philalethes' *Secrets reveal'd*:

> about ye middle of ye Regimen of [tin] fflamel teaches to draw of[f] Azoth ... & imbibe Laton therewith seven times & this he calls washing of Laton, putting ye mother in the belly of her infant, sowing the Dragon's teeth in ye earth to make armed men spring up, & pouring the broth of Medea on ye Dragons of Cholchos to get the horn of Amalthea, & overcoming ye enchanted Bulls wch cast fire & smoke out of their nostrills.

To decode this elaborate and imaginative alchemical symbolism required very considerable labour on Newton's behalf, and in order to invest such labour he had to accept the plausibility of the alchemists' claim that they had inscribed a fundamental truth beneath the artful extravagance of their symbolism. Newton explicitly accepted that this was the case, that the alchemical writings were constructed to conceal sacred and powerful truths from the unworthy, which he frequently glossed as *the vulgar*, while making them available to the penetrating scrutiny of the elect. Secrecy thus played an essential role in Newton's interpretation of alchemical texts; it was in effect the *raison d'être* of this technique. Precisely because it was secret, the alchemical tradition had to contain valuable and powerful knowledge, which made it worth attempting to comprehend. The arcaneness of their style was the guarantee that alchemical writings spoke a profound and ancient truth.

For Newton, the truth of the tradition had a role which complemented that of the truth of experience. Newton oscillated in the course of his alchemical investigations between textual interpretation and concrete manipulations of matter. Dobbs has described in detail five series of experiments which Newton performed in the early 1670s, each of which involved him in a complex process of translation between the symbolic language of the alchemists and the results of his own experimental work. Newton devoted intensive scrutiny to both the textual and the experiential realm, and ascribed to each its appropriate and complementary degree of authority in relation to his ongoing research.

Alchemy and theology

To understand this process better, we need to relate what Newton was doing in his alchemy to his concurrent researches in theology, which are the subject of John Brooke's chapter. Newton's most concentrated work on the interpretation of the alchemists and of the scriptures occurred during the same period of his life—broadly, the 1670s and 1680s. We know almost nothing about the connections which Newton perceived between these fields, but there are two possible links which seem to warrant further consideration.

The first is the comparison of the methods of interpretation in the two fields. In both alchemy and theology, Newton believed that a pure ancient doctrine had been corrupted in the course of its transmission through history, but that it could be recovered by intensive interpretative effort devoted to a wide range of texts. His method for interpreting scriptural prophecies, explained at the beginning of his unpublished manuscript on the subject, could equally have described his approach to the alchemical writings. He was certain that all of the prophets had

Newton believed that alchemical writings preserved a secret knowledge which had been revealed by God. The intimate connection which alchemists perceived between chemical manipulations and divine worship is shown in this plate from Heinrich Khunrath's *Amphitheatrum sapientiae aeternae* (1598). The 'oratorium' (place to pray) stands opposite the 'laboratorium' (place to work). The musical instruments, prominently displayed beside the alchemical equipment, are a reminder of the importance of *harmony* in the mystical traditions.

written in 'one & the same mystical language', which was 'as certain & definite in its signification as is the vulgar language of any nation whatsoever'. He went on:

> The Rule I have followed has been to compare the several mystical places of scripture where the same prophetical phrase or type is used & to fix such a signification to that phrase as agrees best with all the places.

This was very much the same method as he had used to compile his alchemical lexicon.

The second area of connection between alchemy and theology emerged from this kind of process of interpretation. As had many before him in the seventeenth century, Newton came to believe that the account of Creation presented in Genesis was an allegorical description of an alchemical process. In the mid-1670s he copied a manuscript note ascribed to 'Robert Lane', which begins:

> It may seem an admirable & new paradox y^{t} Alchemy should have concurrence wth Antiquity and Theology; ye one seeming merely humane & ye other divine; & yet Moses, y^{t} ancient Theologue describing and expressing y^{e} most wonderful Architecture of this great world tells us y^{t} y^{e} spirit of God moved upon y^{e} waters wch was an indigested chaos, or mass created before by God.

An emblem symbolizing the difficulties of the alchemical quest, from Maier's *Atalanta fugiens* (1618): *He who tries to penetrate the philosophical rose garden without a key, resembles a man who wants to walk without feet.*

Out of this chaos, 'God's great Alchemy' created the order of the world, manipulating matter by means of the spirit as the alchemist tried to do in the laboratory. The alchemist's work was thus analogous to the divine activity at the Creation: both achieved their effects through the manipulation of the subtle vegetative spirit. As Newton explained in a manuscript note from the 1680s:

> [J]ust as the world was created from dark Chaos through the bringing forth of the light and through the separation of the aery firmament and of the waters from the earth, so our work brings forth the beginning out of black chaos and its first matter through the separation of the elements and the illumination of matter.

Newton's researches in alchemy and theology were thus simultaneous and interconnected. In both cases, Newton was engaged in a private process of textual interpretation, devoted to uncovering a secret truth that had been distorted and concealed by its overlying linguistic form. In the case of alchemy, there was the further dimension of his ongoing practice in the laboratory, which was equally intensive and equally private. Newton had taken to heart the injunction he copied from one of his alchemical manuscripts: '*This may be done in your chamber as privately as you will, & it is a great secret*'.

From private to public

There came a point when Newton emerged from the privacy of his chamber, and assumed a role on the public stage. After 1696, when he moved to London, he seems to have abandoned his work on alchemy as he adopted the persona of civil servant, scientific patron and national celebrity. The remainder of this chapter discusses how he constructed a public doctrine out of his hitherto private chemical work, during this stage of his career. This was a problem of *rhetoric*, of using the appropriate techniques to persuade people through public discourse. It was a process which involved manipulating personal relations, experimental apparatus, and written language to convert an audience.

As we have already seen, Newton had previously communicated his chemical ideas only within a limited circle of acquaintances. His rhetoric on these occasions was sometimes strikingly modest. For example, *An hypothesis explaining the properties of light* included the disclaimer:

> while I am describing this I shall sometimes, to avoid circumlocution and to represent it more conveniently, speak of it as if I assumed it and propounded it to be believed ... [But] no man may confound this with my other discourses, or measure the certainty of one by the other, or think me obliged to answer objections.

This was a curious strategy for verbal persuasion. Newton was trying to win over his readers, while avoiding defending himself in debate. He wanted somehow to convey his authority, while absenting himself as author from the scene of dispute. In the event, this rhetorical strategy collapsed. Presumably realizing that not everyone would accept or be convinced by his disclaimer of authorial responsibility (probably the correct assumption in the case of Robert Hooke, at least), Newton refused Henry Oldenburg's request to publish the paper.

Similar disclaimers of responsibility occurred in other letters of Newton's which touched on chemical matters. His 1679 letter to Boyle about the ether ended:

> you will easily discern, whether in these conjectures there be any degree of probability, which is all I aim at. For my own part, I have so little fancy to things of this nature, that, had not your encouragement moved me to it, I should never, I think, have thus far set pen to paper about them.

Likewise a 1681 letter to Thomas Burnet, in which Newton used some of his ideas on the creation as a chemical process, concluded, 'I have not set down anything I have well considered, or will undertake to defend'. Such claims that he had not seriously considered these matters can hardly be taken at face value, in view of the considerable manuscript evidence that he had done so. These statements are better read as elements of the peculiar form of rhetoric which Newton evidently thought appropriate to subjects such as chemistry. He developed a strategy to persuade his readers without explicitly staking his authority on what he said. With readers who were personally known to him and respected him, such as Boyle and Burnet, this strategy was reasonably effective. But with others, such as Hooke, it failed, since Newton could not at this time command the resources to convert everyone to his point of view.

After 1703, however, when his assumption of the Presidency of the Royal Society closely followed the death of his long-standing rival Hooke, Newton gradually accrued more of the means which enabled him to establish and diffuse his natural philosophy. *Newtonianism* had its origin in Newton's mobilization of the social resources which his position conferred, and his rhetoric gained a new strength and effectiveness thereby.

Before 1703, Newton had already begun to build a network of disciples, through exerting his influence on their behalf. In 1692, he secured for David Gregory the Savilian Chair of Astronomy at Oxford, and played a leading role in appointing his favoured candidates to lectureships in mathematics at Christ's Hospital. Around the time that he became President of the Royal Society, he manoeuvred other disciples into important positions, William Whiston into his old Lucasian Chair at Cambridge, and Edmond Halley into the Savilian Chair of Geometry at Oxford. The Royal Society offered him further opportunities to extend the scope of his patronage. Halley, James Jurin, and John Machin were all employed as Secretaries to the Society. Francis Hauksbee and J. T. Desaguliers assumed the vital role of demonstrators of experiments, carrying through programmes of experimental enquiry at Newton's instigation, and being paid according to their results.

Newtonianism as a system of public doctrine was constructed socially through the work of this network. Disciples, such as Henry Pemberton and Colin Maclaurin, wrote textbooks to disseminate and simplify the doctrines of their mentor. Hauksbee and Desaguliers sustained a programme of demonstrations to establish publicly the experimental basis of his theories. For example, as Derek Gjertsen mentioned in his chapter, Hauksbee re-staged the *experimentum crucis* in 1715 for an audience of visiting French academicians, to resolve the controversy which had followed Newton's original announcement of his theory of light and colours in 1672. The formation of an identifiable party among Newton's disciples was one factor in stimulating and maintaining the dispute with Leibniz, which began over the issue of priority in the invention of the calculus, and culminated in the wide-ranging philosophical debate between Samuel Clarke and Leibniz in 1715–16.

The Newtonian doctrine in chemistry was constructed as part of this overall social process. It was initially proposed speculatively, with the usual disclaimers of authorial responsibility, in the *Queries* added in 1706 to the Latin translation of Newton's *Opticks*. The plausibility of the doctrine was bolstered by a series of experimental demonstrations by Hauksbee and Desaguliers, showing the existence of microscopic forces of attraction. It was subsequently taken up and amplified in texts by Newton's followers, John Keill and John Freind, who rested their claims on his personal authority, and proved their loyalty by enrolling themselves on his behalf in the controversy with Leibniz.

Newton introduced his chemical speculations into print in Query 23 of the Latin *Opticks*, which became (with some modifications) Query 31 of the second English edition in 1717. He proposed that microscopic analogues of the force of gravity, acting between the tiny particles of which matter was composed, could explain a variety of chemical phenomena. From his own practical experience, he illustrated his claims by citing examples of precipitation, deliquescence, and displacement reactions among metals. As with Newton's previous writings on chemistry, his proposals were advanced in what was labelled as a hypothetical, speculative style. The *Queries* were constructed as a series of rhetorical questions, in order to insinuate the answers, without actually stating them authoritatively.

In the 1717 version of the *Queries*, Newton inserted an extra passage which had the effect of strengthening his original claim. Where he had earlier asserted the existence of microscopic forces only speculatively, he now insisted that they constituted observable phenomena,

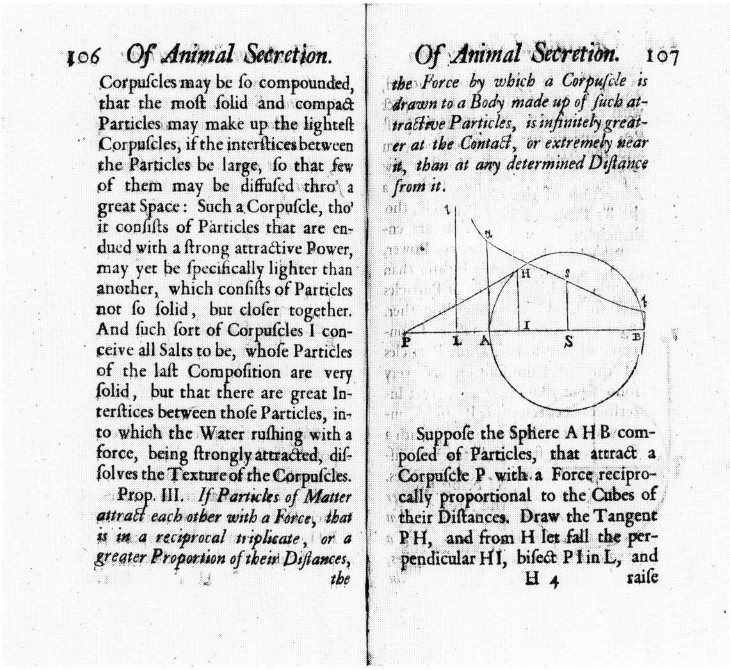

106 *Of Animal Secretion.*

Corpuſcles may be ſo compounded, that the moſt ſolid and compact Particles may make up the lighteſt Corpuſcles, if the interſtices between the Particles be large, ſo that few of them may be diffuſed thro' a great Space: Such a Corpuſcle, tho' it conſiſts of Particles that are endued with a ſtrong attractive Power, may yet be ſpecifically lighter than another, which conſiſts of Particles not ſo ſolid, but cloſer together. And ſuch ſort of Corpuſcles I conceive all Salts to be, whoſe Particles of the laſt Compoſition are very ſolid, but that there are great Interſtices between thoſe Particles, into which the Water ruſhing with a force, being ſtrongly attracted, diſſolves the Texture of the Corpuſcles.

Prop. III. *If Particles of Matter attract each other with a Force, that is in a reciprocal triplicate, or a greater Proportion of their Diſtances,* the

Of Animal Secretion. 107

the Force by which a Corpuſcle is drawn to a Body made up of ſuch attractive Particles, is infinitely greater at the Contact, or extremely near it, than at any determined Diſtance from it.

Suppoſe the Sphere A H B compoſed of Particles, that attract a Corpuſcle P with a Force reciprocally proportional to the Cubes of their Diſtances. Draw the Tangent P H, and from H let fall the perpendicular H I, biſect P I in L, and

H 4 raiſe

A Newtonian physiology was developed by John Keill's brother James. His *Account of animal secretion* (1708), fully equipped with axioms, theorems, and attractive forces, combined Newtonian chemistry with an account of physiological phenomena, and earned him a Fellowship of the Royal Society in 1712.

some aspects of which had long 'been observed by vulgar eyes', and only the causes of which were hypothetical. This strengthened claim of the existence of microscopic forces reflected the successes of the continuing programme to produce them experimentally in the Royal Society. Through the efforts of Hauksbee and Desaguliers, experimental manifestations of forces of electrical attraction, capillarity, and cohesion, had all become regularly reproducible. Although direct demonstrations of chemical forces had not been achieved, their plausibility was heightened by these other experimental successes.

As his chemical claims gained further experimental support, albeit of an indirect kind, Newton's authorial presence also came to be asserted more widely and more weightily in the works of his followers. The relevance of microscopic forces for chemical phenomena was restated in John Keill's 1708 paper in the *Philosophical Transactions*, and in John Freind's *Chymical lectures*, originally given in Oxford and first published in Latin in 1709. In both cases, the doctrine was set out in the form of axioms and deductions, and the axioms were made to depend very firmly on the personal authority of Newton. Freind asserted that Newton's experiments were '*evident to the Sense of all Mankind*', and that the principles he drew from them were '*demonstrative Conclusions*'. All that remained was to put the general principle of an attractive force into practice in the area of chemistry.

In relying on Newton in this way, Freind rested the credit of his own work on the personal authority of his mentor. This had the advantage of enabling him to evade the crucial questions of the relations between chemical and other microscopic forces, and the actual experimental evidence for their existence. The link between gravity and microscopic forces could only be one of analogy, since (as Keill had pointed out) the forces had to obey different distance-relation laws, gravitation varying as $1/r^2$, while chemical forces varied as $1/r^n$, with n greater than 2.

Keill and Freind's claim, that Newton had demonstratively established the existence of chemically active forces, was thus contestable. It was duly contested by Leibniz and his followers. In a highly critical anonymous review of Freind's work which appeared in the Continental journal *Acta Eruditorum* (1710) it was dismissed as a return to *fantastic scholastic philosophy*. In the controversy which followed, Keill and Freind sought to identify their work even more closely with Newton's, thereby cementing their solidarity with other members of the Newtonian party, and attracting the patronage of their master further to advance their careers. Keill was helped by Newton to become Savilian Professor of Astronomy at Oxford, and *Royal Decypherer* to Queen Anne. Freind was elected a Fellow of the Royal Society, and was given Newton's support in building a successful medical career.

The construction of a public image

So the establishment of Newtonian chemistry as a public doctrine was a complex but thoroughly social process. Newton became the epitome of a public figure, a patron in both social and scientific terms. He was characterized by Freind as a patron of natural philosophy as a whole, one whose patronage consisted in dispensing the results of his own investigations to provide the principles of new fields of enquiry. From the evasive private author, Newton had been transformed into a public authority. As his network of disciples was extended, as his clients produced new experimental phenomena to support his speculative claims, and as the solidarity of his party was consolidated in the dispute with Leibniz, Newtonian chemistry was constructed and strengthened as a public system of belief. Its strength was based on the status of Newton as public man and source of philosophical enlightenment, or (as he was addressed in flattering terms by a group of provincial natural philosophers) as '*the great Ornament of the Country and Light of the World*'.

Newton's chemistry had thus been transformed from a private passion to a public doctrine, just as he had himself made the transition from a secretive and reserved individual to a patron of the nation's science. He had sought to abstract chemical theory from its roots in an obscure tradition, and to found it upon replicable public phenomena. Removed from their origins in a doctrine kept secret from the 'vulgar',

The alchemist following in the footsteps of nature, from *Atalanta fugiens*. The caption reads: *May nature, reason, experiment and reading be the guide, staff, spectacles and lamp for him who participates in chemistry*.

the truths of chemistry were to be made 'evident to the Sense of all Mankind'. Newton's ideas were communicated more forcefully and more effectively as he drew allies from his network of disciples who, with their textbooks and experimental work, lent support to his theory.

But acceptance of Newton's chemical doctrines was not universal, and some of the resistance which occurred stemmed from the problems inherent in the transition from private to public realms. The dispute with Leibniz showed that some of Newton's contemporaries were suspicious of the apparently secret sources of his public philosophical authority. Leibniz charged Newton with having reintroduced *occult qualities* into natural philosophy, by invoking the notion of an attractive force to explain natural phenomena. The basis of this charge was the assertion that forces of attraction were unintelligible, and could not be deduced from phenomena. Newton's defence was that the forces *were* phenomena, and that only their *causes* were hidden, and arguably 'occult'. Hence, he maintained, the existence of the forces could be demonstrated, as they had been in his own work and in the experimental programme of his disciples in the Royal Society.

Fundamentally, what was in dispute was whether certain entities (forces of attraction) had been manifested as phenomena—in other words, whether they had been publicly authenticated. Furthermore, the controversy was a contest for public authority between two natural philosophers. As Shapin (1981) and Thackray (1968) have shown, Newton and Leibniz were rivals for political preferment within the Hanoverian court. Leibniz' charge that Newton resorted to occult qualities had the effect of weakening the credibility of his opponent as a public figure. It was therefore impossible, politically and philosophically, for Newton to admit his indebtedness to a secret tradition of alchemical texts. Newton and his followers had to emphasize the observable status of his forces of attraction, and to conceal their origins in his private alchemical work.

This was the context in which the Enlightenment image of Newton was constructed. Newton came to be viewed and portrayed in the way which has dominated to this day, and which has been perpetuated on postage stamps and pound notes. As will be shown in later chapters, he was seen as a national figure, the patron of English science, and his work was presented exclusively in the form of a systematic doctrine, founded securely on experiments conducted in the public realm. In the course of the construction of *Newtonianism*, a new veil of concealment was drawn over Newton's private alchemical work. It has been the purpose of this chapter to lift that veil a little, to bring some light into the shadowy realm of privacy, and to open up the subject of the relations between private and public work in the development of science.

Further reading

For sharply contrasting assessments of the significance of Newton's work on alchemy and chemistry, compare P. M. Rattansi, 'Newton's alchemical studies', in *Science, medicine and society in the Renaissance*, Vol. 2 (edited by A. G. Debus), Heinemann, London, 1972, pp. 167–82; with Marie Boas, 'Newton's chemical papers', in *Isaac Newton's papers and letters on natural philosophy and related documents* (edited by I. B. Cohen), Harvard University Press, Cambridge, Mass., 1978, pp. 241–8.

The work of Betty Jo Dobbs has considerably augmented historians' knowledge of this subject. Her book *The foundations of Newton's alchemy*, Cambridge University Press, Cambridge, 1975, is the most authoritative work, although quite accessible to the general reader, and is available in paperback. Her article, 'Newton's alchemy and his theory of matter', *Isis*, 73 (1982), 511–28, provides a briefer survey of the field; and R. S. Westfall's paper 'Newton and alchemy', in *Occult and scientific mentalities in the Renaissance* (edited by Brian Vickers), Cambridge University Press, Cambridge, 1984, pp. 315–35, gives an up-to-date overview.

An influential article by J. E. McGuire and P. M. Rattansi, 'Newton and the pipes of Pan', *Notes and records of the Royal Society of London*, 21 (1966), 108–

43, discusses Newton's interpretation of ancient philosophy, a preoccupation which related closely to his alchemical work (see Chapter 9).

[illegible] 1662.

[illegible]	1	[illegible]	19
[illegible]	2	[illegible]	20
[illegible]	3	[illegible]	21
[illegible]	4	[illegible]	22
[illegible]	5	[illegible]	23
[illegible]	6	[illegible]	24
[illegible]	7	[illegible]	25
[illegible]	8	[illegible]	26
[illegible]	9	[illegible]	27
[illegible]	10	[illegible]	28
[illegible]	11	[illegible]	29
[illegible]	12	[illegible]	30
[illegible]	13	[illegible]	31
[illegible]	14	[illegible]	32
[illegible]	15	[illegible]	33
[illegible]	16	[illegible]	34
[illegible]	17	[illegible]	35
[illegible]	18	[illegible]	36
		[illegible]	37
		[illegible]	38
		[illegible]	39

CHAPTER EIGHT

The God of Isaac Newton

JOHN BROOKE

At first sight, there should be no problem in describing Newton's God. He gave public definitions of the deity which were exhaustive in their quest for precision. Perhaps the best known example of this occurs in the General Scholium to the 1713 edition of the *Principia*, where the Supreme God is defined as 'eternal, infinite, absolutely perfect'. As *Lord over all* He exercises dominion over His Creation and His servants. From that dominion it follows that He is a 'living, intelligent and powerful' Being—not merely powerful, but omnipotent and omniscient. By His omnipresence He constitutes space. In short, He never misses a trick, for He is *'all eye, all ear, all brain, all arm, all power to perceive, to understand, and to act'*.

At a rough count, Newton's definition of God ran to just over 800 words. Some of these were necessary to show that, whereas we can gain some idea of His attributes, His substance remains elusive. Some were necessary to make the point that divine attributes could only be understood through analogy or allegory. And still more were required to scotch the idea that God ruled as the *soul* of the world. This was an important clarification, because Newton had been fond of an analogy which purported to show that God, as Spirit, could act in the physical world just as human beings can move their limbs.

One of the problems with which advocates of a mechanical philosophy of nature had to contend was how to divest it of its potentially deistic, or even atheistic, connotations. If the universe ran like clockwork, as Descartes had proposed, what scope was left for divine activity? In a polemic directed against 'those who would exclude the Deity from intermeddling with matter', Robert Boyle addressed the problem by emphasizing the power of God to move matter directly, much as a human author is in direct control of what he writes, by the movement of a pen. Our ability to move our limbs at will is sufficient testimony to the fact that matter can be under the immediate control of the Supreme Mind. Newton had no qualms in accepting the analogy, but he came to see that, if taken too literally, it could imply that the physical universe was the body of God, and that would place him on the slippery slope towards pantheism.

How did Newton know, or claim to know, the attributes which should be assigned to God? One way of answering this question would be to trace Newton's manifold sources, and to explore the use he made of them. For example, the reference to God as all eye and all ear, seeing and hearing everything, occurred in Clement of Alexandria, one of

Striking evidence of Newton's teenage turpitude is this notebook where in 1662 he recorded his sins, using the same shorthand (*Shelton's system*) as used by Samuel Pepys for his diary. He apparently committed some 50 sins during his life up to Whit Sunday 1662, which ranged from swimming in a tub on the sabbath and *Making pies on Sunday night* to *Having uncleane thoughts words actions and dreamese*, and *Threatning my father and mother Smith to burne them and the house over them*.

Newton's favourite authorities from antiquity. But a rather different point lies behind the question. In the General Scholium, Newton claimed that God was known 'only by His most excellent contrivances of things and final causes'. If that statement is taken at face value, it seems to imply that Newton's theology was essentially a natural theology in which the God of nature is inferred from His works. From some of his theological manuscripts one is tempted to draw the same implication. He wrote, for example, that there is 'no way to come to ye knowledge of a Deity but by ye frame of nature'—although he added, seemingly as an afterthought, 'without revelation'.

But what is the status of that afterthought? To what extent was Newton's God a construct of natural theology, rather than the outcome of biblical exegesis? These are not pointless questions because R. S. Westfall, while acknowledging that Newton's God was not solely inferred from nature, has recently asserted that He was primarily a '*metaphysical projection of the Creation*'. There are, however, considerations which suggest that such a characterization can be misleading, if taken in isolation.

Let us approach the subject via the following questions:

- How did Newton get from nature to the divine attributes?
- How did Newton's theology influence his interpretation of nature?
- Were there parallels between his scientific and religious quests?
- In his theological manuscripts, what was Newton *against*?
- What was he *for*?

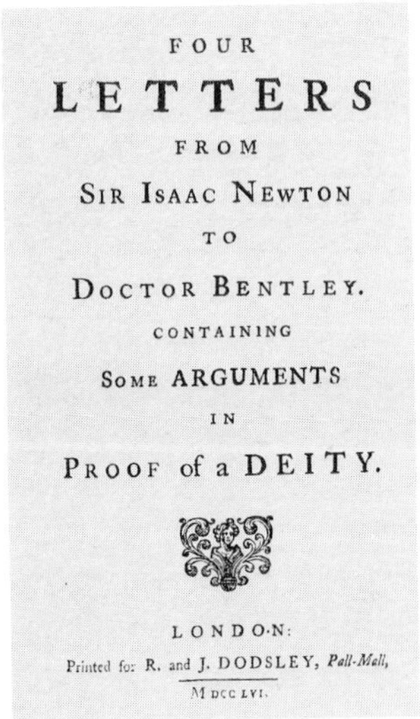
FOUR
LETTERS
FROM
SIR ISAAC NEWTON
TO
DOCTOR BENTLEY.
CONTAINING
SOME ARGUMENTS
IN
PROOF of a DEITY.

LONDON:
Printed for R. and J. DODSLEY, *Pall-Mall*,
MDCCLVI.

From nature to God

It is tempting to say that Newton's God was a projection of Creation, since he approved that style of reasoning which celebrated the existence of order and design in the natural world. His letters to Richard Bentley, the first of the Boyle lecturers, showed that he would assist a project which turned the *Principia* into an argument for providence. In the construction of nature, the will of an active God was manifest. Newton contrasted the aesthetics of planetary motion with the eccentric orbits of the comets, and insisted that there was no natural cause which could give the planets the correct transverse component of their velocity—just the right flick to ensure their assumption of concentric orbits. To make this system required 'a cause which understood and compared together the quantities of matter in the . . . Sun and planets and the gravitating powers resulting from thence'. It was a cause which had to understand and compare the

> several distances of the primary planets from the Sun and of the secondary

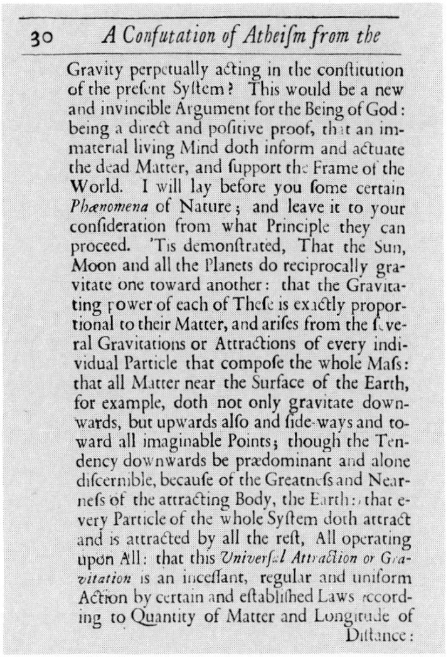
30 *A Confutation of Atheiſm from the*

Gravity perpetually acting in the conſtitution of the preſent Syſtem? This would be a new and invincible Argument for the Being of God: being a direct and poſitive proof, that an immaterial living Mind doth inform and actuate the dead Matter, and ſupport the Frame of the World. I will lay before you ſome certain *Phænomena* of Nature; and leave it to your conſideration from what Principle they can proceed. 'Tis demonſtrated, That the Sun, Moon and all the Planets do reciprocally gravitate one toward another: that the Gravitating power of each of Theſe is exactly proportional to their Matter, and ariſes from the ſeveral Gravitations or Attractions of every individual Particle that compoſe the whole Maſs: that all Matter near the Surface of the Earth, for example, doth not only gravitate downwards, but upwards alſo and ſide-ways and toward all imaginable Points; though the Tendency downwards be prædominant and alone diſcernible, becauſe of the Greatneſs and Nearneſs of the attracting Body, the Earth: that every Particle of the whole Syſtem doth attract and is attracted by all the reſt, All operating upon All: that this *Univerſal Attraction or Gravitation* is an inceſſant, regular and uniform Action by certain and eſtabliſhed Laws according to Quantity of Matter and Longitude of Diſtance:

A page of the Boyle Lecture *A Confutation of Atheism from the Origin and Frame of the World*, in which Bentley developed the argument that the action of gravity was *a new and invincible Argument for the Being of God*.

ones from Saturn, Jupiter, and the Earth, and the velocities with which these planets could revolve about those quantities of matter in the central bodies.

Such a feat argued for a cause '*not blind and fortuitous, but very well skilled in mechanics and geometry*'.

We can hardly escape the conclusion that Newton's God was not only a projection of Creation, but a projection of himself! Moreover, Newton appeared to believe that divine attributes could be read in the book of nature. The fact that the light of the fixed stars is one with the light of the Sun pointed to the unity of the Godhead; the fact that star systems had been placed at such immense distances from each other, preventing what would otherwise be an uncomfortable implosion, was a mark of wisdom and foresight.

Newton was not entirely uncritical of Bentley's plans. To prove the existence of God from the inclination of the Earth's axis seemed a bit askew. But he conceded that it did make the Earth habitable toward the poles. Newton claimed that in nature there was evidence of *choice*, not *chance*. Those very laws, which Pope was to immortalize as hitherto *hid in night*, required a legislator. It was as if Newton had said *Let God be!* and all was light. To those who might protest that such theistic inference belongs to the domain of theology or metaphysics, rather than natural philosophy, Newton had a direct, if unreasoned, reply. To discourse of God from the appearances of things 'does certainly belong to natural philosophy'.

The implications of that remark from the General Scholium are rather striking. If theistic discourse constitutes part of natural philosophy, it becomes anachronistic to ask how Newton *reconciled* his science with his religion. The right question is more likely to be: *how did his distinctive view of God's dominion, in both nature and history, affect his interpretation of nature?* If it affected it at all, would it not then be simplistic to focus entirely on a one-way projection from nature to nature's God? Might there have been other more intimate associations between theological assumptions and the shape of Newton's universe?

From God to nature

In a recent essay on the Scientific Revolution, Amos Funkenstein (1986) has turned a traditional view on its head. Instead of seeing a separation of science and religion during the seventeenth century, he has seen an unprecedented fusion. He has pointed out that seventeenth-century natural philosophers frequently justified scientific ideals in theological language, and conversely, their statements about divine attributes often carried physical meanings. Without debating the merits of his thesis, we should note two points on which he has insisted. First, Newton constitutes an example *par excellence* of the fusion. Secondly, the project of re-defining such concepts as divine providence and omnipresence amounts to considerably more than the construction of a purely natural theology. Let me illustrate how the projection can indeed go the other way—from an analysis of the God of revelation to a particular interpretation of nature.

We begin with Newton's alchemy since, as Jan Golinski pointed out in the previous chapter, the attempt to understand organic processes acquires a certain nobility if the object is to imitate that subtle *vegetable spirit* which was of God's creating. The chemist striving to imitate mechanical changes in nature was practising a common or *vulgar* art. But to induce and imitate the processes of vegetation and organic growth was a more esoteric goal. It promised the adept some share in God's power.

There is, however, a more general consideration. A God who had been active in history, and who had communicated with mankind through the prophets, might also be expected to be active in nature. When Newton was in a more speculative frame of mind, he often seemed to be exploring strategies which would heighten that sense of divine dominion and control. It would seem reasonable to suppose that this was one reason why he was reluctant to make the gravitational force an innate property of matter. The price he paid for that reluctance was an inability to produce a coherent account of how it was supposed to act. However, the connection with his vision of God was quite explicit, as is clear from a draft corollary to Proposition VI of the *Principia*, where causal agency is vested ultimately and directly in the Creator. Newton wrote: '*There exists an infinite and omnipresent spirit in which matter is moved according to mathematical laws.*'

Newton's reference to *omnipresence* introduces a further example, because his understanding of space as absolute and infinite was partly derived from a theology deeply indebted to traditions of biblical exegesis. To elucidate his position, he employed the Hebrew word *maqom*. The Hebrews, he wrote, 'called God *maqom* place, the place in which we live and move and have our being'. In his early essay *De gravitatione*, he argued that space is eternal in duration and immutable in nature, precisely because it is 'an emanative effect of eternal and immutable being'. It was through His presence that God both ruled and discerned things. When Newton wrote in the *Principia* that 'in Him are all things contained and moved', the supporting references included eight from Scripture—notably, St Paul's speech in Acts 17:28.

My next example is perhaps the best known. This is Newton's insistence that the solar system would require a reformation from time to time if it were not to suffer instability and decay. Because Laplace and Lagrange were later to show how the system could be self-stabilizing, Newton has often been accused of invoking a *god-of-the-gaps*, a kind of cosmic plumber with a service contract. But there seem to be at least three things wrong with this popular perception. In the first place, Laplace's demonstration would itself be absorbed within British natural theology: far from being a decisive embarrassment, it could be used to exhibit further the proficiency and foresight of the divine engineer. Secondly, Newton's enterprise cannot be reduced to the proposal that he tried to prove God's existence from what was scientifically inexplicable. There were enough proofs based on what science *could* explain. Thirdly, since he allowed God to use comets as the means of effecting the necessary readjustments, it is not even clear that he was trying to exploit a scientific blank. One reason why the solar system might need a reformation was the loss of material from the Sun through the emission of light and vapours. Struck by how close some comets came to the Sun, he speculated in the 1713 edition of the *Principia* that material from the condensation of their tails might, through the agency of gravity, be used to repair the loss. He had earlier told Thomas Burnet that 'where natural causes are at hand, God uses them as instruments in his works'.

This does not mean, however, that he was not trying to heighten a sense of God's involvement with his creation. With that as his objective, the parameters of his natural philosophy *were* affected—especially what he wished to say about the conservation of motion. It may have been an unfortunate strategy, since it gave Leibniz that glorious opportunity for caricature which he seized with the remark that Newton's God resembled a second-rate watchmaker who had to keep cleaning and rewinding the mechanism. In the celebrated dispute between Leibniz and Newton's spokesman, Samuel Clarke, the political overtones were such that each party would accuse the other of deistic, anti-Christian tendencies, as Shapin (1981) has pointed out. Nevertheless, because Newton's God ruled and discerned everything, He was the very antithesis of a god-of-the-gaps.

A final example showing the relevance of Newton's theology to his science relates to the universality of the gravitational principle. Newton did not take for granted that what was true of our solar system must hold throughout the universe. On certain models of stellar distribution, there was even a sense in which the stability of the stars seemed to constitute a counter-example. He did, however, invoke analogy as a justificatory device, linking the unity of nature to the one God whose omnipresence constituted space. In a draft version of Query 31 of the *Opticks*, he put the argument in this form:

> If there be an universal life and all space be the sensorium of a thinking being who by immediate presence perceives all things in it ... the laws of motion arising from life or will may be of universal extent.

That recurrent motif of a God who perceives all things was, in part perhaps, a carry-over from the somewhat tender puritan conscience of the young man who, in 1662, had compiled a list of his sins: the young man who had made a mousetrap on the sabbath, eaten an apple in God's house, and lied about a louse—all misdemeanours which God had doubtless heard as well as seen!

The parallel between Newton's scientific and religious quest

For later positivists, such as Jean Baptiste Biot and Pierre-Simon Laplace, Newton's religious interests were essentially pathological. More sensitive scholars have pointed out, however, that the rationalism characteristic of his scientific work was not so much *de*flected, as *re*flected in his biblical studies. There are striking parallels between his rules for interpreting nature and rules for interpreting Scripture.

Newton attempted to formalize no fewer than 15 rules for the correct interpretation of the Bible. Just as one paid attention to the analogy of nature, so one respected the analogy of prophetic style. References in the *Apocalypse* to the *'Beast'*, for example, always signified a kingdom or similar body politic. Accordingly, Newton would rebuke those who took the 'Beast' to stand for human vice. Just as one sought certainty in the mathematization of nature, so one tried to choose interpretations of Scripture that converged on a unique and literal meaning. Just as, in debate with Leibniz, Newton would invoke a principle of simplicity to eliminate subtle matter from the heavens, so he insisted that constructions placed on Scripture were to reduce matters to the greatest simplicity. In his ninth rule, he drew the parallel himself:

> It is the perfection of all God's works that they are done with the greatest

Frontispiece of Thomas Burnet's *The Sacred Theory of the Earth*, an influential work which helped to popularize the idea that geological features could change through time. The seven globes show Burnet's ideas on the progress of the Earth through eternity: dark and primordial; smooth and paradisal; flooded, with Noah's Ark riding the waves; in its present fallen state; then the universal conflagration heralding the next stage, paradisal tranquillity for a millennium; and finally transformation into a star.

simplicity . . . And therefore as they that would understand the frame of the world must endeavour to reduce their knowledge to all possible simplicity, so it must be in seeking to understand these visions.

God had revealed Himself in *two* books—the book of His Word, and the book of His Works. The methods by which they were to be deciphered reflected their having a common author, and a common reader. Moreover, a correct knowledge of nature could actually assist a defence of biblical literalism.

A second example of Newton's rationalism comes from just such a context. He tried to persuade Thomas Burnet, author of *The sacred theory of the Earth* (1681–9), that the six days of Genesis (and other facets of the Creation narrative) need not be taken poetically or as an idealization. Newton emphasized that the text had been accommodated to the minds of the unlearned. But the fact remained that one could make the first two days as long as one liked—if the Earth had not yet begun its rotation. This style of apologetic, in which science was pressed into the service of a biblical literalism, was soon taken over by William Whiston, Newton's successor to the Cambridge Lucasian Chair of Mathematics. Whiston set about confirming the Genesis flood with retrospective calculations which showed that a particular comet, which he had observed, would have been in the right place at the right time to have triggered it off.

A third example of rationalism in Newton's biblical study is the manner in which he treated angels, spirits, and devils. There was a certain reductionism in his reading, whereby the *cherubim* and *seraphim* became hieroglyphs of ordinary social groups. Evil spirits bcame mental

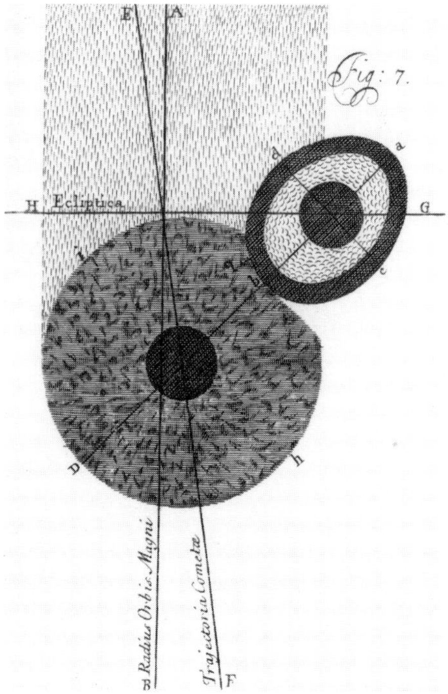

William Whiston (1667–1752) was Newton's successor in 1703 as Lucasian Professor of Mathematics at Cambridge. Theologically as unconventional as Newton, he was far less circumspect, and was forced out of his chair in 1710.

In a *clear, easie, and mechanical account*, Whiston explained Noah's flood as due to a passing comet.

disorders, and devils became the imaginary ghosts of the departed, whom the heathen characteristically worshipped as gods. As John Henry suggested in Chapter 6, Newton's treatment of magic puts him among some of the more radical interpreters of his age, particularly in his deletion of demons. But the fact that his rationalism found expression in both the interpretation of nature and Scripture does not imply that his God was essentially a projection from Creation. If Old Testament prophecy was a privileged source of the most vital knowledge, then no projection from natural laws could suffice.

Newton's understanding of providence emerged from a dialectical process in which the God who had foreknowledge of human history was integrated with the God whose will had been impressed on the natural order. The results of the interplay between scientific and biblical knowledge were sometimes astonishing, as when he paraded his knowledge of the life-span of the locust to vindicate the prophet who had predicted the life-span of the Saracen monarchy. The locusts to which the prophet had referred were interpreted by Newton as signifying the monarchy. Since the prophecy twice referred to the torment inflicted by the locusts, who had a life-span of five months, Newton deduced that 10 months, or 300 days, signified the duration of the empire. One had only to substitute years for days and a perfect fit was then obtained. The Saracens had ceased to torment the Romans in 936, 300 years after their empire had begun in 637.

To emphasize the interplay between Newton's sources is not to deny that he sometimes made a projection from this world to the next. In one of the most striking examples, it was from the dimensions of the Temple of Solomon to that future Temple envisioned in the Apocalypse. In this case, knowledge derived from Old Testament texts was paramount for, as Manuel has observed:

> The Temple of Solomon was the most important embodiment of a future extramundane reality, a blueprint of heaven; to ascertain every last fact about it was one of the highest forms of knowledge, for here was the ultimate truth of God's kingdom expressed in physical terms.

What was Newton against?

To place Newton's work on prophecy and chronology in its social and political context would be an enormous task. His theological manuscripts may, however, give some access to that wider context, especially if one can identify what he was against. As Piyo Rattansi points out in the following chapter, Newton had a distinctive view of human history which, in part, reflected the abhorrence he felt for all who had corrupted Christianity for their own ends. Pre-eminent among Newton's *crafty politicians* was Athanasius, who had grafted the doctrine of the Trinity onto a pristine Christianity, turning it into a false *infernal religion*. Newton did not deny that Christ was the son of God, but early in his theological studies he had sided with Arius against Athanasius. He could not believe that the subordination of Christ's will to that of his Father, as in the Garden of Gethsemane, was consistent with their being co-eternal and of one substance.

If he was against crafty politicians, he was also against the crafty chroniclers of ancient kingdoms who had tried to show that pagan civilizations had preceded the Jewish one. For Newton, it had to be the pagans who learned from Israel: Greeks and Latins, Egyptians and

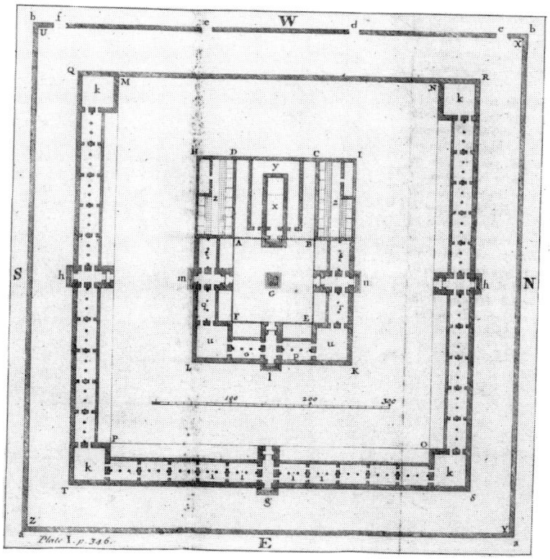

Everything Newton took up was pursued with extraordinary assiduity and concentration. He produced this plan of the *Jewish temple* by minute interpretation of the book of Ezekiel, in Hebrew, Latin and Greek, with much further reading of Jewish commentators and the Church fathers.

Persians, had 'made their first kings a little older than the truth'. The presupposition underlying his own chronology appears to be that the most ancient religion was truly the most perfect, as humanity worshipped the one true God in a society that showed toleration and compassion. There had subsequently been degradation, as idolatry spread through every nation. If there was one thing that Newton was against, it was the *practice of idolatry*.

The poignancy of his position was that he was forced (or chose) to acquiesce in another practice he very much disliked. In a treatise on revelation, he wrote:

> be not ashamed to profess the truth ... but profess it openly and endeavour to convince thy brother also that thou mayst inherit at the resurrection the promise made in Daniel 12.3 that they who turn many to righteousness shall shine as the stars for ever and ever.

He was against any other course but open profession of the truth—and yet to have professed his Arianism openly would have cost him his Fellowship. He had expected to renounce it in 1675, as the deadline for an unacceptable ordination closed in. But if Newton believed in special providence, his belief must have been reinforced in that year, for a special dispensation came in the nick of time, in the form of an exemption from holy orders.

There were other exterior forces that Newton was against. One was *religious enthusiasm* of the kind that had manifested itself in the proliferation of puritan sects, which had earlier threatened the stability of society. He had no time for the 'hot and superstitious part of mankind' who rejoiced in mysteries. In fact, it was precisely their free and easy way with the interpretation of John's revelation that had to be checked by scrupulous research into the true sense. Newton's religion was shorn of mysticism: one worshipped God by obeying his commandments.

Newton was also against *atheism*, and the licentiousness which he believed went with it. Emphatically, there was a God to be feared. Early in his Cambridge days, he would have encountered the sentiment that there were atheists busy exploiting 'the account which may be given of the origin of things from principles of philosophy without the Scriptures'. Five years later, a Cambridge tutor had complained to Henry More that students were deriving from Descartes' philosophy notions of ill consequence to religion. The extent to which Newton's break with Descartes was motivated by such considerations is not entirely clear, but he was soon giving Cartesian mechanisms for the emergence of the solar system unusually short shrift. As he later wrote to Richard Bentley: 'the growth of new systems out of old ones, without the mediation of a divine power, seems to me apparently absurd'.

But Newton was against more than this. He believed that the

doctrine of three equal persons in the Trinity was a form of polytheism. If one was an Arian who believed that Christ was the son of God, but always subordinate to Him, and if one believed the commandment 'thou shall have no other God but me', then there was a stirring conclusion: *Anglican, as well as Catholic, Christianity was guilty of idolatry*. To illustrate a history of idolatry, however, the Catholic church offered the greater scope. In his mature reflections on prophecy he would warn against the dangers of prediction, but as a young man he had ventured to suggest that the 'prevalency yet to come of Popery cannot continue long: it being certain that 1200 of the 1260 years are run out already'.

Newton had had no doubts, then, as to who was Antichrist and who was the whore of Babylon. He vented his spleen against the idolatry of a church which had treasured rotten relics, had encouraged the magical use of the sign of the cross, and had been responsible for the spreading of monkery. He had no time for monks bewailing their lust—it was far better to work hard, as he did, to displace the evil thought. Although popery was theoretically a spent force, its *threat* loomed large in the formation of a Whig ideology during the 1680s. For John Locke, the prospect of a Catholic monarch with allegiance to a foreign power had meant the abandonment of '*the whole kingdom to bondage and popery*'. Newton's every pronouncement indicates that he would have shared Locke's opinion that Roman Catholicism could only appeal to less 'inquisitive heads and unstable minds'. Yet the beast reared its head in Cambridge just as he was completing his *Principia*, and in so ugly a manner, that he sacrificed his privacy to slay it.

The occasion was a mandate from James II, asking Cambridge University to confer the degree of Master of Arts upon Alban Francis, a Benedictine monk, without requiring him to take the usual oath to uphold the Anglican faith. If James could catholicize his army, then this looked like the thin end of the wedge in his bid to control the universities. Newton encouraged the University to resist the Royal will, and was one of its representatives when the Royal fury demanded an explanation. Taking such a stand may have given Newton useful cover for his own heresies, but, like John Locke, he viewed with dismay any development which encouraged the toleration of Catholics. In the Convention Parliament which followed the revolution, he voted with the more extreme Whigs who wished to exclude from public office anyone who had co-operated with James in his revison of corporation charters.

What was Newton for?

Among the obligations of the true Christian, Newton identified what

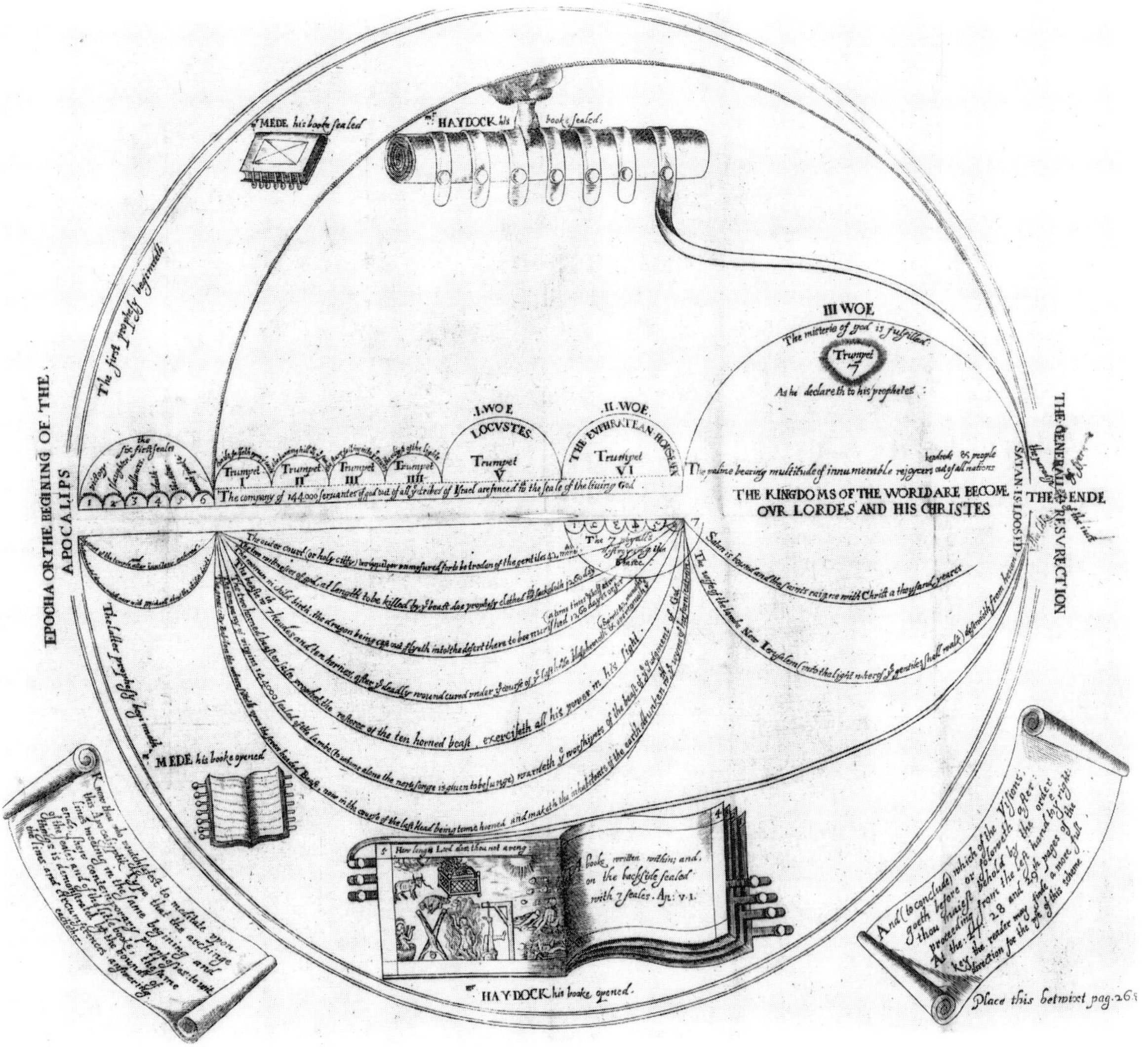

Joseph Mede's biblical interpretations were an inspiration for Newton. This diagram from Mede's *Key of the Revelation* (1627) may be compared with the harmonic design of Fludd's *Cosmic monochord* (p. 100).

he called a '*duty of the first moment*'. It was the duty to come to grips with *prophecy*, especially those pertaining to 'the latter times into which we have fallen'. The reason for urgency he put in the form of a question:

> if God was so angry with the Jews for not searching more diligently into the prophecies which He had given them to know Christ by, why should we think He will excuse us for not searching into the prophecies which He hath given us to know Antichrist by?

One has the sense that Newton felt himself to be on trial. As Christ's parables had been spoken to try the Jews, so the 'mystical scriptures were written to try us'. Beware, he admonished himself, 'that thou be not found wanting in this trial'. The stakes, after all, were high. By rejecting the Messiah through their ignorance of prophecy, the Jews

Although Newton disagreed in detail with Henry More's view of the *seven vials* prophecy from Revelation XVI, it is striking from our perspective how much of the harmonic-structural style of Mede's theology it shares.

had incurred damnation. As protagonist, Newton was for the correct interpretation of prophecy, and he acknowledged his debt to the Puritan expositor Joseph Mede in making it possible.

Mede had developed the technique which allowed the days of many biblical prophecies to be interpreted as years. But he had also looked for structural congruities between prophecies in different parts of Scripture, which allowed one prophecy to illuminate another. For example, Newton insisted (against Henry More) that the prophecy of the seven vials predicted the same events as the prophecy of the seven trumpets. In Newton's mind, the task of the scholar was to show that biblical prophecies had been fulfilled in historical events. One could know, however, only after the event, and it was not for the student of prophecy to become a prophet. Another of Newton's aims was therefore to correct those of his contemporaries who kept fixing dates for Christ's return. Until the event occurred, the prophecies pertaining to it could well remain obscure. This was an important point for Newton, since it meant that the existence of such obscurity was no argument against a true Christian religion. All would become clear in due course.

Even so, Newton tried to clarify it a little. He surmised that the second coming would bring Christ's judgement over all the kingdoms of the Earth—certainly not a spectacular annihilation of the physical world. A true monotheism would be instigated everywhere, and Christ's reign would be for ever, not a mere thousand years. He marshalled text after text to prove that particular point. It is difficult to see how he could have known such things had his God been principally a projection from Creation, but this is not to deny that certain kinds of projection did take place. Thinking again about the future, when Christ would reign, he allowed his imagination to take flight:

> as Christ after some stay in or near the regions of the Earth ascended into Heaven, so after the resurrection of the dead it may be in their power also to

leave this Earth at pleasure and accompany him into any part of the heavens, that no region in the whole Universe may want its inhabitants.

It is tempting to stop with this pleasing vision of a heavenly package tour, but a few further words are necessary.

Instead of seeing Newton as the godfather of the Enlightenment, anticipating the deism of the next generation, we must appreciate that he cannot be so easily categorized. There are many respects in which he looked backwards rather than forwards, and one of these was undoubtedly his desire to protect the analysis of prophecy from the contempt in which it had fallen through bad practice. The argument from fulfilled prophecy was also a way of protecting the dominion of God, whose will was exercised in history as in nature. If there is one motif running through Newton's science, history, and theology, it is that insistence on the power and freedom of the divine will. To take us full circle, even his Arianism was in part a protest against a kind of theology in which certain states of affairs were necessarily the case. Followers of Athanasius had denied that the substance of the son had been generated; to them, His existence had been necessary. Not so for Newton, for whom the son of God had been offspring of the divine *will*.

In presenting the case for Newton as a proto-deist, Westfall has placed particular weight on a manuscript in which Newton discussed the philosophical origins of gentile theology. In a related manuscript, Newton stated that the two basic commandments 'always have and always will be the duty of all nations and the coming of Jesus Christ has made no alteration in them'. This could imply that Christ's visitation added nothing to what Matthew Tindal would call *the religion of nature*. But it can also be read as a more conservative message—that it was not Christ's mission to abrogate the divine commands.

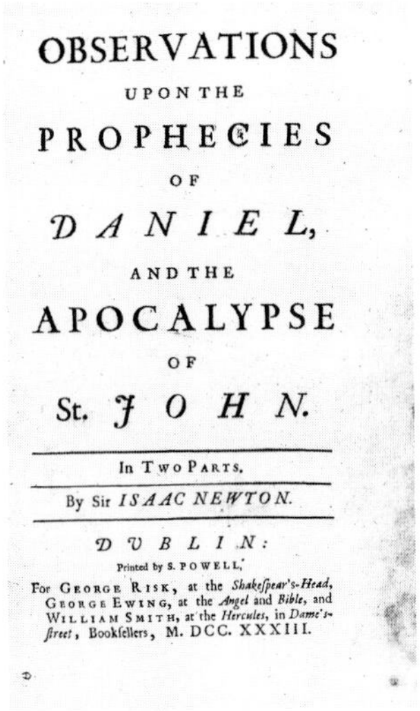
OBSERVATIONS
UPON THE
PROPHECIES
OF
DANIEL,
AND THE
APOCALYPSE
OF
St. *JOHN*.

In TWO PARTS.

By Sir *ISAAC NEWTON*.

DUBLIN:
Printed by S. POWELL,
For GEORGE RISK, at the *Shakespear's-Head*, GEORGE EWING, at the *Angel* and *Bible*, and WILLIAM SMITH, at the *Hercules*, in *Dame's-street*, Booksellers, M. DCC. XXXIII.

This volume of Newton's Biblical studies runs to 323 pages. Although not the most popular of his works, there have been twelve editions between 1733 and 1922.

Moreover to say, as Westfall does, that in Newton's arguments God was identified with law seems unduly reductionist. There are certainly passages in which Newton implied that, once the world had been formed, it might continue by the laws of nature for many ages. But everything hinges on what he meant by the *laws of nature*. On this, as on other aspects of his theology of nature, he seems to have expressed a certain ambivalence. To say that the laws of nature reflect how an intelligent agent chooses normally to act does not seem to be the same as identifying God with those laws. It may also be allowed, as Newton wrote at the end of Query 31, that:

> God is able to create particles of matter of several sizes and figures, and in several proportions to space, and perhaps of different densities and forces, and thereby to vary the laws of nature.

Newton's God surely transcended His laws. As Samuel Clarke put it when he took up the cudgels on Newton's behalf:

> There is no such thing as what men commonly call the course of nature. It is nothing else but the will of God producing certain effects in a continued, regular, constant and uniform manner.

Further reading

Frank Manuel's *The religion of Isaac Newton*, Clarendon Press, Oxford, 1974, is almost certainly the best place to start. This should be complemented by those sections devoted to Newton's religion in R. S. Westfall's *Never at rest: a biography of Isaac Newton*, Cambridge University Press, Cambridge, 1980.

There is a vast literature on the historical relations between science and religion, much of it to be mistrusted because of thinly veiled apologetic intentions. Although written from a distinctive theological position, John Dillenberger's *Protestant thought and natural science*, Collins, London, 1960, remains one of the best introductions. A strong statement of the thesis that the Protestant Reformation created conditions propitious for the growth of science will be found in R. Hooykaas, *Religion and the rise of modern science*, Scottish Academic Press, Edinburgh, 1973. The 18 essays contained in D. C. Lindberg and R. L. Numbers, *God and nature*, University of California Press, Berkeley, 1986, bring out the complexity of the interaction between science and religion within the dominant Christian traditions. This book also includes extensive suggestions for further reading.

That Newton's science was positively welcomed by certain clerics within the Anglican Church is one of the themes of Margaret C. Jacob's controversial book *The Newtonians and the English Revolution*, The Harvester Press, Hassocks, 1976. For an alternative interpretation of the same clerical role in the popularization of Newton's science, see C. A. Russell, *Science and social change 1700–1900*, Macmillan, London, 1983, pp. 52–68.

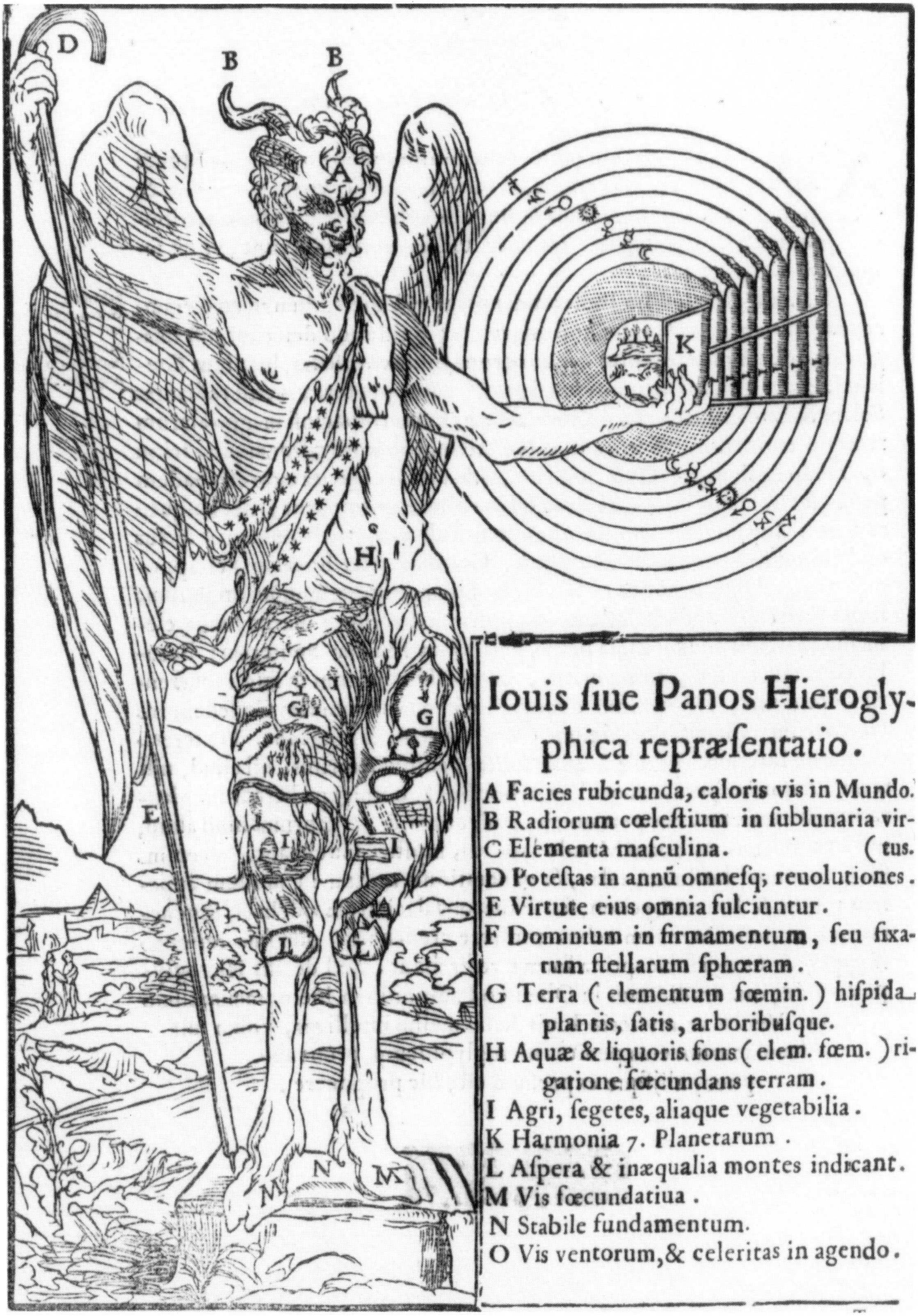

Iouis ſiue Panos Hieroglyphica repræſentatio.

A Facies rubicunda, caloris vis in Mundo.
B Radiorum cœleſtium in ſublunaria virtus.
C Elementa maſculina.
D Poteſtas in annũ omneſq; reuolutiones.
E Virtute eius omnia fulciuntur.
F Dominium in firmamentum, ſeu fixarum ſtellarum ſphœram.
G Terra (elementum fœmin.) hiſpida plantis, ſatis, arboribuſque.
H Aquæ & liquoris fons (elem. fœm.) rigatione fœcundans terram.
I Agri, ſegetes, aliaque vegetabilia.
K Harmonia 7. Planetarum.
L Aſpera & inæqualia montes indicant.
M Vis fœcundatiua.
N Stabile fundamentum.
O Vis ventorum, & celeritas in agendo.

CHAPTER NINE

Newton and the wisdom of the ancients

PIYO RATTANSI

When did the modern age begin? For the *philosophes* of eighteenth-century France—notably, for Voltaire—it began with the publication of Newton's *Principia*. As Voltaire wrote in his notebook, 'Before Kepler, all men were blind. Kepler had one eye, Newton had two'. In his *Lettres philosophiques* (1734), he declared that a genius such as Newton was born perhaps once in a thousand years. Newton exemplified true greatness. Compared with him, even the most famous statesmen and conquerors—never lacking in any age—'shrank until they seemed like figures in a rogue's gallery'. Newton was by far the greatest of the three Englishmen (the other two being Francis Bacon and John Locke) who had helped to lead humanity into the age of enlightenment.

The *philosophes* did not deny that earlier ages had caught glimpses of the enlightenment which had now begun to flood the world with light. It was the Greeks who first inaugurated the search for truth, unfettered by authority. But Aristotle had dimmed that light, and it was almost wholly extinguished after the Gothic invasions. Christianity had prospered among the ruins of Rome, and the world returned to credulity and superstition. The Latin West recovered from Gothic ravages in the high Middle Ages only to pass (in Voltaire's words) from '*savage ignorance to scholastic ignorance*'. The Scholastic philosophy it embraced was '*the illegitimate daughter of Aristotle's philosophy*'.

From ancient times, the god Pan has represented the elemental force in nature, with the power of inspiration and prophecy. This image from Athanasius Kircher's *Oedipus ægyptiacus* (1652) spells out his attributes: he symbolizes the power of the Sun to fertilize and sustain the Earth, and the harmonies of his pipes measure the planets. Newton and some of his contemporaries thought there was an ancient knowledge hidden within such legends, which by diligent enquiry they could uncover.

With the Renaissance came a revival of arts and letters and a new appreciation of the forgotten learning of the classical world: '*In those days Florence was a new Athens*'. By imitating the ancients, men had learnt to write more gracefully and became more rational. Printing and the Reformation supplied a mighty impulse to the new movement.

However, 'true philosophy' began to shine on men, according to Voltaire, only at the end of the sixteenth century with Galileo. In France, René Descartes dedicated himself to the same enterprise. In his *Discours préliminaire* to the great *Encyclopédie*, Jean D'Alembert called Descartes 'the leader of a conspiracy ... to rise up against the despotic and arbitrary power ... [of] the scholastic yoke, of opinion, of authority'. In the end, Descartes had succumbed to those very intellectual deficiencies which had led him to reject the scholastics. He used *a priori* reasoning to establish metaphysical systems, reared speculative hypotheses on flimsy foundations, and mistook tautologies for scientific proofs. Isaac Newton had taken up the fallen standard and in his

The spirit of the *philosophes* is captured in the frontispiece to their great production, the *Encyclopédie* (1751–65). The radiant figure of Truth, attended by Reason and Philosophy, is surrounded by Geometry, Physics, Astronomy, Optics, and others. The mass of working people at the foot of the picture look up to this group as the agent of their deliverance and progress.

masterpiece, the *Principia*, he pointed humanity again to the true path. He had explained facts by facts, a project less daring than Descartes', but how much wiser! A new age was now dawning, in which the methods that Newton had first discovered were being applied to every sphere of knowledge, leading to the transformation of government and society to make men wise and happy.

According to the *philosophes*, Newton was thus the first man truly to emancipate human thought from the despotic power of custom, prejudice, and authority, and usher in an epoch of enlightened rationality.

It seems natural to assume that Newton must have had a similar conception of the originality of his own discoveries, and of their significance. He had no false modesty about the importance of the first piece of work he prepared for publication, his paper on light and colours (1672). He told the Royal Society that his discovery of the compound nature of light was 'the oddest, if not the most considerable, detection, which hath hitherto been made in the operations of Nature'. He fought hard to maintain his claims to priority whenever they became a subject of dispute or challenge. When Hooke claimed credit for the notion of universal gravity, Newton threatened to suppress Book III of the *Principia*. When Leibniz asked the Royal Society to examine their rival claims to the first invention of the infinitesimal calculus, Newton made sure that Leibniz was made to appear to have obtained the first hints of his new method from Newton. Not only did Newton insist on the importance and originality of his great discoveries, he shared with the *philosophes* the hope that those discoveries would help to make men better and wiser (that is, more moral and pious), and he affirmed that sentiment in the closing pages of the English edition of his *Opticks* in 1704.

Discovery and rediscovery

It is all the more surprising, then, to find that in his secret thoughts Newton held a vision of history which would very much have astonished the *philosophes*, had they been acquainted with it. It reduced all he had discovered to a rediscovery of scientific truths well known to some of the great thinkers of the ancient world. One of the few public hints of this attitude was conveyed in a letter which Newton's young *protégé*, the Swiss mathematician Nicolas Fatio de Duillier, wrote some five years after the publication of the *Principia*. For a brief time Fatio had been entrusted with preparing a second edition of the *Principia*. In 1892 he wrote to the great Dutch physicist and Cartesian, Christiaan Huygens, that Newton had discovered that all the chief propositions of the *Principia* had been known to such ancients as Pythagoras and Plato, although those worthies had turned them into a '*great mystery*'. Invited to comment, Huygens was politely sceptical. Could the ancients really have been in possession of the proof of elliptical planetary orbits, which seemed the unique achievement of Newton? No, Newton was being far too reverential to the ancients in crediting them with the depth of mathematical knowledge which had permitted him to arrive at the mathematical demonstrations he had furnished.

Huygens' scepticism did not deter Newton in the slightest degree. He continued to search for anticipations of his work in the writings of the ancients. When the Scottish mathematician David Gregory visited him two years later, spending several months at Cambridge, Newton acknowledged to him his intention, in the forthcoming revised edition, to '*spread himself*' in proving the agreement of his own findings with those of the ancients and '*principally of Thales*', the legendary founder of Greek philosophy. He would demonstrate that what Epicurus and Lucretius had affirmed was true and valid, and that the charge of atheism laid on them was unjust. Thoth, the Egyptian Hermes or Mercury, had been 'a believer in the Copernican system', while Pythagoras and Plato had 'observed the gravitation of all bodies towards all'.

These were not random observations based on a cursory reading in ancient sources. Newton worked on the problem with the same assiduity and concentration that marks his scientific work. Gregory came into possession of a set of 15 folio sheets in which Newton assembled a formidable array of classical authorities to support key propositions of the *Principia*. In logical sequence, they showed these ancients as having held that:

- The Moon was like another Earth, and itself like other celestial bodies; therefore, the planets and their satellites were heavy masses of the same substance as the Earth.
- Bodies in the solar system exercised a mutual gravitation that extended to all other systems (each fixed star being the centre of a gravitational system of planets), that force itself extending indefinitely in all directions.
- All matter was made of atoms, and they were hard, solid, and immutable; gravity accrued to both atoms and to the bodies they composed; gravity was proportional to the quantity of matter in every body.
- The proportion in which gravitational power decreased with distance was analogous to the law governing tension and pitch in a string instrument, and was concealed in the ancient concept of the 'harmony of the spheres'.
- The cause of gravity was explained in the 'mystical philosophy' of the ancients by their supreme divinity, Pan, playing on his pipe—that is, by the direct exercise of God's divine power in all bodies whatsoever.

It is worthwhile examining Newton's contention that the *music of the spheres* was a concealed representation of the inverse-square law of

Pan is also found in alchemical symbolism. He appears in this fourteenth-century manuscript as the son of Mercury—his head is a combination of Sun and Moon which make up the alchemical hieroglyph for mercury. His pipes, too, have taken on the appearance of chemical apparatus.

gravitational attraction, since it typifies the misplaced ingenuity that marked Newton's attempts to find intimations of his ideas among the ancients.

From Macrobius, the late-antique Latin commentator on Cicero, Newton borrowed the story of Pythagoras passing a blacksmith's shop and being intrigued by the different tones emitted as the smith used hammers of different weight (as Penelope Gouk explained in Chapter 5). Making conjectures about the relationship involved, Pythagoras proceeded to test them by attaching various weights to the stretched sinews of oxen and the intestines of sheep. The proportions 'discovered by these experiments', in Newton's words, 'he later applied to the heavens'. That was how he 'learned the ratio of the celestial harmony'.

Newton was not alone among men of science in attempting to draw support for his own scientific discoveries by reinterpreting the ancient notion of the *music of the spheres*. In the sixteenth century, Kepler had justified his ascription of elliptical orbits to the planets by arguing that their angular velocities would generate beautiful and harmonious tones that were audible to God alone. Motion in circular orbits would give rise to single notes and be unvarying and monotonous, like the music of the Greeks. Motion in an ellipse, on the other hand, would give rise to the tones of the polyphonic music newly invented by the moderns, and hence prove much more pleasing to God.

Newton's own interpretation was rather different from Kepler's. In order to support it, Newton used a quantitative relation more recently discovered by Mersenne and Galileo, according to which two equally thick strings stretched by suspended weights would be in unison when the weights were reciprocally as the lengths of the strings. Having learnt this relation, Pythagoras must (Newton contended) have applied it to the heavens, and recognized that the harmony of the spheres required the force of the Sun to act upon the planets in that harmonic ratio of distance by which the force of tension acts upon strings of different length—that is, inversely as the square of the distance. Newton had to admit that the argument was a very subtle one, but

In *The harmonies of the world* (1619), Johannes Kepler examined the relationships between the planets in terms of musical harmonies. The scale he ascribed to a planet is shorter the more nearly circular is its orbit, and the starting note depends on its distance from the Sun. Together, the planets would then make a six-part harmony.

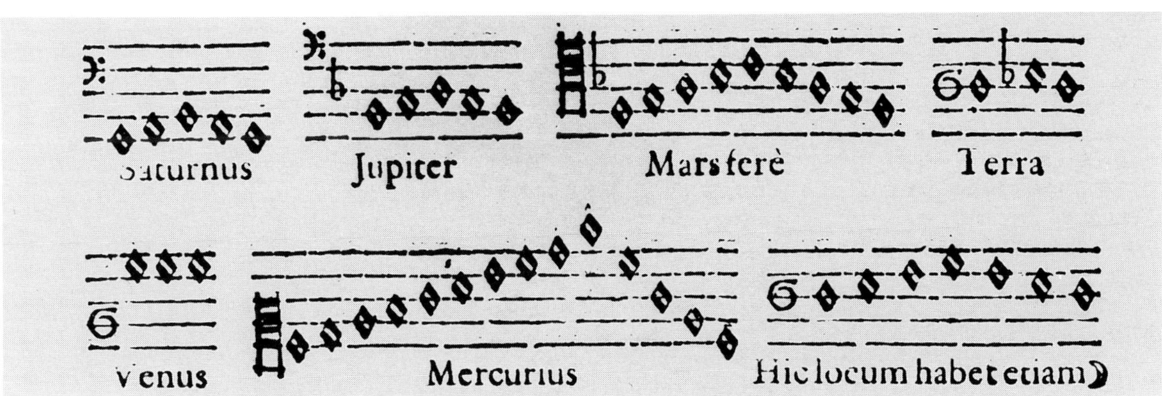

added that it was by no means beyond the mental capacity of the ancients:

Pythagoras and the sages who invented the mystical philosophy of the ancients were men by far the most acute, as Macrobius relates.

Knowledge of this sort had to be kept from the vulgar. In public, Pythagoras presented it beneath the veil of myth. Perhaps it was because they took only the surface literal meaning that Aristotle and his followers, the Peripatetics, had created their monstrous scheme of a system of solid planetary orbs, utterly failing to penetrate the truth that was hidden in it.

Peripatetic crassness, moreover, had given rise to the belief in celestial intelligences to drive the orbs round. In the *mystical philosophy*, Pan was called the supreme divinity, 'inspiring this world with harmonic ratio like a musical instrument and handling it with modulation'. The planets, however, were said to move by the force of their own souls—that is, they moved by their own gravitational power. The Peripatetics turned them into planetary spirits or intelligences. Totally misinterpreted by Peripatetics, the 'mystical philosophy' in its true form survived only among atomists.

The power of gravitation was not conceived as having corporeal origin by those ancients who correctly understood that philosophy. They dismissed the Epicurean conclusion that, if the world consisted of matter and void alone, then it could dispense with the actions of God. It was a patently absurd conclusion. How could two bodies, separated by distance, approach each other by a force of gravity except through the 'mediation of some active principle which comes between them, and by means of which force is propagated from one to the other'? Those who 'more rightly held the mystical philosophy, taught that a certain infinite breath pervades all spaces and contains and vivifies the entire world'. That breath was their supreme divinity, according to the poet cited by the Apostle, who wrote that 'In Him we live, and move, and have our being'. In fact, the mystical philosophy was not Greek in origin. Rather, it had 'flowed down to the Greeks from Egypt and Phoenicia'. Newton hinted that it was even older, for he numbered among its proponents Moschus the Phoenician, 'whom Strabo declares older than the Trojan War'.

Newton never implemented his intention of publishing an edition of the *Principia* embodying these classical annotations. At one time, he seriously contemplated using this type of support in a 'popular' third book on the *System of the world* in its first edition of 1687. But his habitual caution prevailed and he suppressed it, apparently in order to deflect ignorant criticism. He permitted only hints about the authorities he had collected to appear in his own published work. The General Scholium, added to the second edition of the *Principia*, referred

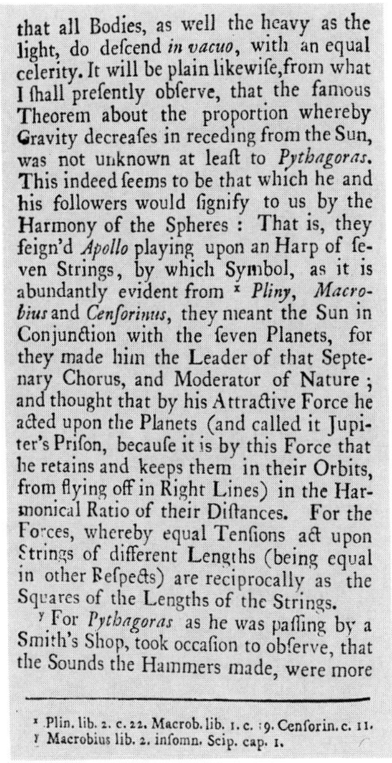

that all Bodies, as well the heavy as the light, do deſcend *in vacuo*, with an equal celerity. It will be plain likewiſe, from what I ſhall preſently obſerve, that the famous Theorem about the proportion whereby Gravity decreaſes in receding from the Sun, was not unknown at leaſt to *Pythagoras*. This indeed ſeems to be that which he and his followers would ſignify to us by the Harmony of the Spheres : That is, they feign'd *Apollo* playing upon an Harp of ſeven Strings, by which Symbol, as it is abundantly evident from [x] *Pliny*, *Macrobius* and *Cenſorinus*, they meant the Sun in Conjunction with the ſeven Planets, for they made him the Leader of that Septenary Chorus, and Moderator of Nature ; and thought that by his Attractive Force he acted upon the Planets (and called it Jupiter's Priſon, becauſe it is by this Force that he retains and keeps them in their Orbits, from flying off in Right Lines) in the Harmonical Ratio of their Diſtances. For the Forces, whereby equal Tenſions act upon Strings of different Lengths (being equal in other Reſpects) are reciprocally as the Squares of the Lengths of the Strings.

[y] For *Pythagoras* as he was paſſing by a Smith's Shop, took occaſion to obſerve, that the Sounds the Hammers made, were more

[x] Plin. lib. 2. c. 22. Macrob. lib. 1. c. 19. Cenſorin. c. 11.
[y] Macrobius lib. 2. inſomn. Scip. cap. 1.

David Gregory (1661–1708) was a young protégé of Newton, who had him appointed to the Savilian chair of astronomy at Oxford. The Preface to his *Elements of astronomy* (1702) expounds Newton's view that the inverse-square law and other matters explained in *Principia* were known to the ancients and coded by them in intellectual structures such as the *harmony of the spheres*.

to many of them. Moreover, when he rejected an etherial explanation of gravity in his English *Opticks* (1704), he invoked the authority of 'the oldest and most celebrated philosophers of *Greece* and *Phoenicia*'. He was perhaps less reluctant to permit disciples to publish those conclusions. In 1702 David Gregory had summarized them in the preface to his introduction to astronomy, the *Elementa astronomiae physicae et geometriae*, without attributing them to Newton.

ASTRONOMIÆ
PHYSICÆ & GEOMETRICÆ
ELEMENTA.

Auctore DAVIDE GREGORIO M. D.
Aſtronomiæ Profeſſore Saviliano OXONIÆ,
& Regalis Societatis Sodali.

OXONIÆ,
E THEATRO SHELDONIANO, An. Dom. MDCCII.

Newton: some dilemmas

How seriously should we take these attempts by Newton to find anticipations of the *Principia* among the ancients? It may at first appear like one of the aberrations of genius on which it would be kinder to draw a veil. In doing so, however, we may be depriving ourselves of a key that may help to unlock the enigma of Newton's total intellectual endeavour. That there is such an enigma must have been uneasily apparent, even to the Enlightenment *philosophes*, who sought to use him as the symbol of the dawning of a new age. Voltaire knew that the Newton who had 'anatomised' the nature of light, invented the infinitesimal calculus, and discovered the true system of the world, had also laboured mightily on the prophetical books of the Bible. The strain of trying to reconcile that aspect of Newton's work with this image of the supreme rationalist is evident in the chapter Voltaire devoted to them in 1738, in his *Elements of Newton's philosophy*.

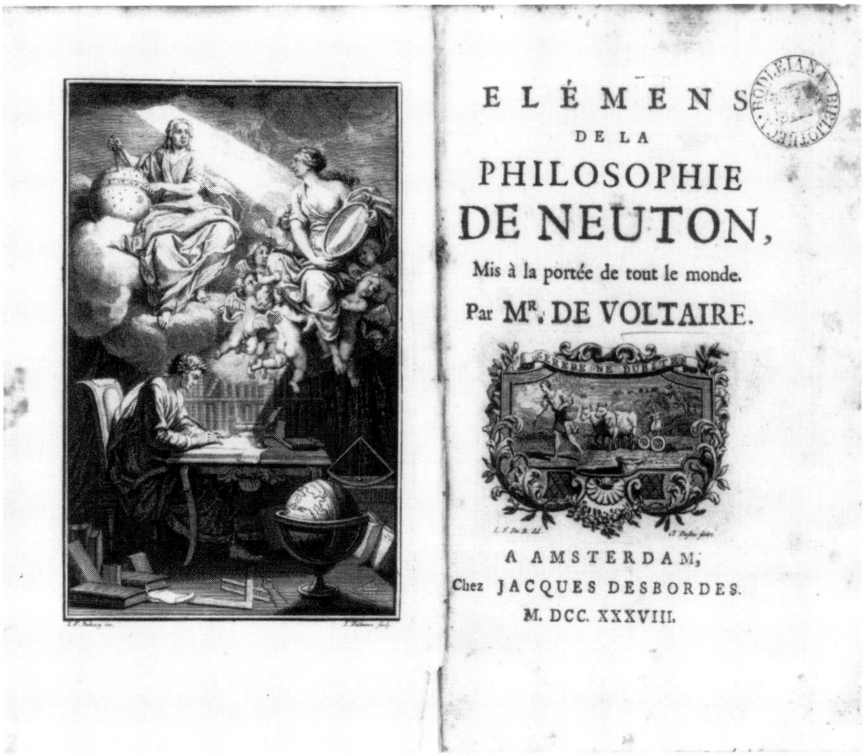

The French enthusiasm for Newton, which grew to ludicrous extremes during the eighteenth century, was especially fostered by Voltaire, in works such as his *Elémens de la philosophie de Neuton* (1738).

Voltaire concentrated on Newton's use of astronomy to provide a surer foundation for biblical chronology—all done by Newton, Voltaire assures us, '*to amuse himself after the fatigue of severer studies*'.

By the late eighteenth century, the French men of science Biot and Laplace despaired of any rational explanation of Newton's biblical work. In the life of Newton that he wrote in 1821 for the *Biographie universelle*, Biot thought that they must date only from the period after Newton's well-chronicled nervous collapse in 1693. His mind crippled, Newton had turned from science to theology.

In 1855, the pious Scottish scientist David Brewster, scandalized by that view, had no difficulty in refuting it after gaining limited access to Newton's manuscripts and using the evidence in the first comprehensive biographical account of Newton. For him, Newton's having been a 'searcher in the scriptures' since early youth was perfectly compatible with having been the greatest of scientists. But, in working through Newton's literary remains, Brewster disposed of one difficulty only to uncover another. He found that a great deal of Newton's creative life must have been spent studying alchemy and in copying, in his fine handwriting, the work of obvious frauds and imposters. A Sotheby's sale of 1936 dispersed the biblical and alchemical manuscripts, and their recent study has considerably enlarged our knowledge of these aspects of Newton's work.

The dilemmas faced by those who tried to sum up Newton's total intellectual endeavour in the past have only become greater with the progress of historical scholarship. Voltaire had claimed that the same intellectual qualities we so much admire and find awe-inspiring in the *Principia* are equally reflected in his theological and biblical work. Recent historical researches do not confirm that judgement. In his *Isaac Newton, historian* (1963), Frank Manuel showed that much of Newton's biblical work was focused on the study of the ancient Near East, in order to demonstrate that biblical prophecy could retrospectively be seen to have predicted the future course of history in minute detail. Newton wished to make Israel the fountain of all the knowledge and wisdom that had flowed to the Mesopotamians and Egyptians. In order to do so he was forced to twist astronomical and other evidence in a very arbitrary way. When compared with the sophisticated historical and philological methods developed for the study of the Bible by the Catholic scholars of his own time, Newton's work seems dated and mediocre—as Voltaire surely must have recognized.

Similarly, any attempt to show that Newton's interest in alchemy is no stranger than that of (say) Robert Boyle, quickly runs into difficulties (as Jan Golinski points out in Chapter 7). Boyle, well-known for 'Boyle's Law', made pioneer contributions to many branches of science and was particularly interested in chemical phenomena. Boyle was dismissive of the ideas and explanations of the alchemists. He was nevertheless prepared to concede that some alchemists may have succeeded in achieving metallic transmutation, when pursuing that dream through practical laboratory operations, since the newly revived particulate notion of matter brought it within the realm of possibility: change the configuration and motion of its subsensible particles, and you could transform one piece of matter into another with quite different properties. Moreover, the alchemists had amassed a vast amount of information on chemical operations over the centuries, and it could be used for other ends by the mechanical philosopher. Newton's attitude to alchemy is similar in some ways. But it displayed far greater credulity about the claims of the legendary succession of alchemical masters and their possession of knowledge of some of the deepest secrets of nature's operations, greatly surpassing that gathered by the practitioners of '*vulgar chymistry*'.

How can we reconcile the Newton of the *Principia* and the *Opticks* with the author of a series of works on biblical chronology and prophecy (such as *The chronology of ancient kingdoms amended* and the *Observations upon the prophecies of Daniel, and the Apocalypse*), and of the half-a-million words on alchemy in the manuscript remains?

Newton's search for anticipations of universal gravitation in the ancient idea of the music of the spheres helps to explain how these apparently incongruous and even contradictory activities of Newton were the expressions of a single intellectual endeavour. They give us a far more integrated picture of the mind and thought of Newton, since they enable us to reconstruct the vision of history which defined for Newton himself the meaning of that endeavour. It was a vision that he shared with some of his contemporaries, although even at that time it was beginning to lose its hold, especially over men of science. That was evident in the *Battle of books*, which raged towards the end of the seventeenth century in England. It was a vision of history rejected by the *philosophes*, who held Newton to be the inaugurator of the new age of reason.

In using classical authority to support the most important propositions of the *Principia*, Newton was obviously employing a defensive and apologetic tactic. The immediate Continental response to the *Principia* could not have pleased him. It combined unbounded admiration for Newton's mathematical genius, with denying the status of a true system of physics to that given in the *Principia*. What Continentals found unacceptable was the 'unintelligible' notion of an attraction, which could not be reduced to any contact action mechanism and was therefore thought to be a reinstatement of 'occult causes' invoked in the old and now discredited science of the scholastics. In seeking the support of the honoured ancients, Newton was trying to lend greater respectability to some of his fundamental conceptions.

But who would have found an argument based on an appeal to the ancients convincing in evaluating scientific work? Who would have thought that Newton's interpretations of ancient sources were at all plausible? It is not just a matter of Newton's being a mediocre or inaccurate historian. Granting legitimacy to novel ideas by appealing to ancient precedents was a characteristic Renaissance tactic, which continued to be employed well into the seventeenth century. The pioneers of the new science knew that doctrines resembling those held by them were to be found among the ancient Greeks. Some of them, like the Frenchman Pierre Gassendi, presented themselves as revivers of the misunderstood corpuscular notions of Epicurus. In order to do so, Gassendi had to demonstrate that Epicurus had not deserved the title of atheist fastened on him by the ancients and by many of the Fathers of the Church.

Notably different was the standpoint of some others, who shared Gassendi's wish to cleanse atomism of the taint of atheism. Relying on dubious classical scholarship, they claimed that the atomic philosophy could safely be embraced by the devout Christian because it was Judaic and Mosaic in origin. That opinion was based on a tradition that Pythagoras had visited Sidon in ancient Phoenicia, and there had met the descendents of a certain *Moschus*. That name in the Phoenician language, it was now claimed, was the same as that designated in

Hebrew by *Moses*. The idea of matter as composed of atoms, which were supposed to be identical to Pythagoras' monads, was therefore really Mosaic. Boyle had also taken account of such claims in *The sceptical chymist* (1661), but conceded that sense-experience and rational argument, rather than the piling up of historical authorities, were to be regarded as decisive in scientific matters.

The tracing of atomism to Moschus/Moses, however, was characteristic of a certain way of viewing history which must be appreciated if we are to grasp the true significance of the line of argument advanced in the Newtonian *Scholia*. In the sixteenth century there were many, especially in Protestant countries, who believed in the imminence of the Millennium and Christ's second coming, and who held that the penultimate age would be marked, not only by the terrible battle with Antichrist, but by a progressive recovery of the wisdom which Adam had possessed before the Fall.

Amidst the devastation of the Thirty Years War (1618–48), various thinkers in central Europe, like J. V. Andreae and J. A. Comenius, dreamed of a great social, educational, and scientific reformation which would restore to humanity the power over the creatures of the Earth which Adam had possessed before the Fall. The invention of printing, the telescope, and the microscope, were as much parts of that historical process as the discovery of America, the Reformation, and the defeat of the Spanish Armada.

Paracelsus, the Swiss-German medical reformer, was one of those who claimed that he had found a genuinely Christian science in the text of Genesis. He wished to install the image of God as an alchemist, and of Creation as a divine chemical distillation. Others followed his lead, in attempting to discover a replacement for 'pagan' science by recourse to the divine word in Scripture, or esoteric traditions—notably, the cabbalistic knowledge said to have been given orally by God to Moses on the mountain, and transmitted through a succession of rabbis. In such a historical perspective, the discovery of new knowledge about nature was really a *recovery* of that which had been lost or corrupted by the Fall. New inventions, for example, repaired the limitations suffered by human senses infected by Adam's sin. It was in this apocalyptic setting that the idea of scientific progress was conceived and propagated by Francis Bacon, and by many others who took up his dream of a *Great instauration*.

Theophrastus Philippus Aureolus Bombastus von Hohenheim (1493–1541), known as Paracelsus, was a controversial and boisterous figure who incorporated ancient occult learning into medical practice and theory, and was associated with religious and social protest.

History and myth

Newton had already absorbed such a vision of history during his last years at school in Grantham. He learnt Greek mythology from Ovid's *Metamorphoses* but, significantly, in an edition which altered but did

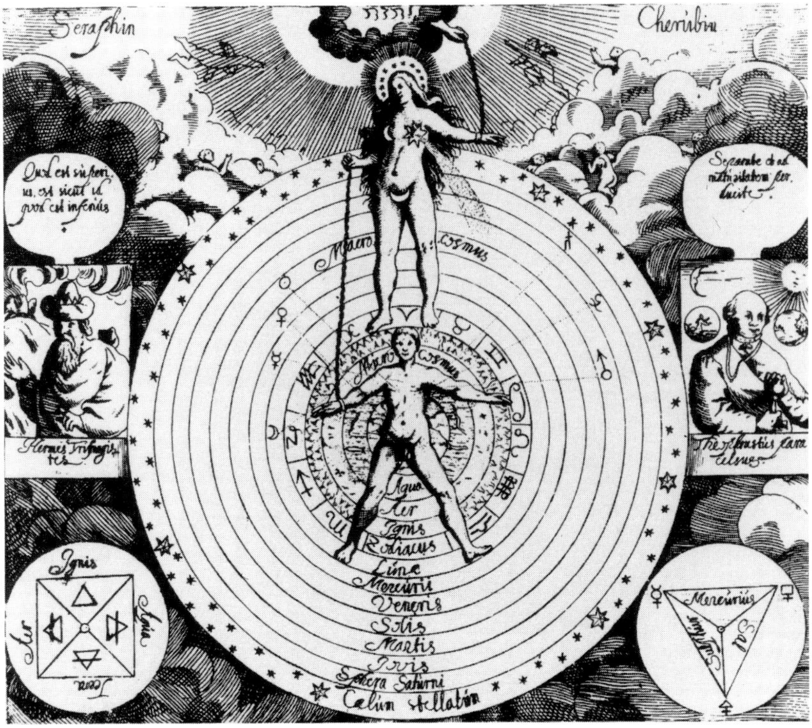

This reworking of Fludd's *Mirror of the whole of nature* (p. 126), from a book of 1654, includes representations of Hermes Trismegistus and Paracelsus to show their importance within the esoteric traditions.

not abandon the medieval allegorizing tradition which had read Christian themes into pagan myth. Ideas that appeared many years later in the suppressed 'popular' third book of the *Principia* were clearly interpretations of themes he first encountered in the *Metamorphoses*—for example, that Pythagoras had learnt the 'Copernican' cosmology from the Jews, and that Numa Pompilius, king of the Romans, in turn came to know about it when he had heard Pythagoras addressing his disciples. Numa had instituted the cult of the Vesta in Rome as a hidden symbol of the true cosmology. Rabelais, in his *Gargantua and Pentagruel* (1533–5), had ridiculed the allegorical interpretation which discovered Christian doctrines beneath the sensous imagery of Ovid. Newton continued to hold fast to a medieval interpretation which other 'moderns' now held in scorn.

Newton's formative years at Cambridge must have served to reinforce this view of history. The Cambridge Platonists were influential thinkers there, when Newton was eagerly beginning to reach out beyond the scholastic natural philosophy prescribed by the statutes to study the novel ideas of the new science. Henry More, the leading Cambridge Platonist, had for a time been the greatest champion of the work of Descartes in England, and had persisted in reading him in terms of the tradition of Mosaic philosophy. He wrote enthusiastic letters in that vein to Descartes himself. However, Descartes, quite unlike Gassendi, believed past intellectual history to be a catalogue of

One influence on Isaac Newton was the Cambridge philosopher Henry More (1614–1687), who hailed from the same part of Lincolnshire. More, a notably pious man whose Christianity was blended with Platonic and occult thought, came to feel that the influential new *mechanical philosophy* of Descartes left no room in the Universe for the workings of God's spirit. Such a perception increasingly appealed to Newton.

errors and acknowledged debts to no preceding thinker. Henry More saw Descartes as offering a genuinely Platonic, or even Mosaic, philosophy when he searched for ideological weapons amidst the turmoil of civil war and regicide in England. He feared that religion was endangered by sectarians who claimed to have been divinely inspired on the one hand, and by Thomas Hobbes and his mechanistic determinism and materialism on the other. Platonic philosophy was, for More, the indispensable but partial moral and metaphysical portion of a lost Mosaical philosophy. That philosophy had originally contained a scientific part, which acknowledged the existence of atoms, but supplemented their purely mechanical interactions by *active principles* planted in nature by God to revitalize continuously the economy of nature—a doctrine which was misunderstood and perverted by the ancient atomists. Descartes had now recovered it and come nearest to reassembling it in its pristine state.

More's enthusiasm for Descartes had cooled considerably by the Restoration. He now thought that Descartes had not safeguarded his doctrine against a deterministic interpretation which failed to emphasize the severe limitations of any purely mechanistic explanations. Triumphant in Hobbes and Spinoza, the perverted mechanistic view now threatened to repeat of the original tearing-apart and division of Mosaic philosophy between Platonist and atheistic atomist in ancient Greece.

A pristine science

This brief sketch of the notion of a Mosaic philosophy and its vicissitudes in England should help us to understand Newton's pristine

The mechanicized political philosophy of Thomas Hobbes, such as in *Leviathan* (1651), whose style was mathematically influenced, led many contemporaries to believe him a dangerous atheist.

endeavours—that is, his attempt to enlist the support of the ancients in the face of what he saw as gross Continental misunderstanding of his scientific work. His biblical work was intended to vindicate the authority of the Bible against those Catholics who had tried to show that only by supplementing it with the tradition of the universal church could it be made authoritative. It served at the same time as a weapon against the free-thinkers who appealed to a purely 'natural' religion, and thereby did away with the unique revelation enshrined in Christian religion. It did so by demonstrating that history was continually shaped according to a providential design which could be shown, only after its fulfilment, to have been prefigured in the divine word. Alchemical texts served an analogous and most significant role. They were a repository of the concealed knowledge of the active principles which prevented the mechanism of the world from running down, but yielded their meaning only when that knowledge had been rediscovered by experiment and induction.

It was not strange, therefore, for Newton to try to prove that his scientific work in the *Principia* was a rediscovery of the mystical philosophy which had passed to the Egyptians and the Greeks from the Jews. It now made it possible to glimpse the truth hidden in ancient riddles, like the *music of the spheres* and the *pipes of Pan* to whose music the whole of creation was said to dance. The rediscovery of the true system of the world must then form an essential part of the process of recovering the lost Adamic knowledge. Once human beings comprehended the infinite power of God, and how He had framed things and continually watched over them, they would be led to a deeper understanding and acceptance of the duties they owed to Him and to their fellow human beings. The recovery of the true scientific account would thus be followed by a restoration of the true morality since it was founded in a genuine conception of God and his providence, both jointly constituting an indispensable part of the preparation for the Millennium that would be brought about by Christ's second coming.

Given his acceptance of such a vision of history, we are much nearer to resolving the intellectual enigma of Newton. The framework in which he viewed the past and the present was not the one elaborated by the *philosophes* as they modified the Renaissance schema—that in which medieval, Renaissance, and modern periods succeeded that of the ancients. It was, rather, that of the four ages of the Book of Daniel in the Old Testament. Called upon in his Babylonian exile to decipher the meaning of the monstrous statue seen by Nebuchadnezzar in a dream, the Hebrew prophet Daniel was said to have identified the parts of the statue with the procession of empires which rose and fell as history marched towards its consummation in accordance with God's

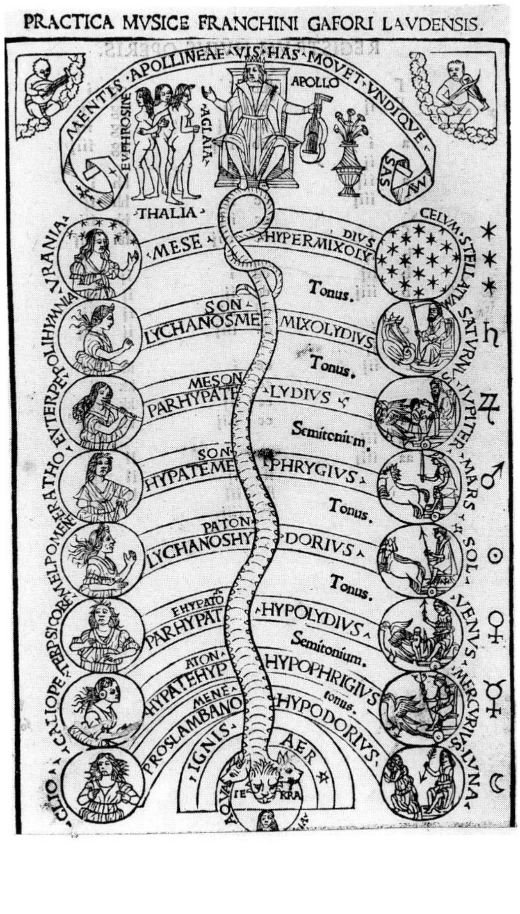

The music of the spheres, from Gafurio's *Practica musice* (1496). This more pagan version of the ideas behind Fludd's *Cosmic monochord* (p. 100) links the planets and the Muses with Greek musical scales, the whole held together by a serpent leading down from Apollo with his lute. The Latin legend at the top says *The strength of Apollo moves the Muses universally*, attesting to a belief in the harmonic foundations of a mathematically structured universe.

The symbolism of Pan and his pipes has lived on into the twentieth century: here is a drawing by Pablo Picasso, *Young men with mirror and Pan-pipes* (1923).

hidden design. Newton followed the Protestant interpretation of Daniel's visions and made the Roman church of later times the kingdom of the Antichrist, which would be overthrown before the final victory of Christ's kingdom.

According to the image of Newton we have inherited from the Enlightenment, his biblical and pristine labours served only (in Voltaire's words) to relieve the fatigue of severer studies. If we are to see him whole, we must recognize how central they were to his intellectual endeavour, serving to define the meaning his life's work held for Newton himself.

The various fields of activity which absorbed Newton's energies over a long and prodigiously creative life were, for him, consistent with the goal of tracing and recovering the wisdom of Creation. This wisdom was manifested not only in the lost knowledge of the structure and the processes of nature, but in divine mysteries which had prefigured the course of history as it progressively disclosed God's eternal purposes.

Further reading

For theological studies relating to Isaac Newton, Frank E. Manuel's books *Isaac Newton, historian*, Cambridge University Press, Cambridge, 1963, and *The Religion of Isaac Newton*, Clarendon Press, Oxford, 1974, can be recommended, as can H. McLachlan's *Sir Isaac Newton: theological manuscripts*, Liverpool University Press, 1950.

Newton's work on alchemy can be found in Betty Jo Dobbs' pioneering book *The foundations of Newton's alchemy*, Cambridge University Press, Cambridge, 1975.

Finally, works on Newton and ancient wisdom include Paulo Casini, 'Newton: the classical Scholia', *History of science*, xxii (1984), 1–58; and J. E. McGuire and P. M. Rattansi, 'Newton and the pipes of Pan', *Notes and records of the Royal Society of London*, (1966), 108–43.

HUTCHIN
NEWTON

CHAPTER TEN

Anti-Newton

GEOFFREY CANTOR

Newton's death on 20 March 1727 triggered an enormous response, and a vast industry grew up dedicated to his memory. Medals were struck; poems poured forth from the presses, heaping praise on England's greatest genius, the man who had discovered the true system of the world; statues were erected; his unconventional theological opinions were conveniently overlooked, and he was buried in Westminster Abbey and an elaborate memorial erected. Newton's epigones wrote numerous condensations of the Newtonian philosophy—there was even a *Newtonianism for ladies* by Algarotti in 1737. His genius was amply praised, along with his method of investigation, his incomparable discoveries, and even his moral purity. Neither before nor since has a British scientist received such public acclaim.

Yet we in the twentieth century have not been entirely negligent. In 1987, symbols of Newton and his synthesis appeared on British postage stamps, and the tercentenary of the *Principia* was celebrated across the world. We are all heirs to one of the most effective publicity stunts in the history of science—*the beatification, indeed the deification, of Newton.*

But did he not discover the theory of gravitation and the composition of white light, and does he not therefore deserve praise? Of course he did, and deserves full credit for these and for his other discoveries. My intention is not to undermine Newton's credibility, nor to deny the historical significance of his work. I would like instead to caution against accepting uncritically the image that was created in the early decades of the eighteenth century and that has subsequently served numerous other functions. In the following chapter, Maureen McNeil analyses the cultural meaning of Newton's image; Derek Gjertsen, for his part, has examined the variety of celebrations that developed in Newton's wake. I shall concentrate on the more limited task of showing that by accepting the image produced in the eighteenth century, we are likely to overlook the numerous and often serious criticisms to which Newton's science was subjected. By drawing attention to these critics of Newton and of Newtonian science, I hope to offer some insight into the reasons for this opposition.

William Hogarth's *Frontiss-piss* to a pamphlet of 1763 attacking the views of the philosopher Francis Hutcheson. The latter, transformed into a witch, washes away with a final stream of nonsense those of his followers (the mice) who have not already died from reading his book. The survivors are attacking the telescope and works of Newton.

Before expanding on this theme, I should point out that the historian cannot simply separate eighteenth-century authors into *Newtonians* and *anti-Newtonians*, as if these were two clearly-defined and self-conscious parties. The map is far more complex; one not only finds numerous different and often incompatible versions of Newtonianism (and, indeed, of anti-Newtonianism), but authors are often impossible to categorize adequately in such simplistic terms.

The latter point can be illustrated by discussing Pope's oft-quoted heroic couplet (published in 1735), which seems to summarize Newton's untrammelled success:

> Nature, and Nature's Laws lay hid in Night.
> God said, *Let Newton be!* and All was *Light*.

Here Newton, the chosen child of God, strips away the world of appearances and shows the divinely ordained laws binding together the whole system. In spite of this deft positive portrayal of Newton in Pope's epitaph, very different perceptions emerge in other writings by the same poet.

In his philosophical poem *Essay on man* (1732–4), Pope appealed to metaphors of stability and order, and he envisaged superior beings looking down who, on seeing

> A mortal Man unfold all Nature's law,
> Admir'd such wisdom in an earthly shape,
> And shew'd a Newton as we shew an Ape.

Thus even Newton, the most intelligent of men, was no different from the stupid ape, for each inhabits its own limited rung on the Great Chain of Being. If, as some people thought, this was an attempt at character assassination, then Pope's main thesis was that reasoning (especially, scientific reasoning) led to pride, and in perpetrating the sin of pride we destroy ourselves: 'In pride, in reas'ning pride, our error lies'.

An even less palatable image of modern science and philosophy emerged in Pope's *Dunciad* (1728), where he brought the charge of *dullness*: Newton and those who adopted the methods of the new science were responsible for destroying language and robbing it of vitality. Moreover, by destroying language Newtonian science was also destroying our very being, our humanity. Far from possessing divine qualities, Newton now emerged as the harbinger of darkness.

That such contradictory images of Newton appeared in the works of a single author should alert us not to accept at face value the numerous examples of over-blown praise for Newton and his science. Moreover, we need to extend our enquiry in another direction, and ask what Newton and his science meant for individuals and groups in different contexts. It is from this perspective that I want to examine a series of criticisms of Newton by eighteenth-century authors. These criticisms cover a considerable range—both in type and in the extent to which they undermine and subvert any holistic conception of the Newtonian world-view. I shall start with relatively minor problems which can be resolved within some recognizably 'Newtonian' frame-

Newton's audience even extended to Italian ladies, or so Francesco Algarotti hoped in packaging Newton's optics for them in 1737.

Later in the century, *young* GENTLEMEN *and* LADIES were encouraged by *Tom Telescope, A.M.*, to understand Newton's ideas.

IL NEWTONIANISMO
PER LE DAME,
OVVERO
DIALOGHI
SOPRA
LA LUCE E I COLORI.

—— *quæ legat ipſa Lycoris.*
Virg. Egl. X.

IN NAPOLI
MDCCXXXVII.

Frontiſpeice.

Lecture on Matter & Motion.

THE
NEWTONIAN SYSTEM
OF
PHILOSOPHY
Adapted to the Capacities of young GENTLEMEN and LADIES, and familiarized and made entertaining by Objects with which they are intimately acquainted:
BEING
The Subſtance of SIX LECTURES read to the LILLIPUTIAN SOCIETY.
By TOM TELESCOPE, A. M.
And collected and methodized for the Benefit of the Youth of theſe Kingdoms,
By their old Friend Mr. NEWBERY, in *St. Paul's Church-Yard.*
Who has alſo added Variety of Copper-Plate Cuts, to illuſtrate and confirm the Doctrines advanced.

O Lord, how manifold are thy Works! In Wiſdom haſt thou made them all, the Earth is full of thy Riches.
Young Men and Maidens, Old Men and Children, praiſe the Lord. PSALMS.

The SECOND EDITION.

LONDON:
Printed for J. NEWBERY, at the BIBLE and SUN, in *St. Paul's Church-Yard.* 1762.

work, and then rise to the numerous attacks which challenged the very foundations of Newtonianism.

Minor tinkering

There are many clear examples of minor tinkering with Newton's system—that is, of alterations which affected only a very limited domain and can in no sense be construed as impugning Newton's natural philosophy. One example concerns Newton's claim that refracting telescopes necessarily introduce chromatic aberration. He based this claim on his discovery of the different *refrangibilities* (degrees of refraction) of the colours of the spectrum, as Casper Hakfoort made clear in Chapter 4. Since red light is the least refracted and violet light

In his frontispiece to John Clubbe's *Physiognomy* (1763), Hogarth was able to rely on a popular recognition of Newtonian catchwords. These worthies are having the gravity of their heads weighed by a machine, and range from *A, absolute Gravity* and *B, Conatus or exertion against absolute Gravity*, to *I, absolute Levity, or Stark Fool.*

is the most, a white source positioned some distance in front of a convex lens will produce an indistinct image, with the red rays brought to a focus at a greater distance from the lens than the violet rays. Newton argued from simple geometrical considerations that a compound lens (consisting of a layer of water sandwiched between two glass lenses) can be used to eliminate spherical aberration, but that chromatic aberration would remain. Indeed, the only way in which chromatic aberration could be reduced was by increasing the telescope's length, which was technologically impracticable. Refractive telescopes were thus doomed, and Newton instead championed instruments with curved mirrors which do not produce this type of image distortion. However, in 1758, the English instrument-maker John Dollond (following up work by a Swedish contemporary) showed that achromatism could be achieved by a compound lens of two types of glass of different dispersive power, such that each coloured ray suffered the same total amount of deviation in passing through the combination. Dollond's work merely corrected an erroneous inference, but did not throw in doubt other parts of Newton's system.

Internal tensions

The concept of tinkering seems to imply that Newton bequeathed a clearly defined conceptual system which could simply be added to or modified. Yet nothing could be further from the truth. As a few writers in the eighteenth century recognized, and as historians now see clearly, there were deep internal contradictions and problems implicit in Newton's published writings. Like shoppers at a supermarket, natural philosophers of the eighteenth and nineteenth centuries had the choice of many different packages marketed under the 'Newton' brand label. In matter theory, for example, one option was to buy a ready-made world consisting of particles of gross matter plus inter-particulate forces, such as the gravitational force. Another was to opt for a world permeated by numerous ethereal fluids—the electric fluid proved one of the most popular purchases. As we shall see later, Newton did not hold the monopoly and other brands could also be found under the counter.

Let us take a closer look at what was on offer, turning to matter theory and some of the issues already introduced in John Henry's chapter. One of Newton's main contentions was that 'God in the Beginning form'd Matter in solid, massy, hard, impenetrable, moveable Particles'. Atomism (or, more precisely, corpuscularianism), a doctrine with a long pre-history, was thus part of Newton's system. But for Newton it was not sufficient that God had merely created these inert particles, since these could not of themselves account for the manifest activity found in nature, such as fermentation or the gravitational

Roger Boscovich (1711–87).

attraction between bodies. Thus God must also have added to the particles what Newton often called *active principles*, which he usually conceived as forces acting at a distance. In short, for Newton, *corpuscles plus forces constituted the physical world.*

Yet, as several writers of the mid-eighteenth century noted, this mixture was conceptually unstable. In his *Theory of Natural Philosophy* (1758), Roger Boscovich, a Catholic priest, made the following criticism: imagine two hard balls or corpuscles; one of these (*Y*) is initially at rest, and the other (*X*) is moving on a collision path with velocity 10. After collision, suppose that *Y* moves with velocity 7, and *X* moves with velocity 3, so that each ball has undergone an abrupt change in velocity: *Y*, which was initially at rest, reaches speed 7, while *X*'s speed falls from 10 to 3. Boscovich recognized that these changes in speed occur instantaneously, since the balls are hard and impenetrable, and that such transitions must undermine the *principle of continuity*.

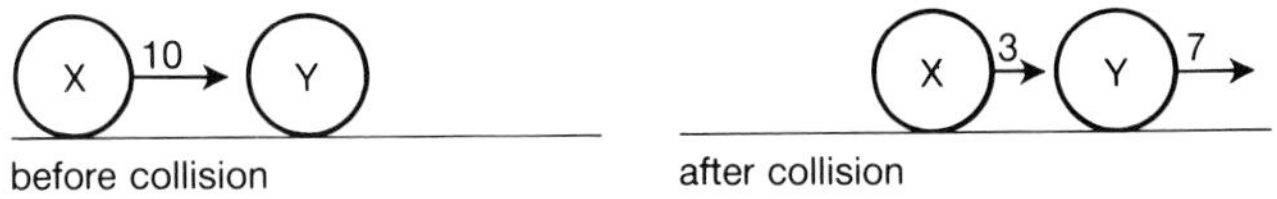

This principle, which Newton and others readily accepted, posits in modern language that in any change, a variable undergoes all intermediate values; so, to give an example, an object accelerating from rest to 60 m.p.h. does not achieve that speed instantaneously, but passes through all intermediate speeds. If we assume that this principle of continuity applies to all changes, then we can appreciate the strength of Boscovich's argument, for he was claiming that Newton's analysis of collision between *X* and *Y* was incompatible with this manifestly true principle. Hence there was a deep problem with Newton's view about corpuscles plus forces.

Boscovich resolved this apparent incompatibility by rejecting the notion of hard extended corpuscles and, like an increasing number of his contemporaries, by attributing the primary role to *force*. The figure below is taken from Boscovich's book, and shows a point atom at *A*:

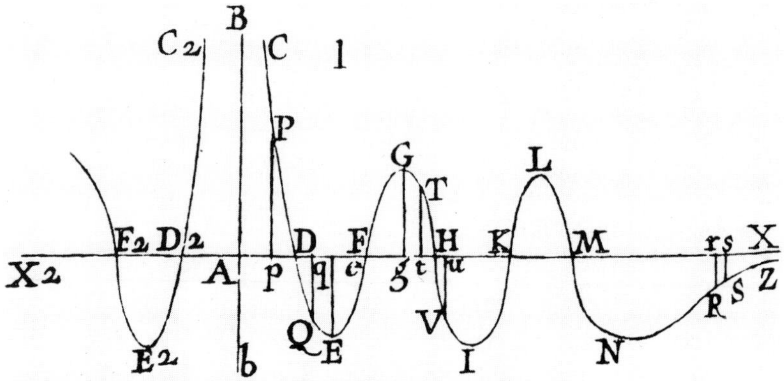

Boscovich's diagram of the force–distance relation between physical points.

a point atom is indivisible, not extended in space, but possesses inertia. Now the curve from *D* to *V* shows the force–distance relationship associated with the point atom at *A*, and since this curve is continuous, the law of continuity is obeyed. The force is repulsive for those parts of the curve above the horizontal axis, and attractive below that axis.

Boscovich sought to explain all physical phenomena by this distribution of force. Consider the force which another point atom would experience at some distance from *A*. At large distances from *A* (such as at *V*), the force is attractive and decreases as the square of the distance; this part of the curve accounts for gravitational attraction. At very small distances, an increasingly strong repulsive force acts, so that the two particles never collide. Instead, a corpuscle aimed at *A* at high speed would be repelled strongly at distances less than *Ab*, and turn back from *A*; throughout this trajectory, its velocity would change continuously.

Alternatively, consider the zero force acting at distance *AE*: it is at an equilibrium point, since if the particle were moved on to *d*, then it would be attracted back towards *E*, whereas if it were moved back to *b*, then it would be repelled towards *E*. Hence, point atoms spaced at a distance *AE* from one another would constitute a geometrically stable substance, such as a stable solid.

Together with other factors, Boscovich's analysis contributed to a significant shift in matter theory during the eighteenth century, with forces playing a more central role and corpuscularianism losing ground. By the early decades of the nineteenth century, forces were used in such various and different contexts that they often bore little relationship to Newton's use of the term.

The next example is more dramatic, and takes us to optical theory. In the *Queries* to his *Opticks*, and in other published writings, Newton had discussed the nature of light. While there is a certain ambiguity in Newton's position, his followers generally read him as providing strong support for the view that light consists of small particles of matter, shot out from a light source and affected by short-range forces. Moreover, he was assumed to have rejected the view that light is some kind of wave motion in an ubiquitous ether. Although a significant proportion of writers did not adopt this position, it was widely held and disseminated through such means as public lectures and natural philosophy texts.

Thomas Young (1773–1829) was a remarkably versatile man. Apart from his work on the wave theory of light, he helped to decipher the Rosetta Stone.

This particulate theory encountered one of its staunchest critics at the beginning of the nineteenth century when Thomas Young, drawing partly on the writings of Leonhard Euler, developed a *wave theory of light*. Young conceived space to be permeated by an ethereal fluid which constitutes light, when set in vibration. The frequency of vibration correlates with colour so that, in the visible spectrum, the red end corresponds to the highest frequency and the blue end corresponds to the lowest. He also introduced a principle of interference which was to prove very powerful in explaining a variety of phenomena.

Looking back at Young's work and the subsequent rise to dominance of the wave theory in the 1830s, it is tempting to see Newton's particulate theory of light as being overthrown by an opposing and incompatible theory. However, this account is inadequate, since it overlooks Young's manifest commitment to a brand of Newtonian natural philosophy. In propounding the wave theory of light, Young saw himself *extending* Newton's work, not undermining it. The luminiferous ether he required for light propagation was derived from Newton's ether, as discussed in the *Queries* to the *Opticks* and in Newton's early optical papers of 1672 and 1675. Viewed from this standpoint, Young's work on the wave theory of light can be located within a Newtonian tradition, and is thus party to the internal conflicts between different intellectual strands found in Newton's writings.

Aiming for the jugular

However broadly one defines the Newtonian tradition, there was a range of criticisms which were highly destructive of the whole enterprise—criticisms that, if taken seriously, attacked Newton's science at its very roots. Such criticisms usually drew on principles from outside Newtonianism, and there were many such alternatives on offer. For example, there existed an extensive literature critically discussing Newton's concept of force. While much discussion drew on various concepts encountered in Newton's writings, some critics rejected the notion of action-at-a-distance as unintelligible, and demanded an account of the physical world in terms of contact-action between particles of matter. In a strong sense, they departed radically from the theories of matter articulated in both the *Principia* and the *Opticks*.

The example I shall discuss at length pertains to another topic—that of calculus. The philosopher George Berkeley was a vehement and highly competent critic of many aspects of Newton's science, and sought to show that Newton's universe was constructed on quicksand. Leaving aside his numerous other criticisms of Newton and his followers, I shall concentrate on a book called *The analyst* (1734), in which he launched a devastating attack on the calculus of both Newton and Leibniz. Here he adopted three main lines of argument.

Inconsistency

Newton had developed the *method of fluxions* which deals with changing quantities—quantities in flux. To find the 'fluxion' of a quantity is to determine its rate of change—for example, the rate of change of velocity gives the acceleration. To determine the fluxion of a function f we need to determine the value of that function for x and for $x+a$, where a is a small finite quantity. The quantity a has to be non-zero since the derivation of the fluxion involves dividing $f(x+a)-f(x)$ by a, and this is unproblematic. However, a few lines further on in the derivation, the quantity a has to be made equal to zero. This is the difficulty, for a cannot both be non-zero and zero; the two requirements are logically incompatible, and this incompatibility renders the whole demonstration void—'a most inconsistent way of arguing', as Berkeley put it. He also noted that in other branches of human knowledge, '*men would hardly admit such a reasoning as this, which in mathematics is accepted for demonstration*'.

The arrow struck deep, since mathematicians in the eighteenth century prided themselves as being the guardians of rationality and of logical scrupulousness.

Relationships between things

Suppose that this is the only book that you and I have so far encountered. By observing this book, we can each form an idea of it, and we can agree to employ the word *book* to signify it. We can use the word *book* in our conversations, and each time I articulate that word, you form a clear conception in your mind of this specific object—the book you hold in your hand.

This procedure works well if we are dealing with a single object. However, as Berkeley pointed out, a problem arises with abstract nouns. In general parlance, the word *book* refers to any book—be it good or bad, green or yellow, octavo or quarto, fat or thin, with pictures or without, and written in English or Mandarin. Unlike the clear idea we can so readily form if the word *book* is applied solely to this particular one, we can form no clear conception of a book in the abstract.

Berkeley's concluson is that we can form no clear conception of abstract terms. This conclusion is directly applicable to mathematics since, for Berkeley, the purveyors of calculus used symbols which do not give rise to clear ideas: if distance is difficult to conceive, then notions like velocity, and velocities of velocities '*exceed ... all human understanding*'. He went on:

> the further the mind analyseth and pursueth these fugitive ideas the more it is lost and bewildered; the objects, at first fleeting and minute, soon vanish out of sight. Certainly, in any sense, a second or third fluxion seems an obscure Mystery.

They are, he said, '*ghosts of departed quantities*'. Hence, Newton's method of fluxions, far from upholding the clear light of reason, was sunk in the mist of conceptual obscurity.

Authority

Berkeley pointed out that when the defenders of calculus were stuck for good arguments they appealed to *authority*, particularly the authority derived from Newton's prestigious name. Thus, contrary to their image, mathematicians were not the guardians of rationality.

Taken together, these arguments (particularly the first) constituted a major criticism of the fluxional method. However, this conclusion went far beyond the bounds of calculus, since calculus was used extensively in physics and astronomy. Thus Berkeley had also cast doubt on the rational basis of these sciences. Moreover, where Berkeley's criticisms of other aspects of science are taken into consideration, we see a wholesale assault on Newtonian science.

Opposing world-views

Let us now proceed beyond the explicit criticisms of particular aspects of Newton's science, and encompass those alternative perspectives from which Newtonianism appeared objectionable and vulnerable to attack. By considering such contexts, we can appreciate why some of the foregoing criticisms were mounted by Berkeley. This approach adds little to my first category—Dollond's tinkering involved solving a technical problem of theoretical, practical, and economic importance. However, it sheds considerable light on the third category, and explains why Berkeley energetically attacked Newton's science.

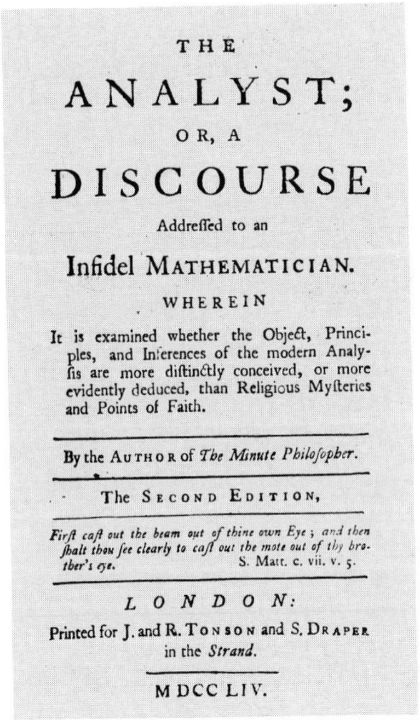
THE

ANALYST;

OR, A

DISCOURSE

Addreſſed to an

Infidel MATHEMATICIAN.

WHEREIN

It is examined whether the Object, Principles, and Inferences of the modern Analyſis are more diſtinctly conceived, or more evidently deduced, than Religious Myſteries and Points of Faith.

By the AUTHOR of *The Minute Philoſopher.*

The SECOND EDITION,

Firſt caſt out the beam out of thine own Eye; and then ſhalt thou ſee clearly to caſt out the mote out of thy brother's eye. S. Matt. c. vii. v. 5.

LONDON:

Printed for J. and R. TONSON and S. DRAPER in the *Strand.*

MDCCLIV.

A 1754 edition of George Berkeley's *The analyst*.

I must first plead guilty to deception. Berkeley's *The analyst* is not simply about calculus, as the book's title page indicates. I also incorrectly called Berkeley a *philosopher*. The term may at first glance seem apposite, since some of Berkeley's works are likely to be encountered by students of philosophy. But it would be more appropriate to think of him as a *clergyman*; he was a member of the High Church faction, who became the Bishop of Cloyne, and he was in addition a Tory. In the light of the book's full title and this redescription of its author, we can now understand more clearly what he was trying to achieve.

Berkeley was greatly exercised by the increasing influence of those who held inimical ideals. The Whigs and the Walpole administration stood for treacherous politics, exemplified by their betrayal of his pet project—a Christian college in Bermuda. The Whigs were in alliance with the Low Church faction, and thus opposed to his own party in the Anglican Church. He considered that their social, political, and religious values would lead to the ruin of Great Britain. Moreover, this unholy alliance also included Newtonian natural philosophy, since the new science was used to underpin conceptions of natural law and natural theology. Under Walpole, another deadly enemy was allowed

George Berkeley (1685–1753).

to flourish: this was *deism*, which threatened to replace Christianity and revealed religion with a pale naturalistic religion based on man's reason. Newton's science and the misuse of reason—Pope's '*reas'ning pride*'—were thus prime targets for Berkeley.

If this was Berkeley's motivation for attacking Newton's science and the pretensions of mathematicians, how does it relate to *The analyst*? The connection is drawn in the work's subtitle, and is stated more fully in the following passage:

> But he who can digest a second or third fluxion ... need not, methinks, be squeamish about any point in Divinity ... But with what appearance of reason shall any man presume to say that mysteries may not be objects of faith, at the same time that he himself admits such obscure mysteries to be objects of science?

Since the foundations of calculus were shrouded in mystery, a wedge could not be driven between mathematics and revealed theology which involved such admittedly obscure notions as the Trinity—the three persons of the Godhead in one. However, the situation with calculus was even less favourable, since the method of fluxions was found to be not only obscure but also logically inconsistent. Hence, Berkeley claimed that his opponents could not legitimately dismiss revelation in the name of reason. Newton's science could not be used as a weapon to undermine the authority of Scripture and Berkeley's system of values.

Whether or not we agree with Berkeley's position, we can appreciate both the reasons underpinning his attacks on Newtonian science and the brilliance of those attacks. Other critics were less sharp intellectually, but were numerous. Reading widely in the eighteenth and early nineteenth centuries, I have been impressed by the sheer volume of works which can be called anti-Newtonian, in this strong sense. From these, let me choose two examples.

As John Brooke argued in Chapter 8, one aspect of Newton's theology emphasized the role of God as Creator and Maintainer of the physical universe. Likewise, for many of Newton's followers the new science provided strong support for a natural theology in which signs of design—particularly, the universal law of gravitation—were taken as indicating the necessity of the Divine Artificer. Moreover, for a number of authors the mutual gravitation of physical bodies, as postulated in Newton's theory, showed God's immanence in the world, since His omnipresence was the source of those active principles which activated the (otherwise inert) particles of matter. However, such a conception of God's relationship to the physical world was, for many, an heretical view, since it omitted the account of Creation given in Genesis, and portrayed God as a mere craftsman (albeit a craftsman, first class). The image of an immanent God was likewise often viewed as heretical and contrary to Scripture. To those (often High Church Tories) who criticized the Newtonian world-view from this position, alternative natural philosophies were available.

The most popular amongst these was propounded in the works of John Hutchinson, and particularly in his appositely titled *Moses's Principia* (1724). Hutchinson rejected the view that knowledge of the natural world should be derived solely from observation, and instead turned to Scripture as a major source of this knowledge (employing a rather idiosyncratic interpretation of the Old Testament). But one of his main criticisms of Newton's matter theory was that it failed to distinguish God from His Creation, since it attributed power—active principles, such as gravitation—to matter. By contrast, Hutchinson conceived (and used his biblical analysis to demonstrate) that power resides only in God, and hence, by attributing power to matter, Newton had opened the door to pagan pantheism.

Hutchinson's God was the God of Genesis, who had created the world and had not interfered with its subsequent normal operations. The opening verses of Genesis were understood by Hutchinson to mean that God had not only created the particles of gross matter, which compose material bodies, but also a fine ethereal matter whose particles fill the rest of space. All observable phenomena were produced by the motions of these ether particles which act only by contact. He thus disposed of Newton's mysterious forces acting at a distance. The ether particles can adopt three modifications—fire, light, and air, which were conceived as the physical analogues of the Father, the Son, and the Holy Ghost. The Sun is not the source of these ether particles, but merely directs them from the centre towards the firmament, and in this rapid motion they are in the form of light. When, however, the ether particles lose their fast translational motion and become associated with gross matter, they manifest themselves as heat; both heat and light were thus often conceived as fluids in the eighteenth century. The ether particles also conglomerate into grains and return to the Sun in that form, causing a centripetal pressure.

Hutchinson likened the universe to a machine, not only because the parts interacted by contact action, but also because in the circulation of ether particles both matter and motion were conserved: God had, in the beginning, produced the perfect perpetual motion machine. Although Hutchinson's natural philosophy may seem fanciful, it was by no means sterile and produced some significant work—especially in the development of *conservation principles* and in the study of both heat and electricity. But its main importance and the source of its popularity lay in the values with which it was associated; it offered an acceptable natural philosophy to those who found Newton's world-view theologically offensive.

Of the many variants of this type of criticism of Newton's science,

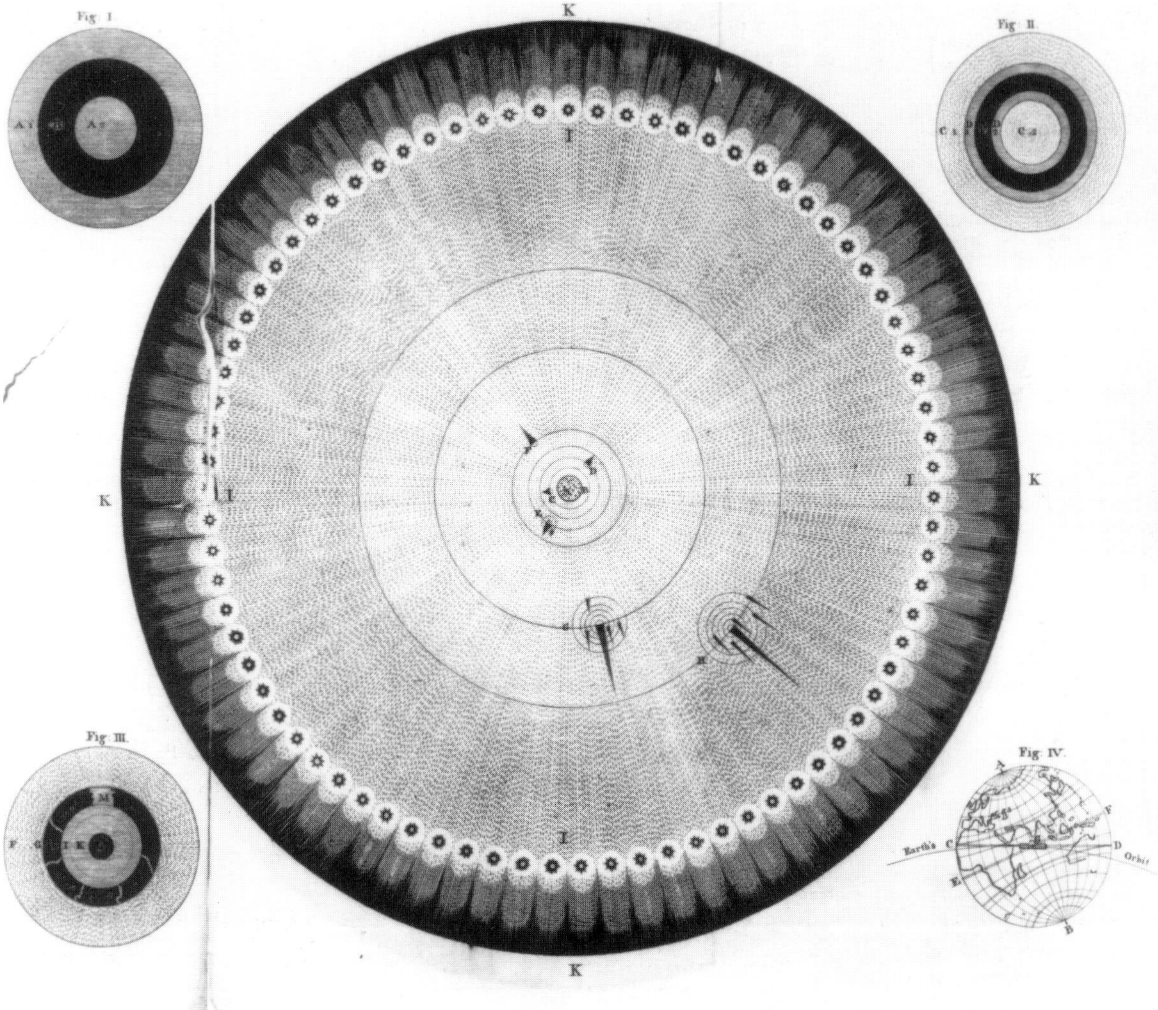
Fig. I.
Fig. II.
Fig. III.
Fig. IV.
K
I
Earth's
Orbit

The poet Samuel Taylor Coleridge (1772–1834) came to take a dismissive, albeit quantitative, view of Newton's creative imagination: *'I believe the souls of five hundred Sir Isaac Newtons would go to the making up of a Shakespeare or a Milton.'*

one which became more emphatic towards the end of the eighteenth century and in the early decades of the nineteenth, is usually described as *Romanticism*. Among those to whom this vague term has been applied, the writer most familiar with Newton's works was probably the poet and critic Samuel Taylor Coleridge. Early in his career, Coleridge declared himself an enthusiastic disciple of both Newton and Locke. He subsequently expressed considerable ambivalence towards Newton's writings, reiterating the latter's view that God directly activates the universe, while simultaneously criticizing severely those passages in which Newton and his followers made the physical world self-sustaining and dependent only on atoms and imponderable fluids. Atomism, Coleridge believed, left no place in the universe for God. Moreover, this false philosophy set itself the impossible task of reducing the diverse forms of activity in nature to the motions and collisions of small, inert particles.

Yet this criticism was not confined to the physical sciences, for Coleridge conceived that Locke held a similar and highly influential view of mind in which human thought was reduced to little, atomistic ideas. Coleridge thus opposed Newton and Locke, not only because of the atheistical implications of their theories, but also because they allowed no place to the creative mind or to imagination. They thus offered a thoroughly corrupt view of man.

Although Coleridge was highly critical of Newtonian science, he should not be construed as opposing science as such. Instead, he pursued an active interest in several branches of science, read attentively such scientific authors as Newton, Hartley, and Priestley. He was a close friend of both Thomas Beddoes, the radical doctor, and Humphry Davy, who fuelled his interest in understanding the natural world. In 1798–9 he was in Germany, fulfilling his plan to study Kant and *Naturphilosophie*: this was a major movement whose members sought to comprehend nature in terms of the interplay of oppositely polarized organic forces.

In Hutchinson's cosmology, physical phenomena are produced by ether particles flowing out from the Sun and flowing back congealed together. From Samuel Pike's *Philosophia sacra: Or, the principles of natural philosophy extracted from divine revelation* (1753)—the title of this book proclaims an approach quite opposite to that of the Newtonian natural theologians, who extracted details *about* God *from* conclusions of natural philosophy.

These studies offered Coleridge just what he found lacking in Newtonian science. Instead of a world of *little things*—of corpuscles, ether particles, atomized ideas, and a highly mechanized view of mind—*Naturphilosophie* portrayed the world (man included) as active and whole. Although at one time he looked upon Davy's work in chemistry as advancing this programme, he subsequently parted from Davy who, he felt, had sold out to atomism. Instead, Coleridge pursued his aim of bringing the insights of *Naturphilosophie* and the truths of the Bible to bear on such subjects as geology, optics, electricity, and biology. More generally, he is recognized as having played a substantial role in helping to import this German intellectual tradition, which achieved only limited popularity in Britain but nevertheless influenced several early Victorian scientists of note.

Newtonian science and conflicting values

As we have seen, Newton's work, although successful in solving scientific problems, was subjected to a wide variety of criticisms. These ranged from minor tinkering with the system, through divergent interpretations, to outright conflict with other opposing natural philosophies. Concentrating on these last criticisms, we should appreciate that the Newtonian system of the world came to be associated with certain *values*—especially social, theological, and political values. Some of these values were inherent in Newton's own work, whereas others were grafted on during the subsequent history of Newtonianism. These values covered a great range, and yet, within this diversity, there were certain recurrent elements among those British writers who opposed Newton. Pope (of the *Dunciad*), Berkeley, Hutchinson, and Coleridge all found Newtonianism inimical to their theologically centred conceptions of the world and, at least Berkeley and Coleridge, found it opposed to their views on the divine creative imaginative spark which we call the human mind.

Such criticisms of Newton arose from both radicals and from conservative High Churchmen. Moreover, the alternative natural philosophies which these opponents articulated differed widely—from Hutchinson's attempt to mechanize the physical world and thus rob

Having descended somewhat from the position occupied by Newton, the natural philosopher by the early nineteenth century was thought suitable for good-humoured mockery by cartoonists.

It's all a farce! I tell you, it's all a farce— there are no clouds, no mountains, no trees, no water— I've proved it, it's nothing, depend on it— nothing— bona fide nothing.
Bishop Berkley
Philosophical Lecturer.

it of all activity, to Coleridge's view that all phenomena resolve into activity and force.

Not only were there many alternatives to Newton's system (or systems), but these alternatives were not merely the untenable pipe dreams of disillusioned men. We have yet to appreciate fully how Berkeley, Hutchinson, or Coleridge fit within the long-term development of science, but it would be premature to dismiss these writers as merely following blind alleys, since studying them casts light on our historical understanding of Newton's science. Moreover, these opponents of Newton can be subsumed under long-term natural philosophical traditions which, in the mid-nineteenth century, led to such developments as field theory and the conservation of energy.

Equally, it can be argued that Newtonianism in Britain offered a very restrictive view of science, and one which was underpinned by a highly authoritarian system. By the time of Newton's death in 1727, his system of the world was being taught by his disciples in universities and at public lectures; it was being preached in sermons, most famously the *Boyle lectures*; it was published in numerous textbooks on natural philosophy; it was discussed in coffee houses, societies and the popular press; it was set to verse in poems such as James Thomson's *The seasons* (1726–30) and Mark Akenside's *The pleasures of imagination* (1744). Moreover, the name of Newton was praised and revered in many

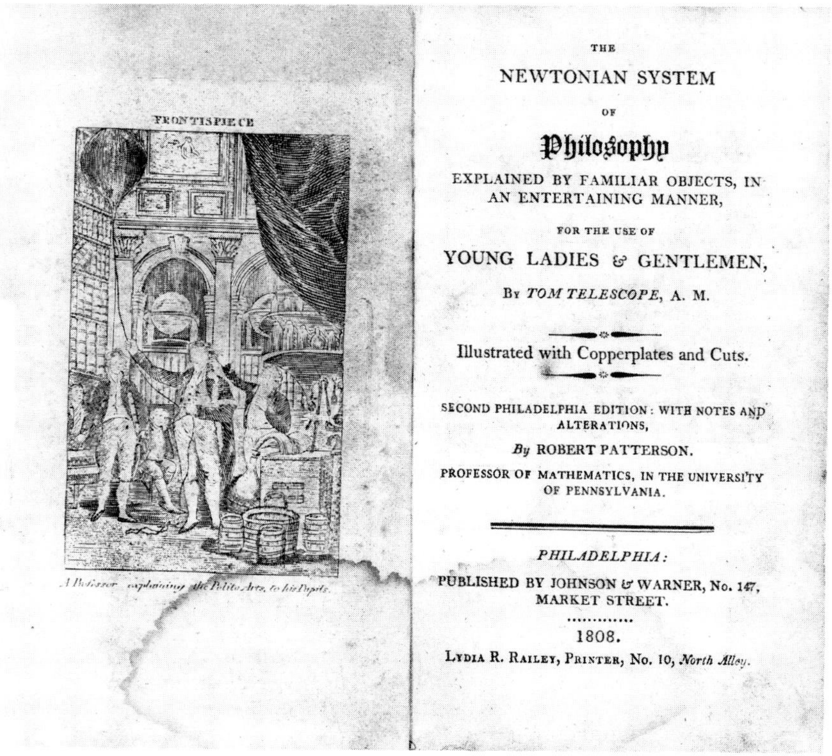

FRONTISPIECE

THE

NEWTONIAN SYSTEM

OF

Philosophy

EXPLAINED BY FAMILIAR OBJECTS, IN AN ENTERTAINING MANNER,

FOR THE USE OF

YOUNG LADIES & GENTLEMEN,

BY *TOM TELESCOPE*, A. M.

Illustrated with Copperplates and Cuts.

SECOND PHILADELPHIA EDITION: WITH NOTES AND ALTERATIONS,

By ROBERT PATTERSON.

PROFESSOR OF MATHEMATICS, IN THE UNIVERSITY OF PENNSYLVANIA.

PHILADELPHIA:

PUBLISHED BY JOHNSON & WARNER, No. 147, MARKET STREET.

....

1808.

LYDIA R. BAILEY, PRINTER, No. 10, *North Alley*.

On into the nineteenth century, and across the Atlantic, Tom Telescope continued to promote Newtonianism.

circles. As Maureen McNeil argues in the following chapter, Newton and his work were adopted for many different, even contradictory, purposes—not only in eighteenth century culture, but also in our time. Yet the Newton industry of the early eighteenth century was particularly successful in creating a positive but highly sanitized image of Newton, and associating the Newtonian system with Enlightenment values such as truth, rationality, and progress.

By its capture of the centre of the public stage and its cultural utility, generations of commentators have readily recognized *Newton's success*, to use Derek Gjertsen's title. While facets of Newtonian science became the dominant establishment view of the universe and were vested with considerable authority, alternative conceptions were not tolerated but were eliminated or driven underground. Thus, to take a particularly instructive example, the powerful form of calculus stemming from Leibniz's work was largely rejected by British mathematicians under the sway of Newton's less efficacious methods. In this area, British mathematicians lagged far behind their Continental counterparts, and it was not until the 1810s that the wind of change blew through Cambridge. More generally, although Newton and his followers made great strides in science, their approach can also be seen as imposing severe restrictions on scientific practice. While such restrictions necessarily focus attention on certain problems, methods, and solutions, they also stifle exploration of alternative approaches to science.

I have attempted to show that, for all its successes, Newton's science was subject to extensive criticism during the eighteenth century, and that there were many writers who not only found it objectionable but propounded alternative natural philosophies. At a time when Newton's name and work is being celebrated throughout the world, we would do well to remember that, during its history, the Newtonian system also encountered strenuous opposition.

Further reading

A useful starting point for exploring eighteenth-century responses to Newton is provided by the essays of Rom Harré, Simon Schaffer, Steven Shapin, and J. L. Heilbron in *The ferment of knowledge: studies in the historiography of eighteenth-century science* (edited by G. S. Rousseau and Roy Porter), Cambridge University Press, Cambridge, 1980; also Simon Schaffer's article, 'Natural philosophy after Newton', in *The companion to the history of modern science* (edited by G. N. Cantor, J. R. R. Christie, M. J. S. Hodge, and R. C. Olby), Croom Helm, Beckenham, 1988.

For disputes over matter theory, see Robert E. Schofield, *Mechanism and materialism: British natural philosophy in an age of reason*, Princeton University Press, Princeton, 1970; and John W. Yolton, *Thinking matter: materialism in eighteenth-century Britain*, Basil Blackwell, Oxford, 1983.

For discussions of some of Newton's opponents, see D. D. Ault, *Visionary physics: Blake's response to Newton*, Chicago University Press, Chicago and London, 1975; Geoffrey N. Cantor, *Optics after Newton: theories of light in Britain and Ireland, 1704–1840*, Manchester University Press, Manchester, 1983; Trevor H. Levere, *Poetry realized in nature: Samuel Taylor Coleridge and early nineteenth-century science*, Cambridge University Press, Cambridge, 1981; and C. B. Wilde's article 'Hutchinsonianism, natural philosophy and religious controversy in eighteenth-century Britain', *History of science*, xviii (1980), 1–24.

CHAPTER ELEVEN

Newton as national hero

MAUREEN MCNEIL

In 1979, the Newton scholar Henry Guerlac was reflecting upon the progress of Newtonian studies in recent years, and observed:

> Besides the technical study of Newton's achievements in mathematics, optics and dynamics, there is a phase of Newtonian scholarship which has attracted renewed interest and which we may call the 'influence', the 'reception', or the 'legacy' of Newton.

This observation well describes the framework in which my initial studies in this field were conceived. My own investigations were at first focused on Newton's *influence* at the end of the eighteenth century in Britain, and the first case study in this chapter derives from that phase of my life when I was interested in the *impact* of Newton and of his ideas.

Looking at Guerlac's quotation now, I feel dissatisfied with the phase of scholarship that he described. It strikes me that the approach needs to be taken further. To understand what Newton—indeed, what any figure in the history of science—*means* should involve investigating not only his writings and their influence, but also other places within the culture where Newton is used as a symbol or lodges as a folk-memory. This is not a simple matter of tracing influence or monitoring impact. It is about understanding the active creative process whereby cultural meanings are generated about who Newton was, why he matters, and what he has come to signify. In this sense, there is no single Newton.

In the second half of this chapter, we look at what might be involved in investigating the cultural meanings accruing to the figure of Newton in contemporary Britain. The two case studies presented here thus reflect a personal trajectory, as well as a movement within modern cultural studies: from work conditioned by the history of science as traditionally practised, to an analysis within a framework orientated towards the cultural dimensions of science.

In the twentieth century, Isaac Newton has become an international symbol of English science. In casting which was imaginative even by Hollywood standards, Harpo Marx played Newton in the 1957 film *The story of mankind*.

Capturing the British imagination

The late eighteenth century is an interesting period for Newtonian studies, for we find a rich vein of Newtonian imagery in the poetry of the time—most notably, in that of Erasmus Darwin and William Blake. Darwin and Blake had much in common. Their social networks to some extent overlapped; they were both thought of as radicals; they

Engraving by William Blake, *The fertilization of Egypt*, for Erasmus Darwin's *Botanic garden* (1791).

explored within their poetry the world of natural philosophy. Indeed, Blake engraved some illustrations for one of Darwin's major poetic works, *The botanic garden*. And yet, their poetic visions were radically different. Newton is a key figure within the poetry of each, but seen rather differently. In each case, though, they hoped to use their image of Newton in the construction of what has been called 'imaginary communities', which might underpin the new sense of *Englishness* that each wished to foster.

The work of Darwin and Blake came towards the end of a long debate about science within poetry which had occupied much of the eighteenth century. Newton was, not surprisingly, a frequently encountered figure within this debate. We shall understand the particular features of Darwin and Blake better if we learn something of the progress of this debate, which can be characterized as having four phases.

In the first phase, Newton's achievement was admired, but in a somewhat guarded or sceptical way, on grounds which are ultimately religious and to do with the position of humankind in the cosmos. This phase is typified in the poetry of Henry Brooke and Alexander Pope. Brooke's 1730s assessment of Newton's importance has a clear perspective:

> For deep, indeed, the ETERNAL FOUNDER lies,
> And high above his work the MAKER flies;
> Yet infinite that work, beyond our soar;
> Beyond what Clarkes can prove, or Newtons can explore!

And in his *Essay on man*, Pope expressed similar reservations about Newton's accomplishments:

> Superior beings, when of late they saw
> A mortal Man unfold all Nature's law,
> Admir'd such wisdom in an earthly shape,
> And shew'd a Newton as we shew an Ape.

These two poets saw Newton as embodying the strengths, but also the limitations, of the human comprehension of the natural world.

In the second phase, it was the imagery which Newton had unleashed that captured the imagination of poets. His *Opticks*, in particular, was a major influence on the work of many poets, for whom Newton had intensified the human experience of the natural world. In the middle of describing a rainbow, James Thomson addressed Newton directly:

> Here, awful Newton, the dissolving clouds
> Form, fronting on the sun, thy showery prism;
> And to the sage-instructed eye unfold
> The various twine of light, by thee disclosed
> From the white mingling maze.

Thomson wrote this poem in 1728, the year after Newton's death. This phase of drawing upon Newtonian imagery was still vigorous in the 1740s, when Mark Akenside conveyed through his poetry his expectation that the human experience of rainbows would be qualitatively improved through Newton's theories.

A rather different response to Newton can be seen in the poetry of Christopher Smart and William Blake. Both of these poets were dissatisfied with the world-picture implied by the works and reputation of Newton and his friend, the philosopher John Locke. Smart and Blake felt that the influence of Newton and Locke was negative, because their views obscured crucial questions of how we know about issues of truth and beauty. Indeed, they seemed to verge on a kind of materialism which left no space in the universe for God. Such a reaction against the earlier admiration for Newtonian views was part of what lie behind Blake's protest in *A vision of the last judgement*:

> The Last Judgement is an Overwhelming of Bad Art & Science. Mental Things are alone Real; what is call'd Corporeal, Nobody Knows of its Dwelling Place: it is in Fallacy, & its Existence an Imposture. Where is the Existence Out of Mind or Thought?

In poetry which appeared in the last decade of the eighteenth century we can see a fourth phase, still inspired by Newton. Poets such as Richard Payne Knight and Erasmus Darwin were optimistic, as Thomson and Akenside had been, about the promise of contemporary natural philosophy. Yet they shared with Smart and Blake doubts

The ambivalence of William Blake's *Newton* has intrigued generations: although he is portrayed staring down at the ground, away from higher aspirations, the figure is noble and not unsympathetically rendered. The symbolism of the dividers recalls a long tradition in western art imagery for representing mathematical activity (see p. 140 for earlier examples).

about whether the picture of a world governed by Newtonian natural laws actually made religious sense. Knight, for example, pondered:

Whether primordial motion sprang to life
From the wild war of elemental strife;
In central chains, the mass inert confined
And sublimated matter into mind?
Or, whether one great all-pervading soul
Moves in each part, and animates the whole;
Unnumber'd worlds to one great centre draws;
And governs all by pre-established laws?

In fact, Knight concluded that he could not tackle these issues, beckoning his readers:

Let us less visionary themes pursue,
And try to show what mortal eyes may view;

Darwin, was more forthright in this respect. For him, the only way of justifying claims to have acquired true knowledge about nature was to frame them in an account of how the natural world and the human mind shared a common origin. By extending the ambition of Newtonian natural philosophy, Darwin sought to bring all social, intellectual, and moral developments under the umbrella of the operations of nature:

By firm immutable immortal laws
Impress'd on Nature by the GREAT FIRST CAUSE.
Say, Muse! how rose from elemental strife
Organic forms, and kindled into life;
How Love and Sympathy with potent charm

Warm the cold heart, the lifted hand disarm;
Allure with pleasures, and alarm with pains,
And bind Society in golden chains.

Later in this poem, *The temple of nature*, we find Newton in Darwin's pantheon of heroes, along with those stalwarts of the Industrial Revolution—Newcomen, Arkwright, Priestley, Savery, Wedgwood, and Boulton:

NEWTON's eye sublime
Mark'd the bright periods of revolving time;
Explored in Nature's scenes the effect and cause,
And, charm'd, unravell'd all her latent laws.

Darwin constructed an *imaginary community* of scientists and industrialists, whose achievements represented to him the culmination of the development of the natural world. Here were true British heroes, and his poetry celebrated their achievements as such.

But there was a further dimension to Darwin's poetic projects which brought him back to Newton. Darwin's poetic images of the natural and social worlds were designed, as he put it, '*to inlist the Imagination under the banner of Science*'. The imagination was to be the vehicle mediating between sensual poetic images and science, which he called 'the ratiocination of philosophy'. But the imagination was also, for Darwin, something that was very visually orientated, as his poetic practice and theory demonstrated. As he explained, 'the Poet writes principally to the eye'. Indeed, Darwin's entire conception of how we

The frontispiece of Darwin's *The temple of nature* (1803), an engraving of a drawing by Fuseli, maintained some of the symbolism of earlier centuries, notably the multi-breasted Nature Goddess.

acquire knowledge was founded on a visual model, and he explored various ideas concerning the physiological dimensions of vision—including speculations about 'luminous music', drawing on Newton's theory of the colour spectrum.

Although his attitude to Newton was very different, William Blake was also concerned with Newton's status as the major figure in contemporary natural philosophy. The core of the appeal of the Newtonian cosmology, in Blake's estimation, was its 'picture-language quality' which drew on both the imagination *and* reason. While Darwin viewed this as a positive feature of Newtonian natural philosophy which he wished to emulate, Blake saw it as a real threat to the human imagination. He endeavoured to extract the imagination from its Newtonian constraints, and was set firmly against Darwin's aim of its mediating between science and poetic images. Blake's intention was to subvert images of vision by transforming them into visionary images:

> The nature of infinity is this: That every thing has its
> Own Vortex, and when once a traveller thro' Eternity
> Has pass'd that Vortex, he percieves [sic] it roll backward behind
> His path, into a Globe itself unfolding like a sun,
> Or like a moon, or like a universe of starry majesty,
> While he keeps onwards in his wondrous journey on the Earth,
> Or like a human form, a friend [with] whom he lived
> Benevolent.

So, Darwin and Blake took opposing stands on the imagination, reason, vision and, indeed, on industrialization. For Darwin, Newton was a hero, and readers were to be drawn into the world of science through poetry, in particular through appeals to the visual sense and an instrumentalist use of the imagination. For Blake, Newton was equally important, something of an anti-hero—linked in his own mythology to the figure Urizen, the tyrant who threatened to dominate and destroy the universe. While the achievements of Newton, Watt, Savery, and Priestley represented progress for Darwin, for Blake they were identified with the impoverishment of the imagination. Urizen symbolized his fears about the dangers of Darwin's goal of enlisting 'Imagination under the banner of Science'. Blake was determined that this and other complementary aims should not be realized on Albion's fair shores.

When I began to examine the issues described above, I was operating, albeit unselfconsciously, within the model described by Guerlac. I too was in pursuit of Newton's influence—in this case, on Darwin and Blake. This framework now seems unsatisfactory. I would argue for a broader perspective than pursuing one particular hare which wanders around late eighteenth-century Newtonian studies—namely, the question of whether Darwin or Blake got Newton 'right'. Instead, I would prefer to see Darwin's and Blake's projects as embodying

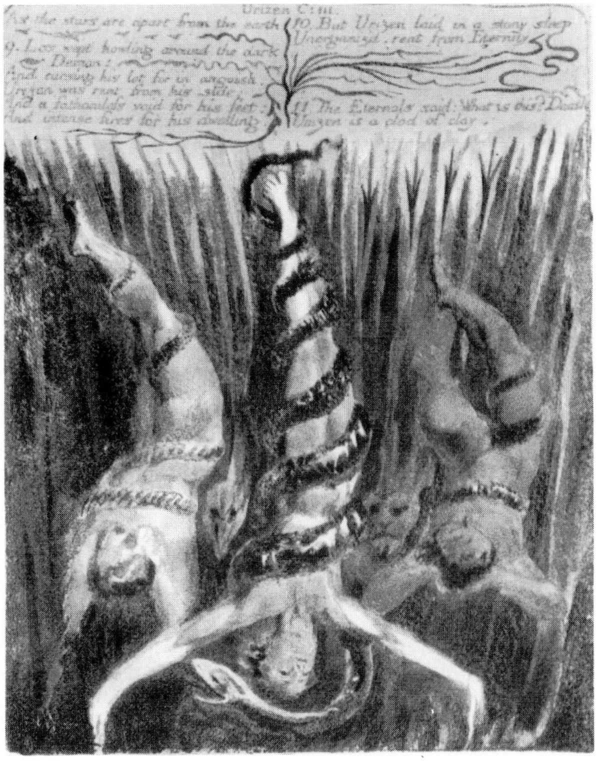

The title page of Blake's *Book of Urizen* (1794) shows the tyrant-demon, with eyes closed, copying from Nature's book what he can read with his toes.

In *Urizen* Blake drew anguished figures, bound with the serpents of constricting imagination, falling into the abyss of Newtonian materialism.

representations, or constructions, or reconstructions of Newton. Each provided the basis for substantive calls for a reorientation in English culture. In Darwin's case, these involved adaptation to the goals of the new innovative industrial bourgeois of the provinces. Blake was seeking an animated anti-industrial, imaginative culture to pose as an alternative. The visions of Darwin and Blake were counterposed: *Newton as hero* or *Newton as anti-hero*; a new England, regenerated 'under the banner of Science', or confined by the 'Loom of Locke' and 'the Water-wheels of Newton'. Each built his aspirations for Albion on different, but complementary, images of Newton.

Imaginary communities today

Many of the contributions to this book are concerned with Newton in his age. Even the first part of this chapter scarcely moved out of the eighteenth and early nineteenth centuries. It is far riskier to tackle the significance of Newton in late twentieth-century Britain. Nevertheless, if we are interested in understanding contemporary British culture and the role of science within it, this is a worthwhile, although difficult, task. For this reason, what follows is limited to some suggestions about starting places for investigating the contemporary meaning of Newton. There are three possibilities:

- situating him within analyses of the components of the national culture;
- identifying key sites where Newton appears as a national hero;
- looking at his position in relationship to the creation of popular myths around scientific heroes.

Components of the national culture

In the late 1960s, some British intellectuals of the left, in an exercise remarkably similar in substance to that of Erasmus Darwin and William Blake, although different in form, reviewed the 'components of the national culture'. Some reached dismayingly negative conclusions. Perry Anderson, for example, concluded that Britain had a culture that was 'mediocre and inert', although it is perhaps significant that he deliberately excluded the natural sciences from his survey. This, and other negative assessments, inspired Edward Thompson to a spirited defence of his national culture. In an article with the marvellously ambiguous title *The peculiarities of the English*, Thompson expounded on the richness of the maligned national culture. In contrast to Anderson, Thompson's main reference point in his rehabilitation was British

Newton as local hero. In 1858, Newton's statue was erected in Grantham, the Lincolnshire market town where he went to school. The ceremony was attended by all the town dignitaries and organizations. Newton still makes a useful contribution to Grantham's finances, as the protagonist of its tourist industry.

natural science. The hero of his version of the national culture was Charles Darwin, and standing in the wings to provide trusty predictable support were those key figures in the British natural philosophy tradition—Francis Bacon and Isaac Newton. Here is the core of the *peculiar* English intellectual tradition, as Thompson identified it. Natural philosophy was highlighted as the English academic discipline *par excellence*.

This leads to my first suggestion about the contemporary significance of Newton within British culture. There is evidently something about this natural philosophy tradition, represented by the triumvirate of Bacon, Newton, and Darwin, which has come to represent British culture to every spectrum of the political arena.

Newton in contemporary popular culture

A second way into the contemporary significance of Newton could be more concretely and empirically rooted. This might begin with the various forms of encounter with Newton which exist in popular culture. This carries us outside the academic context, to the ways that 'the woman or man on the street' meets this scientific hero. This avenue of investigation has not yet been pursued very thoroughly. And yet, it seems a potentially fruitful area of investigation for those concerned with the role of science in culture, with national heroes, with popular culture, and so on.

For this reason, it might be worthwhile to sketch some of the parameters of such research on Newton. The average citizen of late twentieth-century Britain might encounter the figure of Newton in one or all of the following ways:

- in school textbooks, as a major figure in the history of science;
- as a figure represented in substantial statues in some key national settings, such as Westminster Abbey or Trinity College, Cambridge;
- as a person formerly represented on the pound note, thereby joining the notables (such as Shakespeare and the Duke of Wellington) whose images have adorned British currency;
- through the postage stamps issued in 1987 to mark the three-hundredth anniversary of the publication of the *Principia*.

Even this cursory listing is revealing about Newton's role in contemporary British culture. Each of the instances listed involves a key institution of British life: textbooks within the educational system; statues at *the* national church of the state religion (Westminster Abbey) and one of the oldest established English universities (Cambridge); currency and the financial institutions; and the postal service, as one of the oldest and most important components of the national

Roubillac's statue of Newton, before the war memorial in Trinity College, Cambridge. William Wordsworth, a student of the College in the 1780s, remembered seeing from his rooms

> 'The antechapel where the statue stood
> Of Newton with his prism and silent face,
> The marble index of a mind for ever
> Voyaging through strange seas of Thought, alone.'

The English pound note of the late 1970s was a fascinating repository of Newtonian symbolism. Comparing this with other such repositories—for example, that of Newton's tomb—shows us how the balance of Newton's activities and contributions has been perceived at different periods.

communications system. Indeed, currency and postage stamps are perhaps the most tangible and immediate international signifiers of national identity. Westminster Abbey and Cambridge University have double valency, both as seats of major establishment institutions, and as tourist sites where foreigners can pay homage to the relics and paraphernalia of Englishness. Textbooks function, perhaps, more as internal carriers of national identity. Nevertheless, linguists, historians, and cultural analysts have begun to acknowledge their importance in this respect, and to see them as repositories of crucial images of nations.

These representations within key national institutions would seem to denote Newton's status as a powerful signifier of Englishness. Moreover, it is clear that in each of these instances, Newton clearly signifies the *past* achievements of English culture.

This brings us back to the first case study. There we saw Darwin and Blake thrusting Newton into the centre of their projects for major reorientations of English culture. For Darwin, Newton was at the heart of his project for bringing his contemporaries to the world of science and industry, and for making contemporary institutions take account of science and industry (and scientists and industrialists). Blake, in contrast, saw Newton as a major obstacle to a more visionary and imaginative, less materialistic culture. Both poets were inspired by Newton to beckon their contemporaries towards a new kind of Englishness. Theirs was a vision of what Albion might be—a future vision.

Reading the poetry of Darwin or Blake, their contemporaries would link Newton either positively or negatively with a call for change, for a reorientation in British culture. In contrast, the twentieth-century

The four British postage stamps issued in 1987 covered a wide range of Newtonian symbols.

The *Isaac Newton Shopping Centre*, Grantham.

encounter with Newton is not about change, but about what English culture was, and is to remain. Newton inspired Darwin and Blake, and by extension their readers, with a sense of what English culture *could* be. Today, the popular encounter is with a Newton who represents English culture of the past. He is associated with *an Englishness which is to be preserved, and not changed.* He is met as part of what has been called Britain's 'heritage culture', or as 'the historical and sacrosanct identity' of the British nation. Newton's contemporary role would seem to be part of the more general pattern that Patrick Wright has described, whereby 'the past has been secured as a cultural presence in modern Britain'.

Newton and the apple: a key myth

In an intriguing set of essays examining some key contemporary myths, first published in 1957, the French semiologist Roland Barthes turned his attention to Albert Einstein. As his essay title *The brain of Einstein* suggests, Barthes drew attention to what seemed to him to be an obsession with this particular part of Einstein's anatomy. As he saw it, Einstein's brain was the avenue through which this scientist was most frequently encountered in popular culture. This image itself was contradictory, he maintained:

> Einstein's brain is a mythical object: paradoxically, the greatest intelligence of all provides an image of the most up-to-date machine.

But Barthes pursued the mythology surrounding Einstein yet further, considering that 'Through the mythology of Einstein, the world blissfully regained the image of knowledge reduced to a formula'. Even more than this, in Barthes' estimation, Einstein was a crucial figure in popular culture because he:

> fulfills all the conditions of myth, which could not care less about contradictions so long as it established a euphoric security: at once magician and machine, eternal researcher and unfulfilled discoverer, unleashing the best and the worst, brain and conscience. Einstein embodies the most contradictory dreams, and mythically reconciles the infinite power of man over nature with the 'fatality' of the sacrosanct, which man cannot yet do without.

Taking a cue from Barthes, there is a similar sort of job to be done on Newton now. The most popular mythical representation of Newton revolves around the story of the apple. According to this myth, Newton's understanding of gravity, and indeed his subsequent formulation of the laws of motion of bodies, were inspired by the simple experience of having an apple fall on his head as he lay under a tree. Or, in the

In *The story of mankind*, a whole bushel of apples was seen to fall on Newton's head, to hammer home to audiences Hollywood's understanding of scientific discovery. Newton could have no excuse now for not inventing gravity.

From Newton as comic hero, to Newton as romantic hero. This nineteenth-century reconstruction of the young Newton pondering in his apple orchard is barely more plausible an account of scientific discovery than that of 1950s Hollywood.

bold claim of the magazine *Garden answers*, the apple falling on his head 'caused him to discover gravity'. Whatever the sources and reality of the story, it does have extraordinary popular purchase. Indeed, the British Post Office could presume complete public familiarity with the image of the apple as denoting Newton, and thus use it as an appropriate emblem for the stamp which marked the *Principia* tercentenary.

It is precisely the popular appeal of this myth which should draw us back to it for closer scrutiny. What is it which makes it so appealing, such a constant reference? We might return to Barthes' description of Einstein as a mythical figure who 'reconciles the infinite power of man over nature with the "Fatality" of the sacrosanct, which man cannot yet do without'. The myth of Newton's apple seems to fulfil similar needs. Is there not something marvellously reassuring about that tale? Nature quite literally knocks us on the head with the required knowledge! The story bespeaks an amazing integration between humanity and the natural world. And what better endorsement could there be for the potential of the 'gentleman scholar'? In addition, it is fundamentally a pastoral image, as are so many other cherished images of Englishness, including the paintings of Constable: it is, thereby, associated with that touchstone of Englishness—*the countryside*.

Newton's apple speaks to postal users as far apart as Grenada, Nicaragua, and Mali.

This simple and often repeated tale resonates because it is so reassuring. Amidst the insecurities generated by nuclear technology and the big moral questions posed by molecular biology, genetic engineering, and the new reproductive technologies, it offers a more peaceful image of the generation of scientific knowledge—one which is fundamentally without conflict. Moreover, it is also reassuring about Englishness in general, and English science in particular. It reanimates English pastoralism, whilst insisting that, whatever disclaimers are made about the state of British science and technology today, English science has been, and perhaps still is, powerful.

Newton in British culture: the 1790s versus the 1980s

In the two preceding sections, we have explored some dimensions of Newton's role within British culture at two different periods. It is appropriate to draw out some features of these case studies.

In both periods, Newton comes to represent aspects of British science. In Darwin and Blake's era, he represented the potential of natural philosophy: positively for Darwin, negatively for Blake. By contrast, in 1980s Britain, Newton is a figure of reassurance, rather than promise: identified with the past, rather than the future of British science.

It is also interesting to contrast the settings in which we have observed the appearance of Newton. In the first case study, we examined some poetic explorations of Newtonianism. This literary mode was pre-eminent in encouraging public understanding of Newton's natural philosophy. In the twentieth century, the lay encounter with Newton is unlikely to occur via literature, even though there has been at least one novel centred on an historian of science doing research on Newton. In fact, it might even be claimed that Newton is now much more integrated into popular culture at the everyday level.

There are two further dimensions which emerge from juxtaposing the two case studies. One is that Newton has been a pivotal figure within British culture for at least 200 years. His significance for Darwin and Blake was that they regarded him as a linchpin in their efforts to reorientate English culture—he was crucial to their vision of the future of England. Today, Newton is more likely to be taken as a signifier of the past—ensconced as part of the English heritage, and as part of an English culture which is to be preserved, rather than changed. Finally, his potency as a signifier of Englishness has grown since the late eighteenth century. Represented in major institutions of the national establishment and linked to strong pastoral traditions, Newton, like Shakespeare, has come to stand for Englishness.

History of science and cultural studies of science

Despite all the revisions and transformations the history of science has undergone in recent years, it is a discipline which is, to a considerable degree, organized around key figures. This biographical focus still casts

The story of the apple falling on Newton's head is now so far embedded in popular culture that comic allusions to it are immediately understood, as in this *Punch* cartoon.

its shadow over much of the research and teaching undertaken within the discipline. Conferences and books, such as this, have as their organizational core Newton's persona, writings, interests, and activities. There is a certain intellectual quest which motivates much of the input into such productions: identifying the *real* Newton. What were his prime interests? What are his theories and writings really about? Are there elements of his activities and enterprises which have not been adequately acknowledged or analysed?

These are all legitimate and important questions in the history of science. Nevertheless, our historical understanding of science in culture, and of Newton as a particular figure within it, might be enriched if we are sometimes willing to let go of our pursuit of the *right* Newton. On occasion we should shift our focus away from Newton himself, to the appropriations of his ideas and the constructions and reconstructions of his significance. We can learn more from investigating how Darwin and Blake *used* Newton in their reorientations of English culture than from evaluating how *true* their different versions were to the *real* Newton. Likewise, contemporary myths about Newton, including the story of his enlightenment through being knocked on the head by an apple, also merit the attention of those concerned with understanding Newton's significance in contemporary culture.

A second major feature of the history of science is its preoccupation with key texts. This book is itself a testimony to this fact, occasioned as it was by the celebration of the 300th anniversary of the appearance of the *Principia*. Gyorgy Markus has recently argued that the natural sciences themselves have for a long time been structured about key texts which *belong* in a strong sense to their author, like an intellectual patent. The orientation of historical studies of science around major scientific texts seems, then, to parallel the nature of the natural sciences themselves. I do not undermine the importance of this work in suggesting that interpreting Newton as a cultural hero can also involve studies of other texts and other cultural sites. The contemporary meaning of Newton is produced through encounters with stamps and with statues of him, as well as with the *Principia* itself. A cultural studies perspective challenges the narrow text orientation of some history of science.

The final point I wish to draw from my analysis takes me back to the well-trodden terrain of past debates about what kind of factors influence the development of science. It is significant that Newtonian studies have been a battleground for such debates. Was Newtonian mechanics a product of a particular stage in the development of capitalism, or should it be understood as the product of internal developments within the study of the natural world? The fervour animating the clashes between *externalists* and *internalists*—as pro-

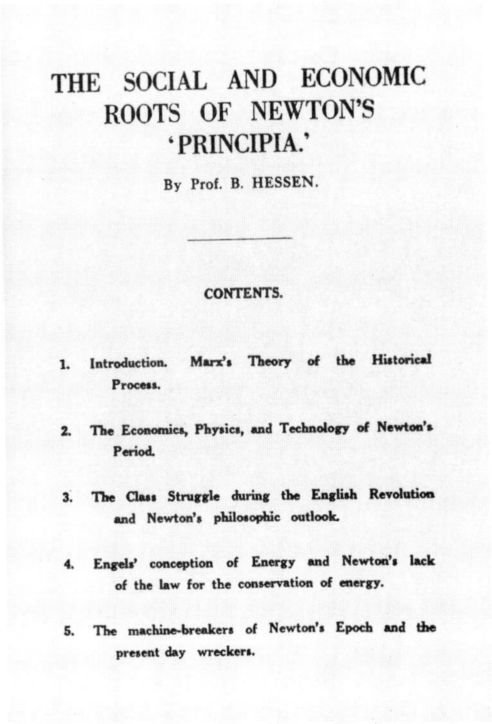

THE SOCIAL AND ECONOMIC ROOTS OF NEWTON'S 'PRINCIPIA.'

By Prof. B. HESSEN.

CONTENTS.

A notable influence on twentieth-century historical studies was the Russian contribution to the 1931 International Congress of the History of Science. Boris Hessen's speech on *The social and economic roots of Newton's 'Principia'* outlined an externalist analysis of seventeenth-century developments. His approach is evident from the section headings of his talk.

ponents of these two positions are called—has made it difficult to note that there is something of a convergence of focus between the two schools. For, whether they draw on internal or external factors, the object in both cases is to explain developments *within* science. In short, they share a common object of study. The history of science has drawn its cues, whether internalist or externalist, from science itself. The understandable logic has gone something like this: to understand science we must begin (at least) with the scientific community, the scientist, the scientific text, and so on, possibly *then* moving outwards in other directions.

I am suggesting that cultural studies of science might undertake rather different projects. Such work is premised on the somewhat radical notion that the meanings of science are not all rooted in the scientific community itself. This is not a straightforward issue of influence, as Guerlac and others have proposed, for it can involve the autonomous generation of meanings about science in a variety of sites. A cultural studies perspective acknowledges that the contemporary meaning of science is not restricted to the domain of its practitioners, but rather is constructed across a range of disparate sites including tourist sites, postage stamps, and so on. Newton's figure in these locations is just as much a locus of meanings as that reconstructed by historians poring over his primary texts. Indeed, this chapter has provided only a cursory sketch of the range of research projects which might be undertaken to provide a fuller picture of Newton's significance in popular British culture.

Such a strategy by no means denigrates the stature of Newton. Indeed, what it proposes is a fuller and more complex investigation of why Newton has been such a crucial national hero.

Further reading

For background on the poetic response to Newton in the eighteenth and early nineteenth centuries, see Donald D. Ault, *Visionary physics: Blake's response to Newton*, Chicago University Press, Chicago and London, 1975; and Marjorie Hope Nicolson, *Newton demands the muse: Newton's opticks and eighteenth century poets*, Princeton University Press, Princeton, 1946. I provide a fuller account of Darwin's poetic project in his historical context in Maureen McNeil, *Under the banner of science: Erasmus Darwin and his age*, Manchester University Press, Manchester, 1987.

Two of the main contributions to the debate about the components of British culture referred to here are Perry Anderson's 'Components of national culture', in *Student power: problems, diagnosis, action* (edited by Alexander Cockburn and Robin Blackburn), Penguin, Harmondsworth, 1969, pp. 214–84; and E. P. Thompson, 'The peculiarities of the English', first published in 1965, and reprinted in *The poverty of theory and other essays*, Merlin Press, London, 1978, pp. 35–91. I find the latter a very rich source on the importance of certain scientific traditions (particularly those associated with Bacon, Newton, and Darwin) to English culture.

For a very interesting attempt to consider the mythologizing of a particular scientist, see Roland Barthes' essay *The brain of Einstein*, in his fascinating collection of essays on myths of contemporary culture, *Mythologies*, Jonathan Cape, London, 1972. For a recent complex (and not always easy) review of some of the features of the natural sciences, including the relationship between text and authors within them, see Gyorgy Markus, 'Why is there no hermeneutics of natural sciences? Some preliminary theses', in *Science in context*, I (1987), 5–51.

アイザック
ニウトン碩
學にして
誇らず

CHAPTER
TWELVE

Newton and the twentieth century—a personal view

SIR HERMANN BONDI

Where do we stand in relation to Newton in this century? Let me start with some very general remarks.

When a scientist makes a useful contribution, he is frequently cited in other people's publications; indeed, it is often thought that one can measure influence by measuring how often papers are cited. The next stage comes when what the scientist has done is so universal, so classical, that one does not give it a citation: when mathematicians write down a *Taylor series* they never refer to Taylor, or when using the *Eulerian equations* they do not refer to Euler. There comes a final stage when it is so difficult to imagine what the world was like before a particular contribution that one can hardly get the contribution into perspective. The landscape has been so totally changed, the ways of thinking have been so deeply affected, that it is very hard to get hold of what it was like before. The landscape of physical science was so completely altered by Newton that it is very hard for us to realize how total a change in outlook he produced.

It is typical of what I am trying to convey that we attach his name most easily and readily to his lesser contributions. When one speaks of *Newton's rings*, seen when there is an oil-film on a puddle, then this was certainly a contribution, but one of his lesser ones. The major contributions have been so influential in forming our picture of the world that one might feel that he really did not do very much; after all, what he found out is what every schoolchild knows! It is an enormously difficult effort to put oneself into the frame of mind of the situation that he revolutionized, first in his thoughts, and markedly later through his great book, the *Principia*.

The way in which that landscape has been changed is certainly too great for me to describe, but it is important to illuminate at least part of it. I will give you a very personal selection. Let me start with my own prejudices about the nature of science.

Isaac Newton, very great head of school but not pompous, according to this Japanese print of about 1869, in which Newton represented Western science in a series of prints of great men of the Western world.

In the philosophy of science I am very much a follower of Karl Popper, and of his notion of the need for scientists to create theories and to subject them to empirical testing. Another follower of Popper, Peter Medawar, particularly stressed what is implicit in Popper's work, that *it is strictly necessary for scientists actually to do something.* To talk about an insoluble problem, even to talk very intelligently about an insoluble problem, is scarcely a recognized contribution to science. In

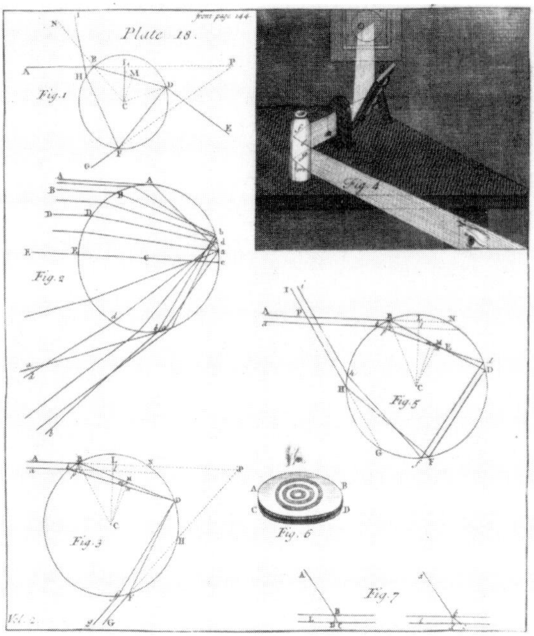

Newton's rings ('*Fig 6*'), which occur between two pieces of glass as well as from an oil-film, have been studied since before Newton's own work on them.

a splendid little book Peter Medawar gave science the title *The art of the soluble*, seeing it as the test of a scientist to attack problems on which some impression can be made, rather than to waste time on insoluble tasks.

It is in the *selection* of these problems that a great deal of the nature of good scientific work, and indeed scientific genius, lies. I like to say that, if you talk about the problems that you meet when you walk about the street, 80 per cent of them are insoluble while $19\frac{1}{2}$ per cent of them are trivial. It is the task of the scientist to select the tiny layer between the insoluble and the trivial, where skill, insight, originality, creativity, and application can make a difference. The difficulty of finding this layer is often overlooked. It is often not appreciated that an enormous amount of the skill and experience and the sheer 'nose' of particularly the older and more experienced members of the profession goes into finding such a layer.

The positive inheritance

In the light of these preliminary remarks, I want to look at what Newton achieved in relation to the solar system. He was given a very jumbled-up heap of data, partly (but only in a very limited way) ordered by Kepler's and by Galileo's work. This enormous heap of data, in which soluble and insoluble items seemed inextricably mingled,

Newton cut neatly in two with surgical precision. His genius separated out the question:

given the positions, velocities, and masses of the bodies of the solar system today, where will they be in the future and where have they been in the past?

He solved this problem so totally that not much was left for others, except a few footnotes and detailed and complex workings-out. So rich a vein did he strike, in fact, that the detailed working-out is not yet finished; indeed, it is amazing how often one finds relatively simple applications of Newton's work in the literature, in papers that are very illuminating in relation not only to the solar system, but also to globular clusters, galaxies and their satellites, and perhaps rings.

So, on one side of the surgical cut he made a clean sweep of the problems, recognizing, with a genius that cannot be overestimated, that this *could* be a clean sweep; the other side of the cut concerns the question:

why do the bodies of the solar system have these particular masses, positions, and velocities?

This is the problem of the origin of the solar system. After 300 years and an enormous amount of work, we are not all that much wiser as regards these issues.

If you ever asked for an illustration of how to divide between the soluble and the insoluble (or, should I say, scarcely soluble), this is surely it. At this very early stage in the evolution of science, most of the people involved had not appreciated the need to leave alone or circumvent those problems for whose solution the time was not ripe. Newton carried out this division with a clarity which seems to me perhaps the most impressive feature of his work.

There are many other features that one can, and must, stress. When we look with the eye of our century at Newton's work, we need to see how he tackled scientific problems and how he selected just those pieces where progress was possible.

Many people could talk better than I about the width of his interests and the wide scale of his contributions. Newton looked at the motion of liquids and their viscosity, and put in the assumption of *linearity*. Today, following his ideas, we describe such fluids as *Newtonian fluids*—in fact, almost all the successes in hydrodynamics have been in the field of Newtonian fluids. The literature on non-Newtonian liquids is of much more recent origin and has been much slower in growing.

As regards his *dynamics*, there are so many features of it that have grown so much into the nature of our thinking that we are perhaps not sufficiently conscious today of all that he did. The differential calculus is not just a necessary tool for studying Newtonian dynamics, which is certainly the case, but it is a widening of mathematics into new fields. Those fields are still among the richest areas for mathematical development and are equally necessary for a large part of physics.

A slightly naughty thought can come to one's mind here. Is it due to the nature of physics that the mathematical tools started by Newton are so essential for many parts of physics through the centuries? Or is our selection of worked-on parts of physics still largely Newtonian? The tools that he gave us stand at the root of so much that goes on now. The parts of physics where rich progress has been made are those where his tools, markedly developed and changed, are still tools of the greatest utility. We may not be doing a lot more than following in his footsteps. We may still be so much under the impression of the particular turn he took that, with all the branching-out and all the widening-out, the direction that he set is still basic to our work. We cannot get it out of our system.

Of course we have gone a long way since Newton. His own field of dynamics has had a tremendous mathematical development, due to people like Euler, Lagrange, Laplace, and Hamilton. It is not always appreciated that, 60 years ago, the makers of modern quantum theory were totally steeped, immersed, educated—brainwashed, if you like—in the mathematical methods of Lagrange and Hamilton; these ideas had grown out of, and were the natural evolution of, Newton's dynamical ideas. Of course, quantum mechanics meant a change and not one to be surprised at. After all, when one enormously extends the range of observations and experiments out of which a theory is grown, it should not cause surprise that some changes in the theory become necessary. But *the roots of quantum theory are firmly in Newtonian dynamics*.

In general, the rails of thinking in physics and astronomy tend to be still very much those that Newton laid down. Indeed, at least some of the areas of spectacular progress are due to the readiness to overcome what were quite often not the prejudices of Newton himself, but of some of his successors. The problematics of an infinite universe, and of absolute and relative space, were problems of which he was aware. He was not nearly as doctrinaire as many of his successors. Changes that became necessary should be regarded as upsetting not so much our Newtonian inheritance, as some of the interpretation of that inheritance.

A very interesting problem is the *theory of light*. He showed us what white light is. This has become so obvious to all, that one does not often think back to the fact—not only that it was not known before his time but that 150 years later even as great a person as Goethe still found the decomposition of white light to be unacceptable and unconvincing. The corpuscular theory of light that Newton proposed has been through many changes. I do not think that it would be

Einstein's brain? Albert Einstein (1879–1955), whose work is arguably simpler to understand than Newton's, was a strong admirer of Newton. He wrote in 1931:

Fortunate Newton, happy childhood of science! ... In one person he combined the experimenter, the theorist, the mechanic and, not least, the artist in exposition. He stands before us strong, certain, and alone.... Newton's discoveries have passed into the stock of accepted knowledge.

sensible to ascribe to Newton what we now know about the corpuscular nature of light, because the kind of experiment to which the modern outlook is due—namely the photoelectric effect—was totally unknown to him. I would, therefore, not wish to say that our present understanding of the corpuscular nature of light can be traced back to Newton. What *can* be traced back to him are the mathematical tools he employed—the fact that the tools of a corpuscular theory, and the application and further development of his picture of dynamics, could be a foundation for a modern theory of light.

Not everything Newtonian has fully entered people's minds. When I try to teach special relativity, I am frequently surprised by how little the revolution of Galileo and Newton has entered students' minds. After years of teaching at school, and possibly even after teaching at university, the relativity of velocity and the absolute nature of acceleration are still somewhat alien to most people's ways of thinking. When I talk on special relativity, I always say that Einstein's contribution has a name for being difficult, but this is quite wrong. Einstein's contribution is very easy to understand, but unfortunately it rests on the theories of Galileo and Newton which are very difficult to understand! I do think that it is the persistent lack of an instinctive understanding of these points that, even 300 to 400 years later, still dogs us in the popular understanding of physics.

The negative inheritance

I have so far stressed the positive inheritance that Newton has given us which is part of the fabric—although perhaps still not fully incorporated into the fabric—of thinking in our century. However, I also want to state the area where there has been a distinctively negative effect, one that is still very much with us.

His solution of the problem of motion in the solar system was so complete, so total, so precise, so stunning, that it was taken for generations as the model of what any decent theory should be like, not just in physics, but in all fields of human endeavour. It took a long time before one began to understand—and the understanding is not yet universal—that his genius *selected* an area where such perfection of solution was possible. This is a rarity in science. It is not universal. If we look at it as a model for what science should be like, we are gravely misled. I think most physical scientists now appreciate this point, although the appreciation took a long time to grow. But when we go outside the physical sciences—first perhaps to the biological sciences, and then to the social sciences, history, economics, or sociology—then so often we find that people have an image, or mirage, of a Newtonian solution as what they should aim for in their fields. They

The behaviour of water, especially where it changes from smooth to turbulent flow, has fascinated people from Leonardo da Vinci onwards. It is still not completely understood, whether by Newtonian or any other techniques.

feel that any proper field of knowledge should aim for the perfection of the Newtonian solution as its target.

I regard this as profoundly misleading. In my view, most of science is not like the Newtonian solar system, but much more like weather forecasting. In a very difficult field like weather forecasting, only a limited amount of success will (in all probability) ever turn out to be possible. Good progress has been achieved and major contributions have been made, but the putative limit lies far ahead.

This example shows what much of science is like. Science does not progress mostly to the perfection and hardness of the *Newtonian clockwork*, but to something much more limited. If one asks when physicists first appreciated the rarity of Newton's kind of solution, then no easy answer can be given. It was perhaps 80 years ago, in the early study of turbulence, when it was first realized that the flow of fluids was such that a perfect answer could generally not be given. However, very useful answers *can* be given, and our aeroplanes could not fly otherwise. Within their limits, these answers are good and rather precise, but they cannot be of unlimited accuracy.

What I am trying to stress is that you do not have to go to the quantum field to see that predictability, so perfect in Newton's solar system, is not a universal (and, indeed, not even a usual) characteristic of science. In the Newtonian solar system, we have a predictability in which there is no theoretical limit to the precision, while the nature of the beast in most other cases is totally different. When you drive on a day with 'scattered showers', you go through a wet patch and then drive a mile or two along a road and find a dry patch. You will feel instinctively that it is in principle impossible to forecast that this place will have rain, the place two miles off will be dry, and the place two miles further on will again be wet. It is only when you appreciate these limitations that you can honour the progress of weather forecasting. Newton gave us so singular an example of perfect prediction, of a perfect solution, that this mirage still impresses us too much.

Indeed, a little consideration shows where the limitations lie. A system subject to differential equations of the kind occurring in a Newtonian system must necessarily have its future *perfectly* predictable from a *perfect* knowledge of the present (positions, velocities, constants such as masses, and so on). But amongst all such systems, there will be some where a *very similar* present will lead to a *very similar* future, and others where the slightest difference in the present will lead to vastly different futures. The solar system happens to be of the first kind, whereas a pin-table is of the second kind. After the lapse of a year the Earth is in almost the same position as it was, and so its motion in the second year is almost the same as in the first year. But the slightest difference in how a ball on a pin-table hits the pin is liable to give it a totally different descent. Although the future follows inescapably from the present in any deterministic system, the only relevant question in science is whether an *approximate* knowledge of the present allows us to predict the future approximately, since *perfect* knowledge of the present never exists.

Oddly, it is only in recent years that there has been serious study of systems where a slight change in present conditions leads to totally different futures, although the link between present and future is rigid and definite. Thus one speaks of *deterministic chaos*. The difficulty of assimilating this has been great, although the example of turbulent flow is quite old. Nobody doubts the precision and firmness of the equations governing fluid flow, yet it is wholly impossible to predict with precision the arrival time of a particular eddy.

Thus the image of the precision of Newton's solar system is so deeply imprinted on our mind that the awakening from this picture has been slow. That in itself is no mean tribute to the genius of Newton.

Further reading

For a stimulating and accessible account of current thinking about prediction in a variety of disciplines, see *Predictability in science and society: symposium of the Royal Society and the British Academy* (edited by Sir John Mason and J. H. Westcott), London, 1986.

Sir Peter Medawar's *Pluto's republic*, Clarendon Press, Oxford, 1982, incorporates *The art of the soluble*, and *Induction and intuition in scientific thought*.

Finally, for discussions of aspects of post-Newtonian physics, see my *Relativity and common sense—a new approach to Einstein*, Heinemann, London, 1965; and also *The nature of time* (edited by R. G. Flood and M. J. Lockwood), Basil Blackwell, Oxford, 1986.

The astronaut who took this photograph was placed in position by technology utilizing Newtonian mechanics. But what he saw—an earth with swirling cloud formations—reminds us that some aspects of everyday experience are still not susceptible to Newtonian analysis.

References and notes

This list gives detailed references to the quotations in the book. For convenience, we use abbreviations for the following frequently cited works:

Correspondence: The correspondence of Isaac Newton, 7 volumes (edited by H. W. Turnbull (Vols I–III), J. F. Scott (Vol. IV), and A. R. Hall and L. Tilling (Vols V–VII)), Cambridge University Press, Cambridge, 1959–77.

Handbook: Derek Gjertsen, *The Newton handbook*, Routledge and Kegan Paul, London, 1986.

Mathematical papers: The mathematical papers of Isaac Newton, 8 volumes (edited by D. T. Whiteside), Cambridge University Press, Cambridge, 1967–84.

Never at rest: Richard S. Westfall, *Never at rest: a biography of Isaac Newton*, Cambridge University Press, Cambridge, 1980.

Optical papers: The optical papers of Isaac Newton, The optical lectures 1670–1672, (edited by A. E. Shapiro), Cambridge University Press, Cambridge, 1984.

Opticks: Isaac Newton, *Opticks* (based on the 4th edition, 1790), Dover Publications, New York, 1979.

Papers and letters: Isaac Newton's papers and letters on natural philosophy and related documents (edited by I. B. Cohen), Harvard University Press, Cambridge, Mass., 1978.

Principia: Sir Isaac Newton, *Principia*, Vols I, II (translated into English by Andrew Motte in 1729, revised edition by F. Cajori), University of California Press, Berkeley, 1962.

INTRODUCTION

1 'He was buried' Voltaire, *Letters on England* (translated by Leonard Tancock), Penguin Books, Harmondsworth, 1980, p. 69.

'Nature, and Nature's laws' Alexander Pope, *Epitaphs*, 1730.

2 'the greatest highth' John Aubrey, cited in Michael Hunter, *John Aubrey and the realm of learning*, Duckworth, London, 1975, p. 60.

3 'Very few persons in London' Voltaire, *Philosophical dictionary*, Edward Trulove, London (article: 'Newton and Descartes'), p. 252.

4 'There are people who think' Voltaire, *Letters on England*, Cassell, London, 1889, p. 71.

5 'Superior beings, when of late' Alexander Pope, *An essay on man*, Dublin, 1732, Epistle II.

6 'Bacon and Newton' William Blake, *Jerusalem*, 1804, Chapter 1.

'one continued course' Robert Routledge, *A popular history of science*, Routledge, London, 1881, p. 182.

'a fellow who believed nothing' Charles Lamb, quoted in *The Autobiography and memoirs of B. R. Haydon*, Vol. i (edited by T. Taylor), London, 1926, p. 269.

'the last of the magicians' John Maynard Keynes, 'Newton, the man', *Newton Tercentenary Celebrations*, Cambridge University Press, Cambridge, 1947, p. 27.

11 'it was said that he was so small' cited in *Never at rest*, p. 49.

14 'In the beginning of the year' cited in *Never at rest*, p. 143.

15 'I believe that the clue' John Maynard Keynes, '*Newton, the man*'.

16 'so few went to hear him' cited in *Never at rest*, p. 209.

17 'Sr/Being of opinion' *Correspondence*, Vol. III, p. 280.

20 'the greatest and rarest' David Hume, *A history of England*, (1754–62), Vol. V, 1864 edition (revised by J. S. Brewer), p. 481.

CHAPTER 1

23 'imaginative integration' S. Toulmin and J. Goodfield, *The fabric of the heavens*, Penguin Books, Harmondsworth, 1963, p. 263.

'grand synthesis' A. R. Hall, *The revolution in science 1500–1750*, Longman, London, 1983, p. 306.

'I. B. Cohen has rejected' see I. B. Cohen, *The Newtonian revolution*, Cambridge University Press, Cambridge, 1980, p. 163.

24 'peculiar happiness' B. de Fontenelle, 'Éloge', *Papers and letters*, p. 465.

'always tranquil' Voltaire, *Letters on England*, Penguin Books, Harmondsworth, 1980, p. 70.

25 'Yet, as D. T. Whiteside noted' see D. T. Whiteside, 'Newton's early thoughts on planetary motion', *British Journal for the History of Science*, 2 (1964), 117–37.

'there was no Keplerian revolution' I. B. Cohen, *The revolution in science*, Cambridge University Press, Cambridge, 1985, p. 132.

'Whereof the present learned' Jonathan Swift, *Gulliver's travels*, Penguin Books, Harmondsworth, 1967, pp. 242–3.

26 'philosophy a form', 'his innumerable discoveries' Jean D'Alembert, 'History of the sciences', in *The age of Enlightenment* (edited by A. H. Eliot and B. Stern), Vol. I, Ward Lock, London, pp. 135–6.

'altogether without a rival', 'indisputably and incomparably' William Whewell, *History of the inductive sciences*, Vol. 2, John Parker, London, 1857, pp. 136–7.

'modern science continues' R. S. Westfall, *The construction of modern science*, Cambridge University Press, Cambridge, 1978, p. 159.

27 'a colossus without parallel', 'The answer is no' Stephen Hawking and Werner Israel, article in *The Times*, London, 27 June 1987.

'apparatus would fall' George Gamow, 'The exclusion principle', *Scientific American*, July 1959, p. 74.

'If I had staid' cited in *Handbook*, p. 561.

'He refused to ignore it' cited in *Never at rest*, p. 217.

28 'Fallacious led philosophy aside', 'in orient beauty bright' M. H. Nicolson, *Newton demands the muse*, Princeton University Press, Princeton, 1966, p. 73.

'How just, how beauteous' ibid., p. 43.

'the greatest and rarest genius' David Hume, *Enquiries concerning the human understanding*, Clarendon Press, Oxford, 1955.

29 'Nearer the gods' *Principia*, Vol. I, p. xv.

30 'When, however, the physicist and novelist' C. P. Snow, *The two cultures*, Cambridge University Press, Cambridge, 1969.

'Whatever reasoning holds' *Principia*, Vol. I.

31 'Every man endeavours', 'Velocities of suspicion' John Craig, 'Theologiae christianae principia mathematica', *History and Theory*, Beihaft 4, 1964.

'counsel and contrivance', 'comets could move in all manner' R. Cumberland, *Four letters from Sir Isaac Newton to Dr. Bentley containing some arguments in proof of a deity*, London, 1756.

32 'the present imperfect condition', 'all the sciences', 'the science of Man' David Hume, *A treatise of human nature*, Vol. I, Dent, London, 1911.

'Were ideas entirely loose' ibid.

'A picture naturally leads', 'Here is a kind of attraction' David Hume, *Enquiries concerning the human understanding*, Clarendon Press, Oxford, 1955.

33 'We are to admit' *Principia*, Vol. II.

'treat with contempt hypotheses' Thomas Reid, *The Works of Thomas Reid*, Vol. I, Edinburgh, 1785, p. 235.

'The authors who have treated', 'Thought in the mind' ibid., pp. 200–2.

34 'with that general law', 'in the inverse ratio' Comte de Buffon, *Historie naturelle*, Vol. 13, 1765.

'the affinity of mercury' A. Thackray, *Atoms and powers*, Harvard University Press, Cambridge, Mass., 1970, p. 214.

35 'a certain cure', 'bind his head strait' *Correspondence*, Vol. IV, p. 152.

'A large particle' James Keill, *An account of animal secretion, the quantity of blood in the humane body, and muscular motion*, London, 1708.

37 'He had no relish' John Conduitt, 'Memoirs of Sir Isaac Newton', in *Collections for the history of the town and soke of Grantham* (edited by Edmund Turnor), William Miller, London, 1806.

38 'If I have seen further' *Correspondence*, Vol. I, p. 416.

'What a lesson to the vanity' see Sir David Brewster, *The life of Sir Isaac Newton*, John Murray, London, 1831.

41 'the diameter of the Earth' *Principia*, Vol. II, pp. 424–8.

CHAPTER 2

43 'Indeed, Newton's masterpiece' *Principia*, Vol. II, pp. 544–6.

'I now demonstrate' *Principia*, Vol. II, p. 397.

44 'There have appeared edited' *Isaac Newton's Philosophiae Naturalis Principia Mathematica* (edited by A. Koyré and I. B. Cohen), Vol. II, Cambridge University Press, Cambridge, 1972, Appendix viii.

'Newton laid the mathematical' *Never at rest*, Chapter 5.

'he would make no necessities' cited in *Handbook*, p. 178.

'The immediate impetus' see *Never at rest*, Chapter 10.

45 'Mr Hook said' *Correspondence*, Vol. II, p. 442.

'Sr Isaac replied immediately' cited in I. B. Cohen, *Introduction to Newton's 'Principia'*, Cambridge University Press, Cambridge, 1971, p. 297.

46 'The third I now designe' *Correspondence*, Vol. II, p. 437.

47 'at last brought your book' cited in *Handbook*, p. 250.

'cried out with admiration' cited in *Never at rest*, p. 473.

48 'I contrive no hypotheses' *Principia*, Vol. II, p. 547.

50 'D. T. Whiteside has argued' D. T. Whiteside, 'The mathematical principles underlyuing Newton's *Principia Mathematica*', *Journal for the History of Astronomy*, 1 (1970), 118–19.

'According to B. Goldstein' B. Goldstein, personal communication.

'Newton then stated the laws' see M. Jammer, *Concepts of force*, Harvard University Press, Cambridge, Mass., Chapters 5, 6, 7.

52 'According to Kepler's second law' see M. Caspar, *Kepler* (translated by C. Doris), Hellman, London, 1959, Section 3.

54 'Its validity has been disputed' see H. Brougham and E. J. Routh, *Analytical view of Sir Isaac Newton's Principia*, Longman, Brown, Green, and Longman, London, 1855, pp. 57–8.

56 'the force by which the moon' *Principia*, Vol. II, p. 408.

59 'the solid of revolution' S. Zdravkovska, 'Conversation with Vladimir Igorevich Arnol'd', *Mathematical Intelligencer*, Vol. 9, no. 4 (1987), 30.

'the logical structure' D. T. Whiteside, 'The mathematical principles underlying Newton's *Principia Mathematica*', *Journal for the History of Astronomy*, 1 (1970), 116.

'The quantity of matter' *Principia*, Vol. I, p. 1.

'The answer is possibly to be found' ibid., pp. 6–12.

60 'He wrote that the meanings of words' ibid., p. 10.

'If I may so say' ibid., p. 23.

CHAPTER 3

The following references give further details of the mathematical topics and papers mentioned in this chapter. Full details can be found in the eight volumes of *Mathematical papers* (edited by D. T. Whiteside). In the following, the abbreviation *Reader* refers to J. Fauvel and J. Gray, *The history of mathematics—a reader*, Macmillan, London, 1987.

65 Roberval's work on the cycloid see *Reader*, pp. 376–7.

The fundamental theorem of calculus see *Never at rest*, pp. 123–8.

66 Subnormals and curvatures see *Never at rest*, pp. 110–12.

Newton's calculus (method of fluxions) see *Reader*, pp. 381–6; *Handbook*, pp. 213–15; or *Mathematical papers*, Vol. III.

67 Infinite series see *Handbook*, pp. 72–4; *Reader*, pp. 402–6; or *Never at rest*, pp. 113–23; see also D. T. Whiteside, 'Newton's discovery of the general binomial theorem', *Mathematical Gazette*, 45 (1961), 175–80.

68 *De analysi* see *Handbook*, pp. 149–52; or *Mathematical papers*, Vol. II.

69 Cubic curves see *Reader*, pp. 410–12; or *Never at rest*, pp. 199–202.

71 The *Epistola prior* and *Epistola posterior* see *Handbook*, pp. 198–9; or *Reader*, pp. 402–8.

74 *Specimen of a universal system of mathematics* see *Handbook*, pp. 345–6; or *Mathematical papers*, Vol. IV.

Arithmatica universalis see *Handbook*, pp. 33–6; or *Mathematical papers*, Vol. V.

75 Newton's dynamics see Chapter 2, and the references given there.

76 *Tractatus de quadratura curvarum* see *Handbook*, pp. 578–81; or *Mathematical papers*, Vols VII and VIII.

78 *Commercium epistolicum* see *Never at rest*, pp. 725–8; or *Handbook*, pp. 127–9.

CHAPTER 4

81 'experiments which Mr Newton' N. Malebranche, *Oeuvres* (edited by A. Robinett), Bibl. des textes phil., Paris, 1958–70, Vol. 3, p. 302.

82 'Although Mr Newton is not at all' ibid., Vol. 19, pp. 771–2 (emphasis added).

86 'It is affirmed that these propositions', 'although colours may belong', 'Hence the former' *Optical papers*, pp. 87–98.

87 '*Light* consists of *Rays differently refrangible*' *Correspondence*, Vol. I, p. 95.

88 'it can no longer be disputed' ibid., p. 100.

89 '[a] naturalist would scearce' ibid., p. 96.

90 'an "illustration" for the convenience' *Papers and letters*, pp. 178–9.

91 'These speculations have been taken' R. S. Westfall, *The construction of modern science: mechanisms and mechanics*, Cambridge University Press, Cambridge, 1977, p. 140.

'I suppose light is neither', 'multitudes of unimaginable' *Papers and letters*, p. 184.

'received a continual impulse' ibid., p. 185.

92 'not at all considering' *Principia*, Vol. I, pp. 230–1.

94 'some Queries, in order' *Opticks*, p. 339.

'[a]re not the rays' my translation from I. Newton, *Optice: sive de reflexionibus, refractionibus, inflexionibus et coloribus lucis*, London, 1706, p. 315; see also *Opticks*, p. 370.

'[w]hat I call Attraction' *Opticks*, p. 376.

97 '[f]or a Bell or Cannon' ibid., p. 363.

98 'a crucial experiment' C. Huygens, *Oeuvres*, The Hague, 1888–1950, Vol. 10, p. 613.

CHAPTER 5

101 'never was at more than one Opera' Rev. William Stukeley, *Diary*, 18 April 1720.

'Newton, hearing Handel play' Quoted by Joseph Warton, *Works of Alexander Pope*, London, 1797.

102 'the *seven liberal arts and sciences*' see *The seven liberal arts in the Middle Ages* (edited by D. L. Wagner), Indiana University Press, Bloomington, Indiana, 1983.

'During the Middle Ages' ibid., pp. 171–8.

103 'A substantial part of Greek harmonic science' see W. Burket, *Lore and science in ancient Pythagoreanism* (translated by E. L. Minor, Jr.), Cambridge University Press, Cambridge, 1972.

105 'those two which gave' Boethius, *On music* I, *A source book in Greek science* (edited by M. R. Cohen and I. E. Drabkin), Harvard University Press, Cambridge, Mass., 1948, pp. 298–9.

106 'Most of his early notes on the subject' Newton's notes on music are to be found in the Cambridge University Library, Additional MSS 4000 (fols 104–13, 137–43), 3958 (B) (fol. 31), and 3970 (fols 1–15).

107 'His work seems to have been based' see W. Brouncker, *Renatus Des-Cartes excellent compendium of musick: with necessary and judicious animadversions thereupon by a person of honour*, London, 1653; see also D. P. Walker, *Studies in musical science in the late Renaissance*, London, 1978, pp. 117–18.

For discussions of various scales, see H. F. Cohen, *Quantifying music: the science of music at the first stage of the scientific revolution, 1580–1650*, Dordrecht, 1984; J. M. Barbour, *Tuning and temperament: a historical survey*, Michigan State University Press, East Lansing, 1951 (reprinted New York, 1972); and M. Lindley, *Lutes, viols and temperaments*, Cambridge University Press, Cambridge, 1984. These books are referred to below as Cohen (1984), Barbour (1951), and Lindley (1984).

109 The just intonation scale is discussed in Cohen (1984), pp. 34–41.

'While temperament was accepted' see Barbour (1951), pp. 45–87, and Lindley (1984), pp. 19–42.

110 '(*multiple division*)' see Barbour (1951), pp. 107–32.

Newton's scale is discussed in P. M. Gouk, *Music in the natural philosophy of the early Royal Society*, Ph.D. thesis, University of London, 1982, pp. 261–4. This thesis is referred to below as Gouk (1982).

113 'From the very beginning' see Gouk (1982), pp. 34–9; and Cohen (1984), pp. 116–79.

'Newton himself always made' see *Never at rest*, pp. 155–74; A. E. Shapiro, 'Newton's "achromatic" dispersion law: theoretical background and experimental evidence', *Archive for the History of Exact Sciences*, 17 (1979), 91–218, and 'The evolving structure of Newton's theory of white light and colour', *Isis*, 71 (1980), 211–35; and Z. Bechler, 'Newton's search for a mechanistic model of colour dispersion', *Archive for the History of Exact Sciences*, 11 (1973), 1–37.

114 'Newton sent a description of his discovery' *Correspondence*, Vol. I, pp. 92–107; *Never at rest*, pp. 211–15, 238–43.

'Hooke also suggested in his letter' *Correspondence*, Vol. I, pp. 110–14; A.I. Sabra, *Theories of light from Descartes to Newton*, Oldbourne, London, 1967, pp. 187–92, 233–4.

'Similarly, the analogy' see P. M. Gouk, 'The role of acoustics and music theory in the scientific work of Robert Hooke', *Annals of Science*, 37 (1980), 573–605, 585–7. This work is referred to below as Gouk (1980).

115 'The most systematic experiments' see M. Mersenne, *Harmonie universelle*, Paris, 1636–7; see also Cohen (1984), pp. 78–114.

'*coincidence theory* of consonance' see Cohen (1984), pp. 94–7.

116 'for particles that are all similar' Robert Hooke, *Micrographia*, London, 1665 (reprinted by Dover Publications, New York, 1961), p. 15.

117 'as there are produced in sounds' *Correspondence*, Vol. I, pp. 110–14.

'Hooke extended this principle' see Gouk (1980), p. 587.

'Newton here outlined a general theory' *Correspondence*, Vol. I, pp. 362–89; see also B. J. T. Dobbs, *The foundations of Newton's alchemy*, Cambridge University Press, Cambridge, 1975, pp. 204–10.

118 'as the harmony and discord' *Correspondence*, Vol. I, p. 376.

'hardly visible to the keenest judge' *Optical papers*, pp. 544–5.

'The difficulty that Newton found' these topics in the *Opticks* may be found in Book I, Part II, Prop. VI; Book II, Part I, Obs. XIV; and Book II, Part IV, Obs. VIII.

120 'Unpublished draft material reveals' Cambridge University Library, Additional MS 3970 (fols 348–9).
'As is now well known' see *Never at rest*, pp. 281–334.

121 'In contrast, his own heliocentric' see S. Schaffer, 'Newton's comets and the transformation of astrology' in *Astrology, science and society* (edited by P. Curry), Woodbridge, Suffolk, 1987.

122 'and consequently by comparing' J.E. McGuire and P.M. Rattansi, 'Newton and the pipes of Pan', *Notes and Records of the Royal Society, London*, 21 (1966), 116–17.

'Pythagoras numbered the musical tones' ibid., p. 117.

'It was Johannes Kepler' D.P. Walker, *Studies in musical science in the late Renaissance*, London, 1978.

CHAPTER 6

127 'I wish we could derive' *Principia*, Vol. I, p. xviii.

131 'the natural philosopher knows' Daniel Sennert, *Thirteen books of natural philosophy* (translated by Nicholas Culpeper and Abdiah Cole), London, 1660, p. 434.

133 'And thus by simple enumeration' René Descartes, *Principles of philosophy* (translated by V.R. Miller and R.P. Miller), Reidel, Dordrecht, 1983, Principle 199, pp. 282–3.

'*The first law of nature*' ibid., Principles 37, 39, 40, pp. 59–62.

134 'If you think that the *vis inertiae*' Isaac Newton, draft manuscript for Query to *Opticks*, written around 1710, Cambridge University Library, Additional MS 3970 (fol. 619^{r}).

'Seeing therefore the variety'. 'Particules have not only' *Opticks*, Query 31, pp. 399, 401.

135 'Gravity must be' letter from G. W. Leibniz to the Abbé Conti, 1715, quoted from A. Koyré and I. B. Cohen, 'Newton and the Leibniz–Clarke Correspondence', *Archives Internationales d'Histoire des Sciences*, 5 (1962), 63–126, 70. This paper is referred to below as Koyré and Cohen (1962).

'These Principles I consider' *Opticks*, Query 31, p. 401.

136 'occult qualities are decried' Newton, draft MS letter to the Abbé Conti, written about February 1716, Koyré and Cohen (1962), p. 74.

139 'Natural magic is that which' Henry Cornelius Agrippa von Nettesheim, *De incertitudine et vanitate scientiarum et artium*, Paris, 1531, Chapter 42.

140 'Magick is nothing else' G. B. della Porta, *Natural magick*, London, 1658, pp. 1–2.

141 'But hitherto I have not' *Principia*, Vol. II, General Scholium, p. 547.

143 'certain aetherial spirits' Newton, 'An hypothesis explaining the properties of light' (1675), *Papers and letters*, pp. 180–1, 185; letter from Newton to Henry Oldenberg, 25 January 1676, ibid., p. 254.

'ye aether is but a vehicle' Smithsonian Institution, Washington, DC, Burndy MS. 16 (fol. 4^r).

'Do not Bodies', 'Are not gross Bodies', 'Have not the small particles of Bodies' *Opticks*, pp. 339, 374–6.

CHAPTER 7

149 'There is no problem' Sir David Brewster, *Memoirs of the life, writings, and discoveries of Sir Isaac Newton*, Vol. II, Constable, Edinburgh, 1855, p. 372.

'peculiar bent of his mind' ibid., p. 375.

'*a rational, experimental scientist*' M. Boas and A. R. Hall, 'Newton's chemical experiments', *Archives Internationales d'Histoire des Sciences*, 11 (1958), 151–2.

154 'The noble author' *Correspondence*, Vol. II, pp. 1–2.

155 'political inconveniences that may ensue' Robert Boyle, 'Of the incalescence of quicksilver with gold, generously imparted by B. R.', *Philosophical Transactions*, 10 (1675–6), 515–16, 529.

157 'about ye middle of ye Regimen' B. J. T. Dobbs, *The foundations of Newton's alchemy*, Cambridge University Press, Cambridge, 1975, p. 155. This book is referred to below as Dobbs (1975).

159 'The Rule I have followed' David Castillejo, *The expanding force in Newton's cosmos*, Ediciones de Arte y Bibliofilia, Madrid, 1981, p. 32.

'It may seem an admirable' King's College, Cambridge, Keynes MS 33 (Tract 'Manna' not in Newton's hand, with his annotations and additional notes at the end) (fol. 5^r). This manuscript is referred to below as Keynes.

160 '[J]ust as the world' Dobbs (1975), p. 164.

'This may be done in your chamber' Keynes (fol. 6^r).

'While I am describing this' *Correspondence*, Vol. I, p. 364.

161 'You will easily discern' *Correspondence*, Vol. II, p 296.

'I have not set down anything' *Correspondence*, Vol. II, p. 334.

163 'evident to the Sense of all Mankind' John Freind, *Chymical lectures* (translated by J.M.; 2nd English edition, J.W.), Christian Bowyer, London, 1729, pp. 175–6.

CHAPTER 8

169 'eternal, infinite, absolutely perfect', 'living, intelligent and powerful', 'all eye, all ear, all brain' *Principia*, Vol. II, London, 545.

170 'only by His most excellent contrivances' Isaac Newton, quoted in R.S. Westfall, 'The rise of science and the decline of orthodox Christianity: study of Kepler, Descartes, and Newton', *God and nature: historical essays on the encounter between Christianity and science* (edited by D.C. Lindberg and R.L. Numbers), University of California Press, Berkeley, 1986, p. 233. This paper is referred to below as Westfall (1986).

172 'In a recent essay' Amos Funkenstein, *Theology and the scientific imagination from the Middle Ages to the seventeenth century*, Princeton University Press, Princeton, 1986.

'The price he paid' see E. McMullin, *Newton on matter and activity*, University of Notre Dame Press, Notre Dame, Indiana, 1978, Chapters 3, 4.

'There exists an infinite' see *Never at rest*, p. 509.

174 'If there be an universal life' see R.S. Westfall, *Force in Newton's physics: the science of dynamics in the seventeenth century*, MacDonald, London, 1971, p. 397.

'It is the perfection' F.E. Manuel, *The religion of Isaac Newton*, Clarendon Press, Oxford, 1974, p. 120. This book is referred to below as Manuel (1974).

175 'Whiston set about confirming' see J.E. Force, *William Whiston: honest Newtonian*, Cambridge University Press, Cambridge, 1985, pp. 47–53.

177 'The Temple of Solomon' F.E. Manuel, *Isaac Newton, historian*, Cambridge University Press, Cambridge, 1963, p. 162.

178 'be not ashamed' Manuel (1974), pp. 112–13.

179 'prevalency yet to come' ibid., p. 99.

180 'if God was so angry' ibid., p. 109.

181 'as Christ after some stay' ibid., pp. 135–6.

182 'Westfall has placed particular weight' Westfall (1986), pp. 230–4.

CHAPTER 9

185 'Before Kepler, all men were blind' *Voltaire's notebooks* (edited by T. Bestermann), Geneva, 1952, Vol. I, p. 63.

'shrank until they seemed like figures' Voltaire, *Lettres philosophiques*, Basle, 1734, Lettre XII.

'In those days Florence was a new Athens' Voltaire, 'Essai sur les moeurs', *Oeuvres Complètes* (edited by L. Molland), Paris, 1877–83, Vol. I, pp. 638, 766–7; see also Peter Gay, *The Enlightenment: an interpretation*, London, 1967, Vol. I, *passim*. These works are referred to below as Voltaire (1877–83) and Gay (1967).

'true philosophy' Voltaire (1877–83), Vol. II, p. 172; Gay (1967) Vol. I, p. 228.

'the leader of a conspiracy' Jean D'Alembert, 'Discours préliminaire', *Mélange de littérature, d'histoire, et de la philosophie*, Vol. I, 1757, pp. 130–6; Gay (1967), Vol. II, p. 149.

186 'the oddest, if not the most considerable' *Correspondence*, Vol. I, pp. 82–3.

187 'great mystery' *Correspondence*, Vol. III, pp. 193–5.

'No, Newton was being far too reverential' *Correspondence*, Vol. III, pp. 196–8.

'a believer in the Copernican system', 'observed the gravitation' *Correspondence*, Vol. III, pp. 338–9, 384.

189 'discovered by these experiments', 'he later applied to the heavens', 'learned the ratio' Royal Society, Gregory MS 247, reproduced in P. Casini, 'Newton: the classical Scholia', *History of Science*, xxii (1984), p. 32; see also J.E. McGuire and

P.M. Rattansi, 'Newton and the pipes of Pan', *Notes and Records of the Royal Society*, London, 21 (1966), 108–43, 116. These works are referred to below as Casini (1984), and McGuire and Rattansi (1966).

190 'Pythagoras and the sages who invented' Casini (1984), p. 32.

'inspiring this world with harmonic ratio' Casini (1984), p. 38.

'flowed down to the Greeks', 'whom Strabo declares older' Casini (1984), p. 36; McGuire and Rattansi (1966), p. 115; Cambridge University Library, Additional MS 3965.6 (fol. 269), cited in *Never at rest*, p. 511.

191 'the oldest and most celebrated philosopher' *Opticks*, Book III, pp. 1, 369.

'In 1702, David Gregory had summarized' D. Gregory, 'The author's preface', *Elementa astronomiae physicae et geometriae* (English edition), 1725, cited in Casini (1984), pp. 47–58.

192 'to amuse himself after the fatigue' Voltaire, *Lettres philosophiques*, Basle, 1734, Lettre XV.

'His mind crippled, Newton had turned' Biot, 'Life of Newton', *Biographie universelle*, Vol. XXXI, 1821, p. 180.

'a searcher in the scriptures' Sir David Brewster, *Memoirs of the life, writings, and discoveries of Sir Isaac Newton*, Vol. II, Constable, Edinburgh, 1855, p. 314; see also H. McLachlan, *Sir Isaac Newton: theological manuscripts*, Liverpool University Press, Liverpool, 1950, p. 1.

193 'vulgar chymistry' 'Nature's obvious laws and processes in vegetation', Burndy MS, cited in P.M. Rattansi, 'Newton's alchemical studies', in *Science, medicine and society in the Renaissance*, Vol. II (edited by A.G. Debus), Science History Publications, New York, 1972, p. 176.

'a series of works on biblical chronology' I. Newton, *The chronology of ancient kingdoms amended*, London, 1728, and *Observations upon the prophesies of Daniel and the Apocalypse*, London, 1733.

'The immediate Continental response' see, for example, *Journal des Savants*, 16 (1688), 237–8.

195 'sense-experience and rational argument' Robert Boyle, *The sceptical chymist* (1661), Vol II, Everyman edition, London, 1911, pp. 71–2.

'He learnt Greek mythology' Item 1224 in J. Harrison, *The library of Isaac Newton*, Cambridge University Press, Cambridge, 1978.

197 'a doctrine which was misunderstood' see, for example, Henry More, *The immortality of the soul*, London, 1659, Book 1, Chapter xi, p. 7.

CHAPTER 10

203 '*Newtonianism for ladies*' F. Algarotti, *Sir Isaac Newton's theory of light and colours, and his principle of attraction, made familiar to ladies in several entertainment*, 2 volumes, London, 1742.

207 'God in the Beginning' *Opticks*, p. 400.

208 'the strength of Boscovich's argument' see R.J. Boscovich, *A theory of natural philosophy*, Harvard University Press, Cambridge, Mass., 1966, pp. 31–42.

210 'Looking back at Young's work' Thomas Young, 'On the theory of light and colours', *Philosophical Transactions of the Royal Society of London*, 92 (1802), 12–48.

211 'a most inconsistent way of arguing' George Berkeley, *The analyst*, in *Works*, Vol. 3, Clarendon Press, Oxford, 1871, p. 266.

'men would hardly admit' ibid., p. 268.

'exceed ... all human understanding' ibid., p. 260.

'ghosts of departed quantities' ibid., p. 283.

213 'this unholy alliance' see Steven Shapin, 'Of gods and kings: natural philosophy and politics in the Leibniz–Clarke disputes', *Isis*, 72 (1981), 187–215.

214 'But he who can digest' George Berkeley, op. cit., pp. 261–2.

CHAPTER 11

223 'Besides the technical study' Henry Guerlac, 'Some areas for further Newtonian studies', *History of Science*, XVII (1979), 75.

224 'imaginary communities' Benedict Anderson, *Imagined communities: reflections on the origin and spread of nationalism*, Verso, London, 1983.

'For deep, indeed,' Henry Brooke, 'Universal beauty' (written in 1735), *Collection of the pieces*, London, 1778, p. 42, ll. 319–22.

225 'Superior beings, when of late' Alexander Pope, *An essay on man* (written in 1733), London, 1753, p. 34, ll. 31–4.

'Here, awful Newton' James Thomson, 'To the memory of Sir Isaac Newton' (written in 1728), *The complete poetical works of James Thomson* (edited by J. L. Robertson), London, 1908, p. 11, ll. 208–12.

'when Mark Akenside conveyed' Mark Akenside, *The pleasures of imagination*, London, 1744, ll. 100–20.

'The Last Judgement is' William Blake, '[A Vision of the Last Judgement] from the Note-Book for the year 1810', in *William Blake: complete writings with variant readings* (edited by Geoffrey Keynes), Oxford University Press, London, 1969, p. 617.

226 'Whether primordial motion' Richard Payne Knight, *The progress of civil society: a didactic poem*, London, 1796, p. 3, ll. 1–8.

'Let us less visionary themes' Richard Payne Knight, ibid., p. 3, ll. 15–16.

'By firm immutable immortal laws' Erasmus Darwin, *The temple of nature; or, the origin of society*, London, 1803, Canto I, p. 1, ll. 1–8.

227 'NEWTON's eye sublime' Erasmus Darwin, ibid., Canto IV, p. 148, ll. 233–6.

'to inlist the Imagination' Erasmus Darwin, Advertisement of *The botanic garden: a poem in two parts; Part I; The economy of vegetation* (4th edition); *Part II; The loves of the plants* (5th edition), London, 1799.

'the ratiocination of philosophy' ibid.

'the Poet writes principally' ibid.

228 'picture-language quality' Donald D. Ault, *Visionary physics: Blake's response to Newton*, Chicago, 1974, p. 50.

'The nature of infinity is this' William Blake, 'Milton' (written and etched 1804–8), in *William Blake: complete writings with variant readings* (edited by Geoffrey Keynes), Oxford University Press, London, 1972, p. 497.

230 'components of the national culture' Perry Anderson, 'Components of the national culture', in *Student power: problems, diagnosis, action* (edited by Alexander Cockburn and Robin Blackburn), Penguin Books, Harmondsworth, 1969, pp. 214–84.

'mediocre and inert' ibid., p. 215.

233 'heritage culture' Seamus Heaney, as quoted in Robert Hewison, *Too much: art and society in the sixties*, Methuen, London, 1986, p. 308.

'the historical and sacrosanct identity' Patrick Wright, *On living in an old country: the national past in contemporary Britain*, Verso, London, 1985, p. 2.

'the past has been secured' ibid., p. 3.

234 'Einstein's brain is' Roland Barthes, *Mythologies* (first published in 1957; selected and translated from the French by Annette Lavers), Paladin, London, 1973, p. 68.

'Through the mythology' ibid., p. 69.

'fulfills all the conditions' ibid., p. 70.

235 'caused him to discover gravity' *Garden Answers*, September 1982, p. 29.

Notes on contributors

Sir Herman Bondi is Master of Churchill College, Cambridge. Previously, he was Chairman and Chief Executive of the Natural Environment Research Council. He was Professor of Mathematics at King's College London, and is known internationally for his work in cosmology, gravitation, relativity, and astrophysics.

John Brooke is Senior Lecturer in the History of Science at Lancaster University. He is currently completing a book on the historical relations between science and religion.

Geoffrey Cantor is Senior Lecturer in the History of Science at Leeds University. Amongst his books is *Optics after Newton* (1983), and he is currently preparing a biographical study of Michael Faraday.

John Fauvel is Lecturer in Mathematics at the Open University. He has been an editor of several books, including *Darwin to Einstein: Historical studies on science and belief* (1980), *Conceptions of inquiry* (1981), and *The history of mathematics: a reader* (1987).

Raymond Flood is Staff Tutor in Computing and Mathematics at the Department for External Studies, Oxford University. His main research interests are in mathematical statistics.

Derek Gjertsen taught philosophy and the history of science at the University of Ghana from 1960 to 1979. He is the author of *The classics of science* (1984) and *The Newton handbook* (1986).

Jan Golinski is a Research Fellow at Churchill College, Cambridge. He is currently working on a book about public science in the eighteenth-century Enlightenment.

Penelope Gouk is a Research Fellow at Linacre College, Oxford. She is presently completing a study of the relations between music and natural philosophy during the seventeenth century.

Casper Hakfoort teaches in the History Department in the Faculty of Philosophy and Social Sciences at the University of Twente, The Netherlands. His research interests include the shift from classical to modern physics and the history of industrial science.

John Henry is a Research Fellow at the University of Edinburgh. His research interests embrace the interactions in the early modern period between magic, medicine, science, and religion.

Maureen McNeil is a Lecturer at the Cultural Studies Department, Birmingham University. She is author of *Under the banner of science: Erasmus Darwin and his age* (1987), and is editor of *Gender and expertise* (1987).

Jon Pepper is Head of the Mathematics Department at the North East London Polytechnic. He is the author of several papers on Thomas Harriot's unpublished scientific and mathematical manuscripts.

Piyo Rattansi is Professor of the History of Science at University College London. He is the author of *Isaac Newton and gravity* (1974), and his biographical study of Newton has recently appeared in the Oxford University Press Past Masters series.

John Roche teaches history of science at Linacre College, Oxford, and physics at Oxford Polytechnic. His chief research interest is in using history as a clinical instrument in modern physics.

Michael Shortland teaches history and social studies of science at the University of Oxford. His current projects include a history of science in films, and a study of nineteenth-century scientific controversies.

Robin Wilson is Senior Lecturer in Mathematics at the Open University. He has written and edited a number of books on graph theory and combinatorics, including *Introduction to graph theory* (1972), and *Graph theory 1736–1936* (1976).

Picture credits

Frontispiece: Engraving by G. Bickham, 1732. Courtesy of Museum of the History of Science, Oxford.

facing p. 1: Drawing by H. Gravelot, engraved by C. Grignion. Courtesy of the Dean and Chapter, Westminster Abbey, London.

2 Nicolas Copernicus, *De revolutionibus orbium coelestium*, Nuremberg 1543, p. 9^v^. Bodleian Library, Oxford.

2 Frontispiece of René Descartes, *Opera philosophica*, 1692.

4 MS Add. 3965, f. 109^r^, University Library, Cambridge. By permission of the Syndics of Cambridge University Press.

4 Courtesy of Trinity College, Cambridge.

5 Drawing by William Stukeley, c. 1719. Courtesy of the Royal Society.

8 An alchemist and his assistant, woodcut by Hans Weiditz, c. 1520.

9 Francis Bacon, *Instauratio magna*, 1620, title-page. Bodleian Library, Oxford.

9 Frontispiece to Thomas Sprat, *History of the Royal Society of London*, 1667, designed by John Evelyn, engraved by Wenceslaus Hollar. Courtesy of the Royal Society.

12 Woolsthorpe Manor, near Grantham, Lincolnshire. Courtesy of the National Trust.

12 Free Grammar School of King Edward VI, Grantham.

12 Window sill in King Edward VI Grammar School, Grantham. From P. M. Rattansi, *Isaac Newton and gravity*, Wayland Press, 1974.

13 Engraving by David Loggan, from his *Cantabrigia illustrata*, Cambridge, 1690, Plate xxix. Courtesy of the Royal Society of Antiquaries, London.

16 *Philosophical transactions of the Royal Society of London*, no. 81, vol. 7, 1672, Plate 1. Bodleian Library, Oxford.

18 Nicolas Fatio de Duillier, by an unknown artist. Pastel. Courtesy of the Bibliothèque Publique et Universitaire, Geneva.

19 Engraving from James Beeverell, *Les délices de la Grande-Bretagne*, Leiden, 1707, IV, 802.

20 Engraving after Sir Godfrey Kneller.

22 Giovanni Battista Pittoni, *Allegorical monument to Isaac Newton*, oil painting on canvas. Courtesy of the Fitzwilliam Museum, Cambridge.

25 Johannes Kepler, *Astronomia nova*, Prague, 1609, p. 289. Bodleian Library, Oxford.

26 William Hogarth, *The rake's progress*, 1735, Plate VIII. From Joseph Burke and Colin Caldwell, *Hogarth: the complete engravings*, Thames & Hudson, 1968. Reproduced by permission of the Trustees of the British Museum.

27 Stamps courtesy of Robin J. Wilson.

28 Temple of British Worthies, Stowe, Buckinghamshire. Photographs John Fauvel.

29 Etienne-Louis Boullée, *Cénotaphe de Newton*, 1784. Bibliothèque Nationale, Paris, HA 57, nos. 7 and 8. Reproduced from Helen Rosenau, *Boullée & visionary architecture*, 1976, courtesy of Academy Editions, London.

31 John Craig, *Theologiae christianae principia mathematica*, 1699, title-page. Bodleian Library, Oxford.

32 William Derham, *Physico-theology*, 1798 edition, title-page.

35 Add. MS 3975, f. 15, University Library, Cambridge. By permission of the Syndics of Cambridge University Press.

36 *Sistême Astronomique de la Révolution Françoise*, broadside from the collection of Professor I. B. Cohen. From I. Bernard Cohen, *Revolution in science*, Harvard University Press, 1985.

39 From R. B. Merton, *On the shoulders of giants*.

42 Isaac Newton, *Philosophiae naturalis principia mathematica*, 1687, title-page.

44 Isaac Newton, *The mathematical principles of natural philosophy*, tr. Andrew Motte, 1803 edition, title-page.

44 Isaac Newton, *Principes mathématiques de la philosophie naturelle*, tr. Emilie du Châtelet, Paris, 1759, title-page.

44 Isaac Newton, *Principiile matematice ale filozofiei naturale*, tr. Victor Marian, Bucharest, 1956, title-page.

45 George Cruikshank, *The courtship of Sir Isaac Newton*. From P. M. Rattansi, *Isaac Newton and gravity*, Wayland Press, 1974.

46 Isaac Newton, *Principia*, Book III, Example following Proposition 41, Problem 21.

47 Add. MS 3965, 7 f. 55^r^, University Library, Cambridge. By permission of the Syndics of Cambridge University Press.

48 The Octagon Room, Royal Observatory, Greenwich, designed by Christopher Wren. Etching

by Francis Place, after drawing by Robert Thacker. Courtesy of the Master and Fellows of Magdalene College, Cambridge.

48 Isaac Newton, *Principia*, Cambridge, 1713, title-page.
51 *Principia*, 1687, pp. 12–13.
51 George Atwood, *A treatise on the rectilinear motion and rotation of bodies*, Cambridge, 1784, frontispiece. Bodleian Library, Oxford.
52 Photographs Mike Levers.
57 *traité de l'opinion, ou mémoires pour servir à l'histoire de l'esprit humain*, Paris, 1733, vol. 3, plate 2. From Allen G. Debus, *Man and nature in the Renaissance*, Cambridge University Press, 1978.
58 Isaac Newton, *A treatise of the system of the world*, 1728, plate 1.
58 Willem 'sGravesande, *Mathematical elements of natural philosophy, confirmed by experiments*, 1726, vol. 1, plate 9. Bodleian Library, Oxford.
59 Isaac Newton, *Principia*, Book II, Scholium to Proposition 34, Theorem 28.
62 Isaac Newton, *The method of fluxions and infinite series; with its application to the geometry of curve-lines*, 1736, frontispiece. Bodleian Library, Oxford.
64 Apollonius of Perga, *Opera*, Venice, 1537, title-page. Bodleian Library, Oxford.
67 Stamps courtesy of Robin J. Wilson.
68 Isaac Newton, *Analysis per quantitatum series, fluxiones, ac differentias*, edited by William Jones, 1711. Turner Collection, University of Keele.
69 Isaac Newton, *The method of fluxions*, 1736, title-page. Bodleian Library, Oxford.
70 Isaac Newton, *Opticks*, 1704. Bodleian Library, Oxford.
71 Add. MS 4294 f. 119^{v}, University Library, Cambridge. By permission of the Syndics of Cambridge University Press.
72 Add. MS 4004 f. 81^{v}, University Library, Cambridge. By permission of the Syndics of Cambridge University Press.
73 University Library, Cambridge. By permission of the Syndics of Cambridge University Press.
74 Isaac Newton, *Universal arithmetick*, 1728, title-page.
75 Isaac Newton, *Universal arithmetick*, 1728, p. 69. Bodleian Library, Oxford.
76 Isaac Newton, *Opticks*, 1704, p. 170. Bodleian Library, Oxford.
78 *Philosophical transactions of the Royal Society of London*, vol. 29, February 1715, p. 204. Bodleian Library, Oxford.
80 Engraving by J. A. Houston. Mansell Collection.
83 René Descartes, *Les météores*, Leiden, 1637, p. 258.
83 Willem 'sGravesande, *Mathematical elements of natural philosophy, confirmed by experiments*, 1726, vol. II, plate 19. Bodleian Library, Oxford.
84 René Descartes, *Les météores*, Leiden, 1637, p. 257.
85 Add. MS 3996 f. 122^{r}, University Library, Cambridge. By permission of the Syndics of Cambridge University Press.
86 Isaac Newton, *Optical lectures*, 1728, title-page. Bodleian Library, Oxford.
87 By kind permission of the Master and Fellows, New College, Oxford.
89 *Philosophical transactions of the Royal Society of London*, no. 80, February 1672, p. 3075. Bodleian Library, Oxford.
90 University Library, Cambridge. By permission of the Syndics of Cambridge University Press.
92 Isaac Newton, *Opticks*, 1704. Bodleian Library, Oxford.
96 Isaac Newton, *Principia*, 1787, Proposition 42, Theorem 33.
97 Christiaan Huygens, *Traité de la lumière*, 1690. Bodleian Library, Oxford.
100 Robert Fludd, *De metaphysico macrocosmi ... [= Utriusque cosmi ... historia*, tom. I, tract.i], Oppenheim, 1617, p. 90. Wellcome Institute Library, London.
102 Gregor Reisch, *Margarita philosophica*, Freiberg, 1503. Museum of the History of Science, Oxford.
104 MS Ii.3.12, f. 61^{v}. Cambridge University Library. By permission of the Syndics of Cambridge University Press.
105 Franchino Gafurio, *Theorica musice*, 1492, p.ci. Bodleian Library, Oxford.
108 Gioseffo Zarlino, *Istitutione harmoniche*, Venice, 1573, p. 31. Bodleian Library, Oxford.
111 Add. MS 3958.2, f. 31^{r}, University Library, Cambridge. By permission of the Syndics of Cambridge University Press.
112 Marin Mersenne, *Harmonie universelle*, Paris, 1636. Bodleian Library, Oxford.
113 P. M. Rattansi, *Isaac Newton and gravity*, Wayland Press, 1974, p. 42.
114 Robert Hooke, *Micrographia*, 1665, pp. 60, 175. Bodleian Library, Oxford.
116 Marin Mersenne, *Harmonie universelle*, Paris, 1636, frontispiece. Bodleian Library, Oxford.
119 Voltaire, *Elémens de la philosophie de Neuton*, Amsterdam, 1738, p. 182. Bodleian Library, Oxford.

123 Robert Fludd, *De naturae simia seu technica macrocosmi historia* [= *Utriusque cosmi . . . historia*, tom. I, tract. ii], Oppenheim, 1618, folding plate. Wellcome Institute Library, London.
126 Robert Fludd, *Ultriusque cosmi . . . metaphysica physica atque technica historia*, tract. ii, Oppenheim, 1617–18, pp. 4–5. Wellcome Institute Library, London.
129 Galileo Galilei, *De systemate mundi*, Leiden, 1635, title-page. British Library.
130 Cornelius Petraeus, *Sylva philosophorum*, 17th century, Bibliotheek der Rijkuniversiteit, Leiden.
131 Athanasius Kircher, *Regnum naturae magneticum*, Rome, 1667, title-page. Bodleian Library, Oxford.
132 René Descartes, *Principia philosophiae*, Amsterdam, 1644, p. 272.
136 Pavement in Siena Cathedral. Mansell Collection.
137 Michael Maier, *Symbola aureae mensae duodecim nationum*, Frankfurt, 1617.
138 *Musaeum hermeticum*, 1625, plate II. Museum of the History of Science, Oxford.
139 Henry Cornelius Agrippa, *Three books of occult philosophy*, 1651, pp. 204–5. Bodleian Library, Oxford.
140 Michael Maier, *Atalanta fugiens, hoc est. Emblemata de secretis naturae chymia*, Oppenheim, 1618, p. 93. Bodleian Library, Oxford.
140 Robert Fludd, Mystical Compass. From Frances Yates, *Giordano Bruno and the hermetic tradition*, Routledge and Kegan Paul, 1964.
142 John Baptista della Porta, *Natural magick*, 1658, title-page. Bodleian Library, Oxford.
143 Drawing by Isaac Newton, accompanying his copy of John de Monte-Snyder's *Metamorphosis of the Planets*. Yale Medical Library.
146 Courtesy of the Provost and Fellows, King's College, Cambridge.
148 Michael Maier, *Symbola aureae mensae duodecim nationum*, Frankfurt, 1617.
149 Courtesy of the Provost and Fellows, King's College, Cambridge.
149 Michael Maier, *Symbola aureae mensae duodecim nationum*, Frankfurt, 1617.
151 Michael Maier, *Tripus aureus*, 1618, title-page. Bodleian Library, Oxford.
152 Engraving by David Loggan, from his *Cantabrigia illustrata*, Cambridge, 1690, Plate xxix. Courtesy of the Royal Society of Antiquaries, London.
154 Courtesy of the Provost and Fellows, King's College, Cambridge.
155 Courtesy of the Provost and Fellows, King's College, Cambridge.
156 From Richard S. Westfall, *Never at rest*, Cambridge, 1980. Courtesy of the Babson College Library.
158 Heinrich Khunrath, *Amphitheatrum sapientiae aeternae*, Hanover, 1609. Bodleian Library, Oxford.
159 Michael Maier, *Atalanta fugiens*, Oppenheim, 1617, p. 117. Bodleian Library, Oxford.
163 James Keill, *Essays on several parts of the animal oeconomy*, 2nd edition, 1717, pp. 106–7. Bodleian Library, Oxford.
165 Michael Maier, *Atalanta fugiens*, Oppenheim, 1618, p. 177. Bodleian Library, Oxford.
168 By courtesy of the Fitzwilliam Museum, Cambridge.
170 *Four Letters from Sir Isaac Newton to Doctor Bentley*, published in 1756.
171 Richard Bentley, Eighth Boyle Lecture, preached at St Mary-le-Bow on December 5th 1692.
175 Thomas Burnet, *The sacred theory of the earth*, 1690.
176 Portrtait of William Whiston, artist unknown. By kind permission of Sir John Conant, Bart.
176 William Whiston, *A new theory of the earth, from its original, to the consummation of all things*, 1696, figure 7.
177 Isaac Newton, *The chronology of ancient kingdoms amended*, 1728, plate 1, p. 346. Bodleian Library, Oxford.
180 Joseph Mede, *The key of the revelation, searched and demonstrated out of the naturall and proper charecters of the visions, with a coment thereupon*, trans. R. More, 1650 edition, p. 26. Bodleian Library, Oxford.
181 Henry More, *Opera theologica*, 1675, p. 29. Bodleian Library, Oxford.
182 Isaac Newton, *Observations upon the prophecies of Daniel, and the Apocalypse of St. John*, Dublin, 1733, title-page.
184 Athanasius Kircher, *Oedipus aegyptiacus*, Rome, 1652–4, p. 428. Bodleian Library, Oxford.
186 Denis Diderot *et al.*, *Encyclopédie*, Paris, 1751–65, allegorical frontispiece. From I. Bernard Cohen, *Album of Science: from Leonardo to Lavoisier*, Charles Scribner's Sons, 1980.
188 MS Ashburn 1166, f. 18. Biblioteca Mediceo-Laurenziana, Florence. From Stanislas Klossowski de Rola, *Alchemy*, Thames and Hudson, 1973.
189 Johannes Kepler, *Harmonice mundi*, Linz, 1619, book V.
191 David Gregory, *Elements of astronomy*, English translation of 1715, author's preface.
191 David Gregory, *Astronomiae physicae & geometriae elementa*, Oxford, 1702, title-page.
192 Voltaire, *Elémens de la philosophie de Neuton*, 1738, frontispiece and title-page. Bodleian Library, Oxford.

195 From H. Kearney, *Science and change 1500–1700*, World University Library, 1971.
196 Tobias Schütz, *Harmonica macrocosmi cum microcosmi*, 1654. From Allen G. Debus, *Man and nature in the renaissance*, Cambridge, 1978.
197 Engraving by William Faithorne, 1675. From Frank E. Manuel, *A portrait of Isaac Newton*, Muller, 1980.
198 Thomas Hobbes, *Leviathan*, 1651, title-page.
199 Franchino Gafurio, *Practica musice*, 1496, By permission of the Syndics of Cambridge University Press.
200 Courtesy of Thames & Hudson, London.
202 Royal Library, Windsor Castle. By gracious permission of Her Majesty the Queen.
205 Francesco Algarotti, *Il newtonianismo per le dame*, Naples, 1737. The frontispiece shows Algarotti in conversation with Emilie du Châtelet.
205 Tom Telescope, *The newtonian system of philosophy*, 1761. Bodleian Library, Oxford.
206 From Joseph Burke and Colin Caldwell, *Hogarth: the complete engravings*, Thames & Hudson, 1968. Reproduced by permission of the Trustees of the British Museum,
208 Roger Boscovich, painted by Robert Edge Pine, 1760. Franciscan Monastery, Dubrovnik. From L. L. Whyte (ed.), *Roger Joseph Boscovich*, George Allen & Unwin, 1961.
208 R. J. Boscovich, *Theoria philosophiae naturalis*, Venice, 1763.
209 From Vasco Ronchi, *The nature of light*, Heinemann, 1970.
212 George Berkeley, *The analyst*, 1734. Turner Collection, University of Keele.
213 Courtesy of the Open University.
216 Samuel Pike, *Philosophia sacra*, 1753. Bodleian Library, Oxford.
217 Engraving by W. Say, after J. Northcote. Mansell Collection.
218 Copyright British Museum, London.
219 Tom Telescope, *The Newtonian system of philosophy*, Philadelphia, 1808. Bodleian Library, Oxford.
222 Courtesy The National Film Archive.
224 Erasmus Darwin, *The botanic garden*, 1791. This engraving by Blake, after a wash drawing by Fuseli, faces p. 145 of the 1799 edition.
226 Tate Gallery, London.
227 Erasmus Darwin, *The temple of nature*, 1803, frontispiece, engraved by Houghton from a design by Fuseli.
229 Bodleian Library, Oxford.
229 Bodleian Library, Oxford.
230 *Illustrated London News*, 2 October 1855.
232 Trinity College, Cambridge.
232 Courtesy of the Bank of England, London.
233 Courtesy of the Post Office.
233 Photograph Robin J. Wilson.
234 H. Medved and M. Medved, *The golden turkey awards*, Angus & Robertson, London, 1986.
235 Courtesy of the Open University.
235 Stamps courtesy of Robin J Wilson.
236 *Punch*, 28 September 1960, p. 468. By permission of *Punch*.
238 N. I. Bukharin and others, *Science at the cross roads*, 1931, p. 149.
240 Print in collection of Stillman Drake, reproduced by kind permission.
242 Willem 'sGravesande, *Mathematical elements of natural philosophy*, volume II, plate 18. Bodleian Library, Oxford.
245 Stamp courtesy of Robin J. Wilson.
246 The river Nith, Dumfries. Photograph John Fauvel.
248 Courtesy of NASA, Houston, Texas, USA.

Index

Readers may wish to supplement the sketchy identifications given here with the much fuller details available in reference books. (Unless otherwise stated, people can generally be taken to be English.) The following volumes are especially useful, and have valuable entries on many of the people mentioned in this book: *Dictionary of scientific biography*, 16 volumes, edited by C. C. Gillespie, Charles Scribner's Sons, New York, 1970–80. (Dates or approximate dates are given in parentheses.)